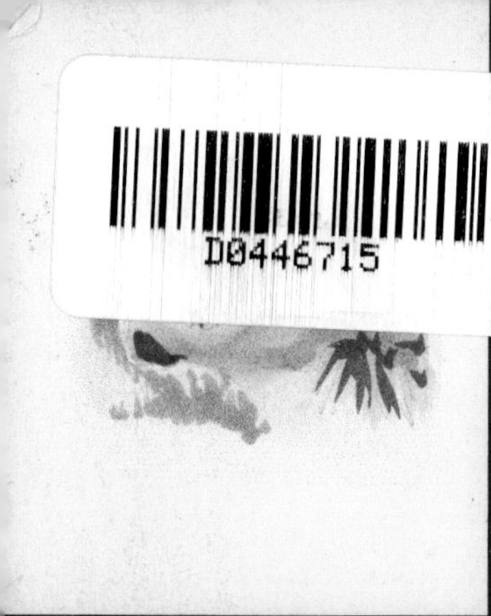

went to the National
useum of Nature and
cience in Ueno the other
y and saw a Tyrannosaurus.
was so cool. If I weren't
manga artist, I think I
ould've been a Hercules
beetle or a Tyrannosaurus.
That's how much I love them.

-Tite Kubo

BLEACH is author Tite Kubo's second title. Kubo made his debut with *ZOMBIEPOWDER.*, a four-volume series for *WEEKLY SHONEN JUMP*. To date, *BLEACH* has been translated into numerous languages and has also inspired an animated TV series that began airing in the U.S. in 2006. Beginning its serialization in 2001, *BLEACH* is still a mainstay in the pages of *WEEKLY SHONEN JUMP*. In 2005, *BLEACH* was awarded the prestigious Shogakukan Manga Award in the *shonen* (boys) category.

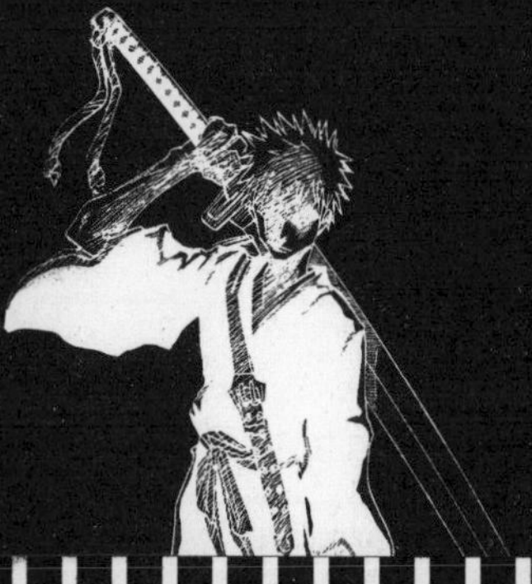

BLEACH
Vol. 40: THE LUST
SHONEN JUMP Manga Edition

STORY AND ART BY
TITE KUBO

English Adaptation/Lance Caselman
Translation/Joe Yamazaki
Touch-up Art & Lettering/Mark McMurray
Design/Yukiko Whitley, Kam Li
Editor/Alexis Kirsch

Published by VIZ Media, LLC
P.O. Box 77010
San Francisco, CA 94107

10 9 8 7 6 5 4 3 2 1
First printing, June 2012

PARENTAL ADVISORY
BLEACH is rated T for Teen and is recommended
for ages 13 and up. This volume contains
fantasy violence.

ratings.viz.com

www.viz.com

THE WORLD'S
MOST POPULAR MANGA
SHONEN JUMP
www.shonenjump.com

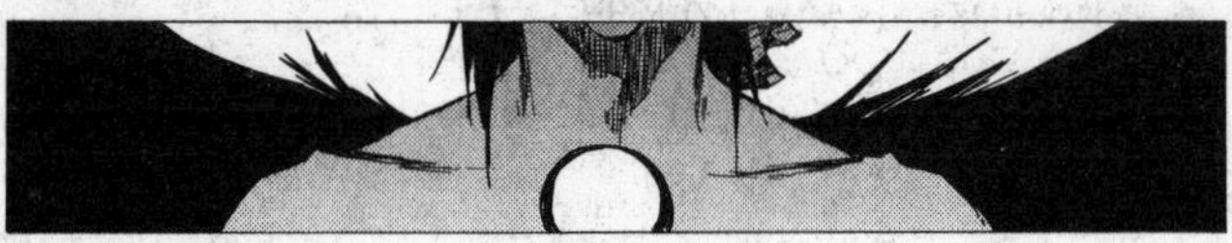

Envious because I have a heart

Gluttonous because I have a heart

Greedy because I have a heart

Prideful because I have a heart

Slothful because I have a heart

Wrathful because I have a heart

Because I have a heart

I lust for all that you are

BLEACH 40 THE LUST

Shonen Jump Manga

STARS AND

Ichigo Kurosaki

Ulquiorra

plot

When high school student Ichigo Kurosaki meets Soul Reaper Rukia Kuchiki his life is changed forever. Soon Ichigo is a soul-cleansing Soul Reaper too, and he finds himself having adventures, as well as problems, that he never would have imagined. Now Ichigo and his friends must stop renegade Soul Reaper Aizen and his army of Arrancars from destroying the Soul Society and wiping out Karakura as well.

The battle finally begins! The Thirteen Court Guard Companies head to Karakura while Ichigo remains in Hueco Mundo to fight Ulquiorra. As Orihime watches, the fight goes back and forth. Who will come out on top?!

BLEACH ALL
STORIES

井上織姫

Orihime Inoue

BLEACH 40

THE LUST

Contents

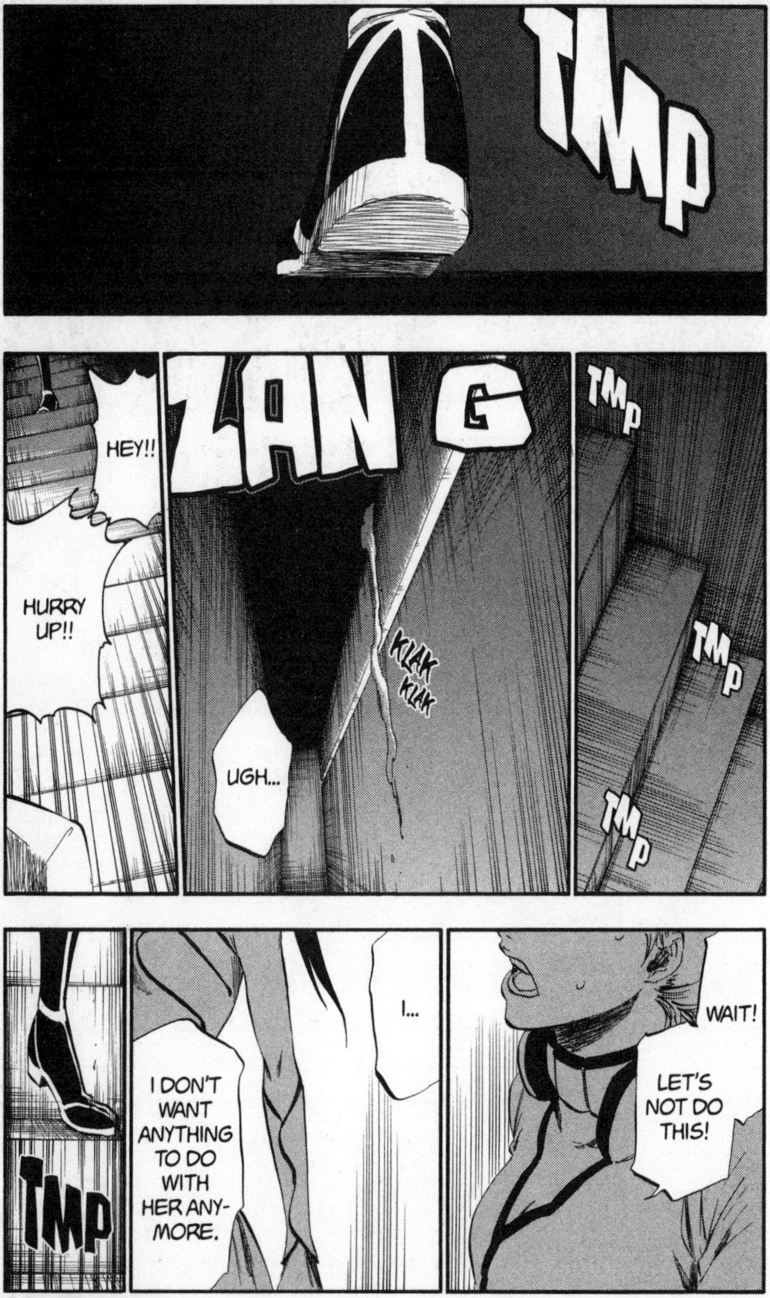
TMP
TMP
TMP
TMP
ZANG
KLAK KLAK
UGH...
HEY!!
HURRY UP!!
WAIT!
LET'S NOT DO THIS!
I...
I DON'T WANT ANYTHING TO DO WITH HER ANY-MORE.
TMP

341. The envy

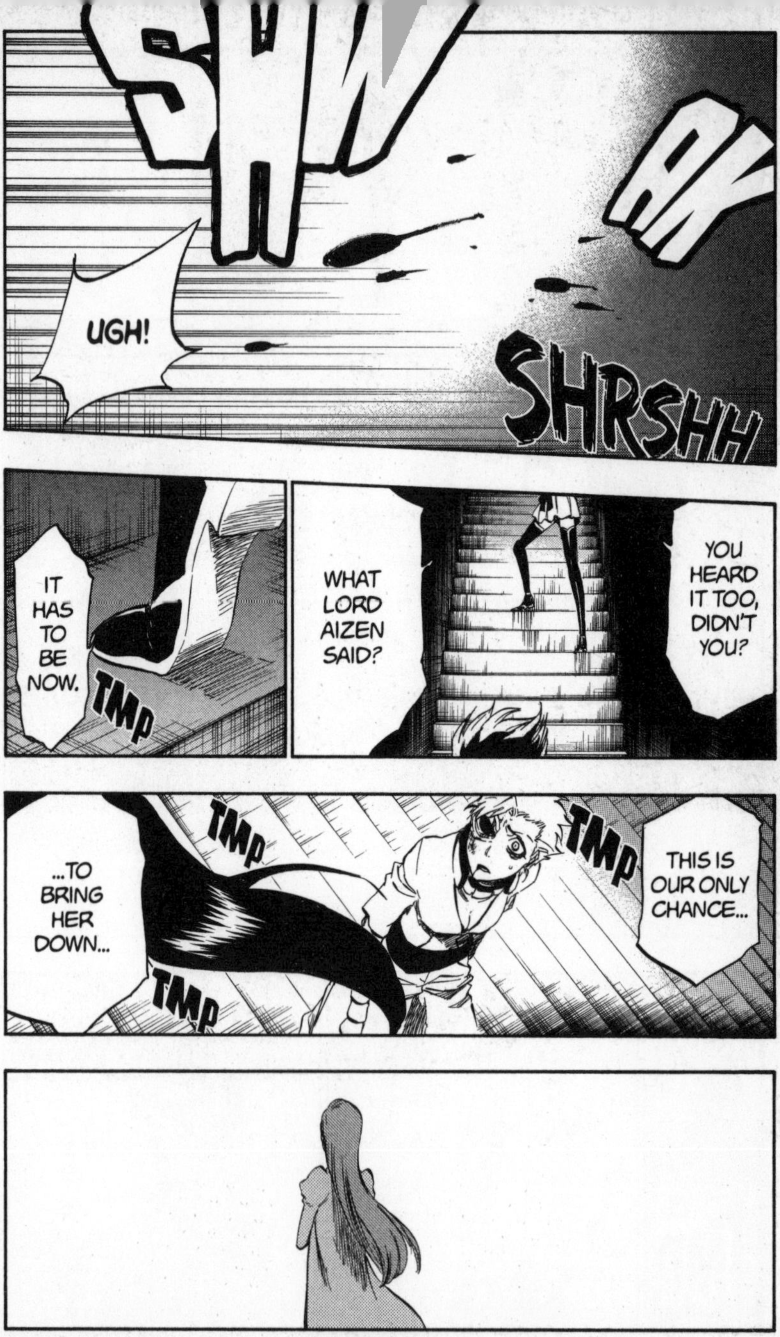
SHWAK
SHRSHH
UGH!
YOU HEARD IT TOO, DIDN'T YOU?
WHAT LORD AIZEN SAID?
IT HAS TO BE NOW.
TMP
TMP
THIS IS OUR ONLY CHANCE...
TMP
...TO BRING HER DOWN...
TMP

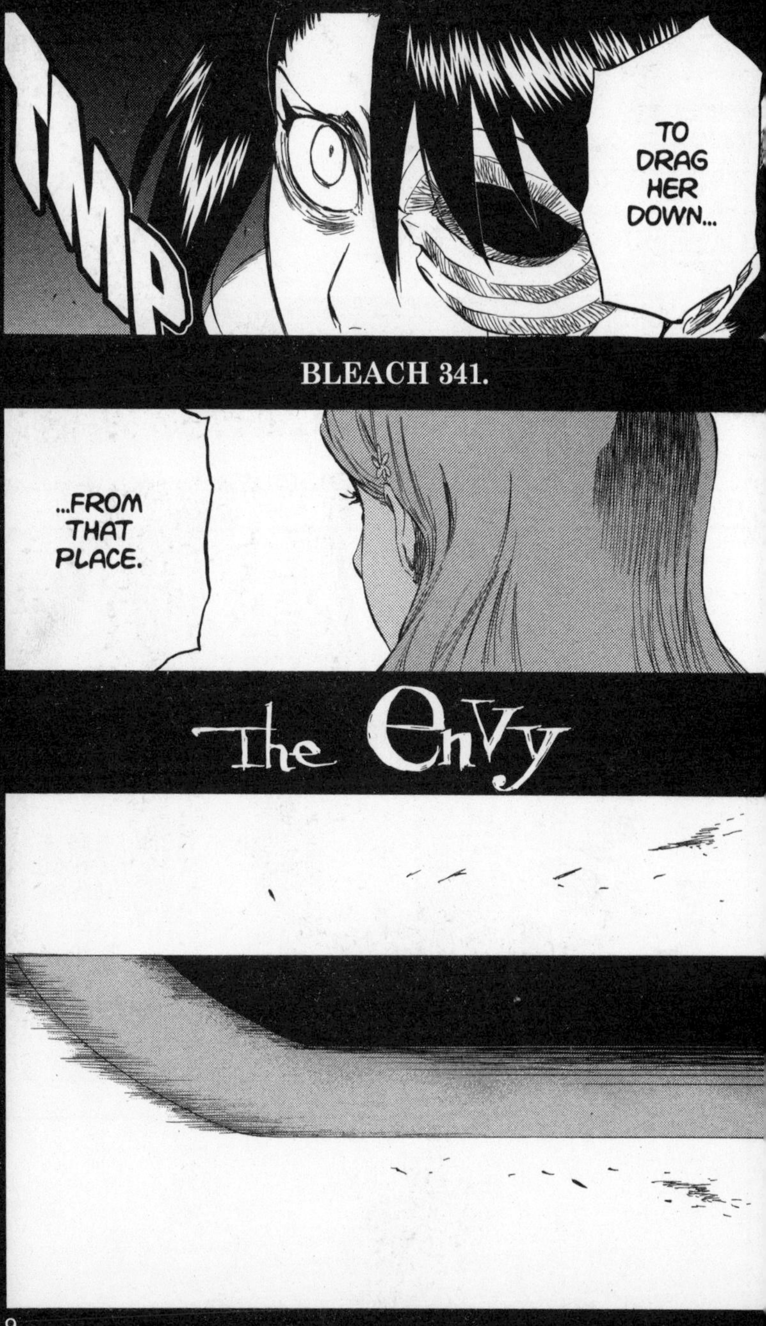
TO DRAG HER DOWN...
TMP
BLEACH 341.
...FROM THAT PLACE.
The Envy

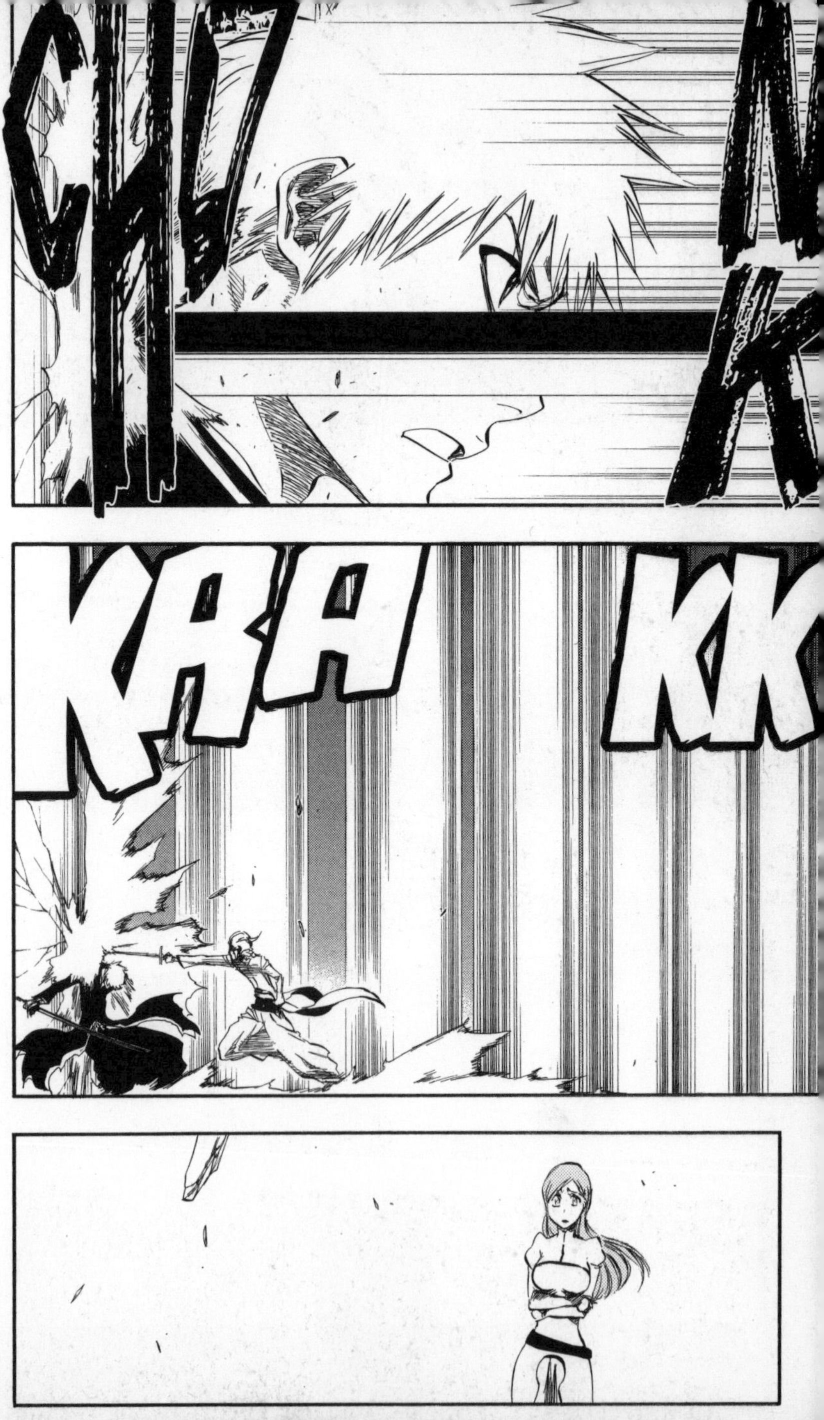
CHU
KRA KK

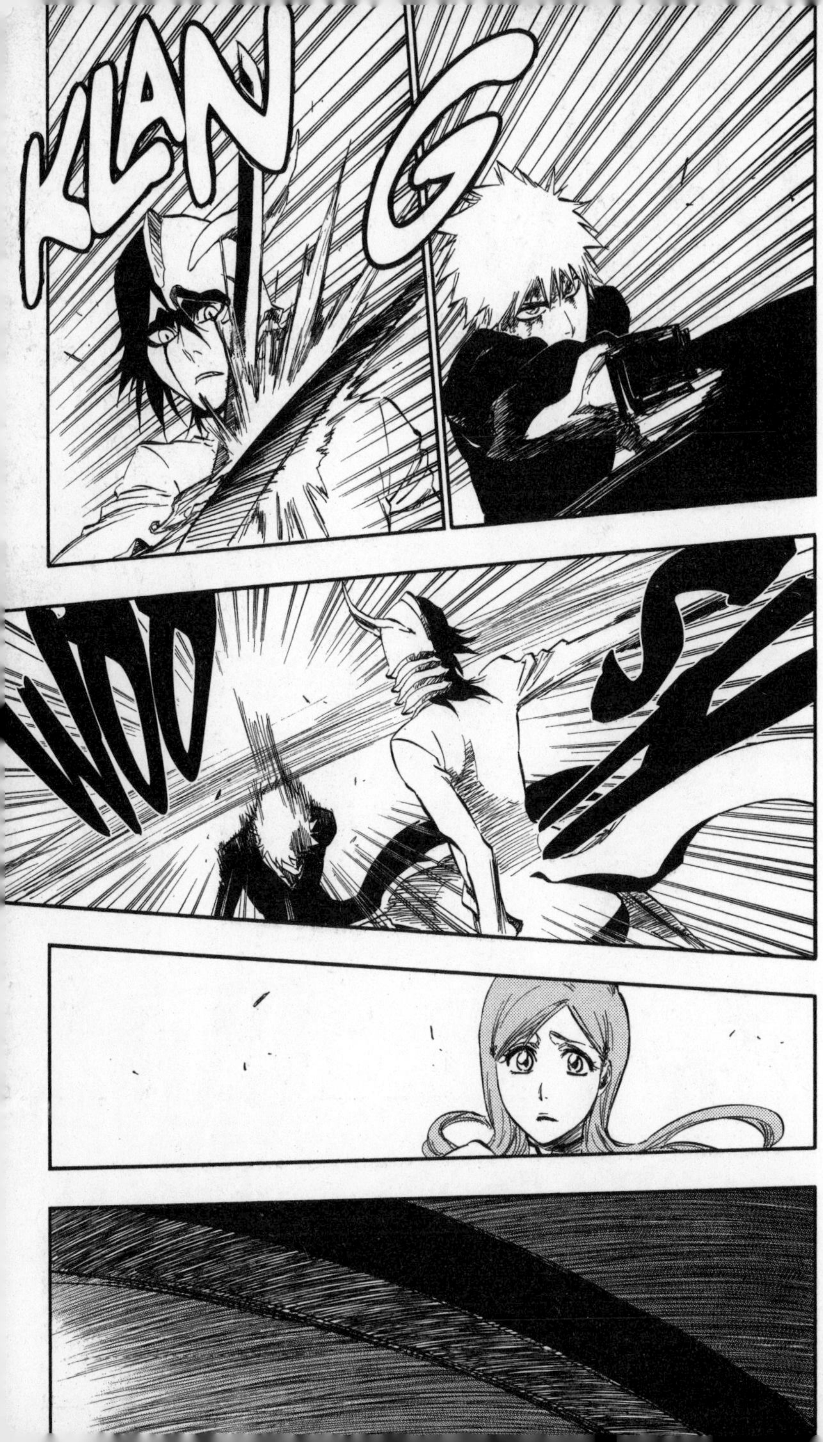
KLANG
WOOSH

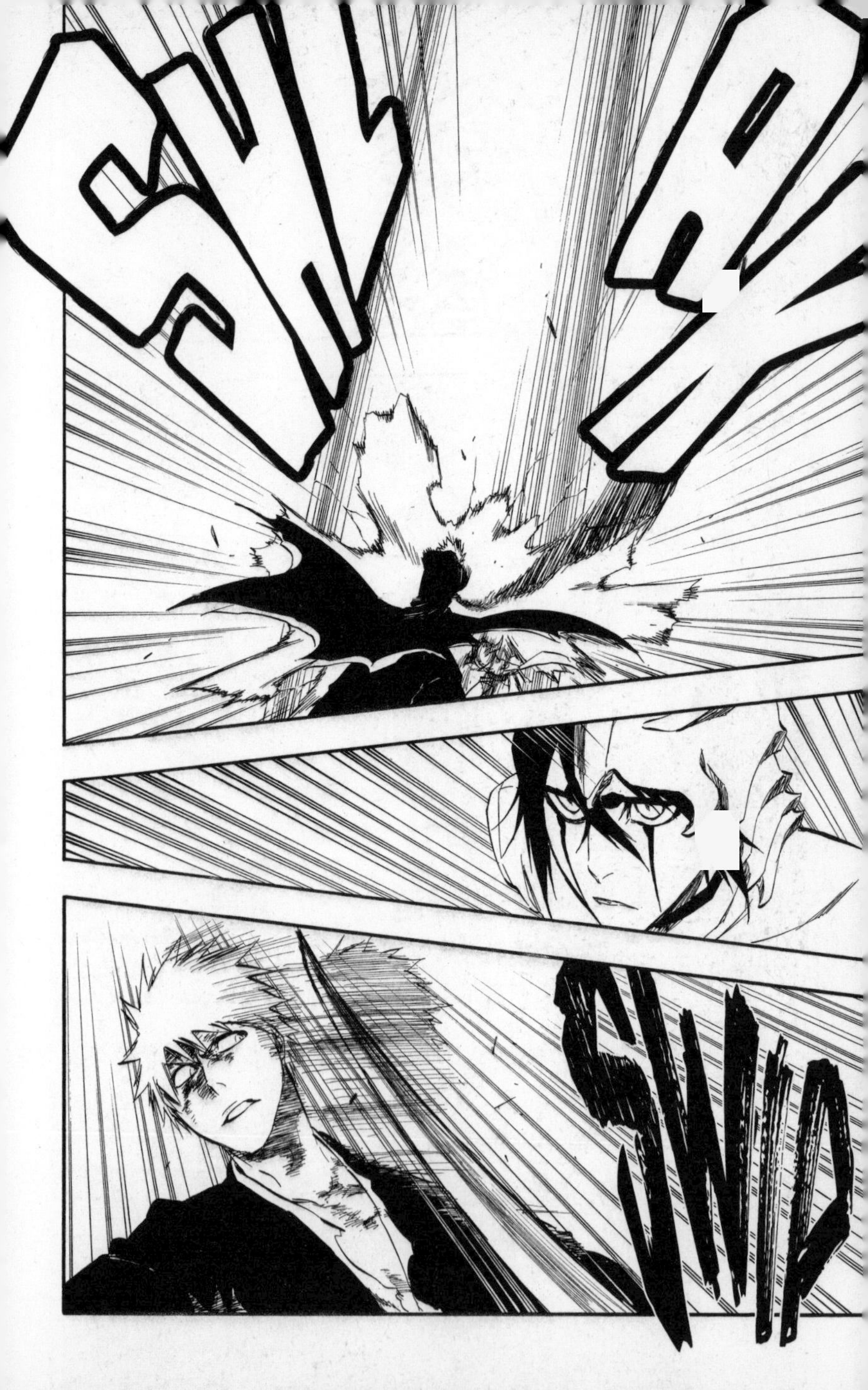
SWIP

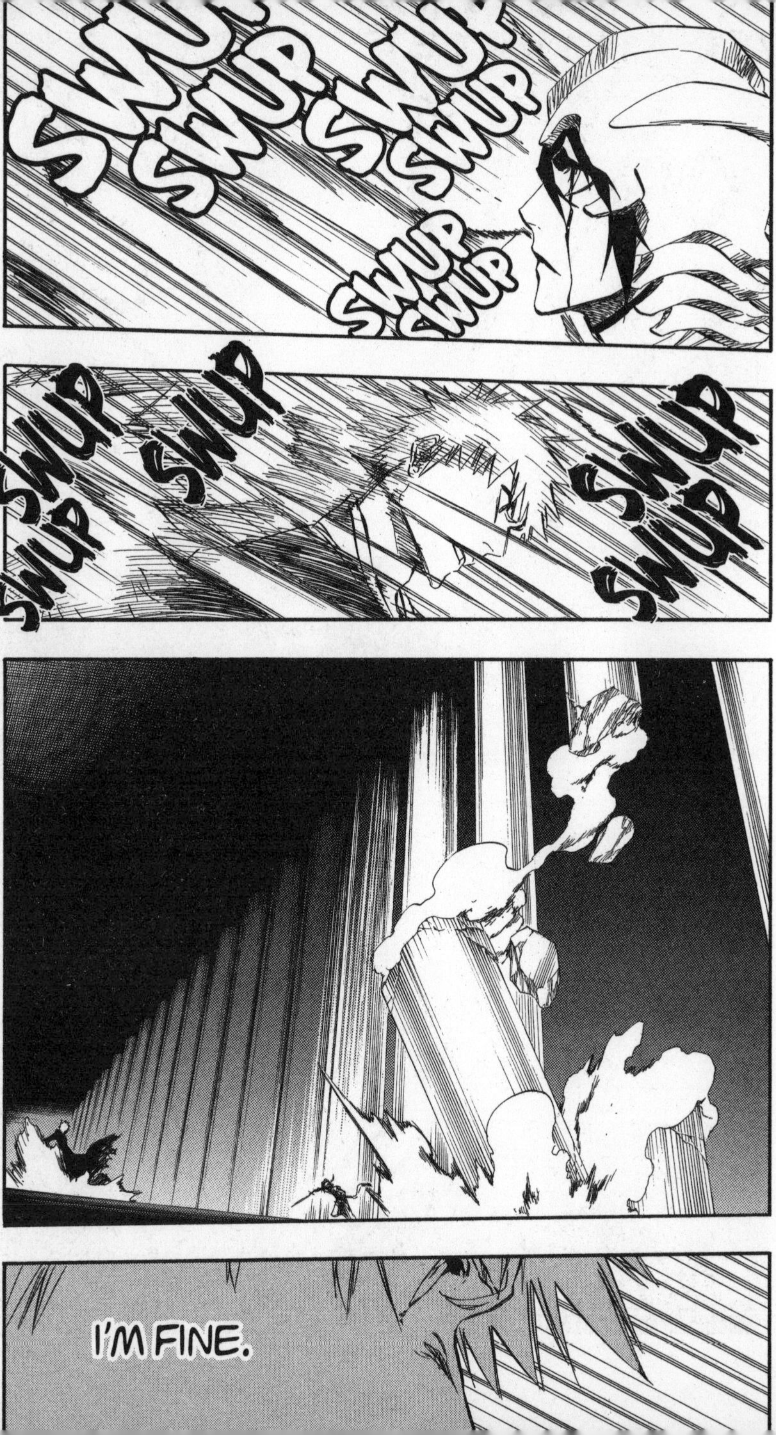
SWUP SWUP
SWUP SWUP
SWUP SWUP
SWUP SWUP
SWUP SWUP
SWUP SWUP
I'M FINE.

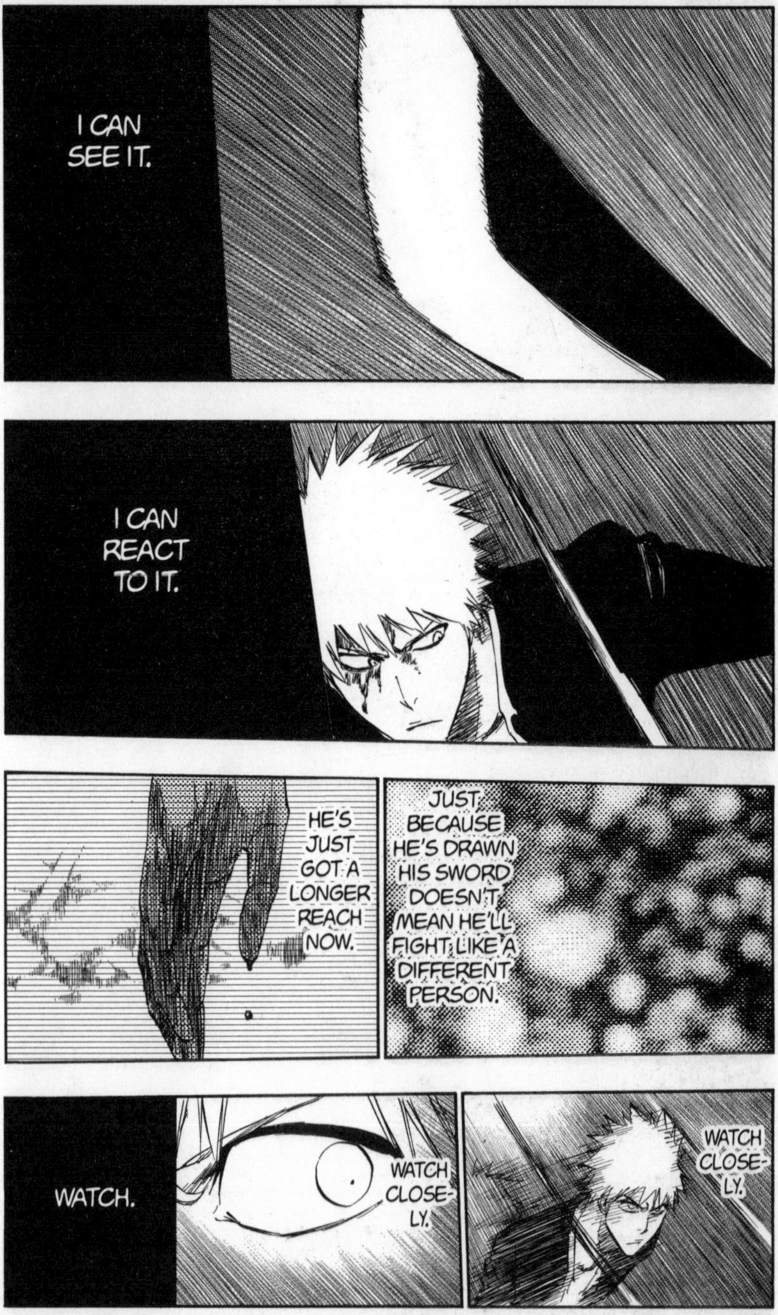

I CAN SEE IT.
I CAN REACT TO IT.
JUST BECAUSE HE'S DRAWN HIS SWORD DOESN'T MEAN HE'LL FIGHT LIKE A DIFFERENT PERSON.
HE'S JUST GOT A LONGER REACH NOW.
WATCH CLOSE-LY.
WATCH CLOSE-LY.
WATCH.

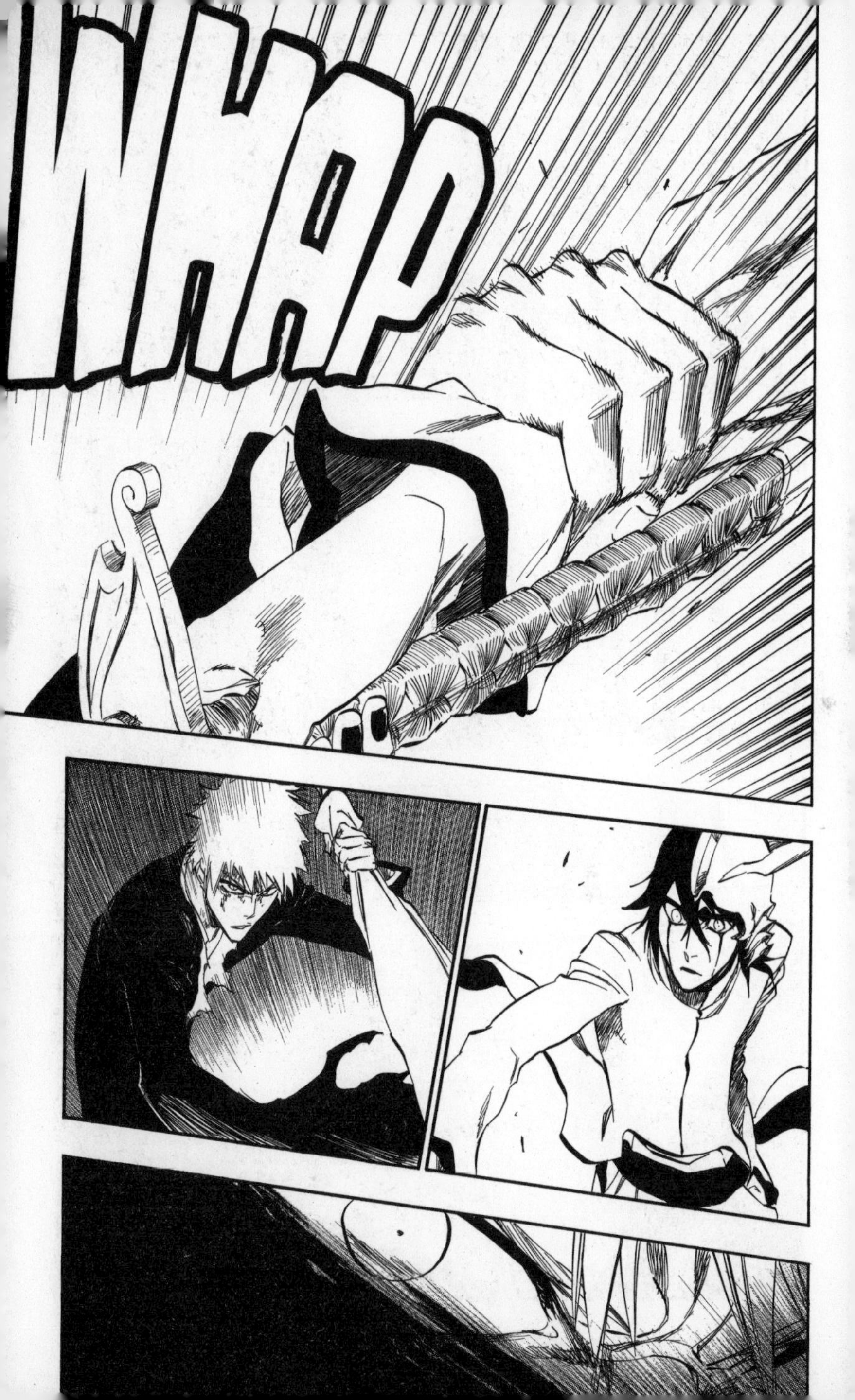
WHAP

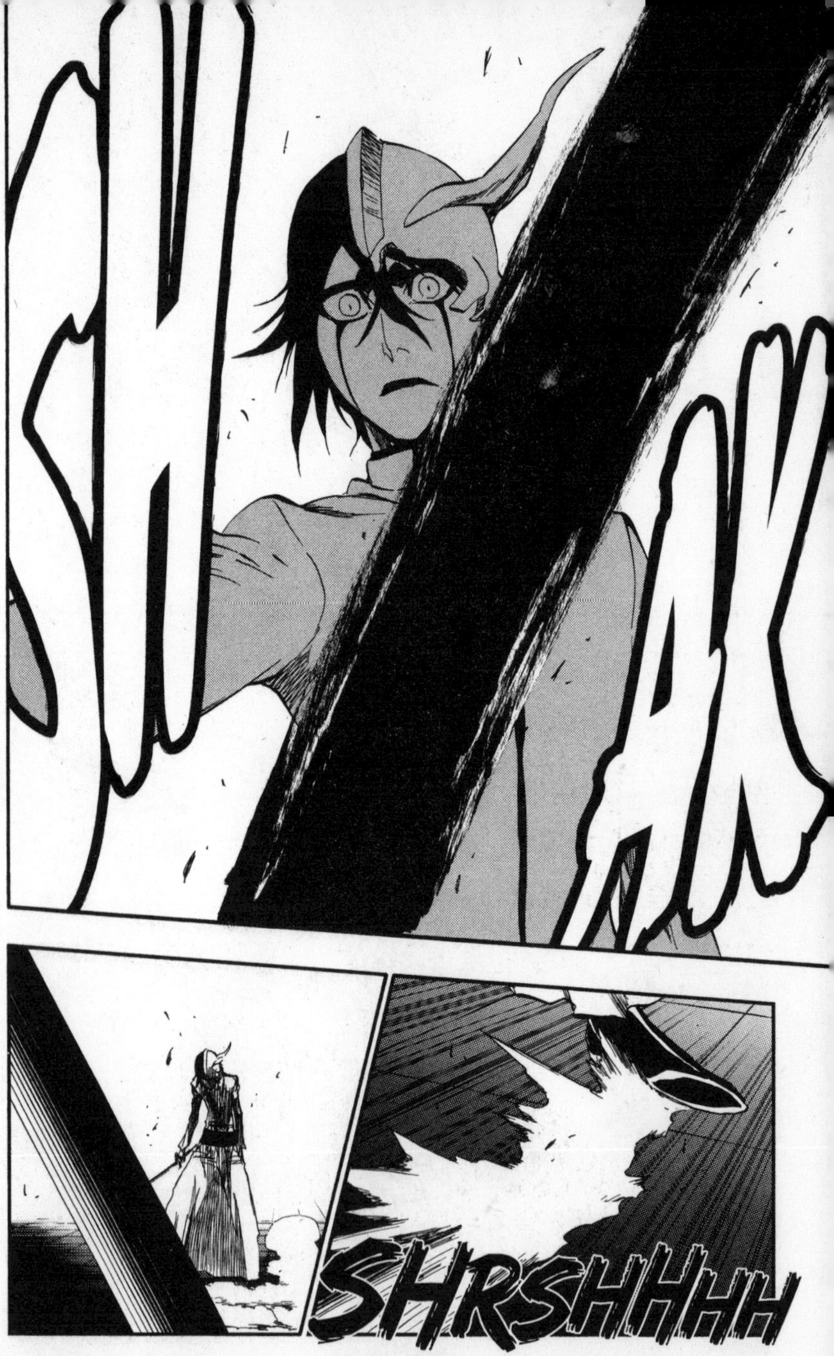
SHRSHHHH

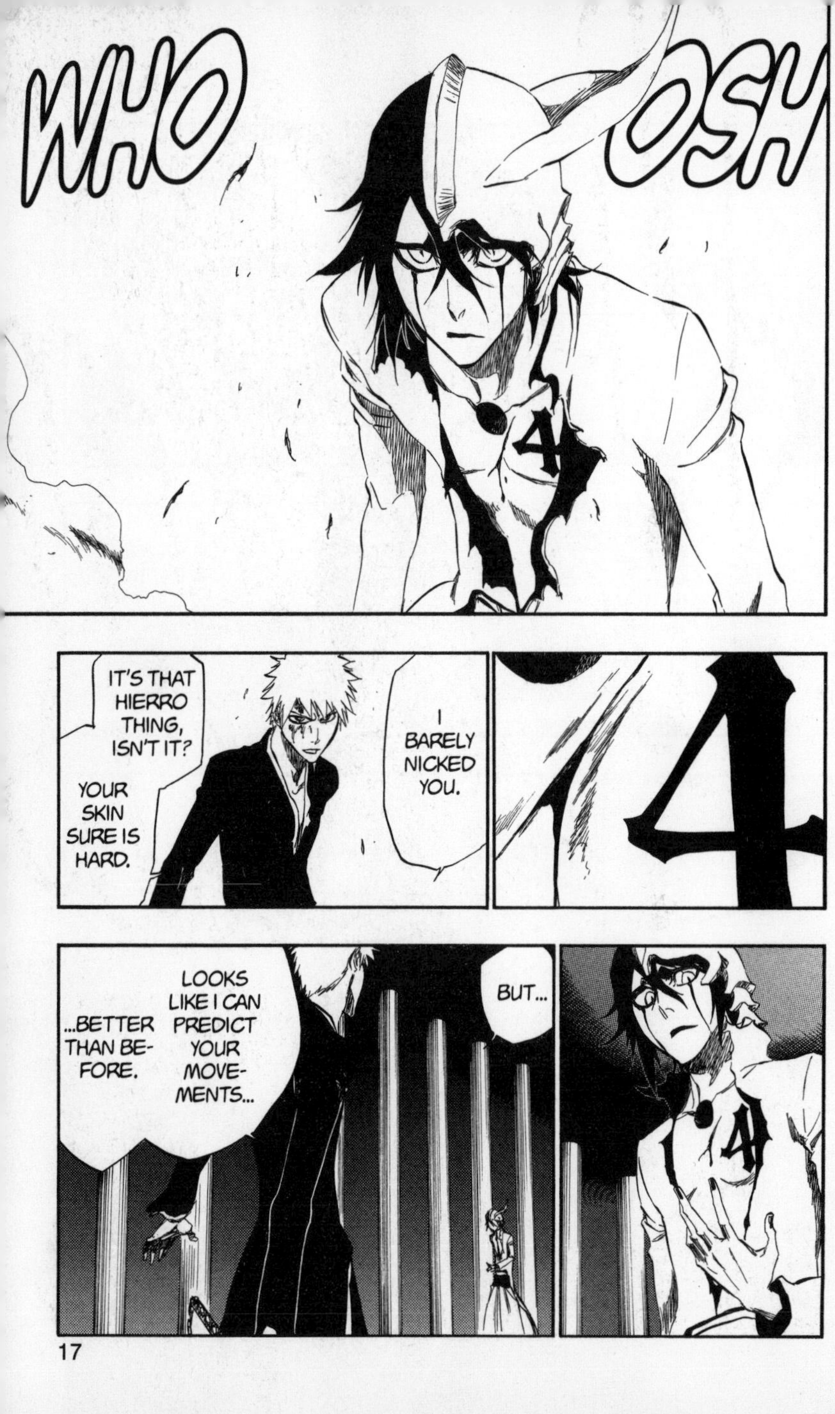
WHOOSH
I BARELY NICKED YOU.
IT'S THAT HIERRO THING, ISN'T IT?
YOUR SKIN SURE IS HARD.
BUT...
LOOKS LIKE I CAN PREDICT YOUR MOVE-MENTS...
...BETTER THAN BE-FORE.

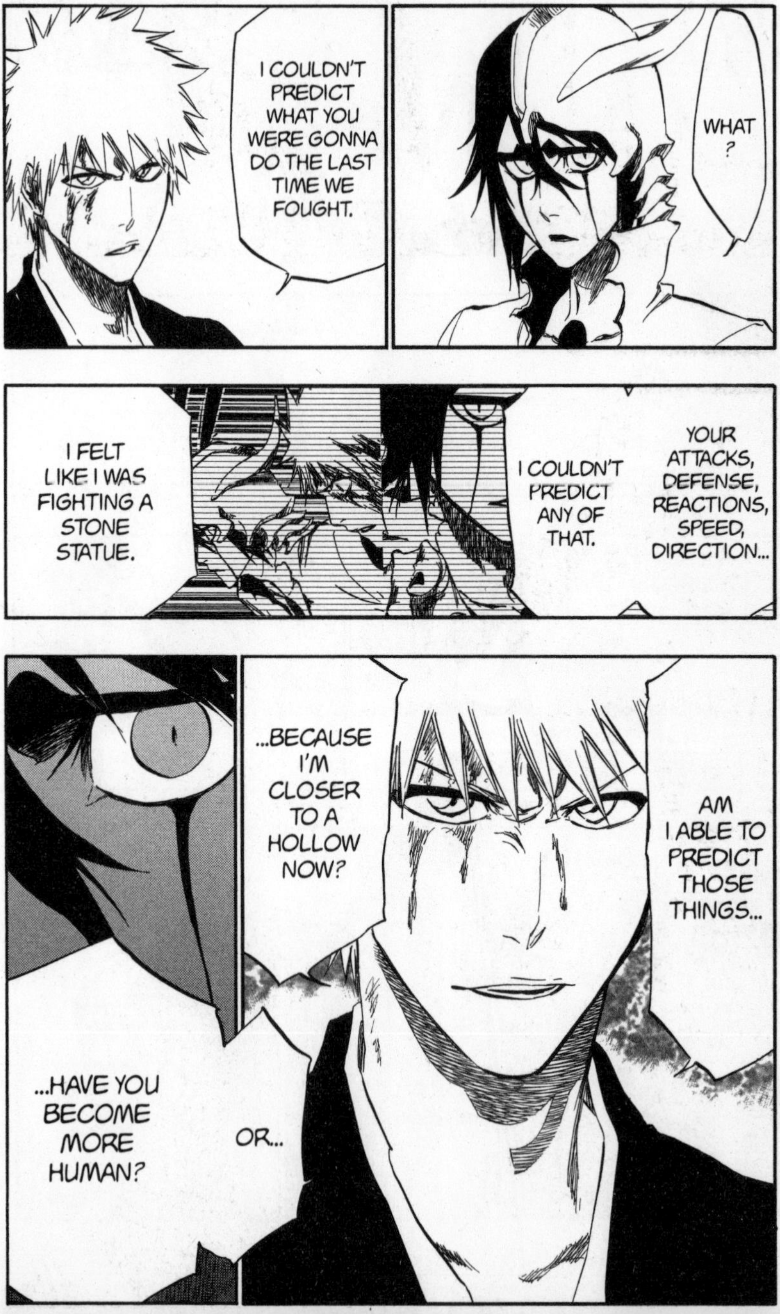
WHAT?
I COULDN'T PREDICT WHAT YOU WERE GONNA DO THE LAST TIME WE FOUGHT.
YOUR ATTACKS, DEFENSE, REACTIONS, SPEED, DIRECTION...
I COULDN'T PREDICT ANY OF THAT.
I FELT LIKE I WAS FIGHTING A STONE STATUE.
AM I ABLE TO PREDICT THOSE THINGS...
...BECAUSE I'M CLOSER TO A HOLLOW NOW?
OR...
...HAVE YOU BECOME MORE HUMAN?

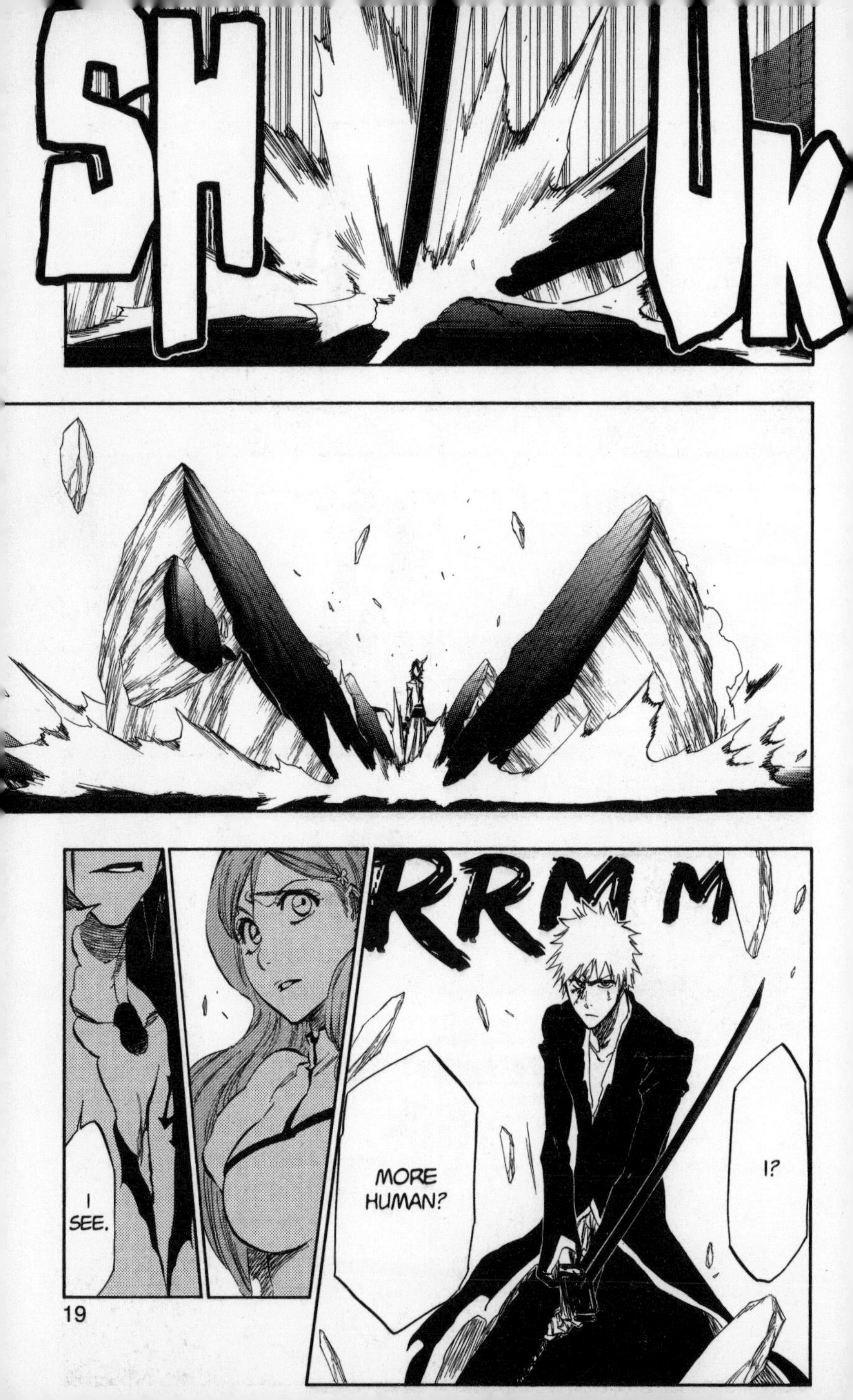
SH UK
RRMM
I?
MORE HUMAN?
I SEE.

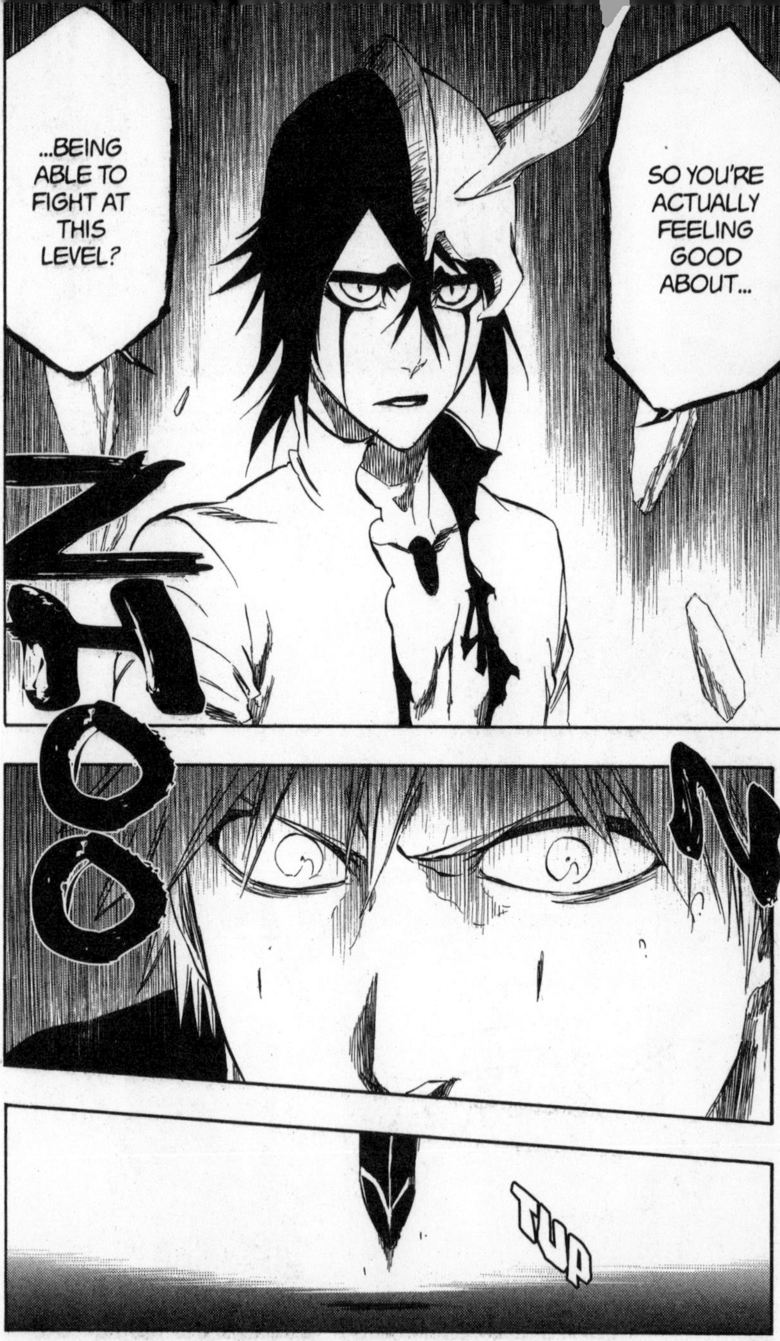
SO YOU'RE ACTUALLY FEELING GOOD ABOUT...
...BEING ABLE TO FIGHT AT THIS LEVEL?
TUP

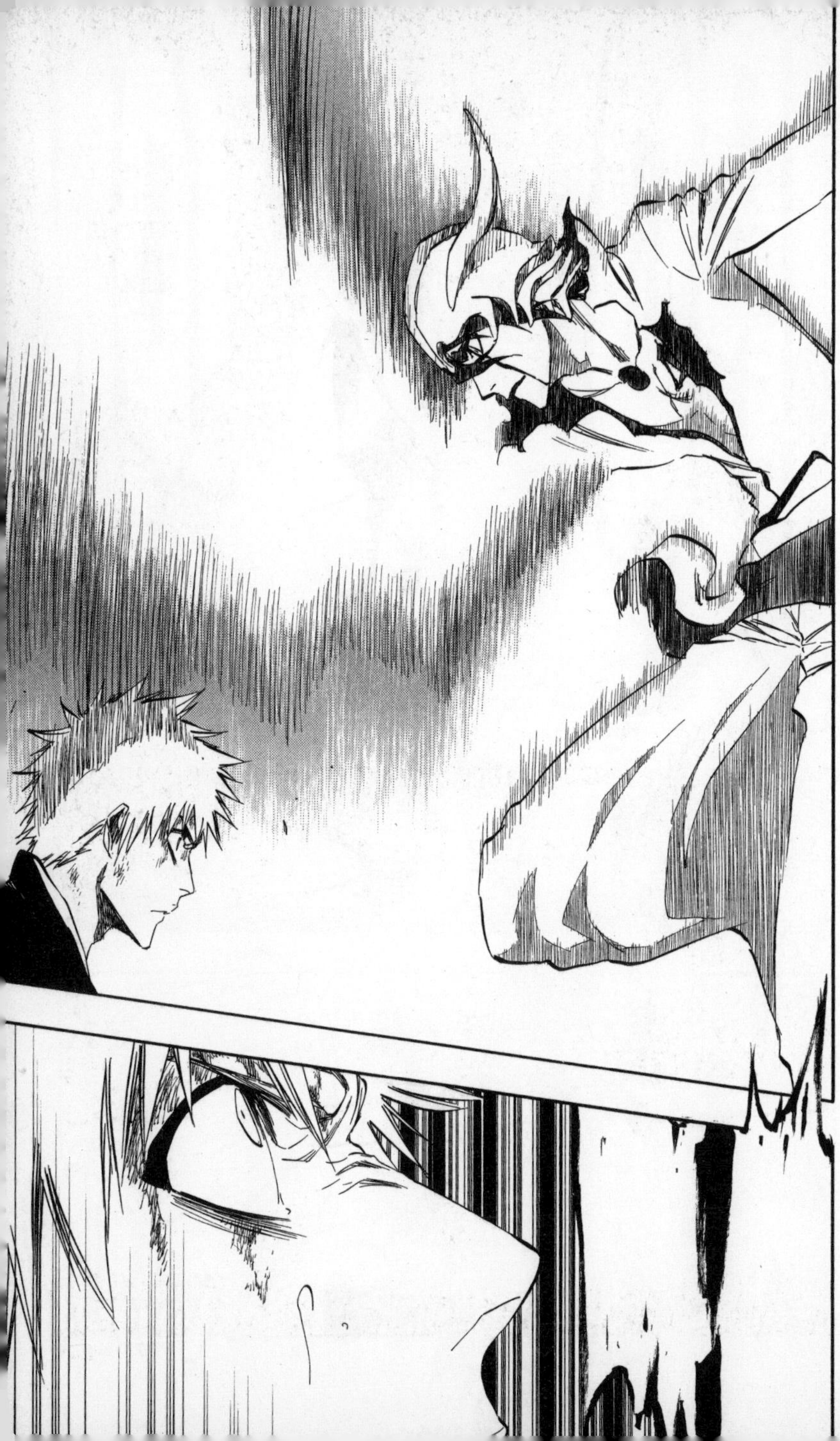

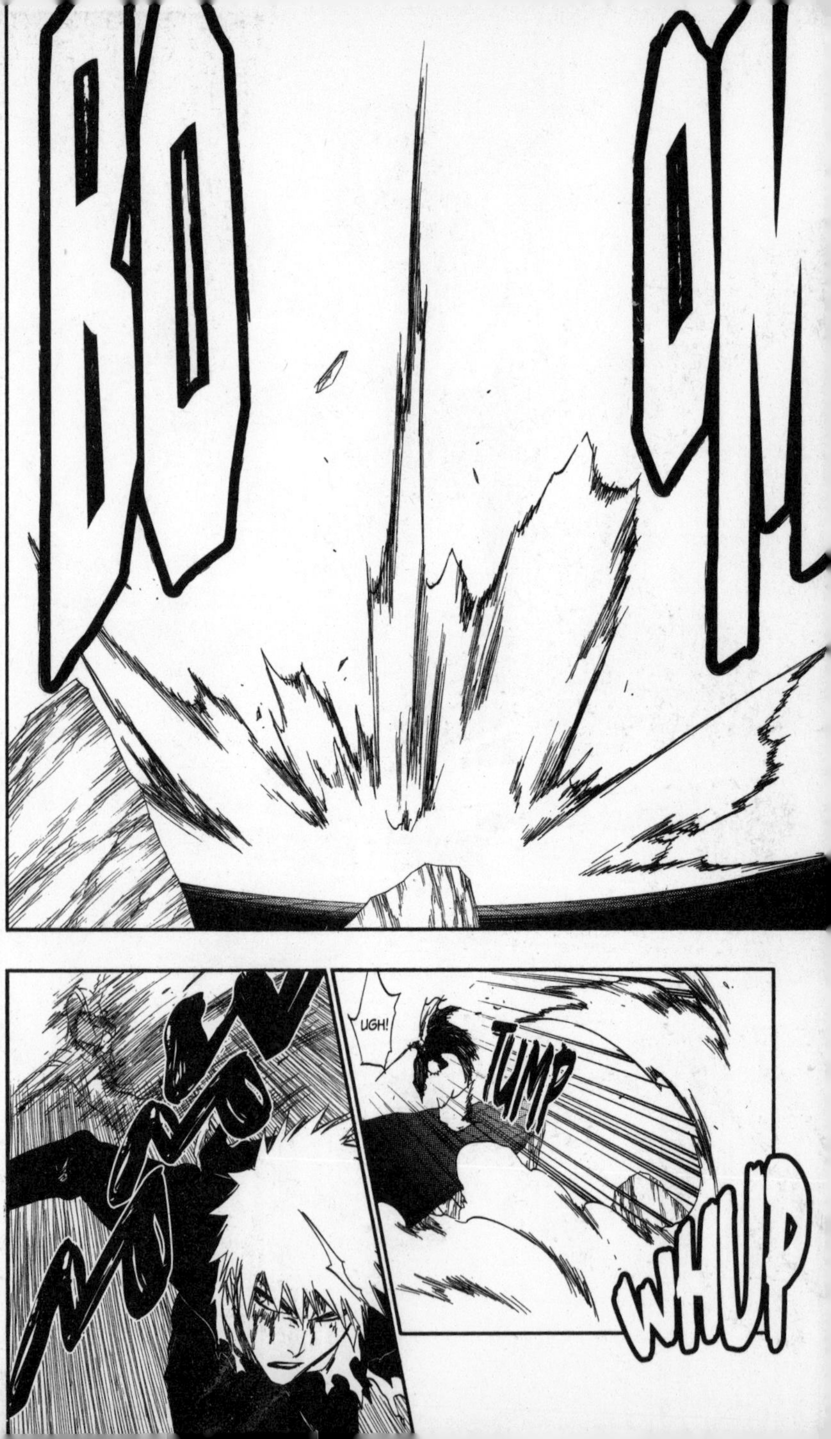
UGH!
TUMP
WHUP

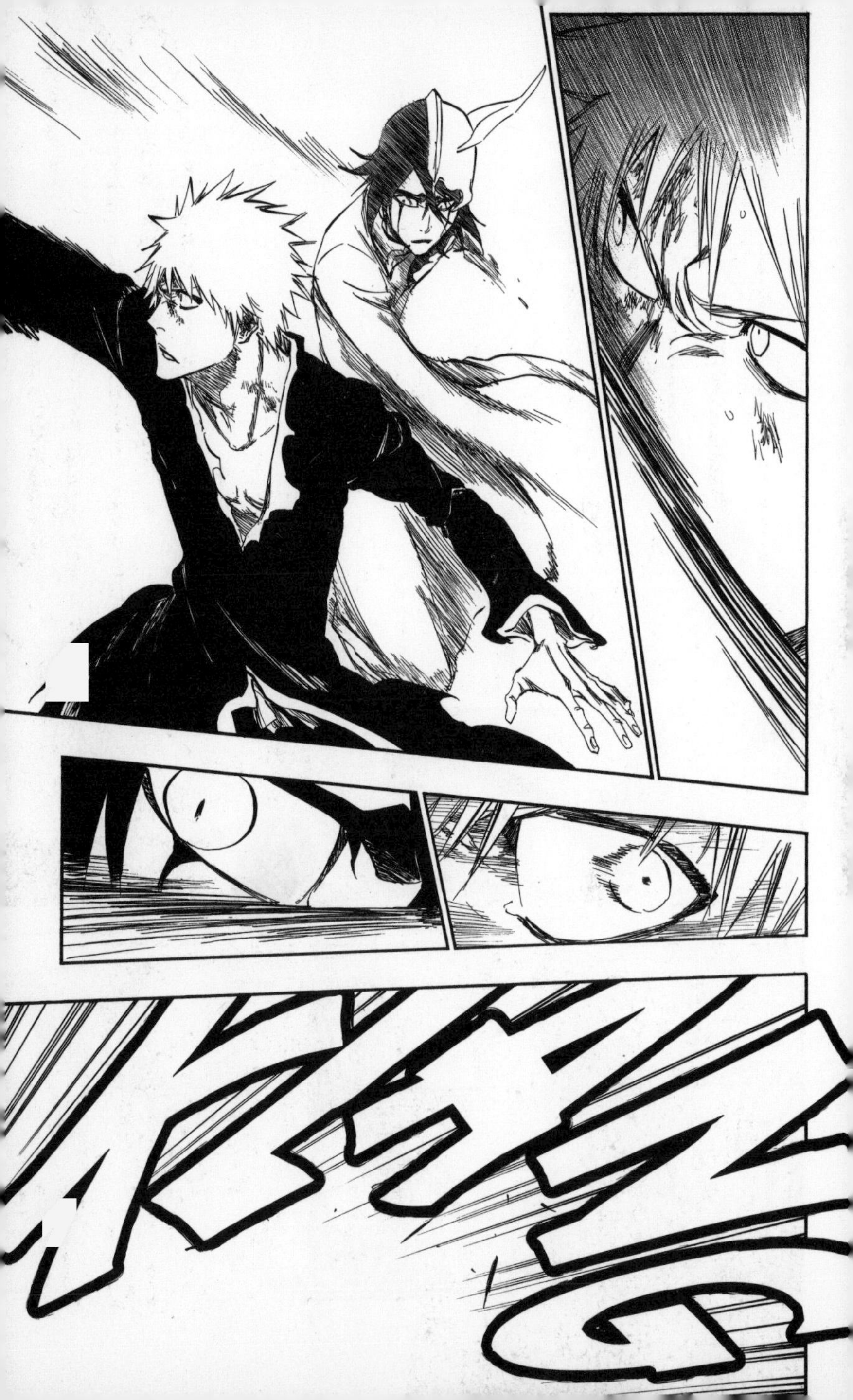

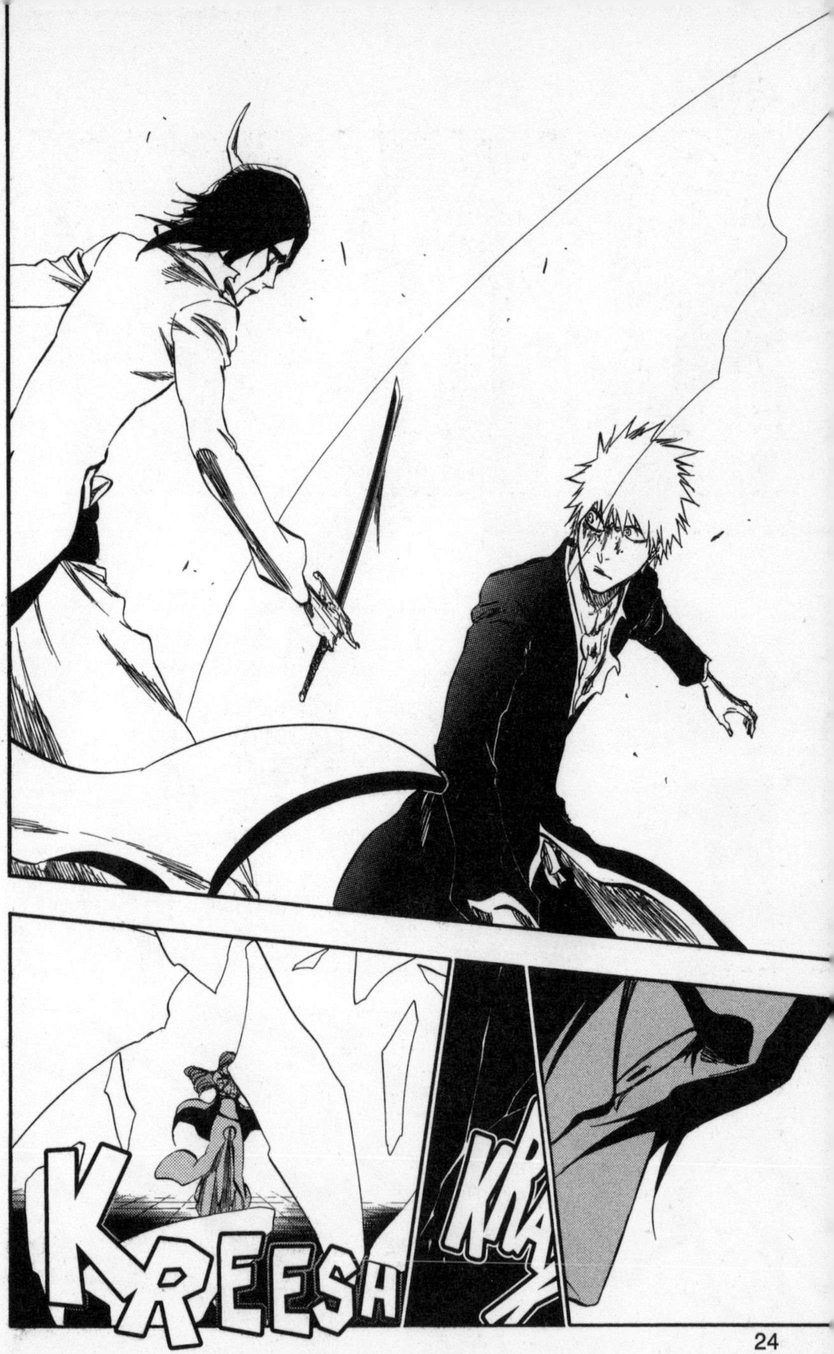
KRA
KREESH

READ THIS WAY

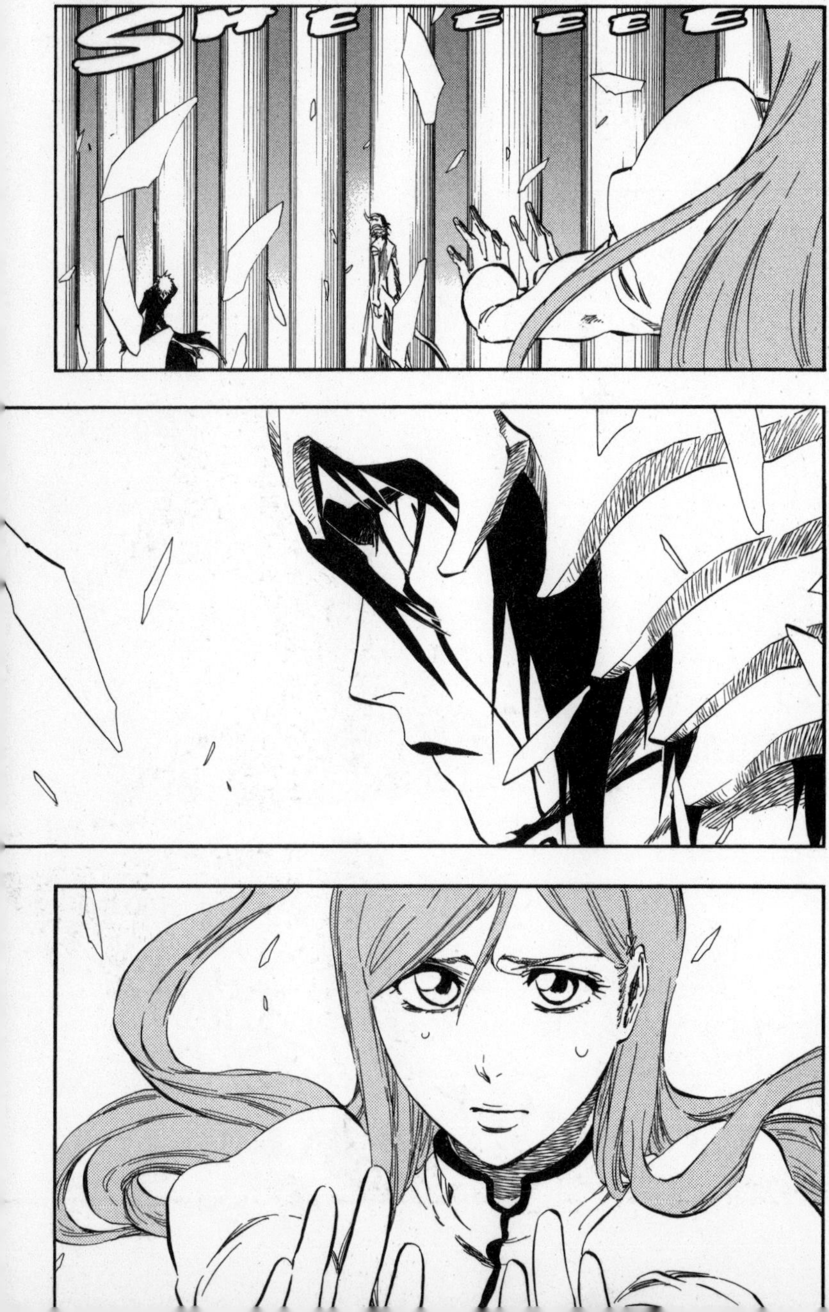
SHEEEEE

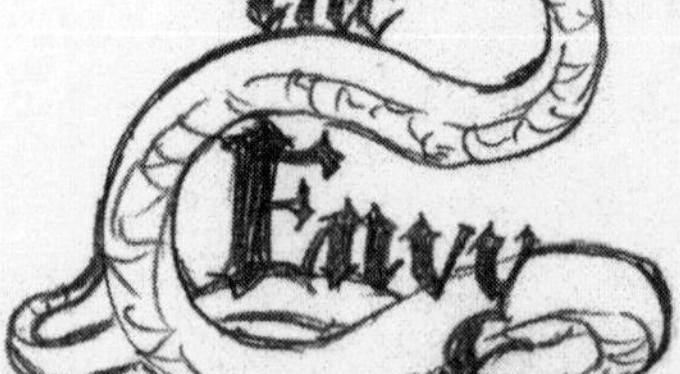
the Envy

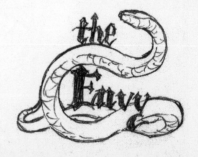

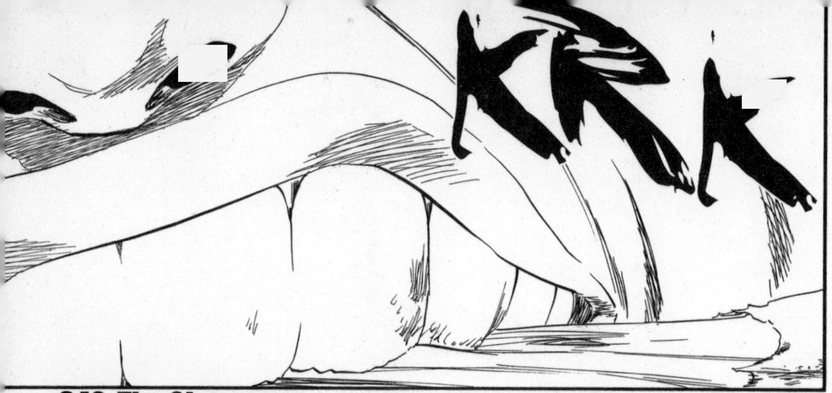
KRK

342. The Gluttony

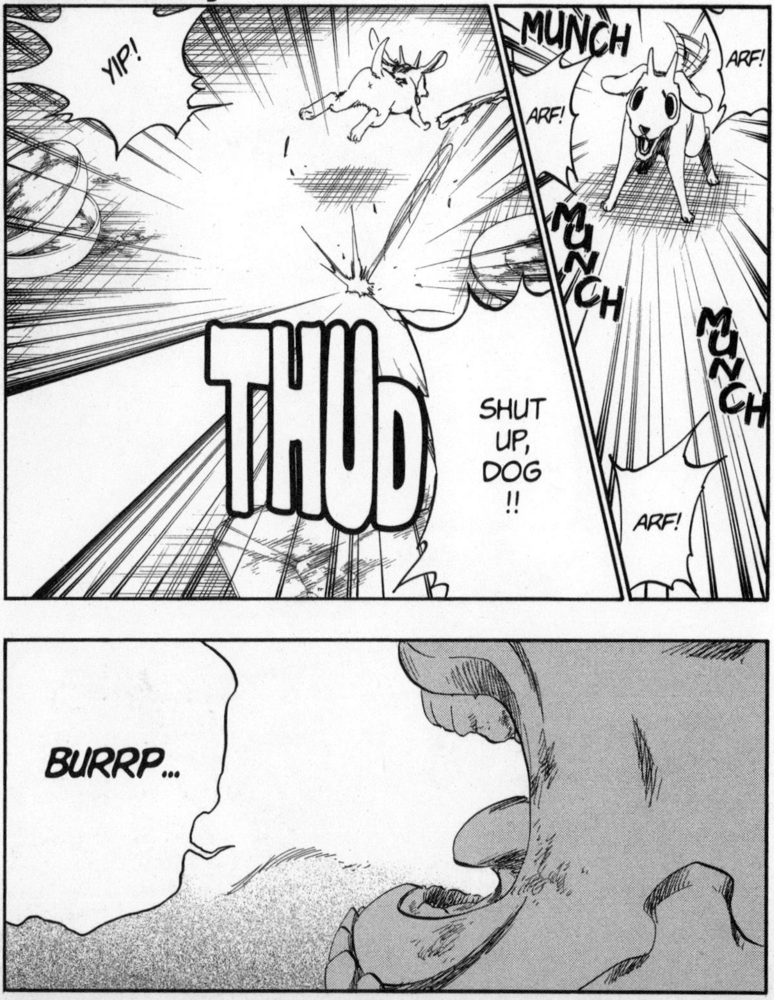
MUNCH
ARF!
ARF!
MUNCH
MUNCH
ARF!
YIP!
THUD
SHUT UP, DOG!!
BURRP...

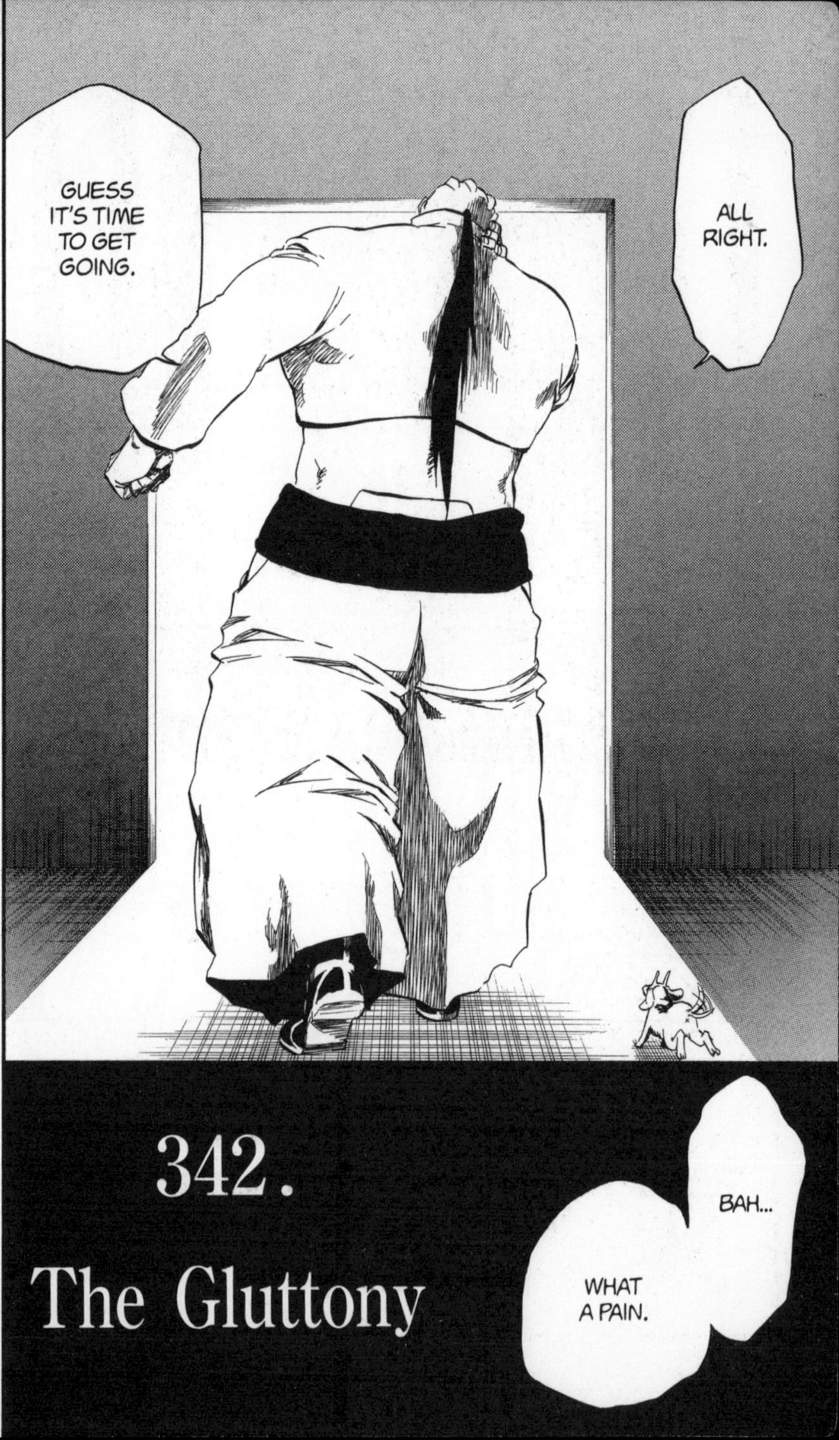
ALL RIGHT.
GUESS IT'S TIME TO GET GOING.
BAH...
WHAT A PAIN.

342. The Gluttony

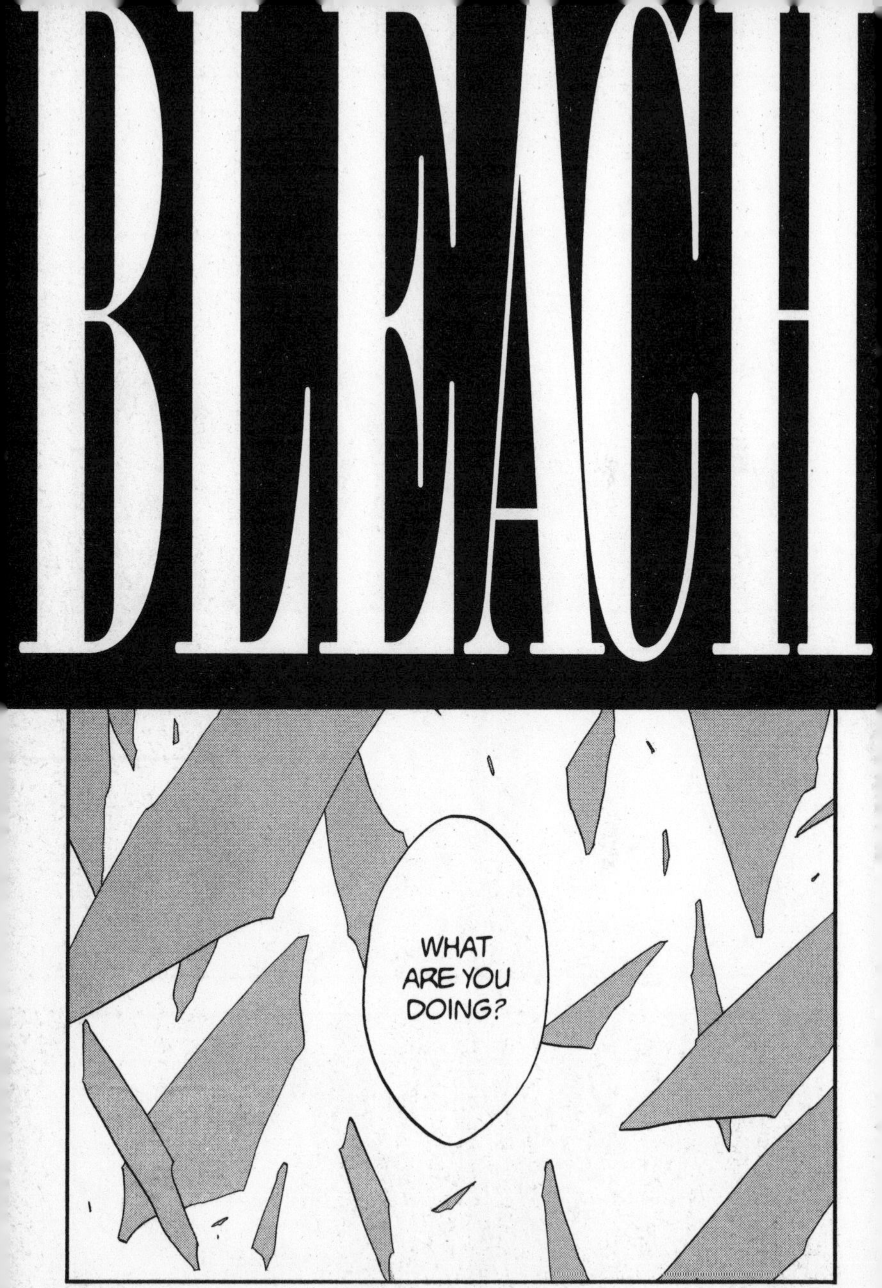
BLEACH
WHAT ARE YOU DOING?

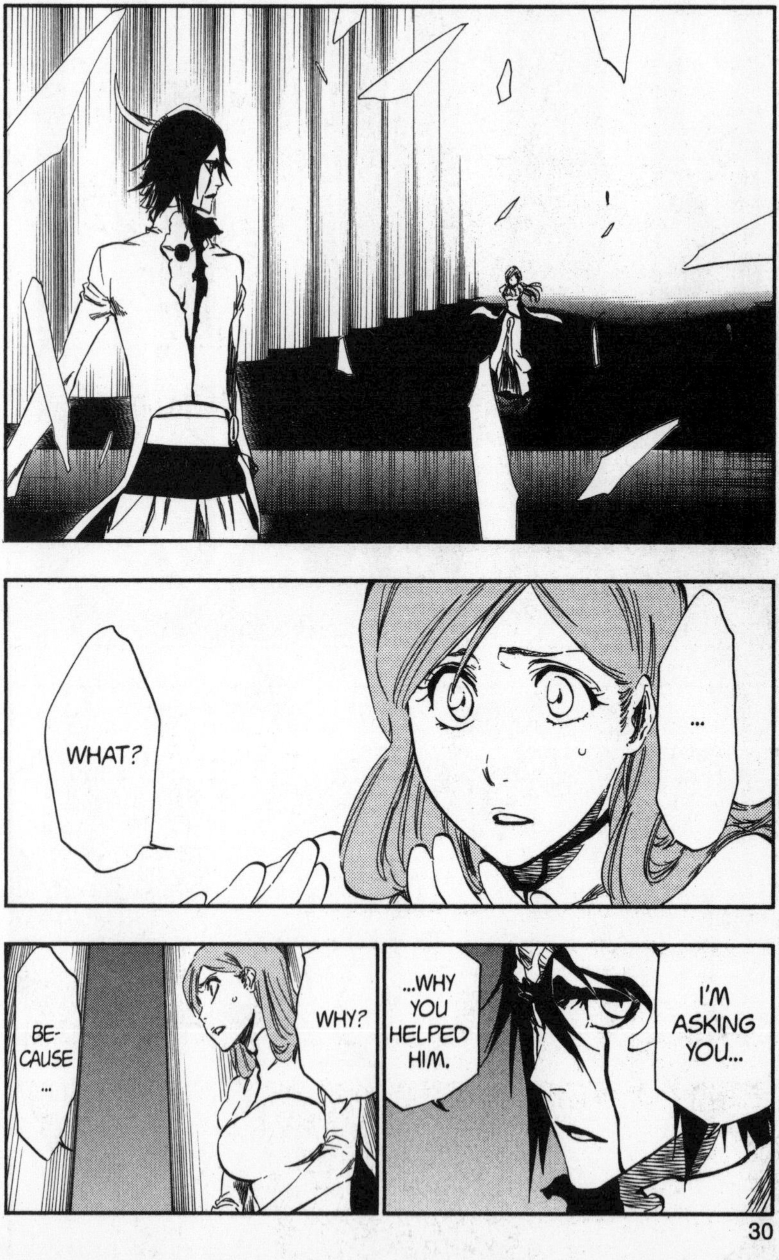
...
WHAT?
I'M ASKING YOU...
...WHY YOU HELPED HIM.
WHY?
BE-CAUSE ...

READ THIS WAY

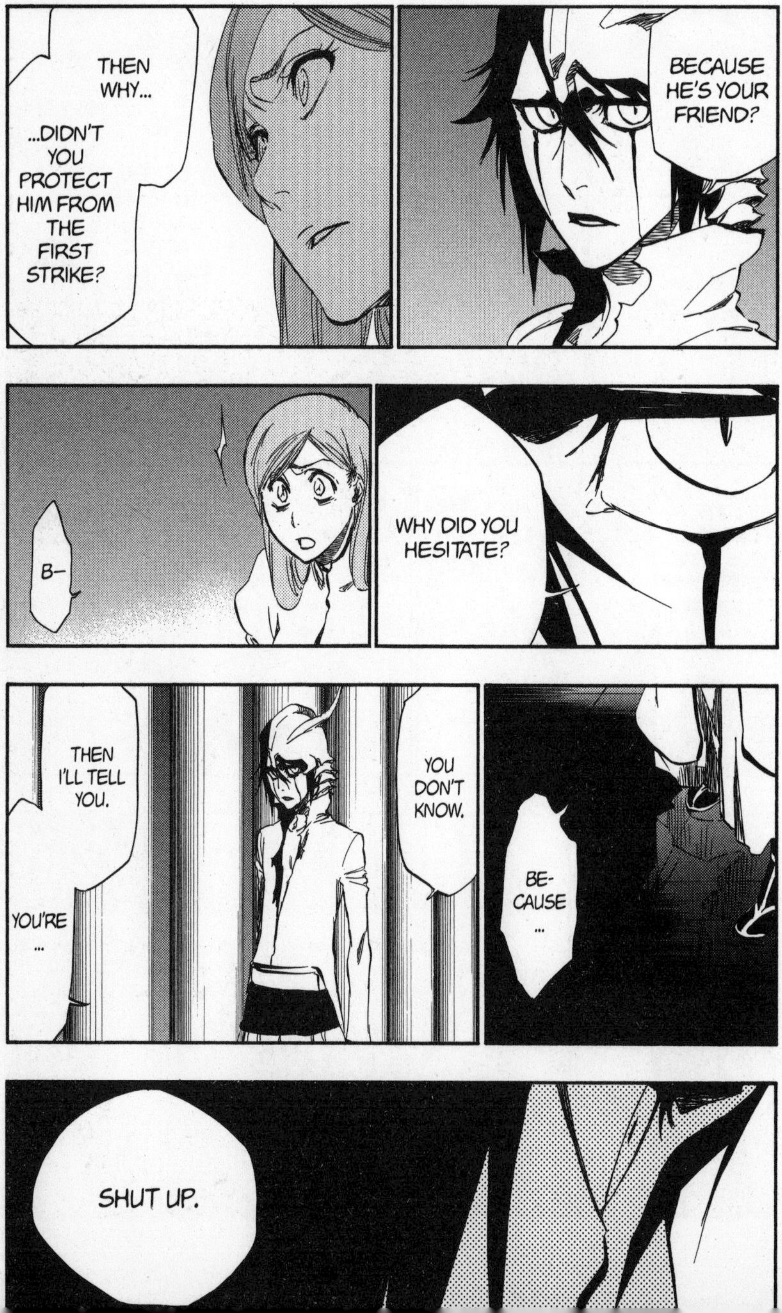
BECAUSE HE'S YOUR FRIEND?
THEN WHY...
...DIDN'T YOU PROTECT HIM FROM THE FIRST STRIKE?
WHY DID YOU HESITATE?
B—
BE-CAUSE ...
YOU DON'T KNOW.
THEN I'LL TELL YOU.
YOU'RE ...
SHUT UP.

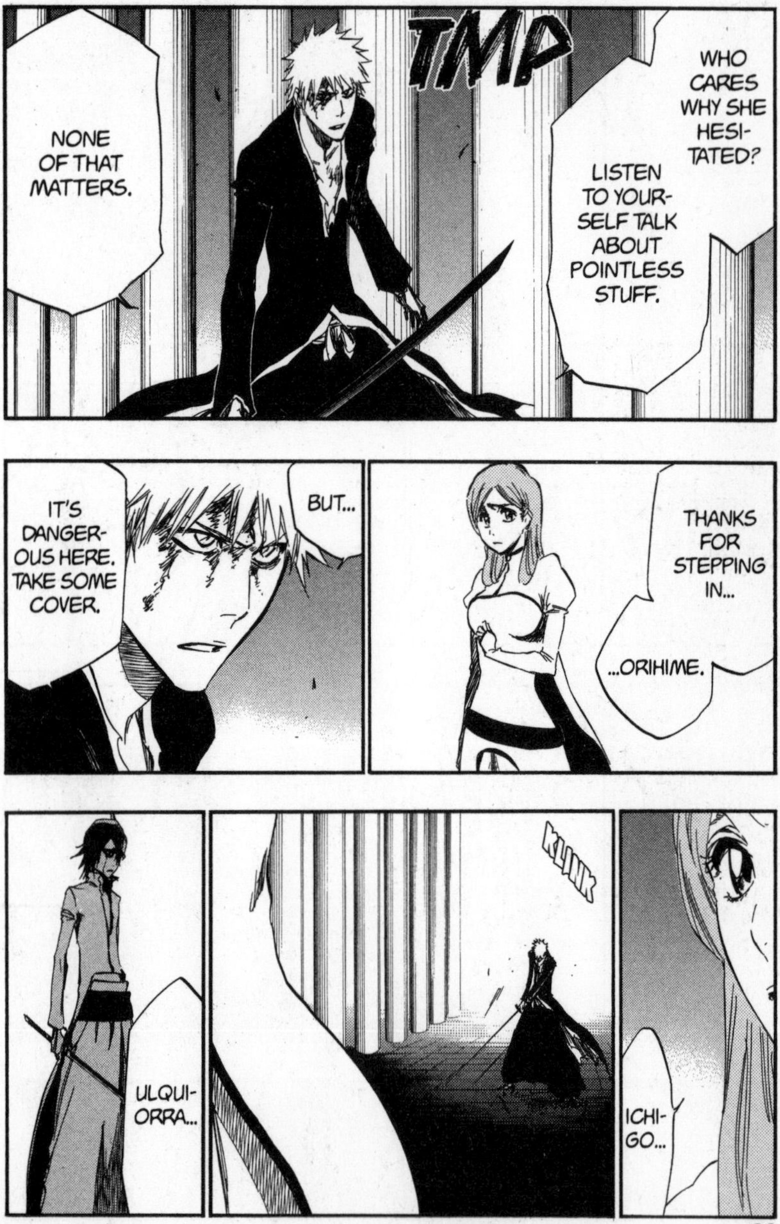

WHO CARES WHY SHE HESITATED?
LISTEN TO YOURSELF TALK ABOUT POINTLESS STUFF.
TMP
NONE OF THAT MATTERS.
THANKS FOR STEPPING IN...
...ORIHIME.
BUT...
IT'S DANGEROUS HERE. TAKE SOME COVER.
ICHIGO...
KLINK
ULQUIORRA...

READ THIS WAY

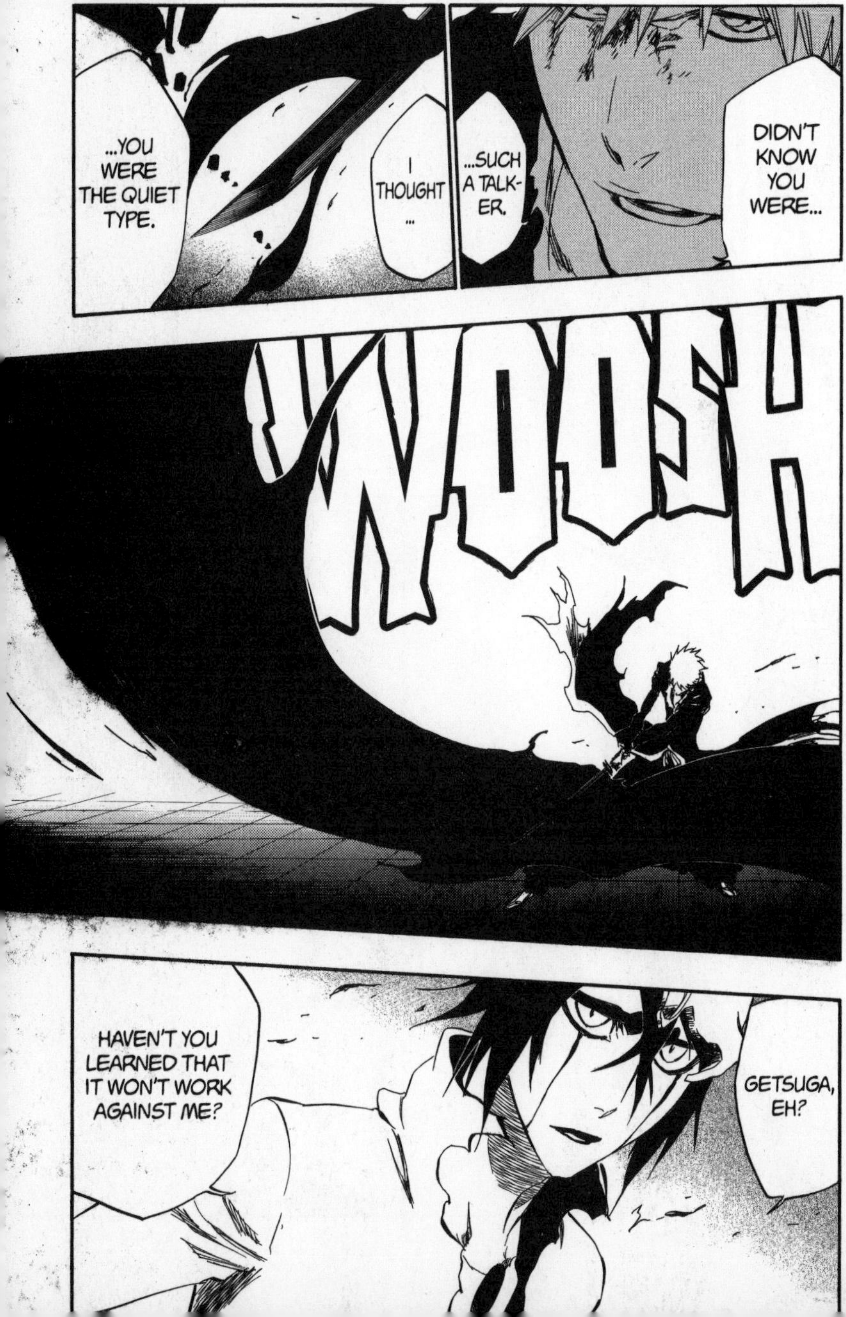
DIDN'T KNOW YOU WERE...
...SUCH A TALK-ER.
I THOUGHT...
...YOU WERE THE QUIET TYPE.
WOOSH
GETSUGA, EH?
HAVEN'T YOU LEARNED THAT IT WON'T WORK AGAINST ME?

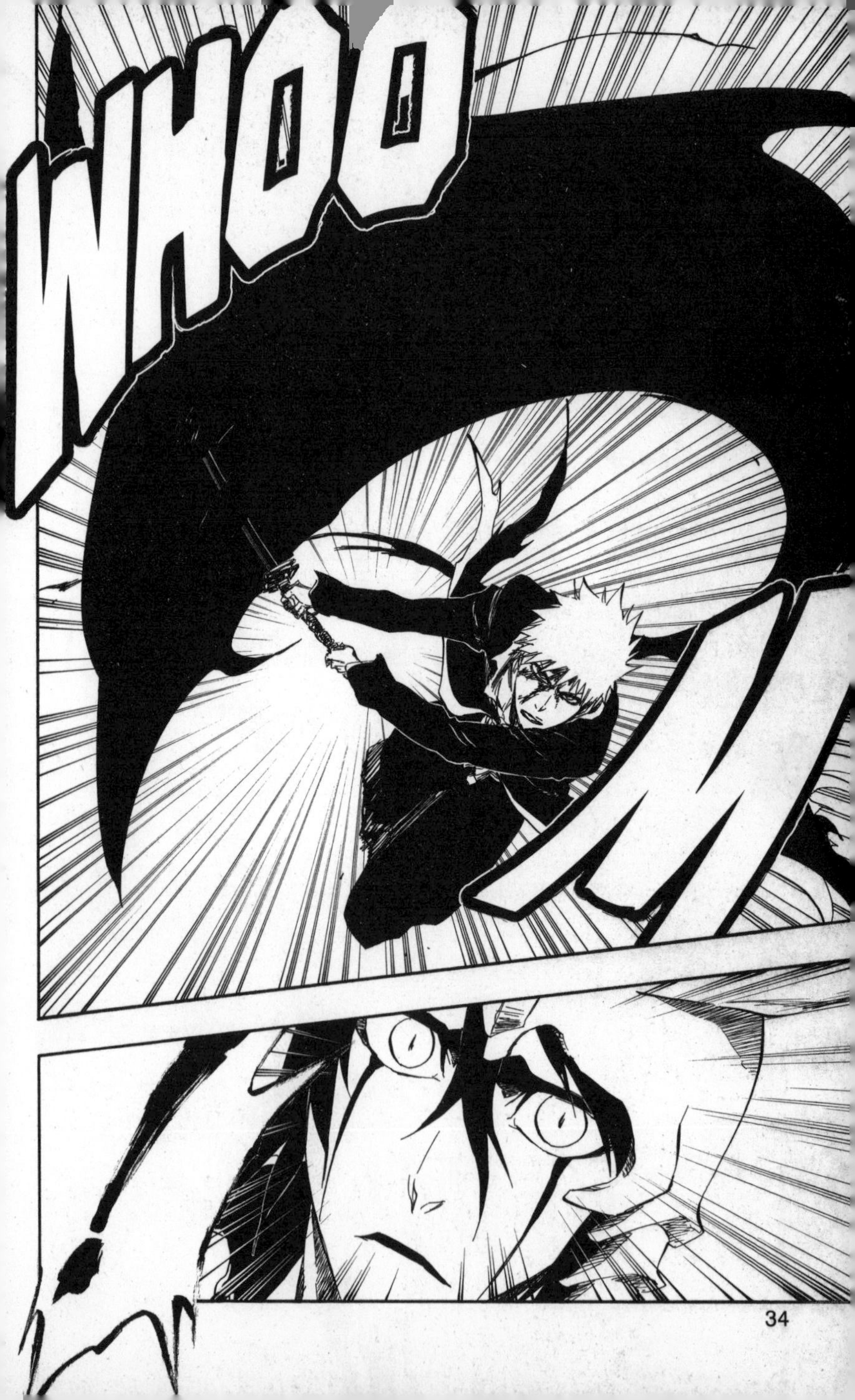
WHOOM

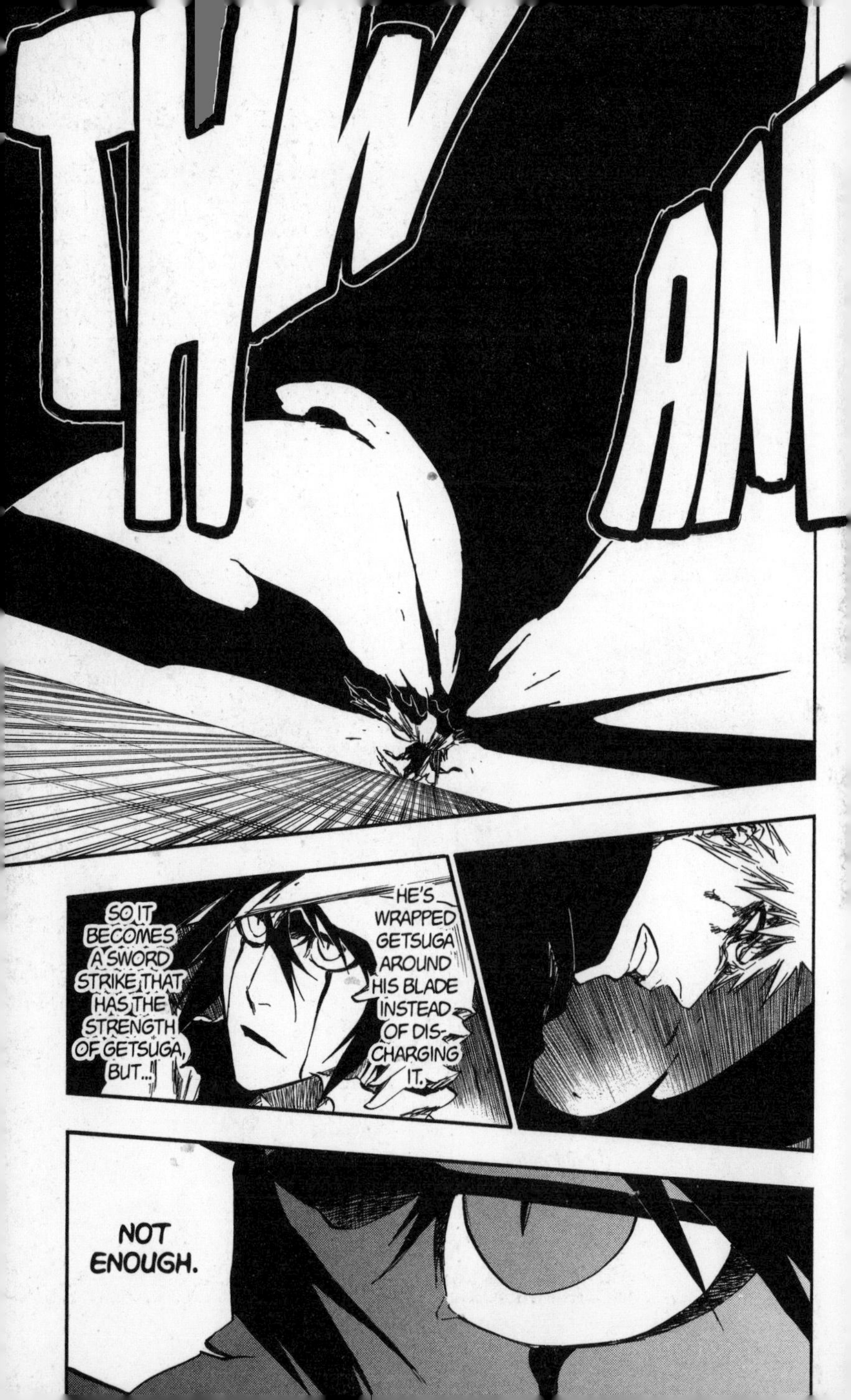
THWAM
HE'S WRAPPED GETSUGA AROUND HIS BLADE INSTEAD OF DIS-CHARGING IT.
SO IT BECOMES A SWORD STRIKE THAT HAS THE STRENGTH OF GETSUGA, BUT...
NOT ENOUGH.

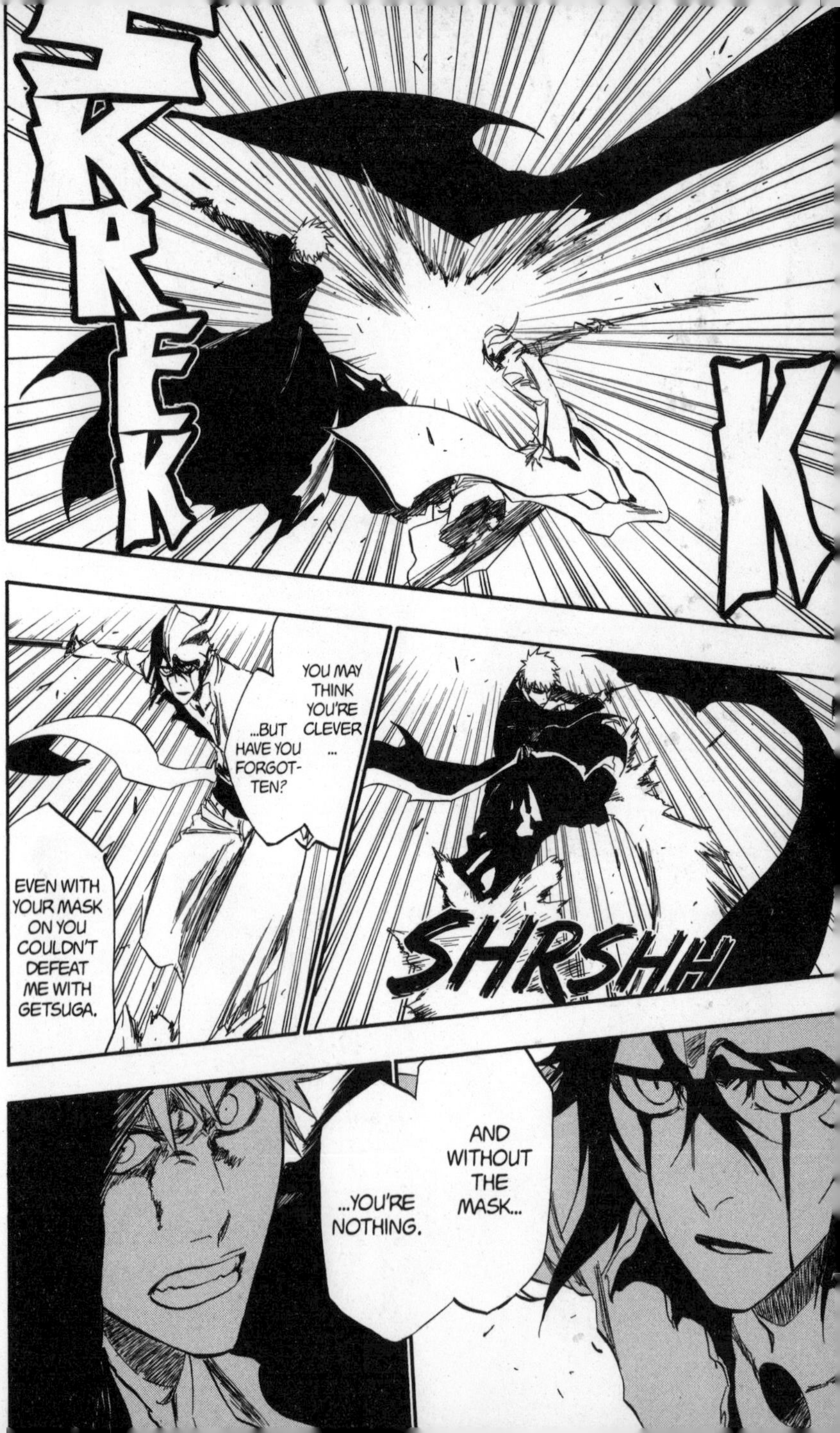
KREK
K
SHRSHH
YOU MAY THINK YOU'RE CLEVER...
...BUT HAVE YOU FORGOTTEN?
EVEN WITH YOUR MASK ON YOU COULDN'T DEFEAT ME WITH GETSUGA.
AND WITHOUT THE MASK...
...YOU'RE NOTHING.

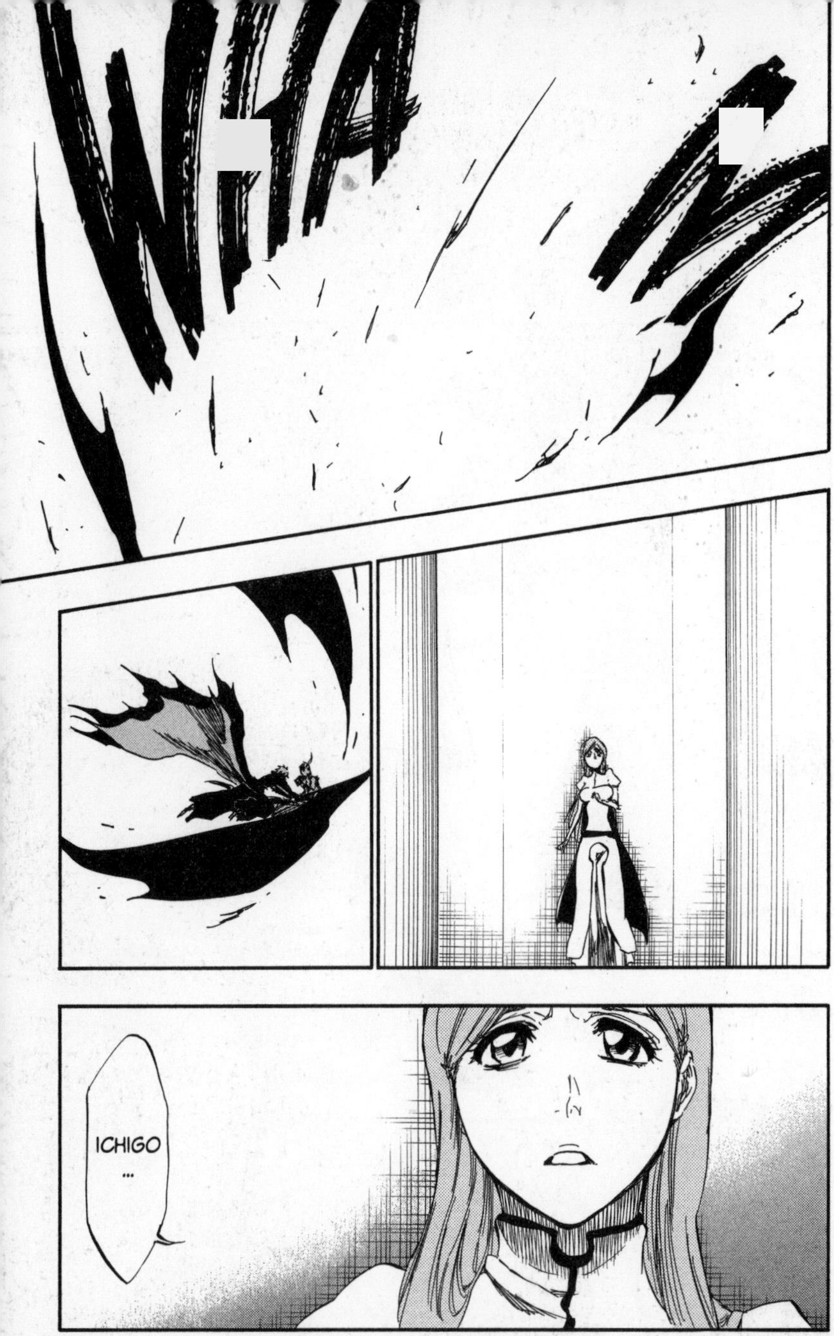
WHAM
ICHIGO
...

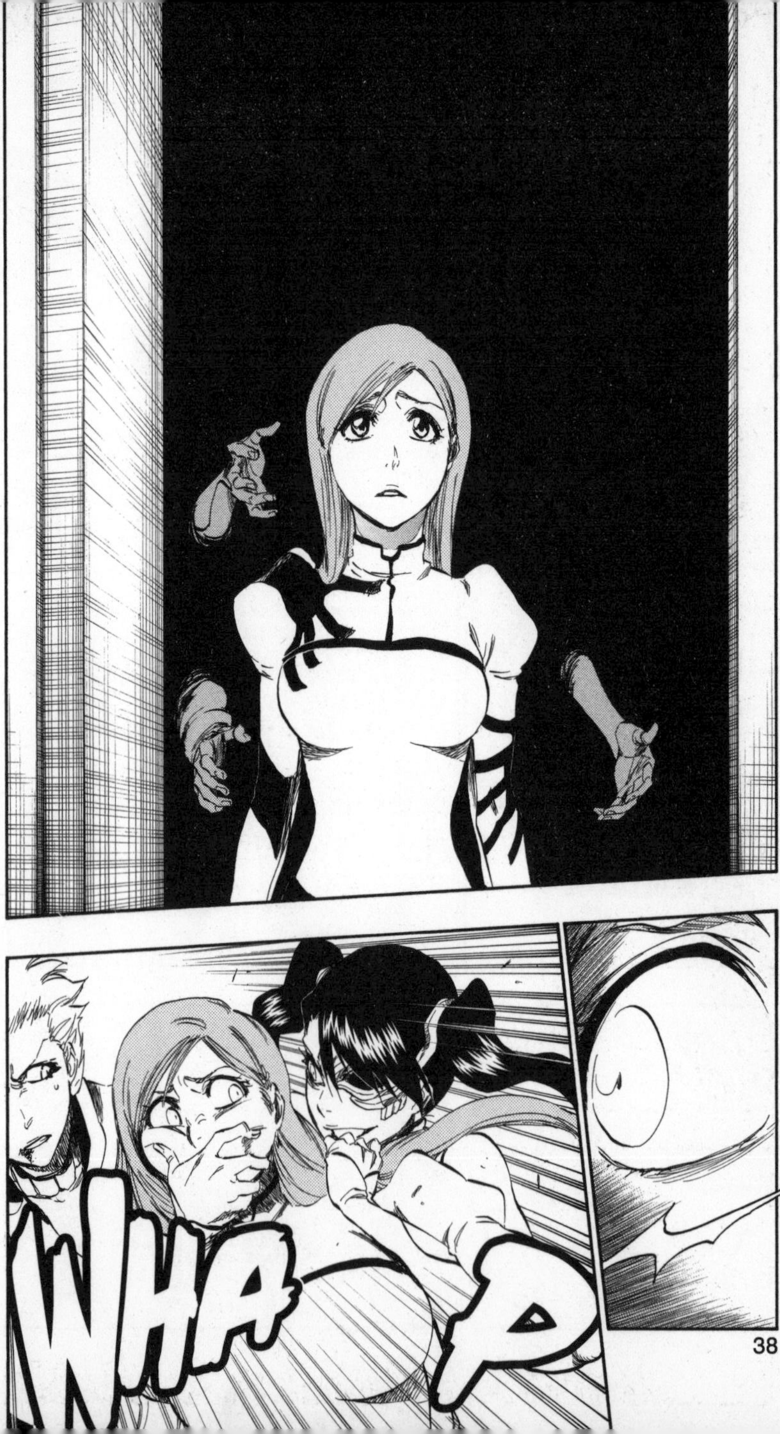
WHAP

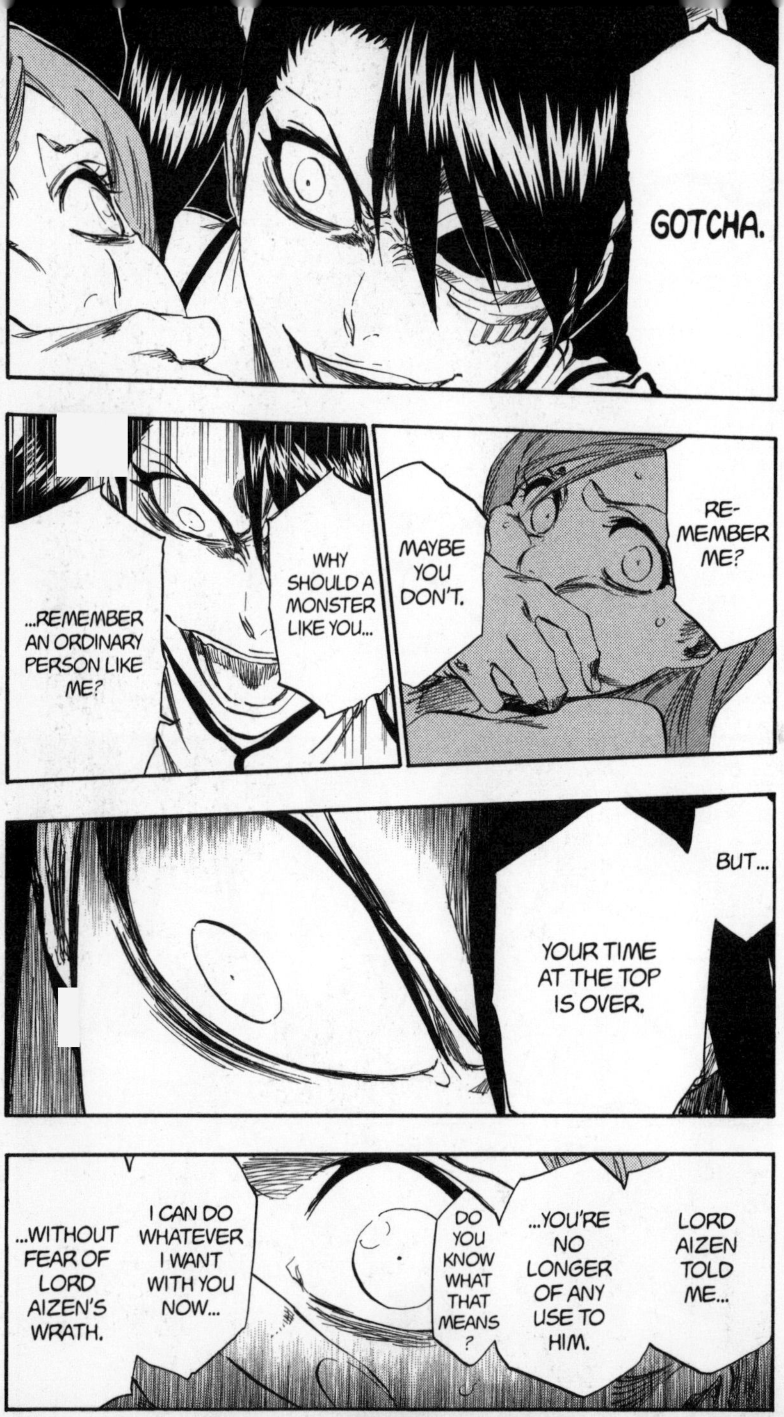
GOTCHA.
REMEMBER ME?
MAYBE YOU DON'T.
WHY SHOULD A MONSTER LIKE YOU...
...REMEMBER AN ORDINARY PERSON LIKE ME?
BUT...
YOUR TIME AT THE TOP IS OVER.
LORD AIZEN TOLD ME...
...YOU'RE NO LONGER OF ANY USE TO HIM.
DO YOU KNOW WHAT THAT MEANS?
I CAN DO WHATEVER I WANT WITH YOU NOW...
...WITHOUT FEAR OF LORD AIZEN'S WRATH.

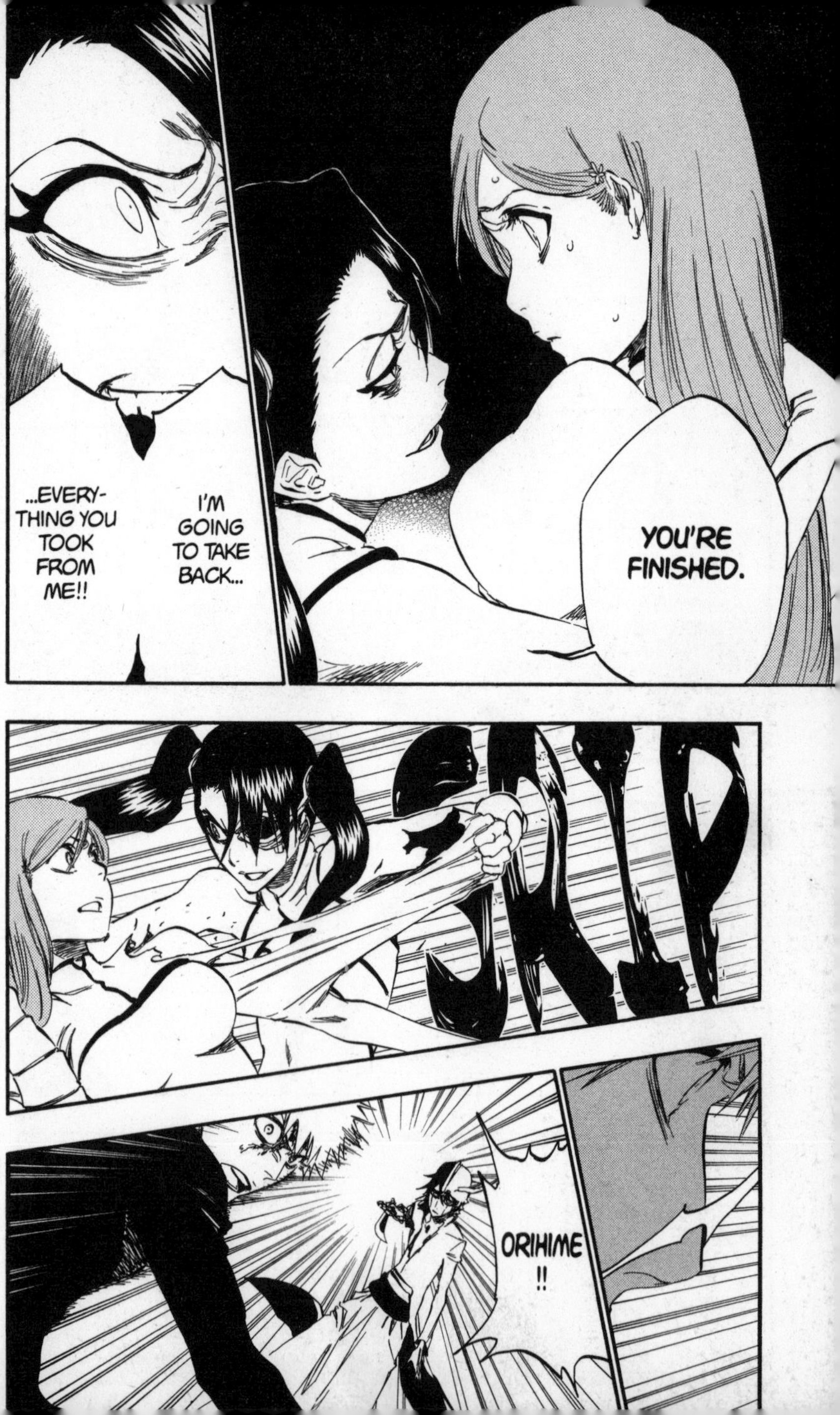
YOU'RE FINISHED.
I'M GOING TO TAKE BACK...
...EVERY-THING YOU TOOK FROM ME!!
SKRIP
ORIHIME!!

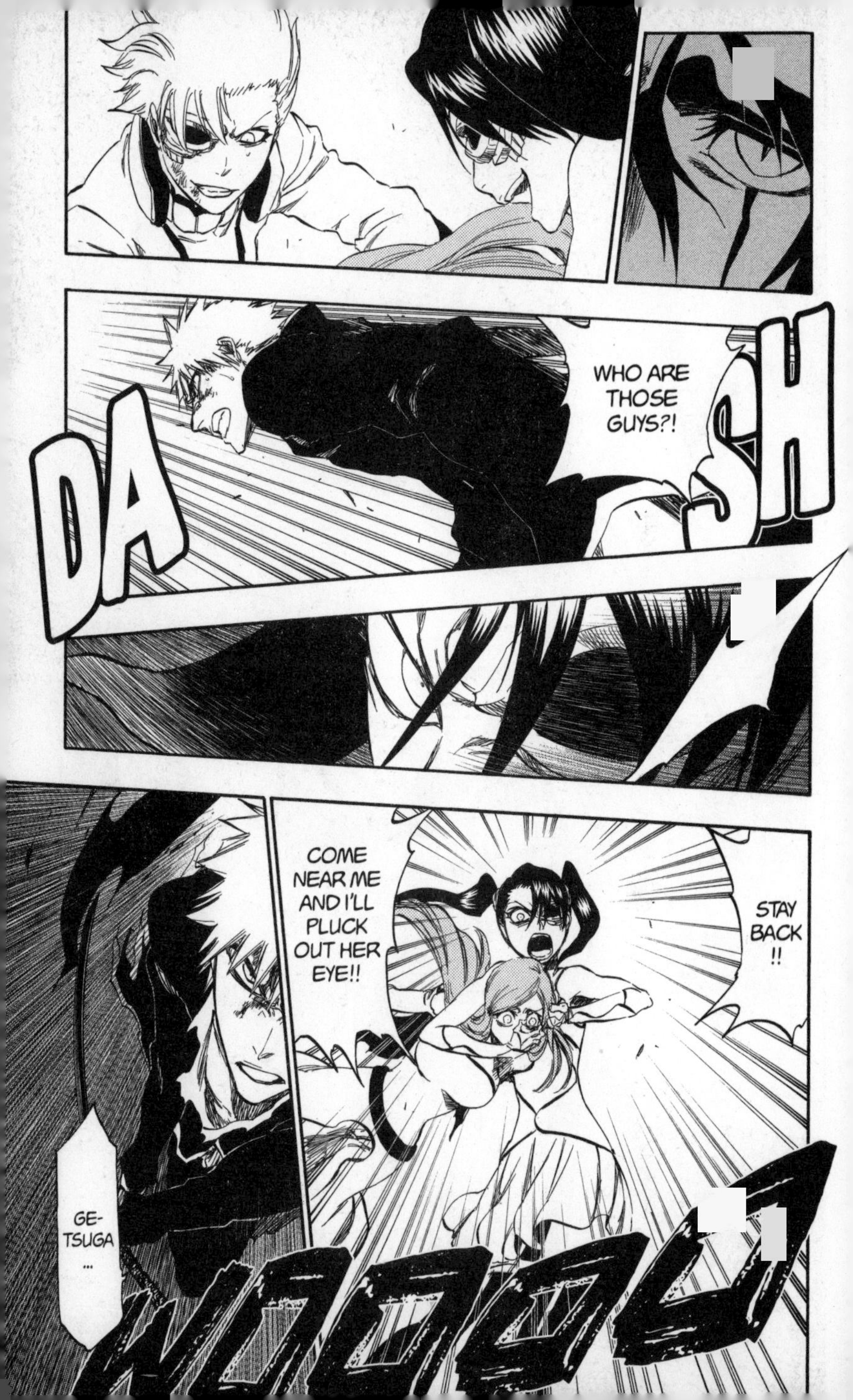
WHO ARE THOSE GUYS?!
DA
SH
STAY BACK!!
COME NEAR ME AND I'LL PLUCK OUT HER EYE!!
GE-TSUGA...

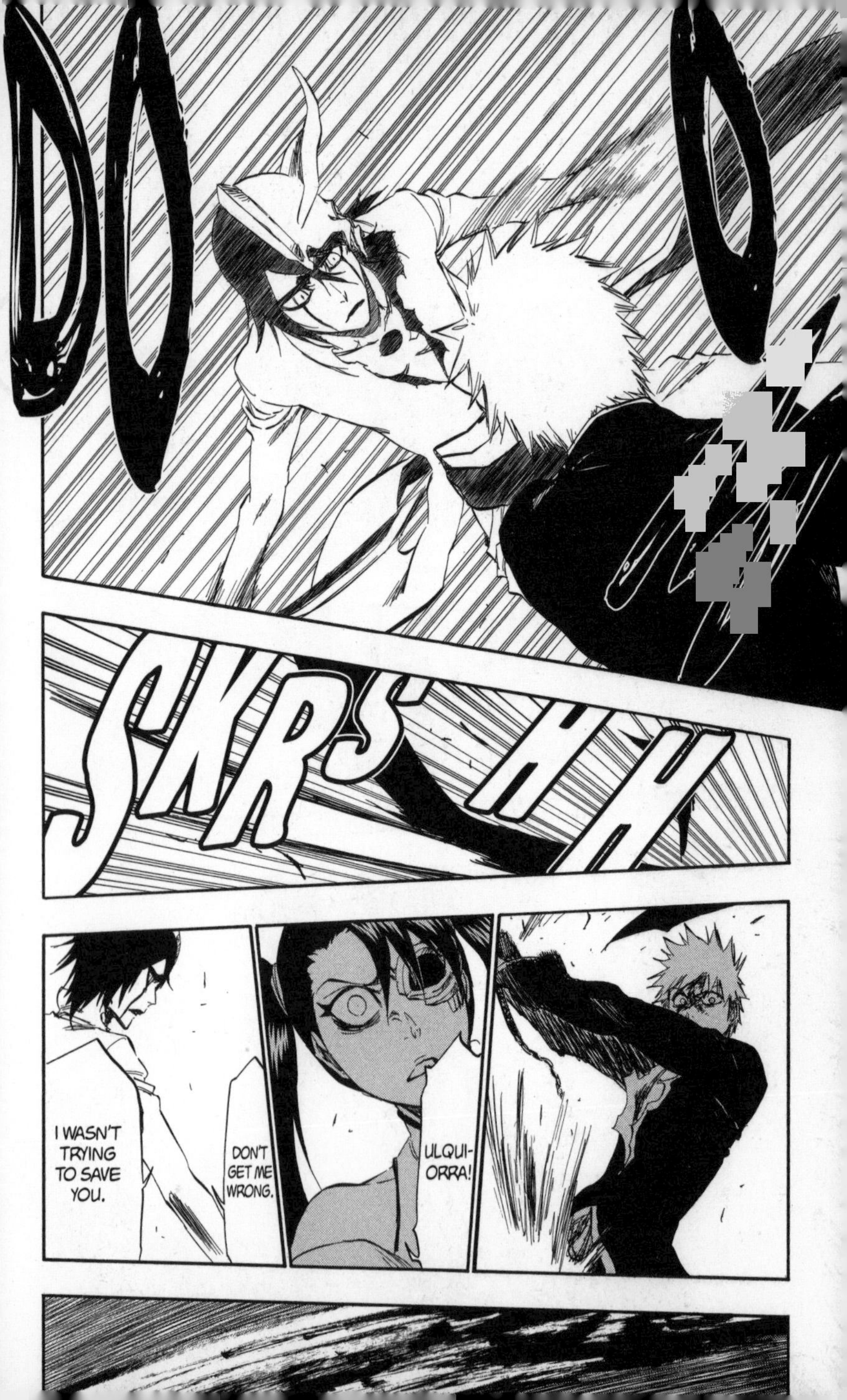
SKRSHH
ULQUI-ORRA!
DON'T GET ME WRONG.
I WASN'T TRYING TO SAVE YOU.

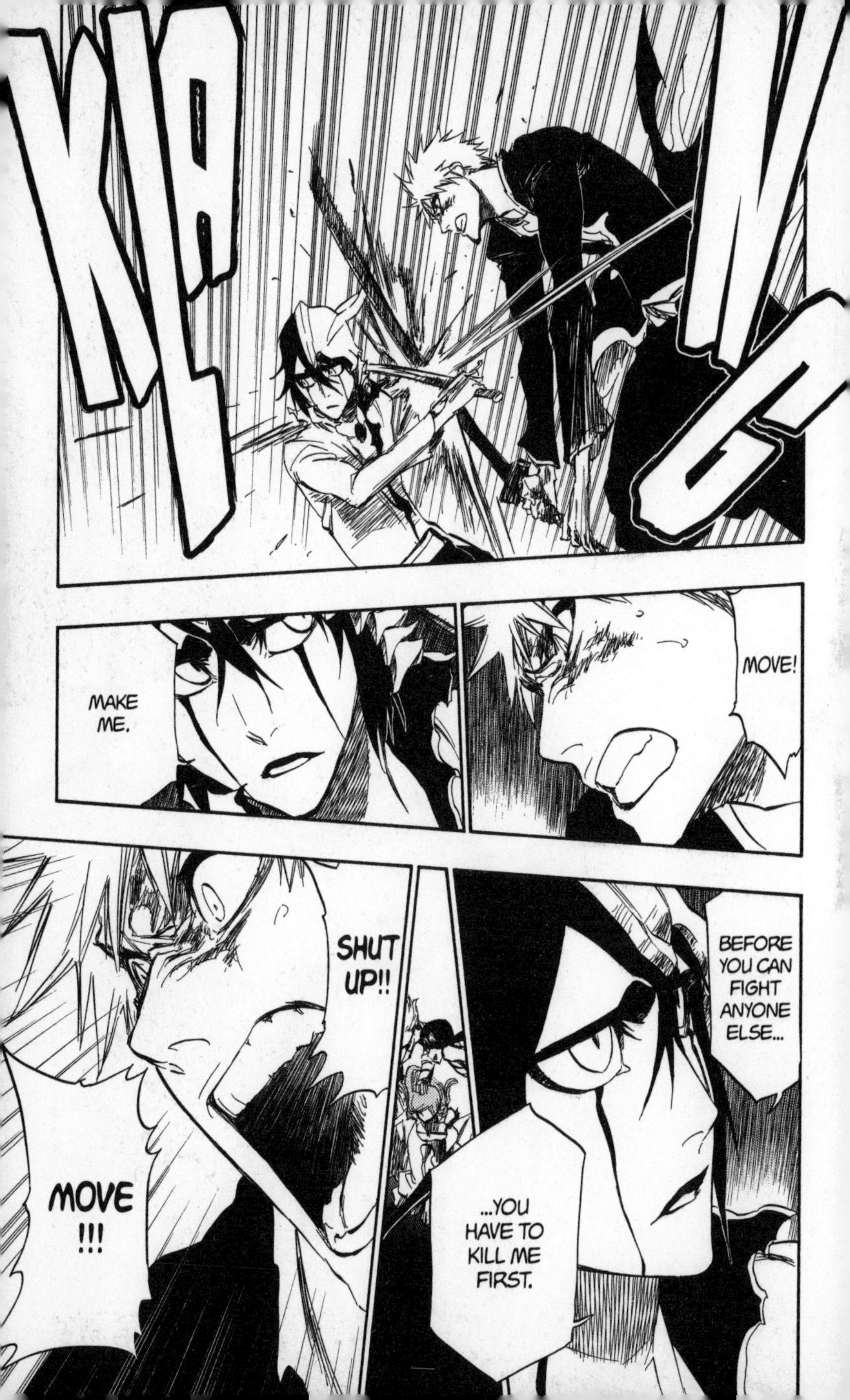
MOVE!
MAKE ME.
BEFORE YOU CAN FIGHT ANYONE ELSE...
...YOU HAVE TO KILL ME FIRST.
SHUT UP!!
MOVE !!!

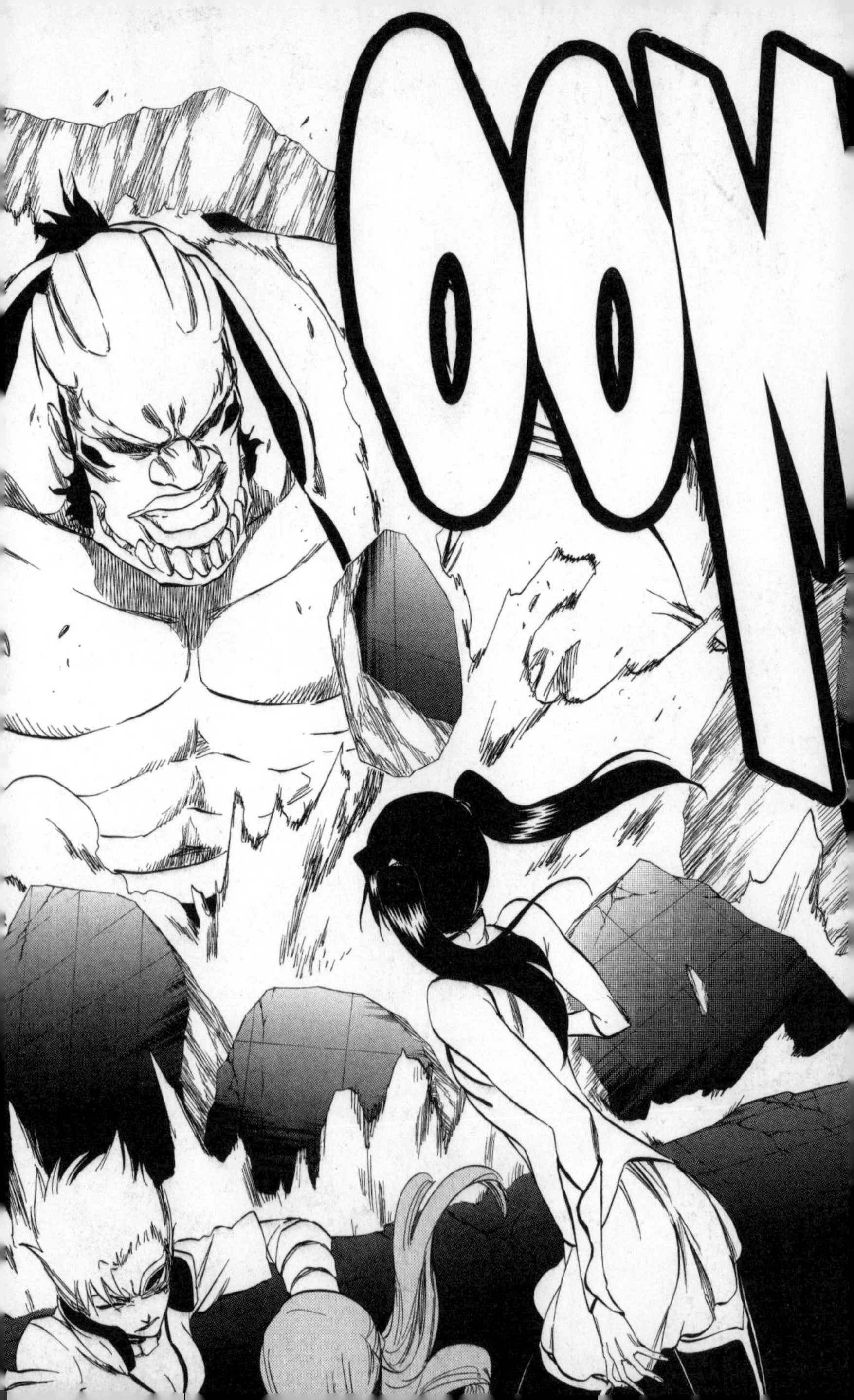
OOM

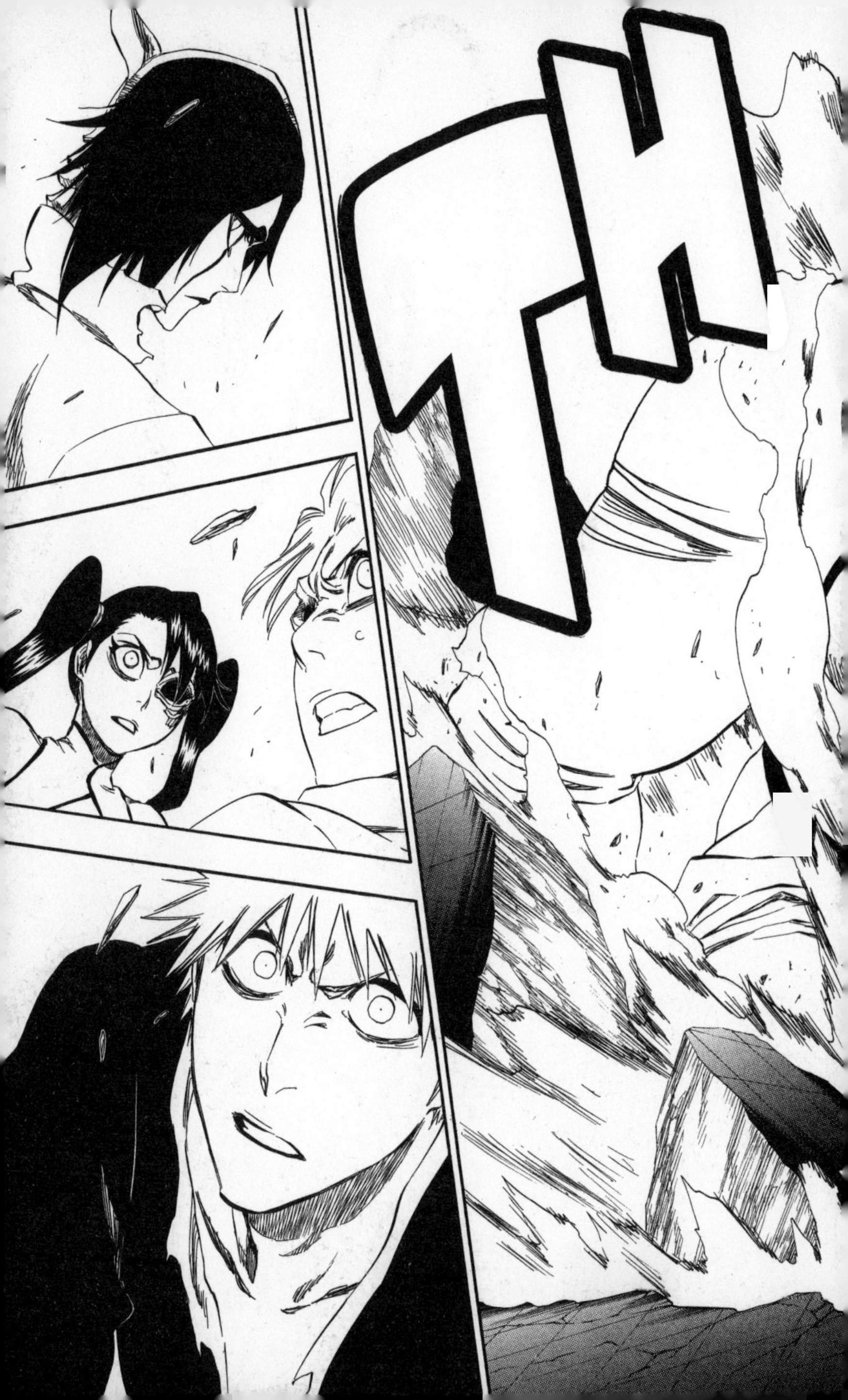
TH

The Gluttony

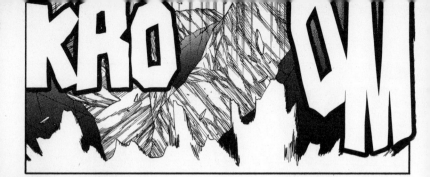

KRO OM

ULQUIORRA!

TUMP

BLEACH

343. The Greed

WHEN DID I SAY I NEEDED YOUR HELP...

...YAMMY?

I CAME TO HELP.

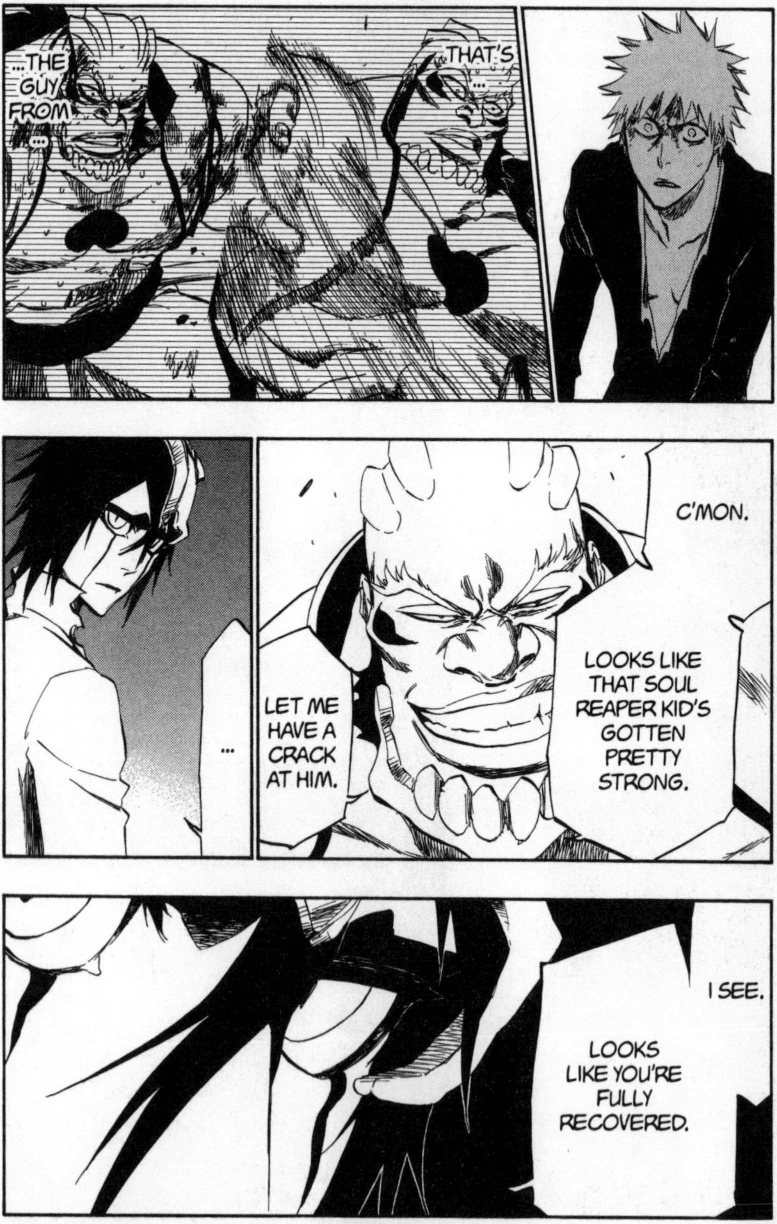
THAT'S ...
...THE GUY FROM ...
C'MON.
LOOKS LIKE THAT SOUL REAPER KID'S GOTTEN PRETTY STRONG.
LET ME HAVE A CRACK AT HIM.
...
I SEE.
LOOKS LIKE YOU'RE FULLY RECOVERED.

READ THIS WAY

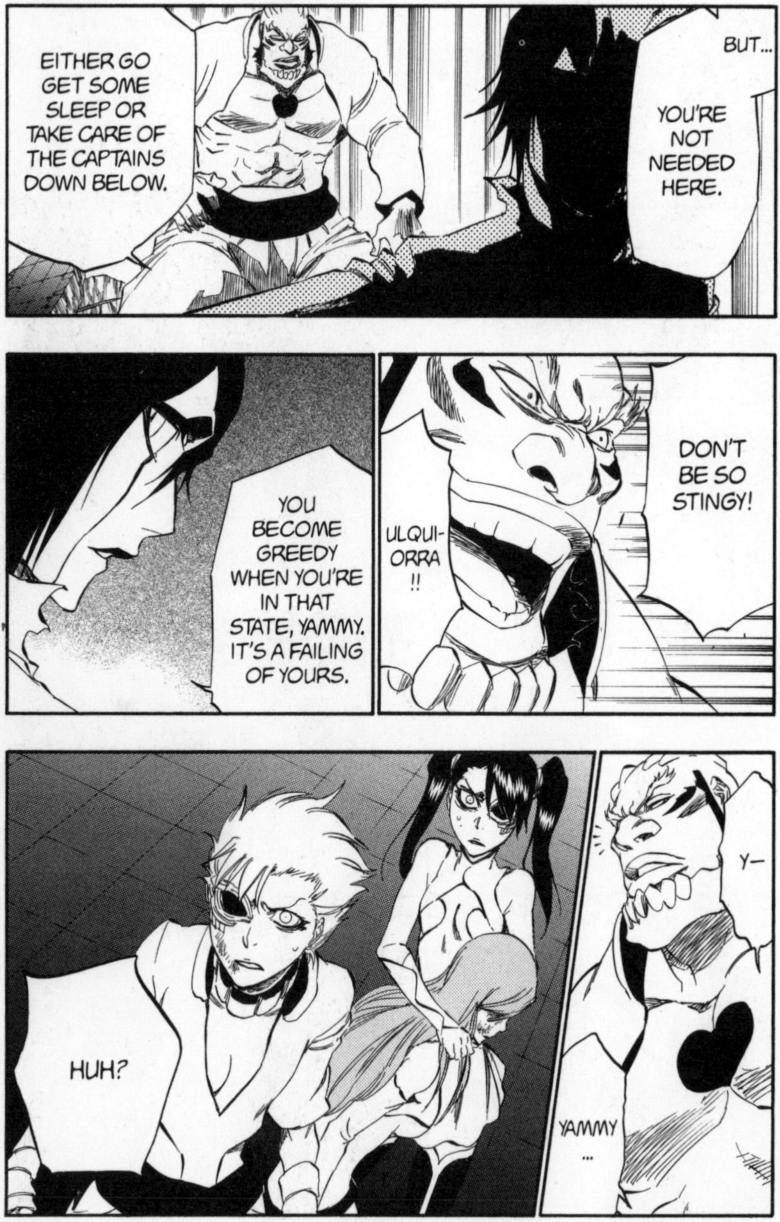
BUT...
YOU'RE NOT NEEDED HERE.
EITHER GO GET SOME SLEEP OR TAKE CARE OF THE CAPTAINS DOWN BELOW.
DON'T BE SO STINGY!
ULQUI-ORRA !!
YOU BECOME GREEDY WHEN YOU'RE IN THAT STATE, YAMMY. IT'S A FAILING OF YOURS.
Y—
YAMMY ...
HUH?

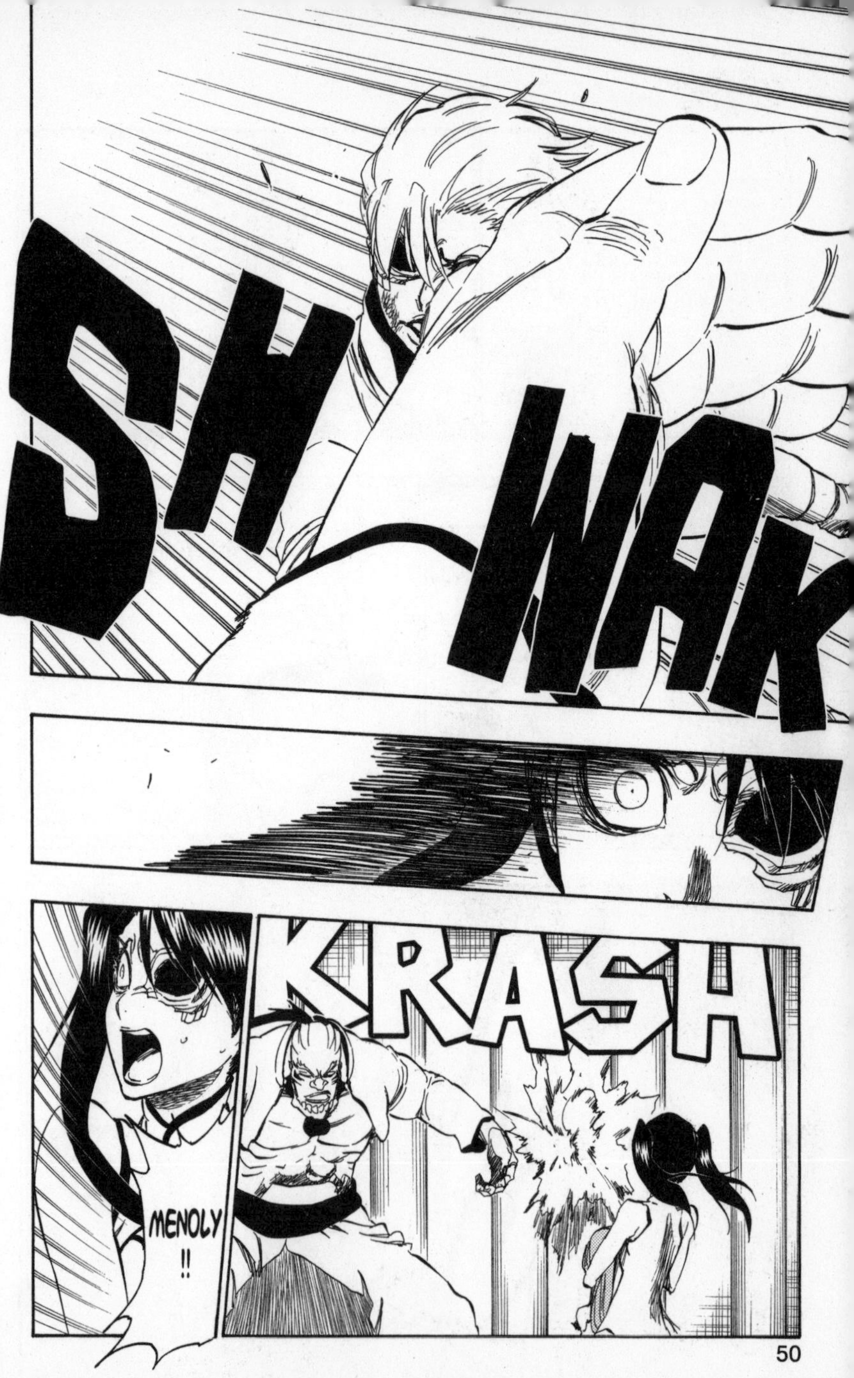
SHWAK
KRASH
MENOLY !!

READ THIS WAY

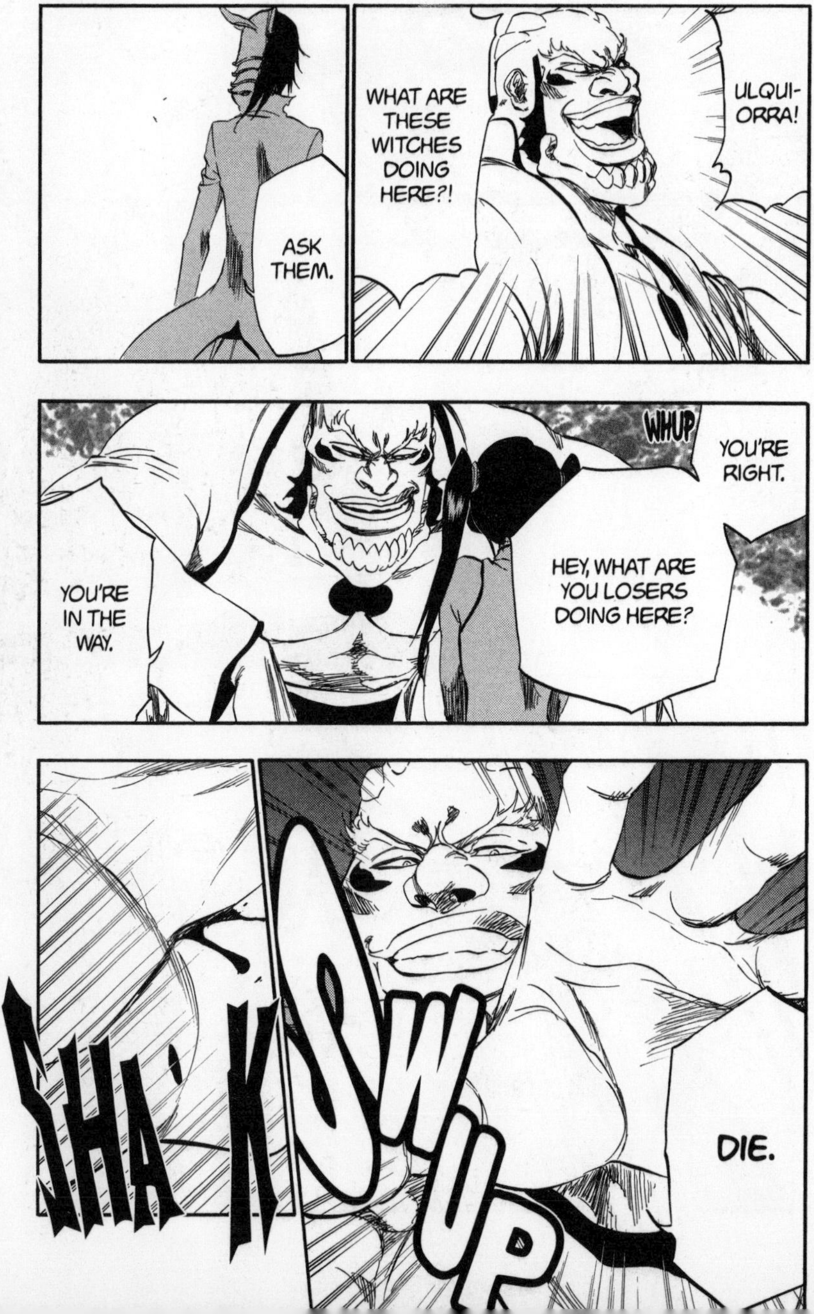
ULQUI-ORRA!
WHAT ARE THESE WITCHES DOING HERE?!
ASK THEM.
WHUP
YOU'RE RIGHT.
HEY, WHAT ARE YOU LOSERS DOING HERE?
YOU'RE IN THE WAY.
DIE.
SHA-KOWUP

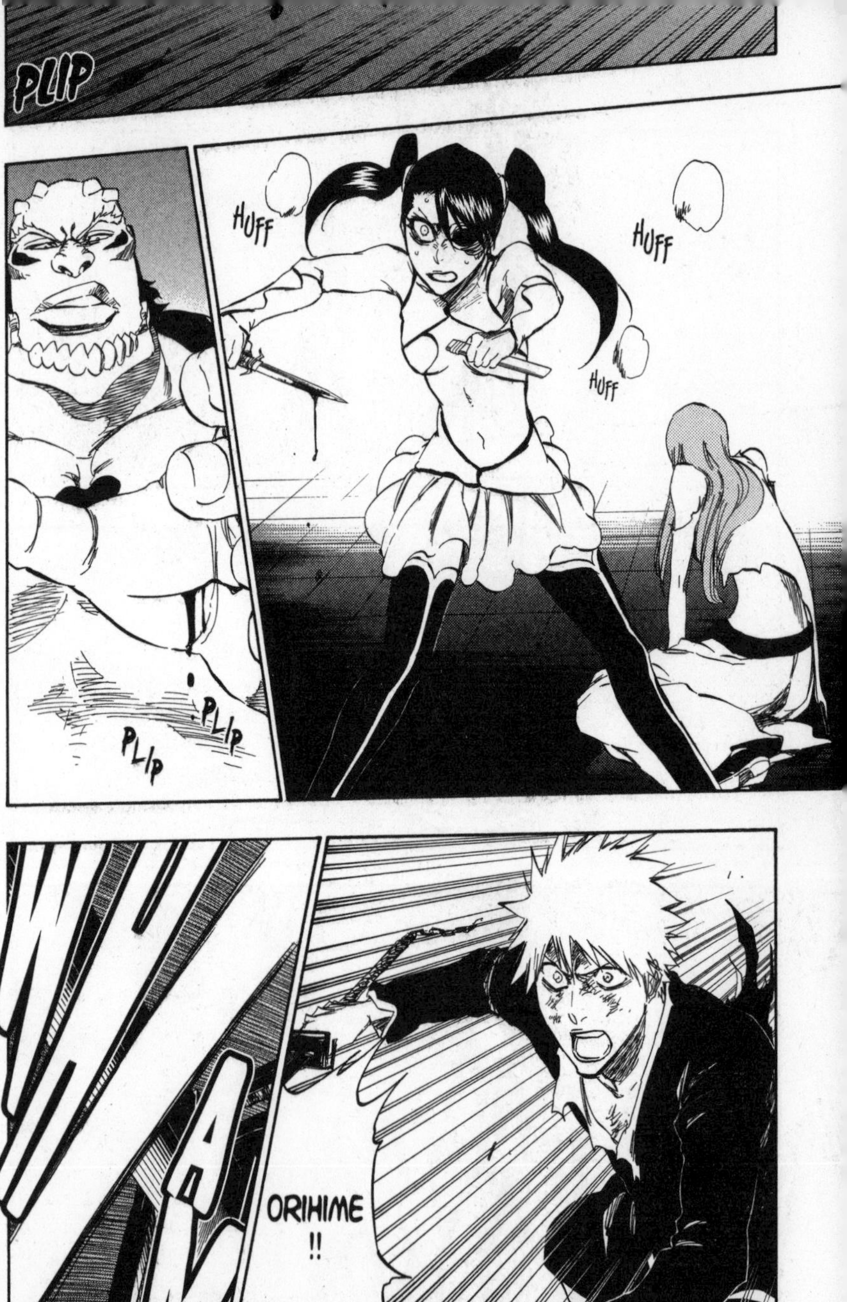
PLIP
HUFF
HUFF
HUFF
PLIP
PLIP
ORIHIME !!
WHAM

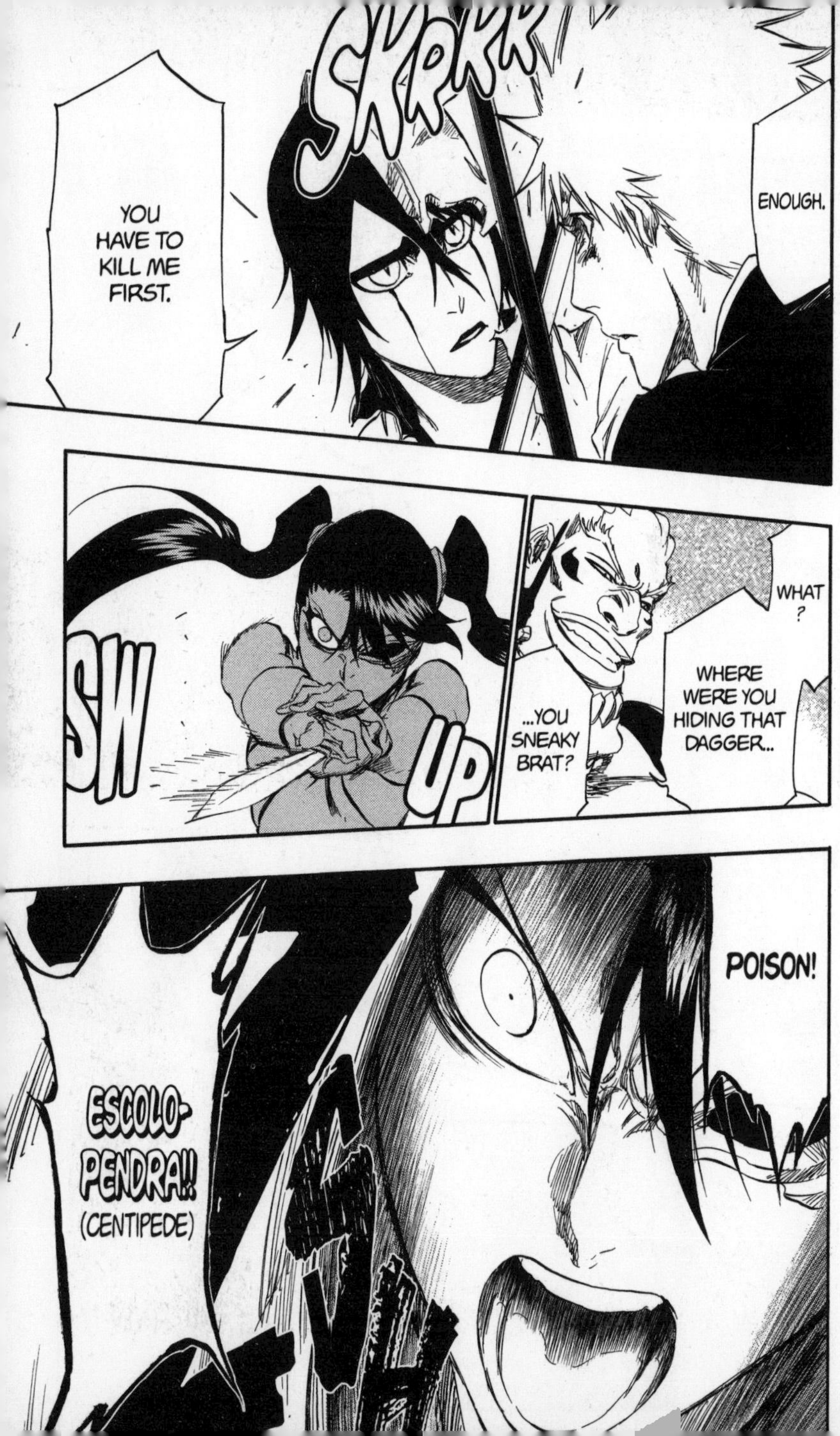
SKRRK
ENOUGH.
YOU HAVE TO KILL ME FIRST.
WHAT?
WHERE WERE YOU HIDING THAT DAGGER...
...YOU SNEAKY BRAT?
SWUP
POISON!
ESCOLO-PENDRA!!
(CENTIPEDE)

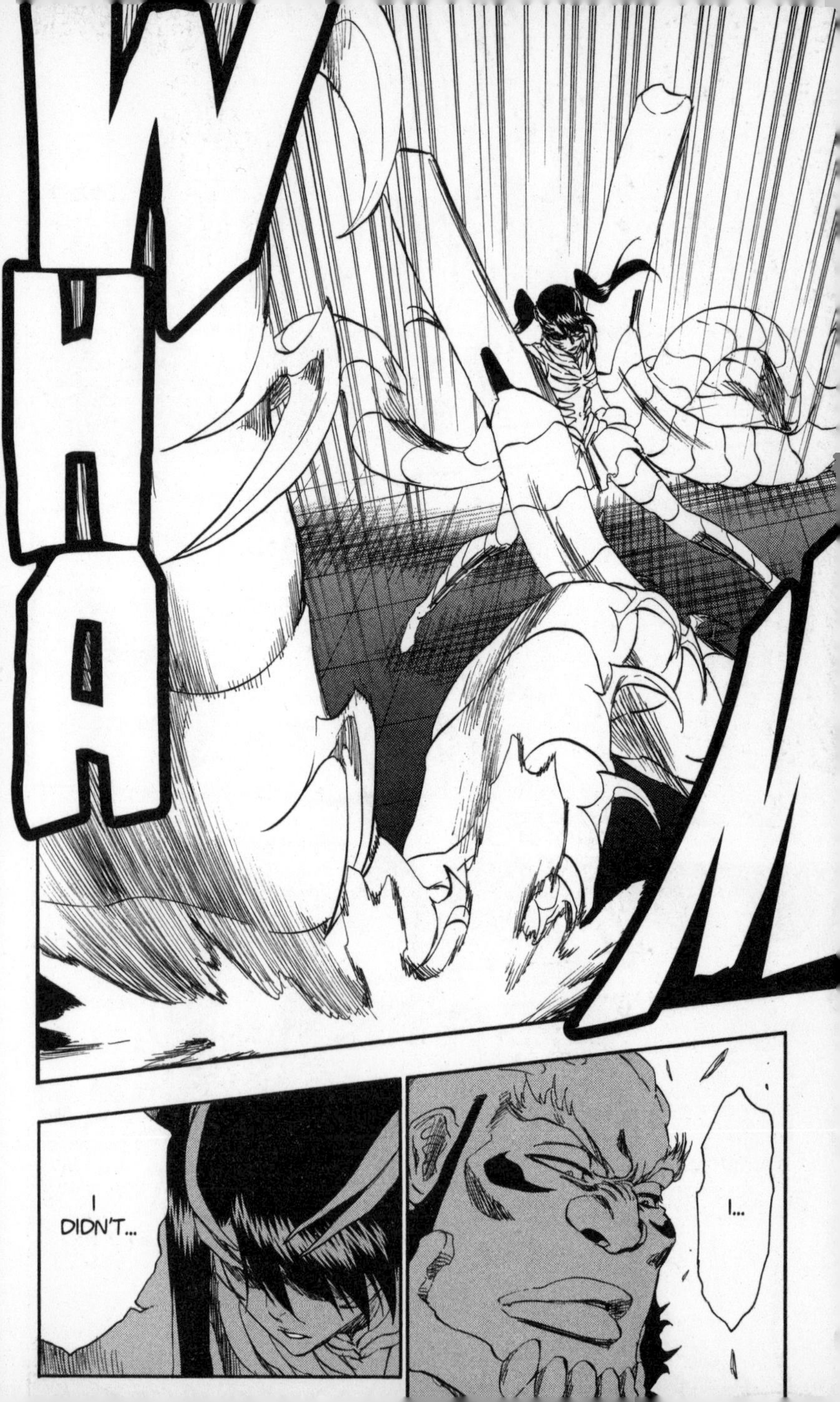
WHAM
I...
I DIDN'T...

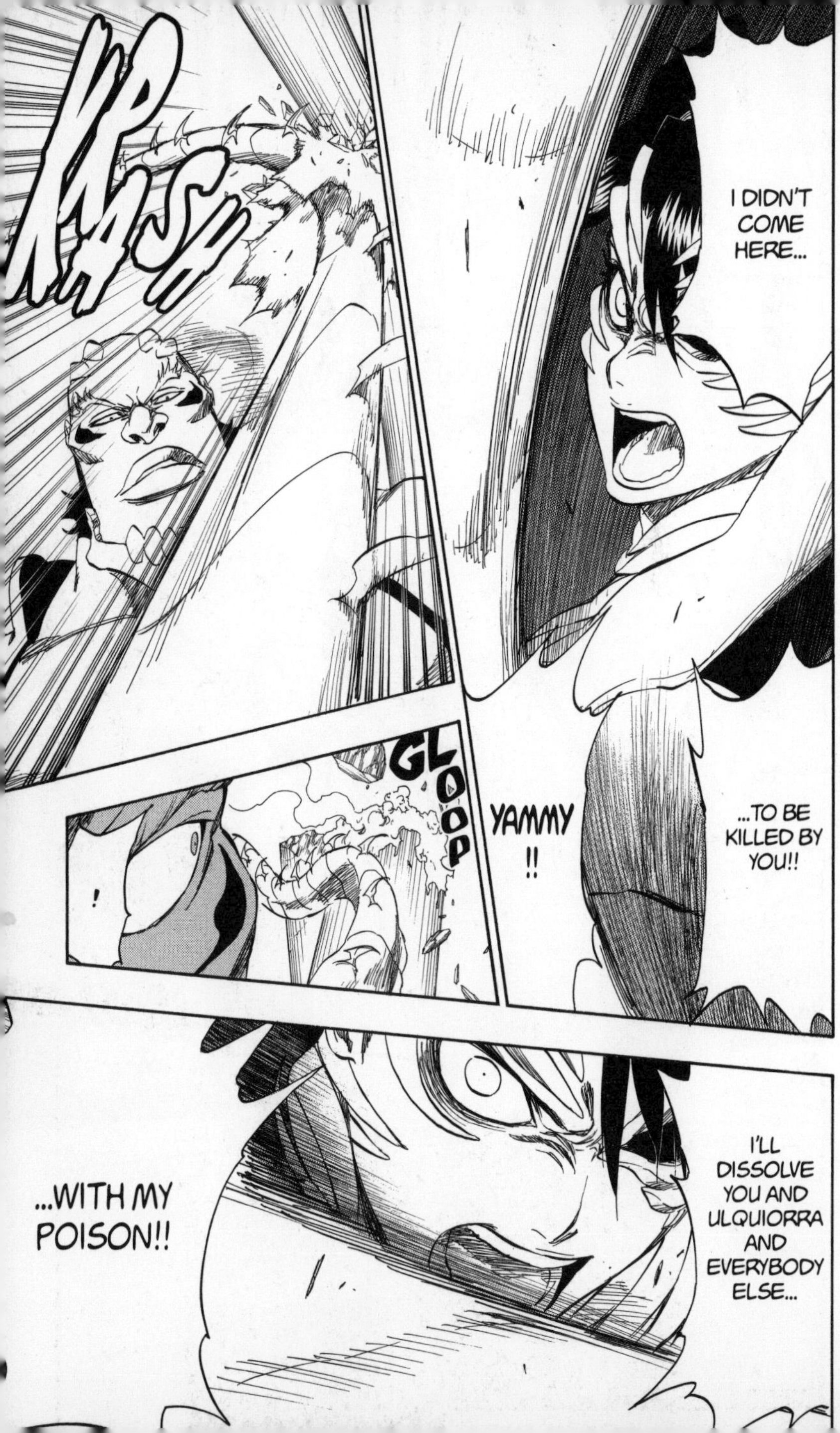
I DIDN'T COME HERE...
...TO BE KILLED BY YOU!!
YAMMY !!
KRASH
GLOOP
!
I'LL DISSOLVE YOU AND ULQUIORRA AND EVERYBODY ELSE...
...WITH MY POISON!!

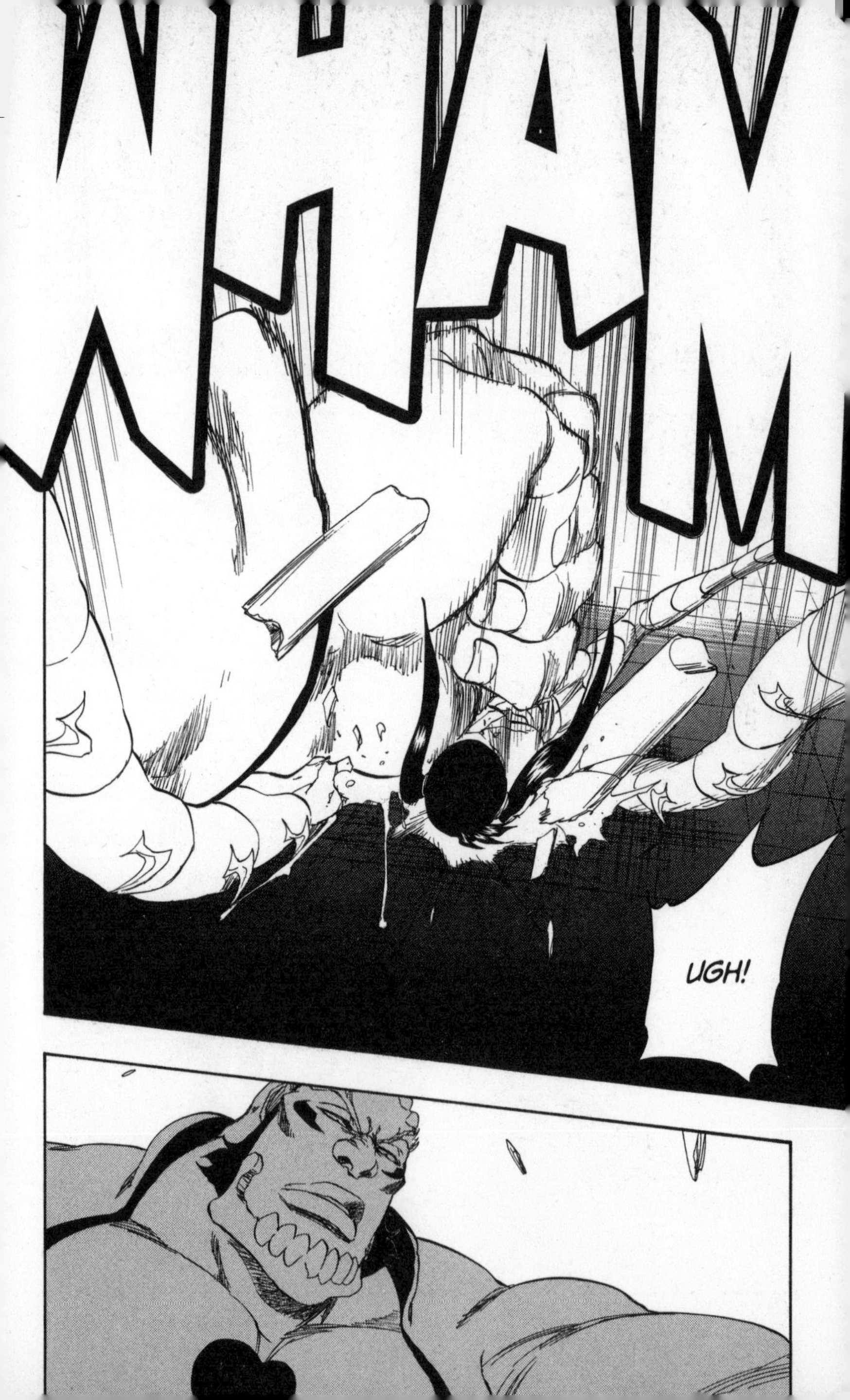
WHAM
UGH!

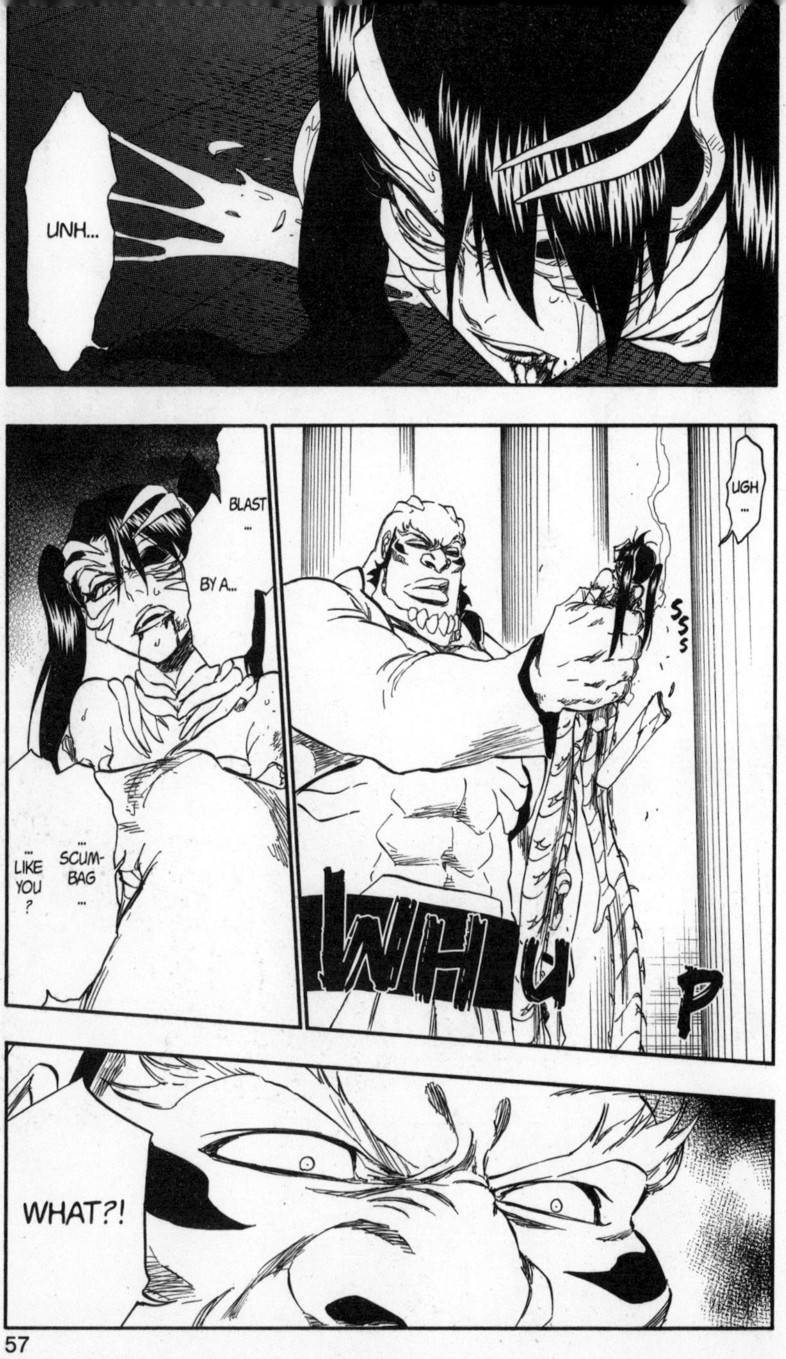
UNH...
UGH ...
SSS
WHUP
BLAST ...
BY A...
... SCUM-BAG ...
... LIKE YOU ?
WHAT?!

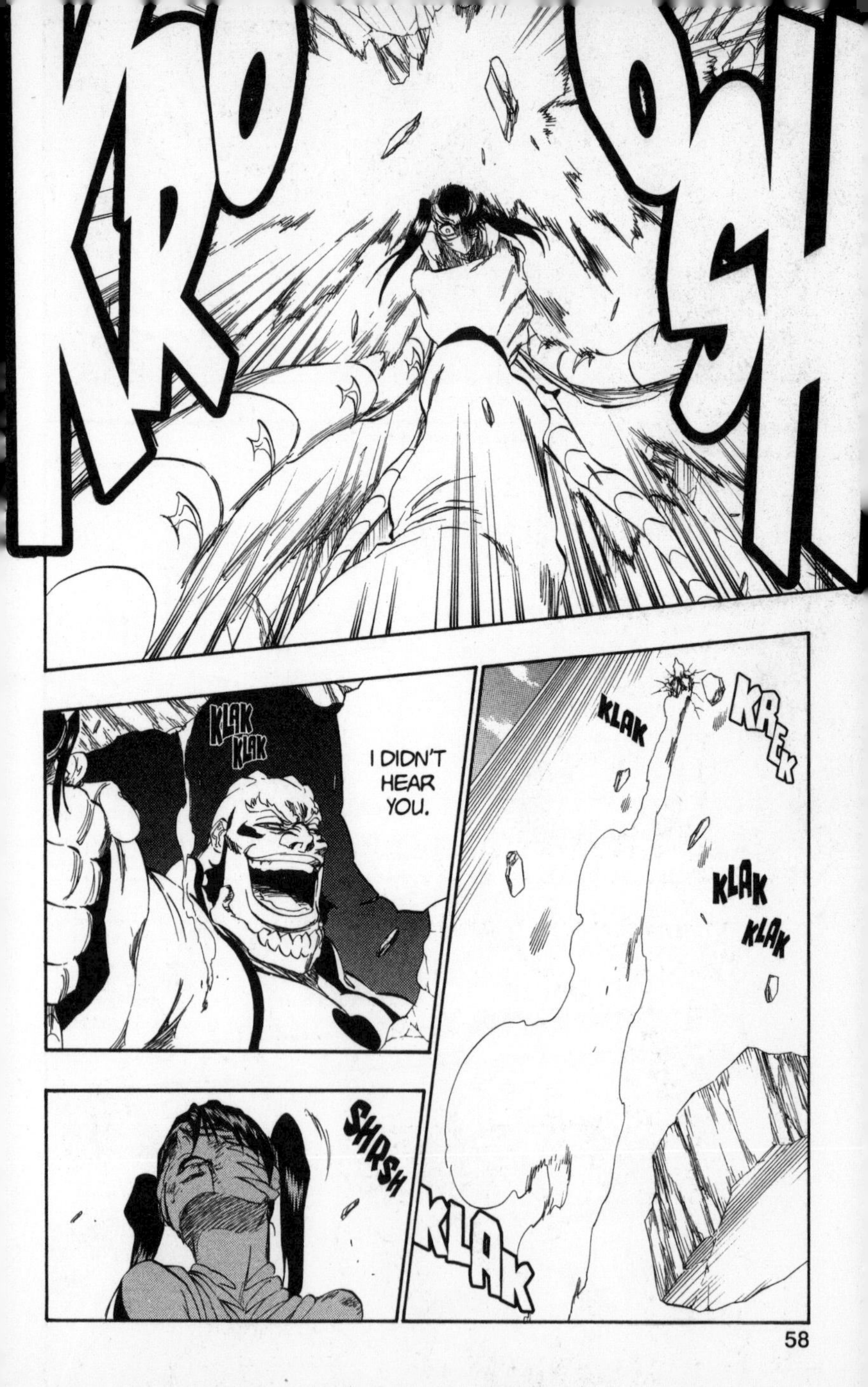
KROOSH
KLAK
KRAEK
KLAK
KLAK
KLAK
KLAK KLAK
I DIDN'T HEAR YOU.
SHRSH

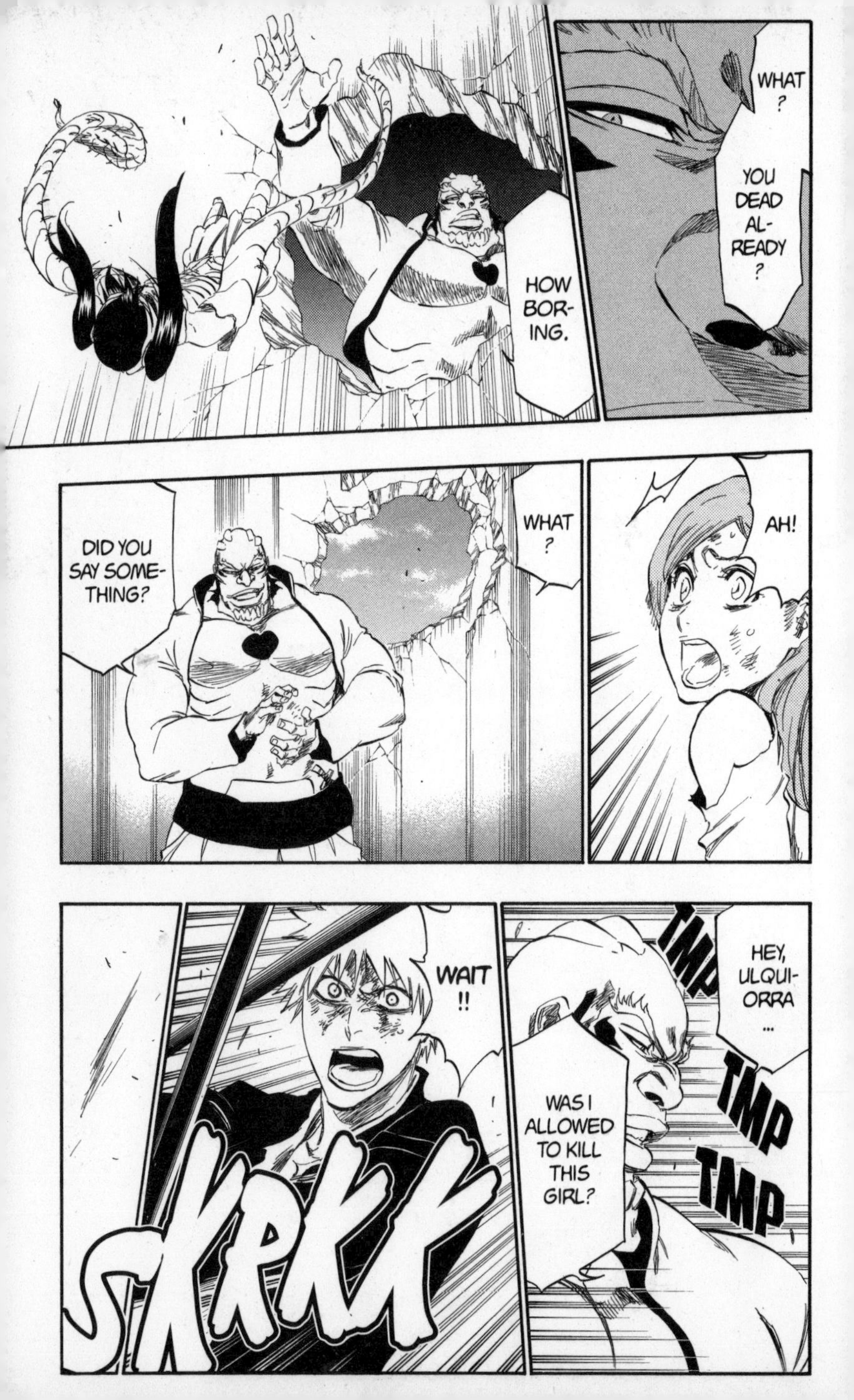
WHAT? YOU DEAD ALREADY?
HOW BORING.
AH!
WHAT?
DID YOU SAY SOMETHING?
TMP
HEY, ULQUIORRA...
TMP
TMP
TMP
WAS I ALLOWED TO KILL THIS GIRL?
WAIT!!
SKRKK

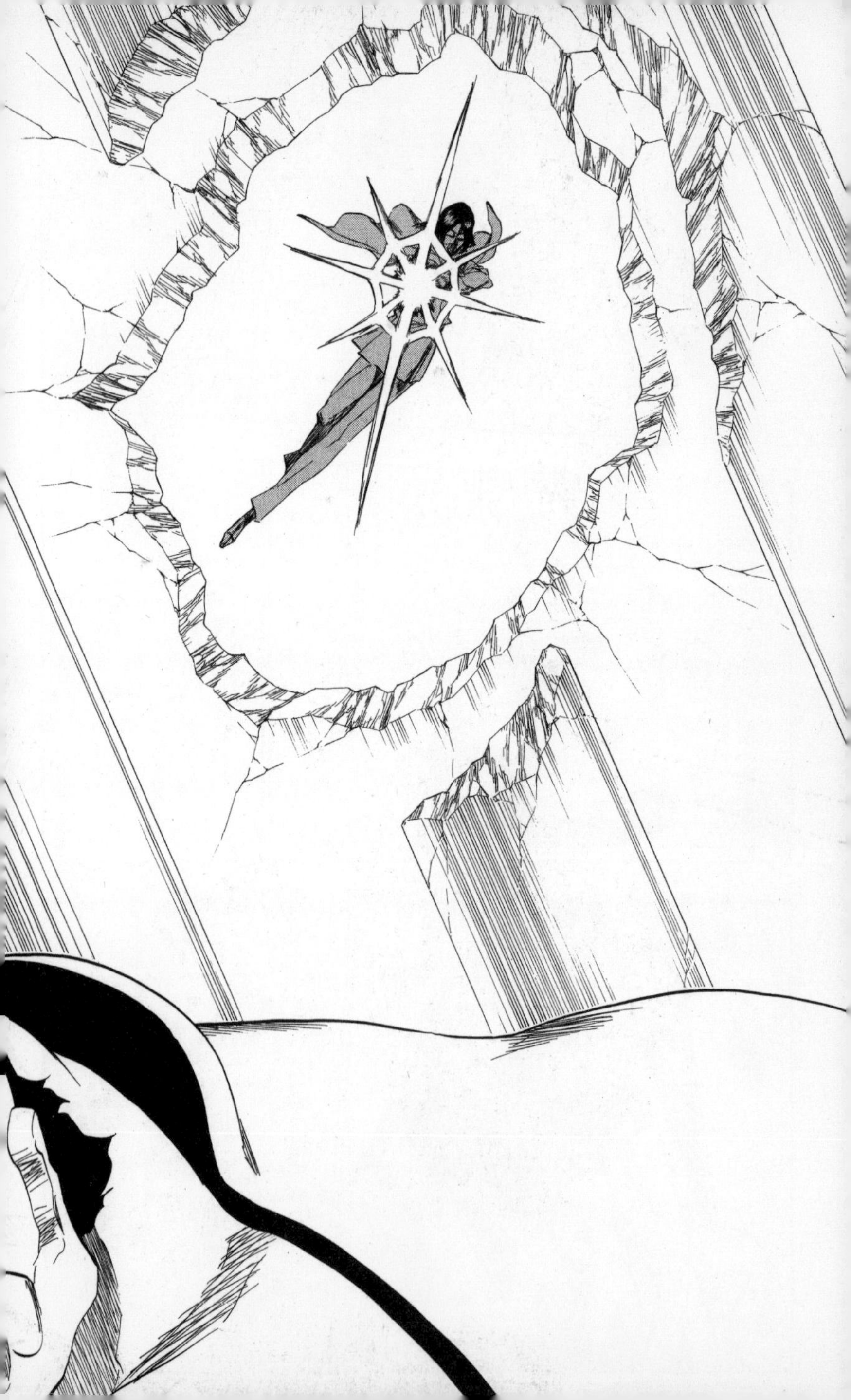

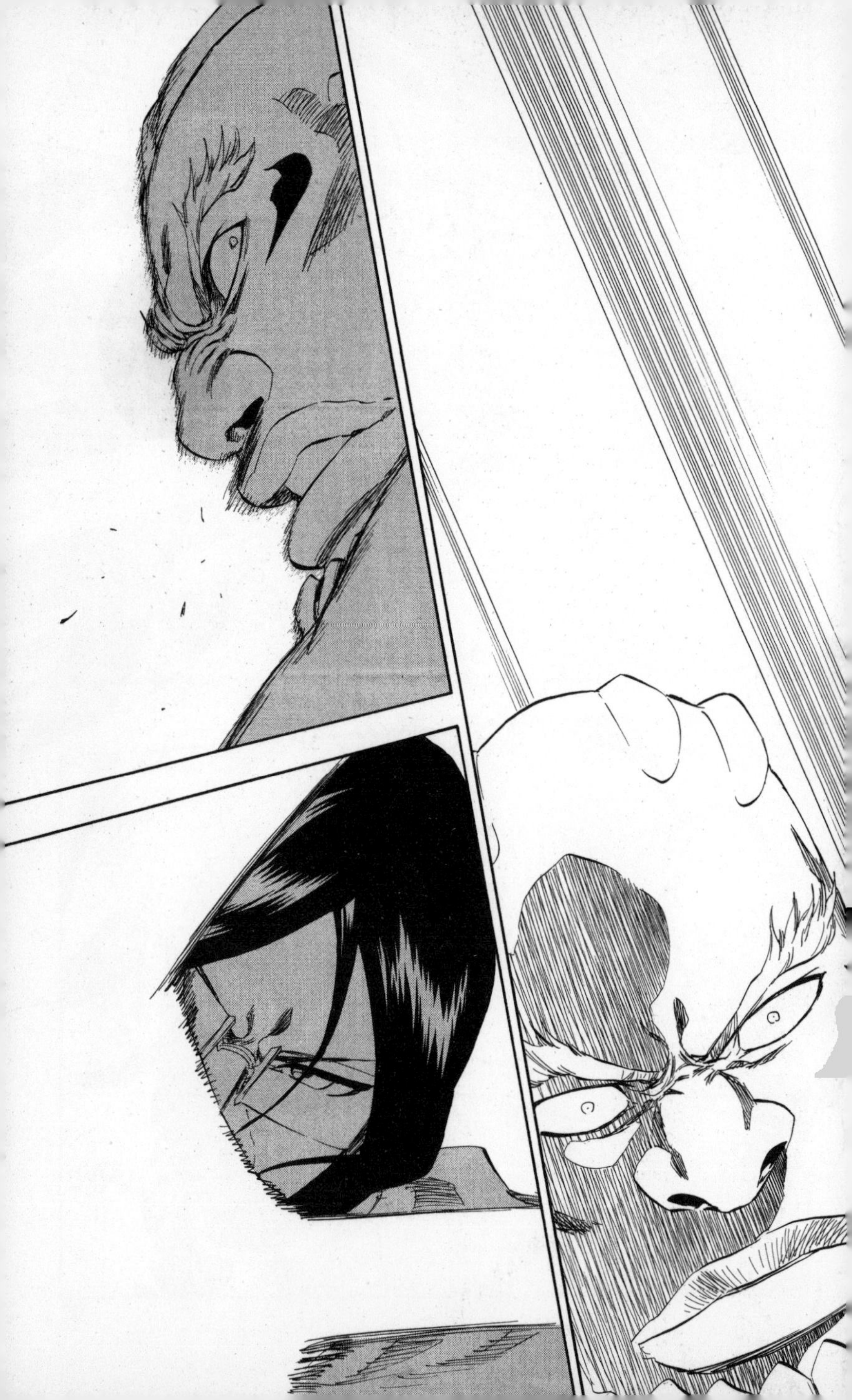

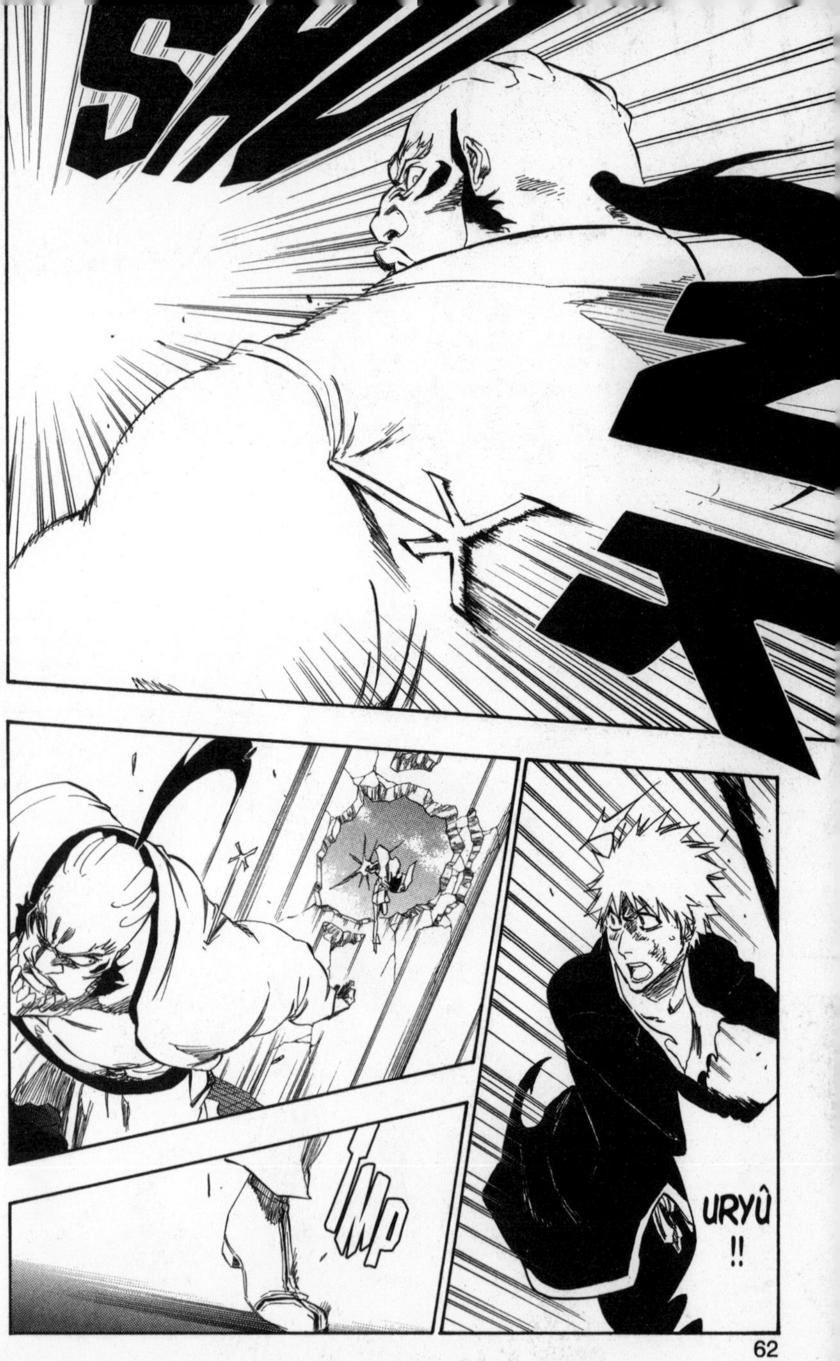
URYÛ
!!
TMP

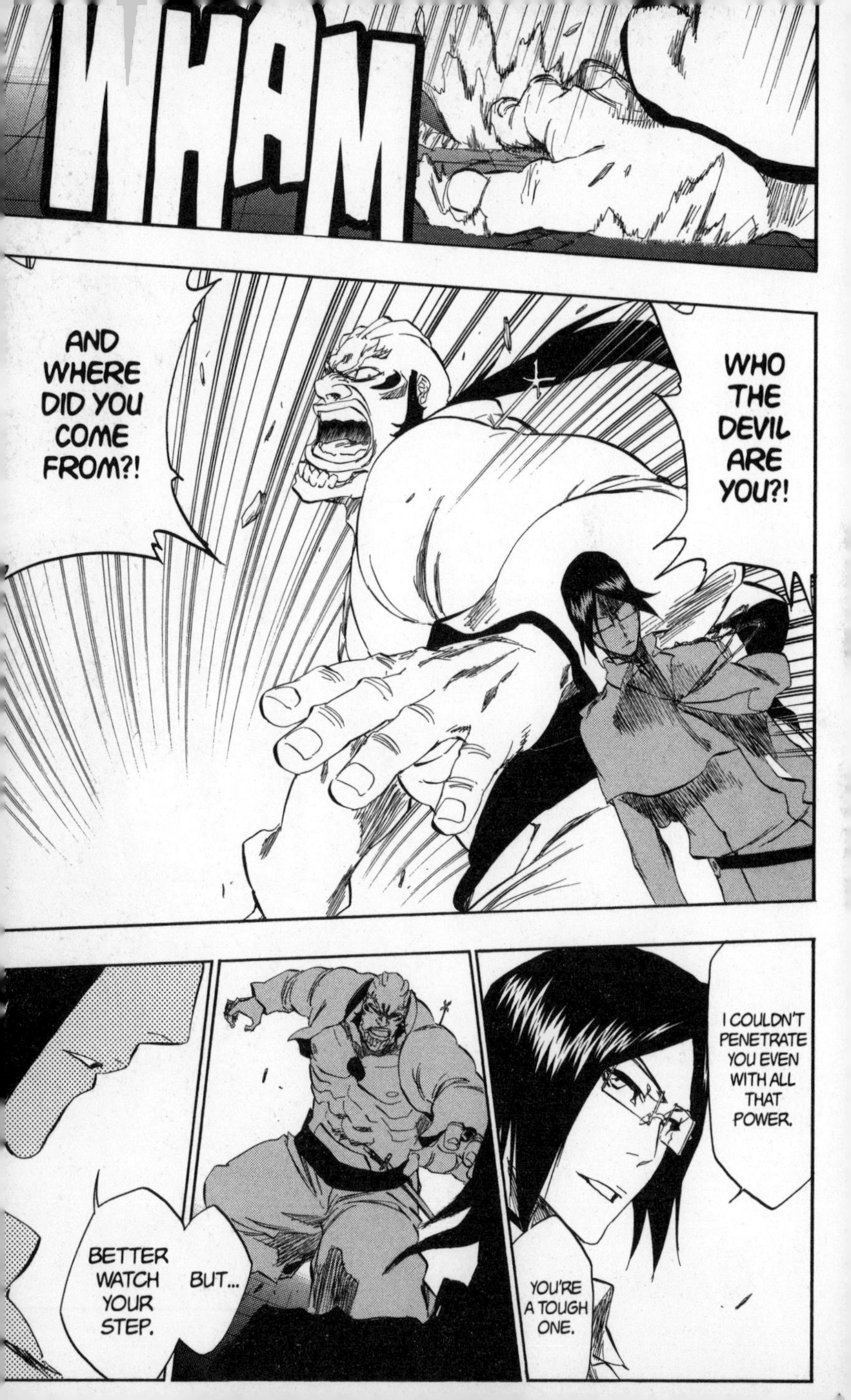
WHAM
WHO THE DEVIL ARE YOU?!
AND WHERE DID YOU COME FROM?!
I COULDN'T PENETRATE YOU EVEN WITH ALL THAT POWER.
YOU'RE A TOUGH ONE.
BUT...
BETTER WATCH YOUR STEP.

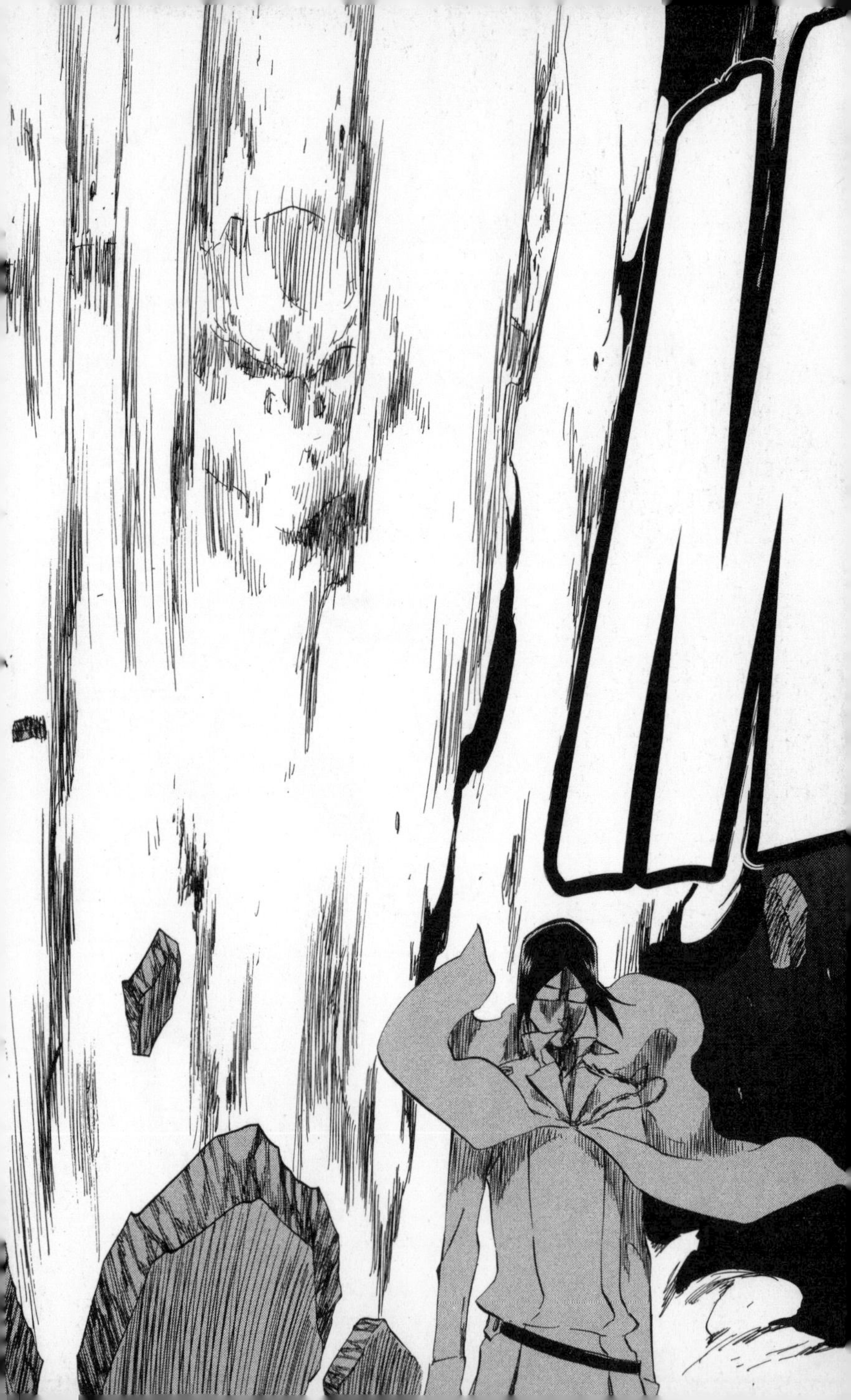

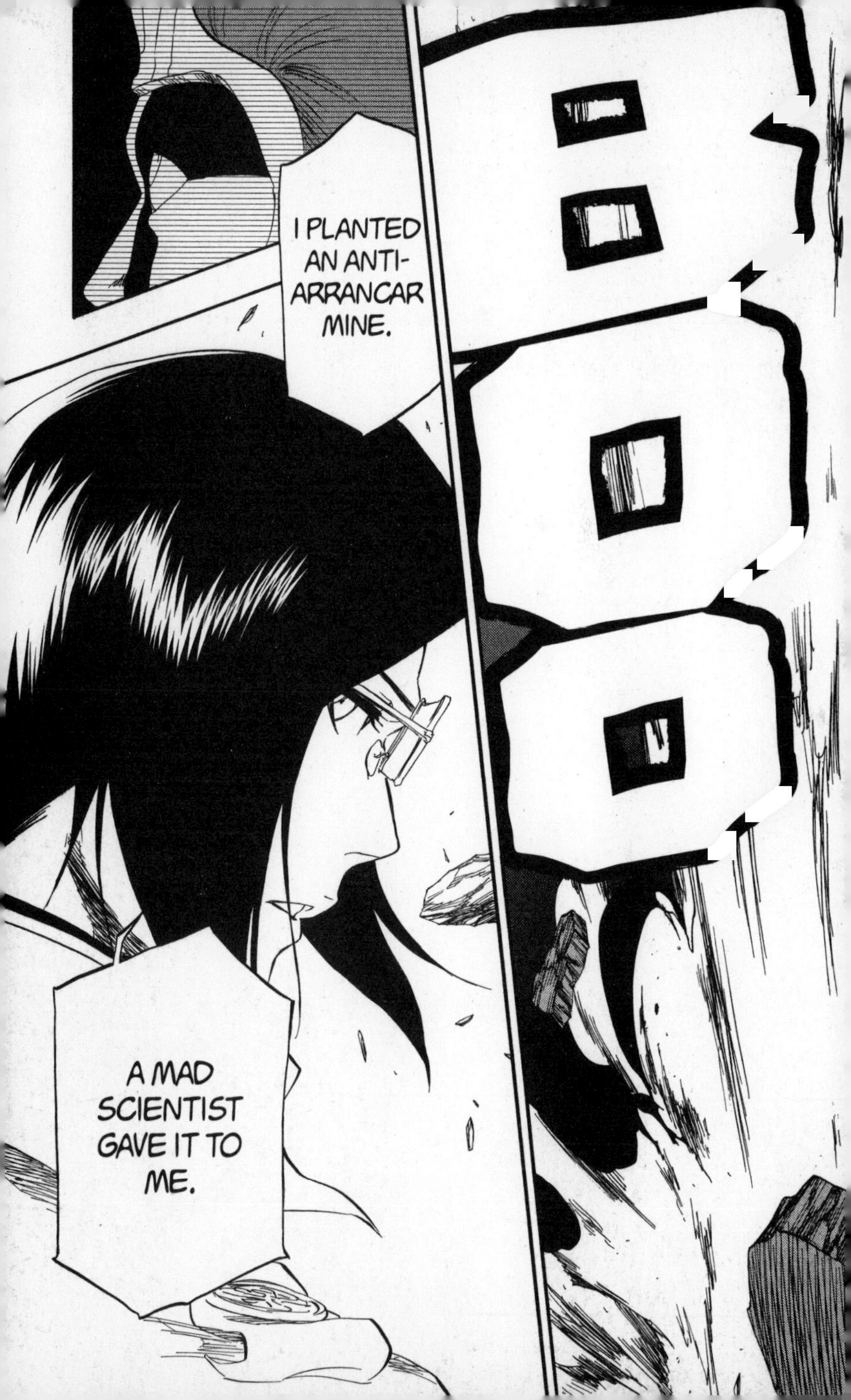
I PLANTED AN ANTI-ARRANCAR MINE.
A MAD SCIENTIST GAVE IT TO ME.

the Greed

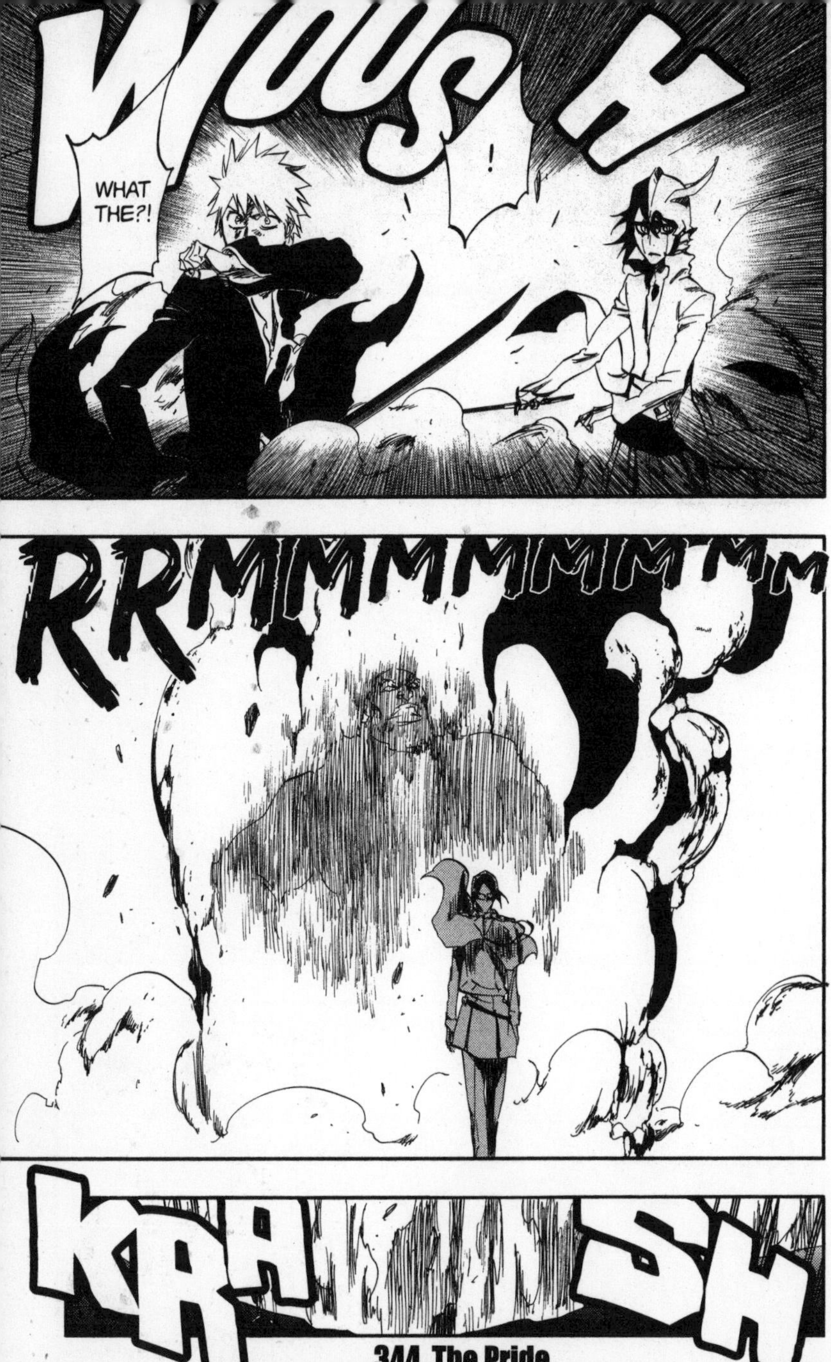
WHOOSH
WHAT THE?!
RRMMMMMMMMM
KRAAASH

344. The Pride

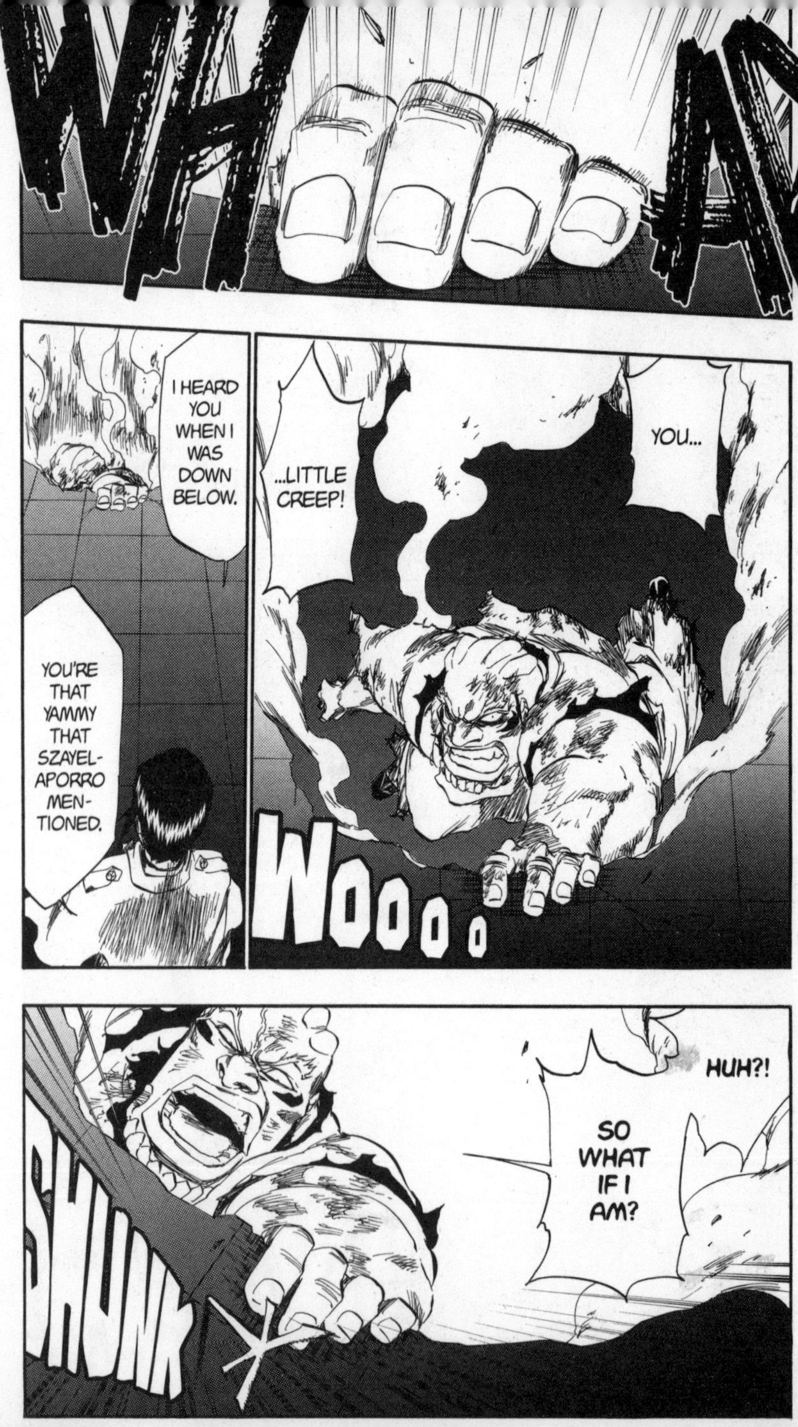
WHAP
YOU...
...LITTLE CREEP!
WOOOO
I HEARD YOU WHEN I WAS DOWN BELOW.
YOU'RE THAT YAMMY THAT SZAYEL-APORRO MEN-TIONED.
HUH?!
SO WHAT IF I AM?
SHUNK

READ THIS WAY

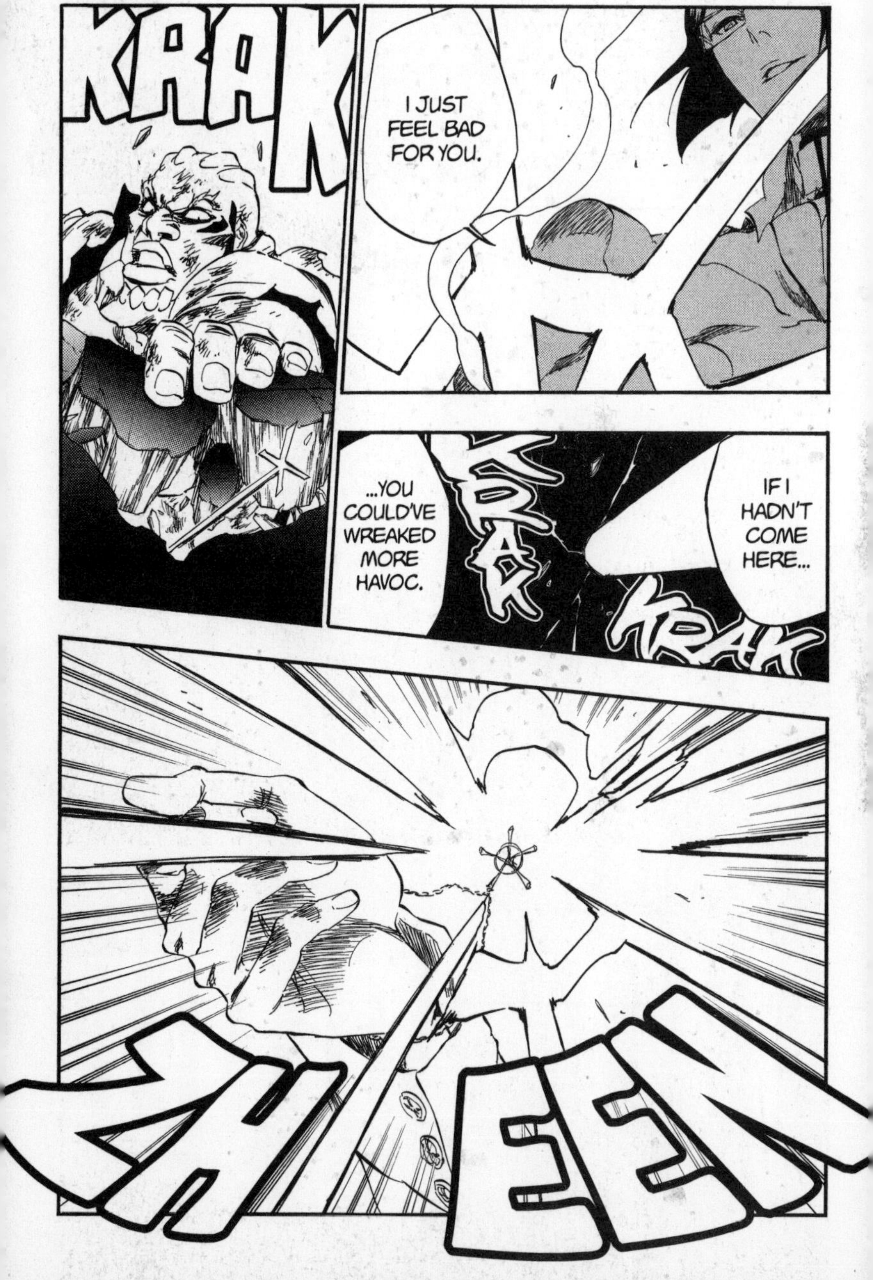
I JUST FEEL BAD FOR YOU.
IF I HADN'T COME HERE...
KRAK
...YOU COULD'VE WREAKED MORE HAVOC.
KRAK
KRAK

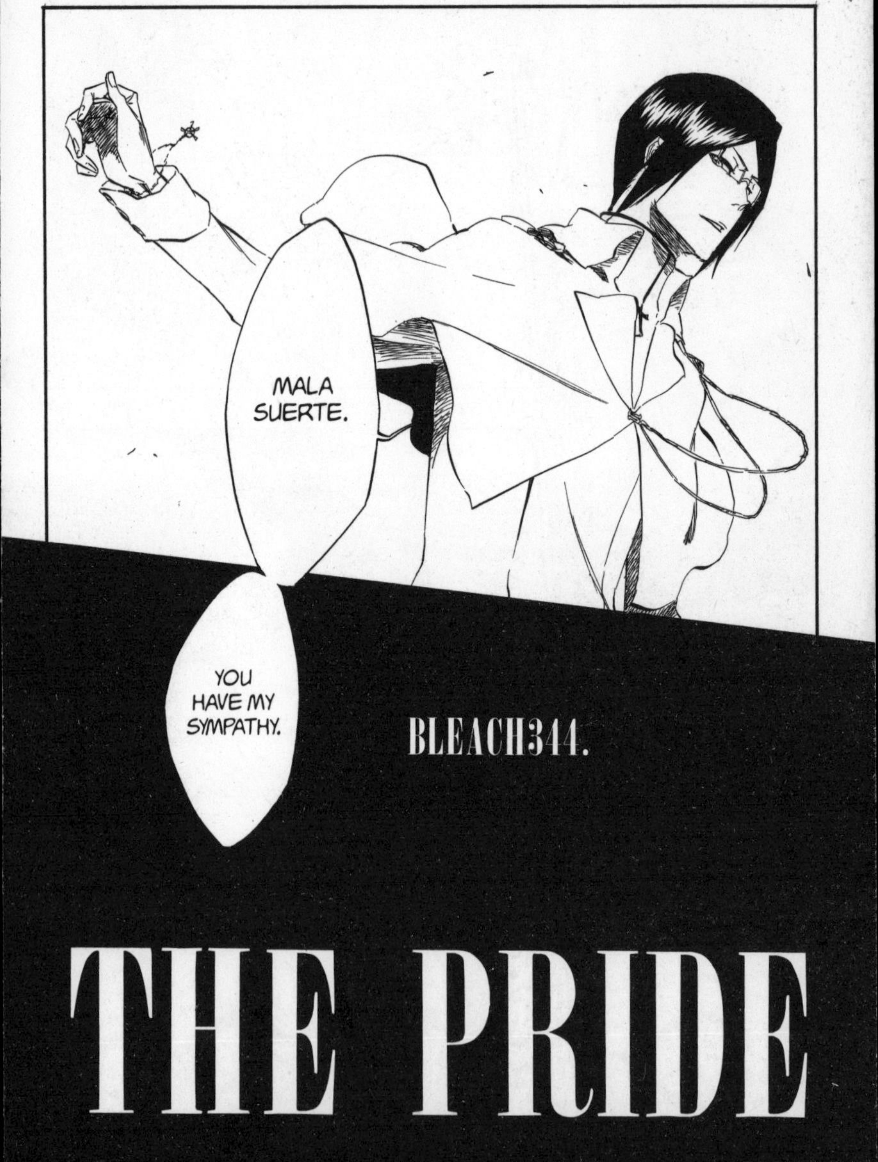
MALA SUERTE.
YOU HAVE MY SYMPATHY.
BLEACH344.
THE PRIDE

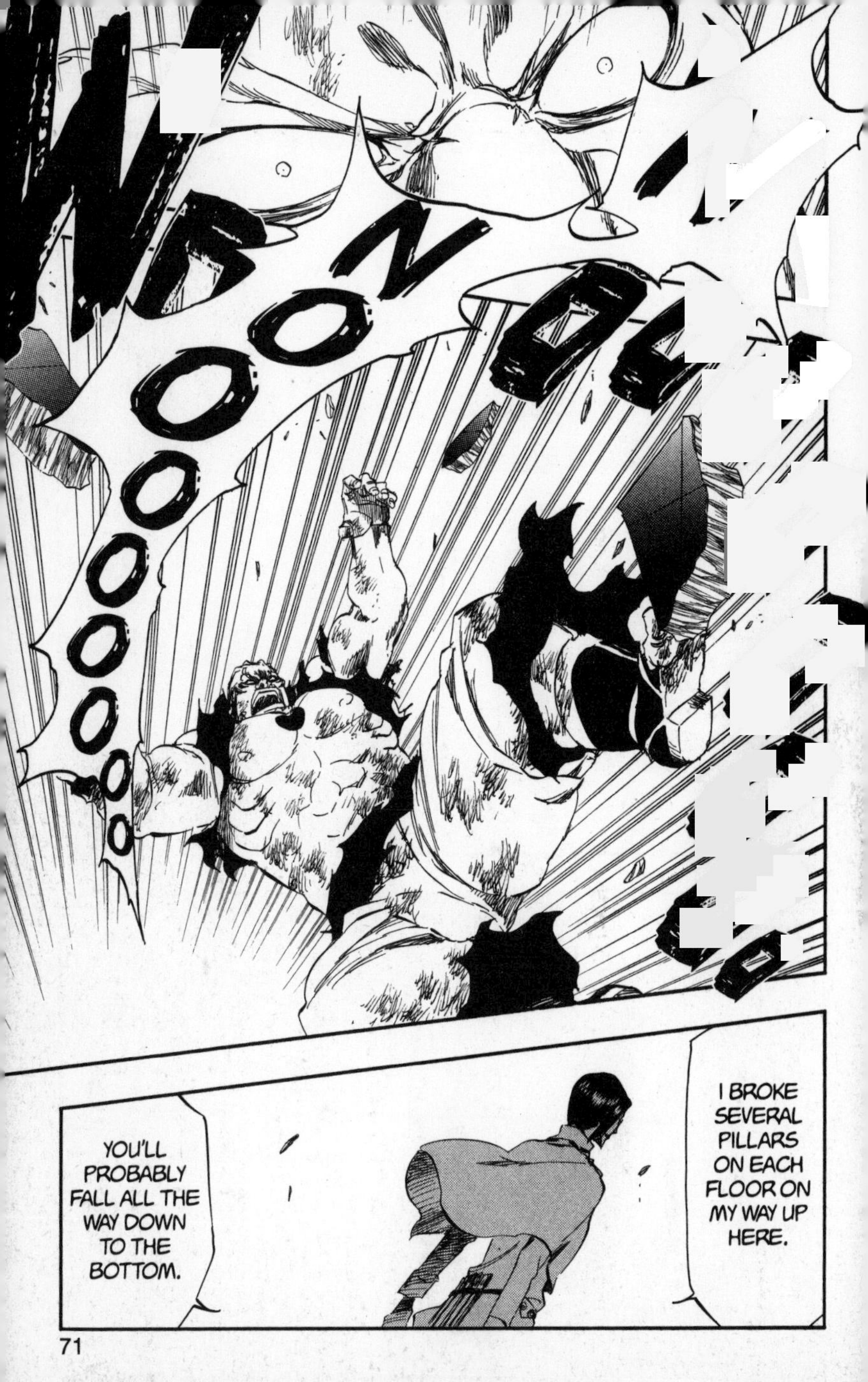
I BROKE SEVERAL PILLARS ON EACH FLOOR ON MY WAY UP HERE.
YOU'LL PROBABLY FALL ALL THE WAY DOWN TO THE BOTTOM.

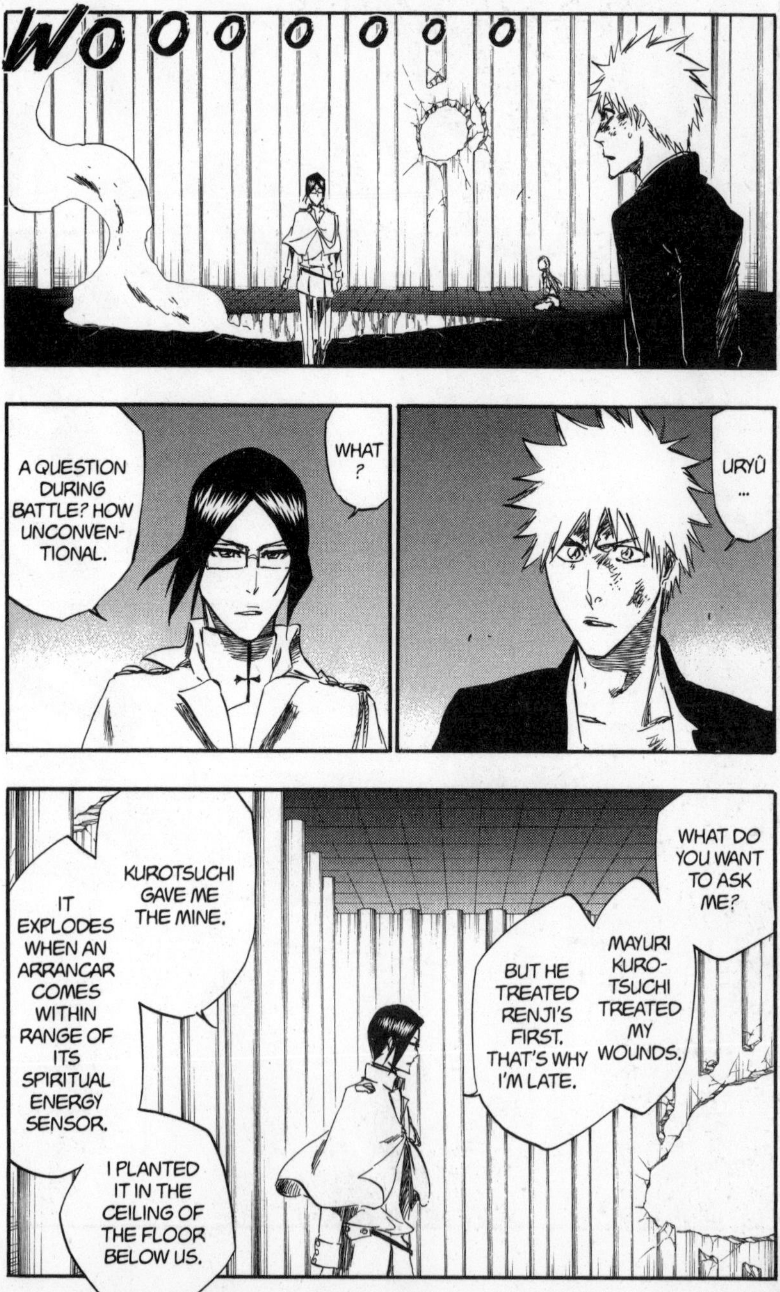
WOOOOOOO
URYÛ ...
WHAT ?
A QUESTION DURING BATTLE? HOW UNCONVENTIONAL.
WHAT DO YOU WANT TO ASK ME?
MAYURI KUROTSUCHI TREATED MY WOUNDS.
BUT HE TREATED RENJI'S FIRST. THAT'S WHY I'M LATE.
KUROTSUCHI GAVE ME THE MINE.
IT EXPLODES WHEN AN ARRANCAR COMES WITHIN RANGE OF ITS SPIRITUAL ENERGY SENSOR.
I PLANTED IT IN THE CEILING OF THE FLOOR BELOW US.

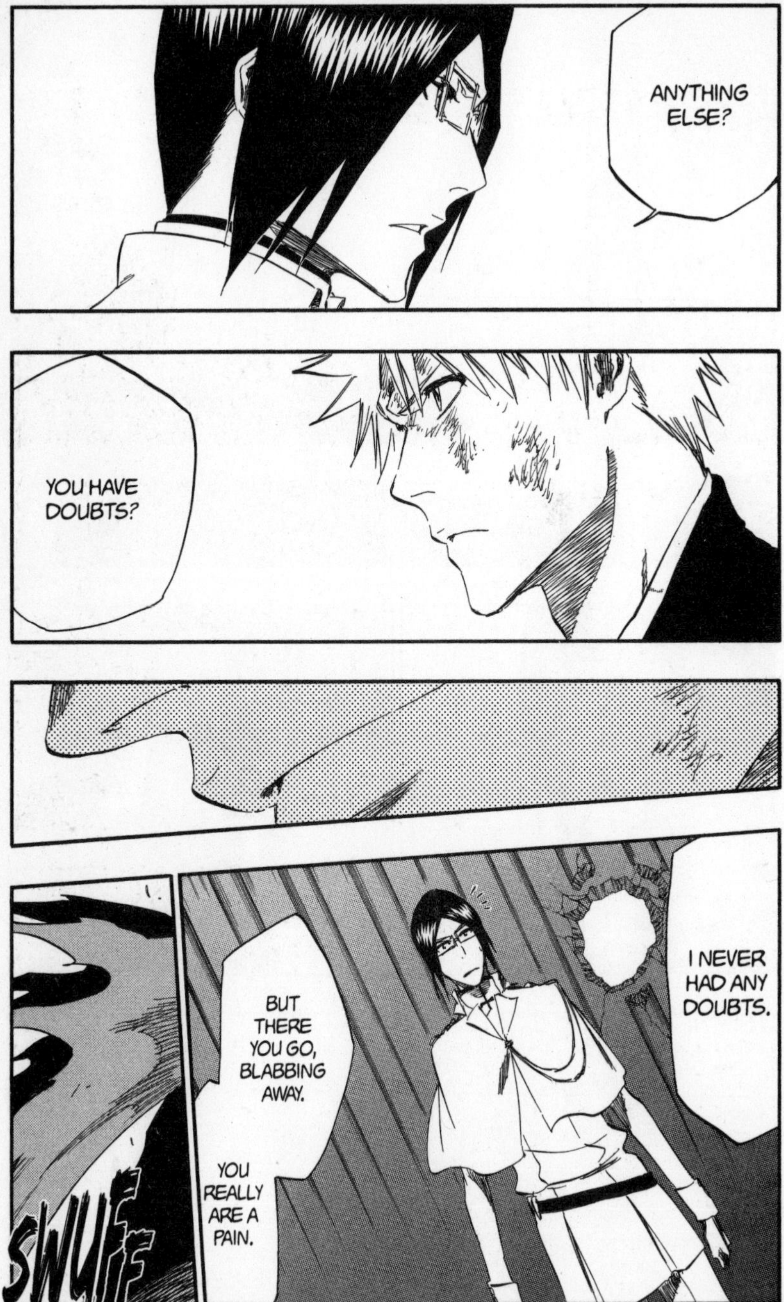
ANYTHING ELSE?
YOU HAVE DOUBTS?
I NEVER HAD ANY DOUBTS.
BUT THERE YOU GO, BLABBING AWAY.
YOU REALLY ARE A PAIN.
SWUFF

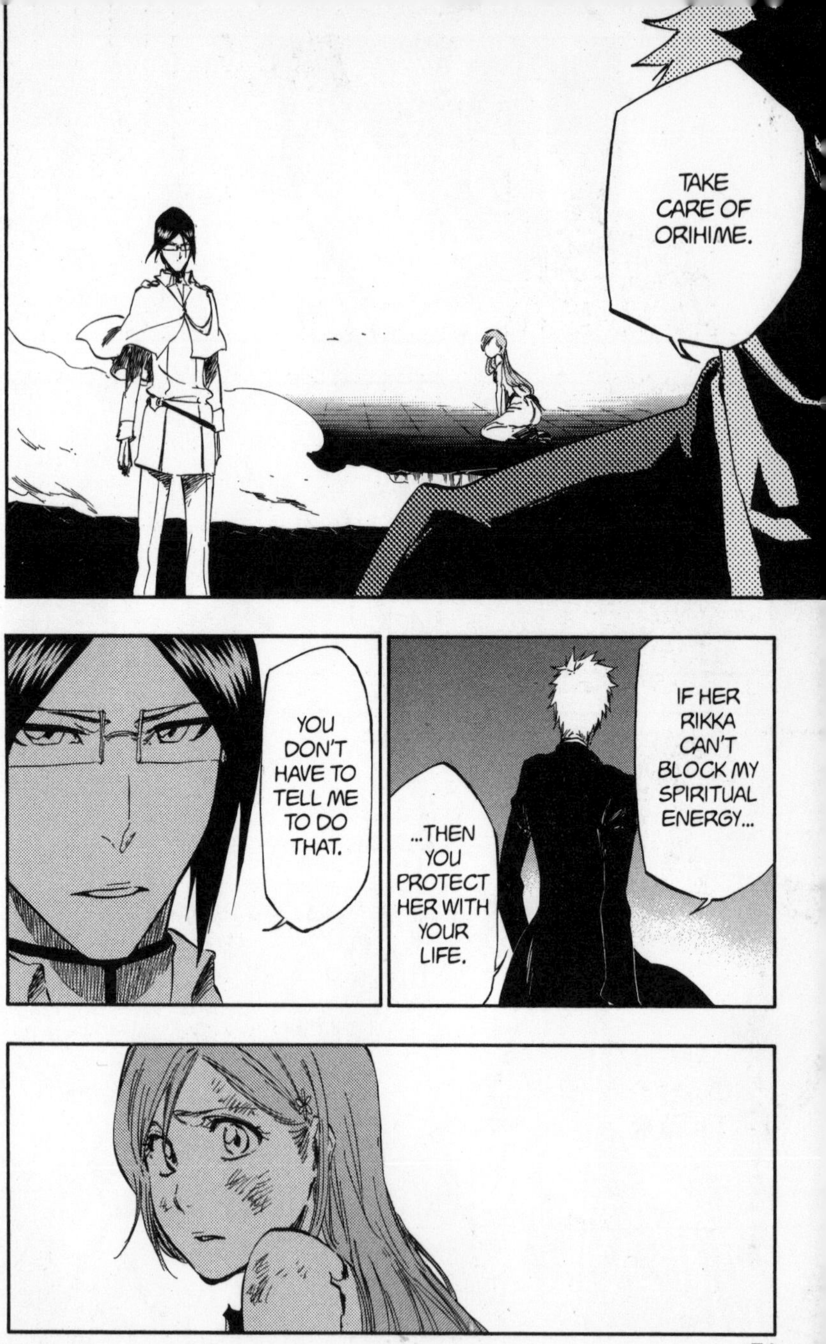
TAKE CARE OF ORIHIME.
IF HER RIKKA CAN'T BLOCK MY SPIRITUAL ENERGY...
...THEN YOU PROTECT HER WITH YOUR LIFE.
YOU DON'T HAVE TO TELL ME TO DO THAT.

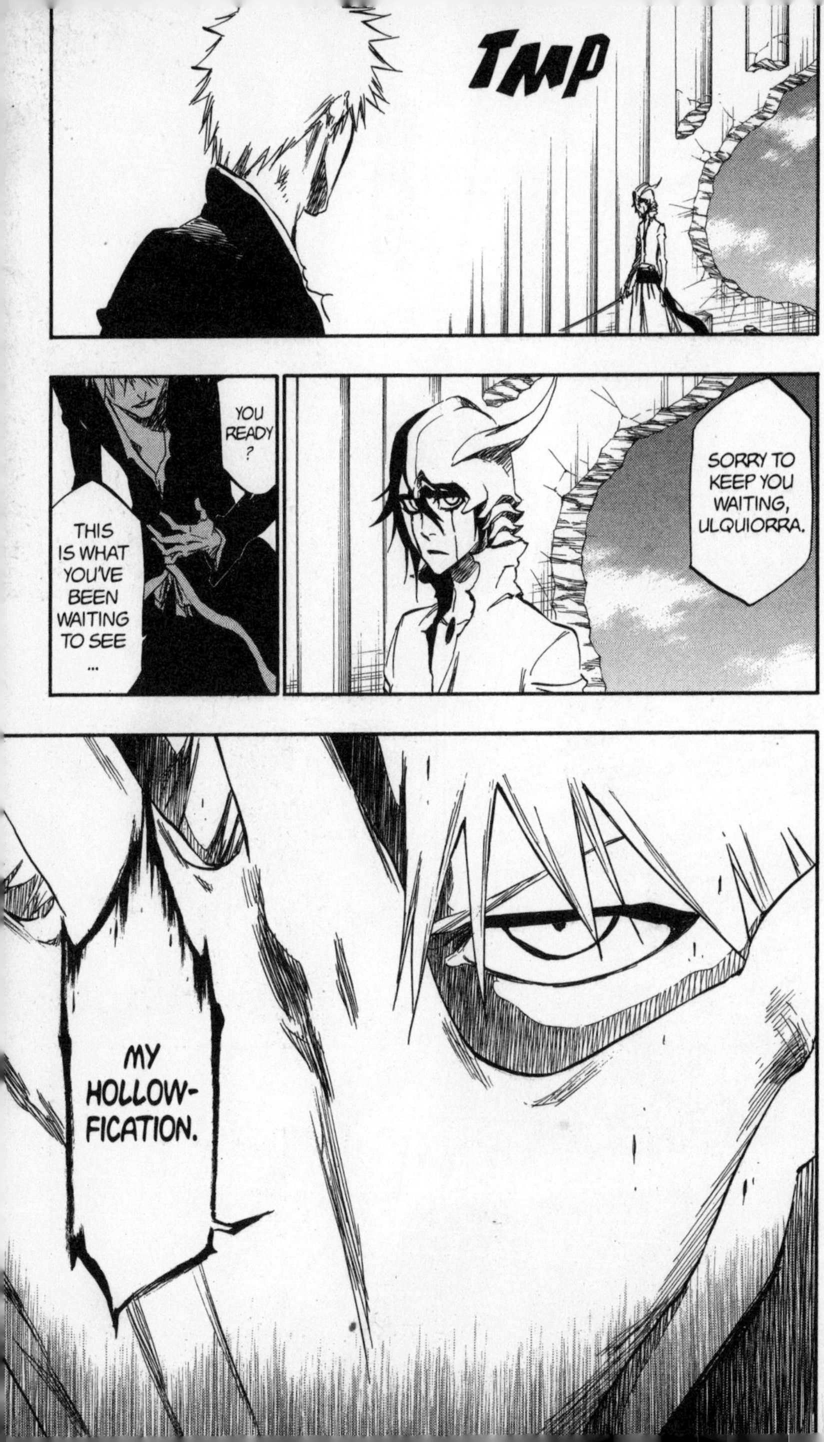
TMP
SORRY TO KEEP YOU WAITING, ULQUIORRA.
YOU READY?
THIS IS WHAT YOU'VE BEEN WAITING TO SEE...
MY HOLLOW-FICATION.

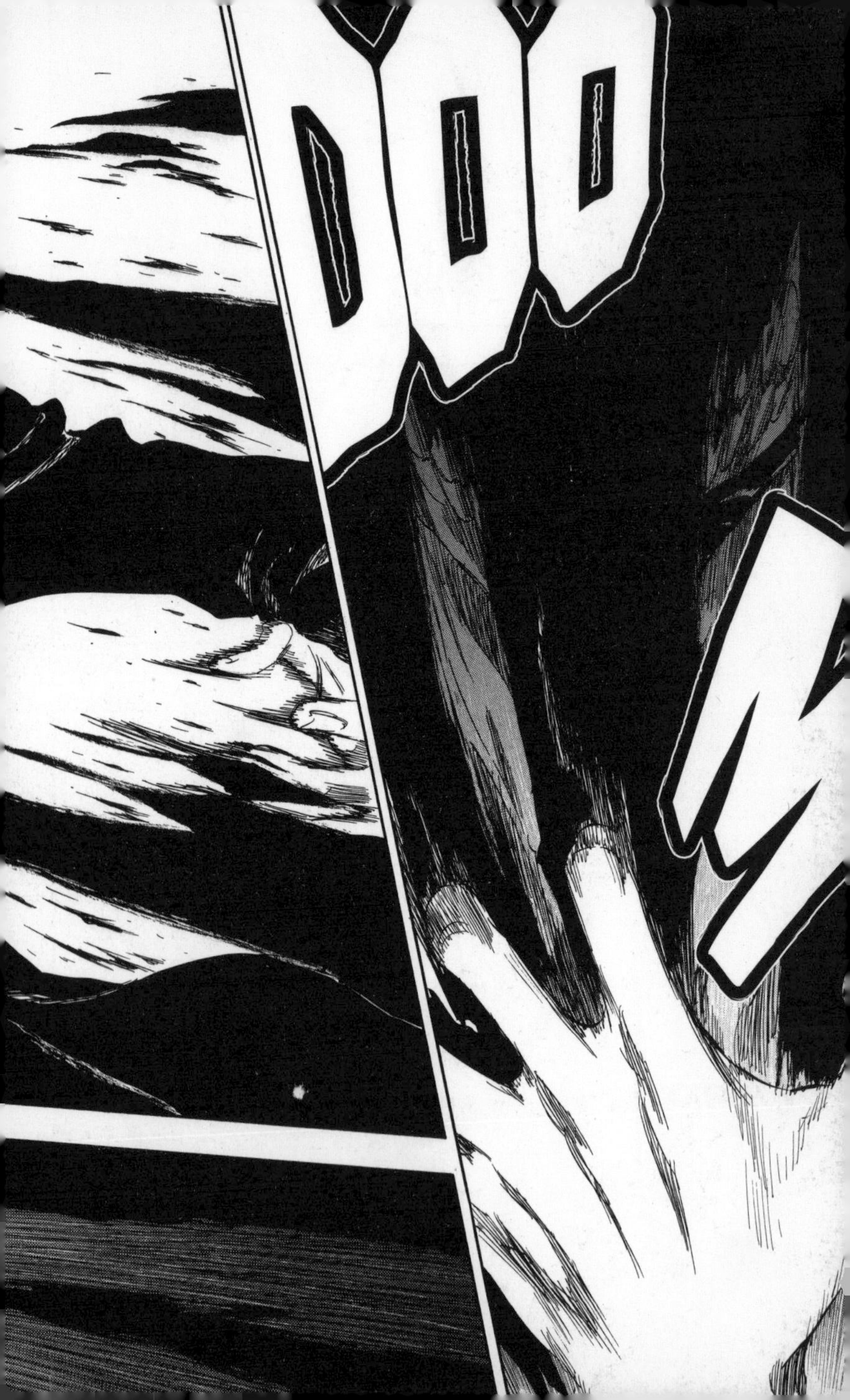

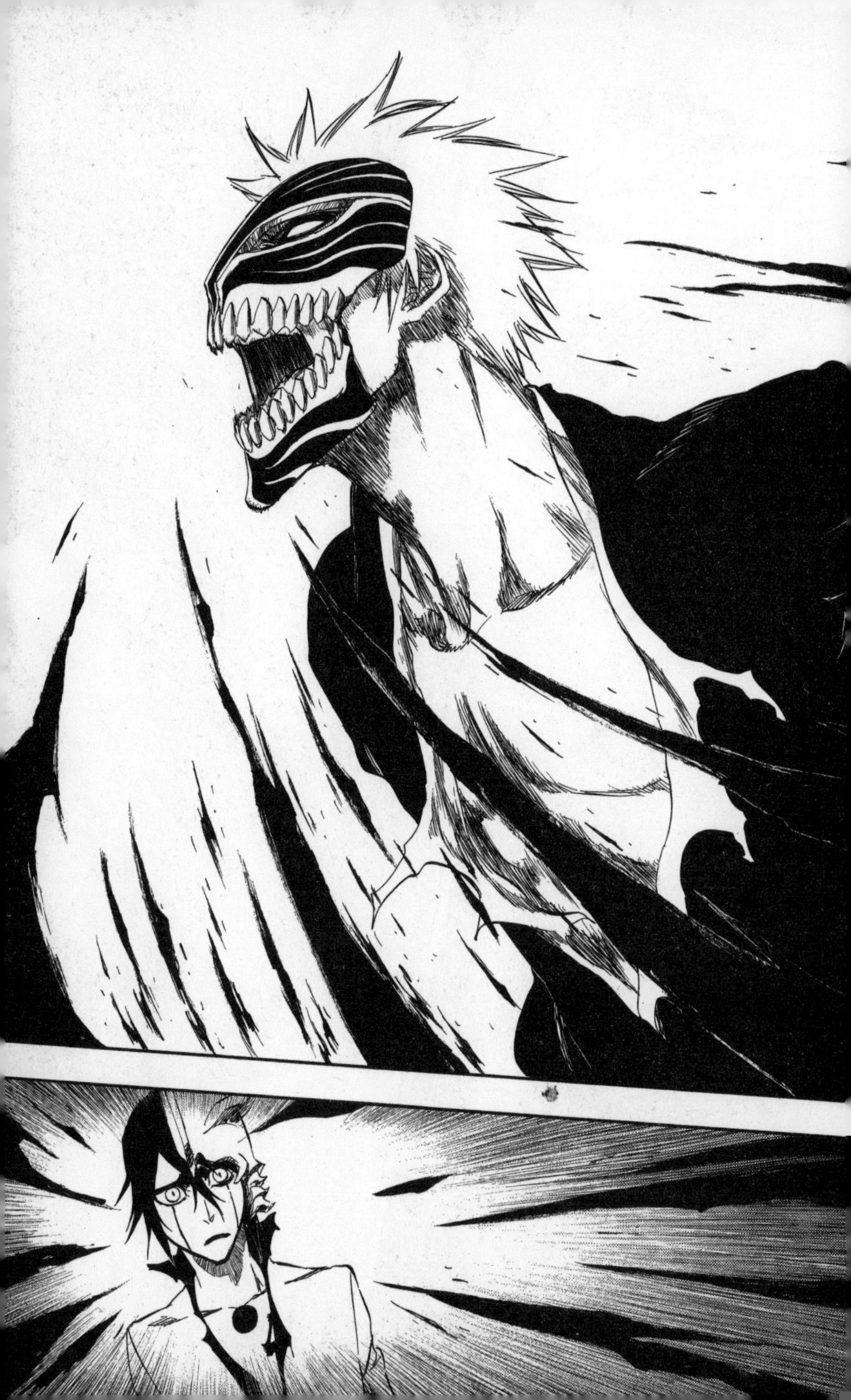

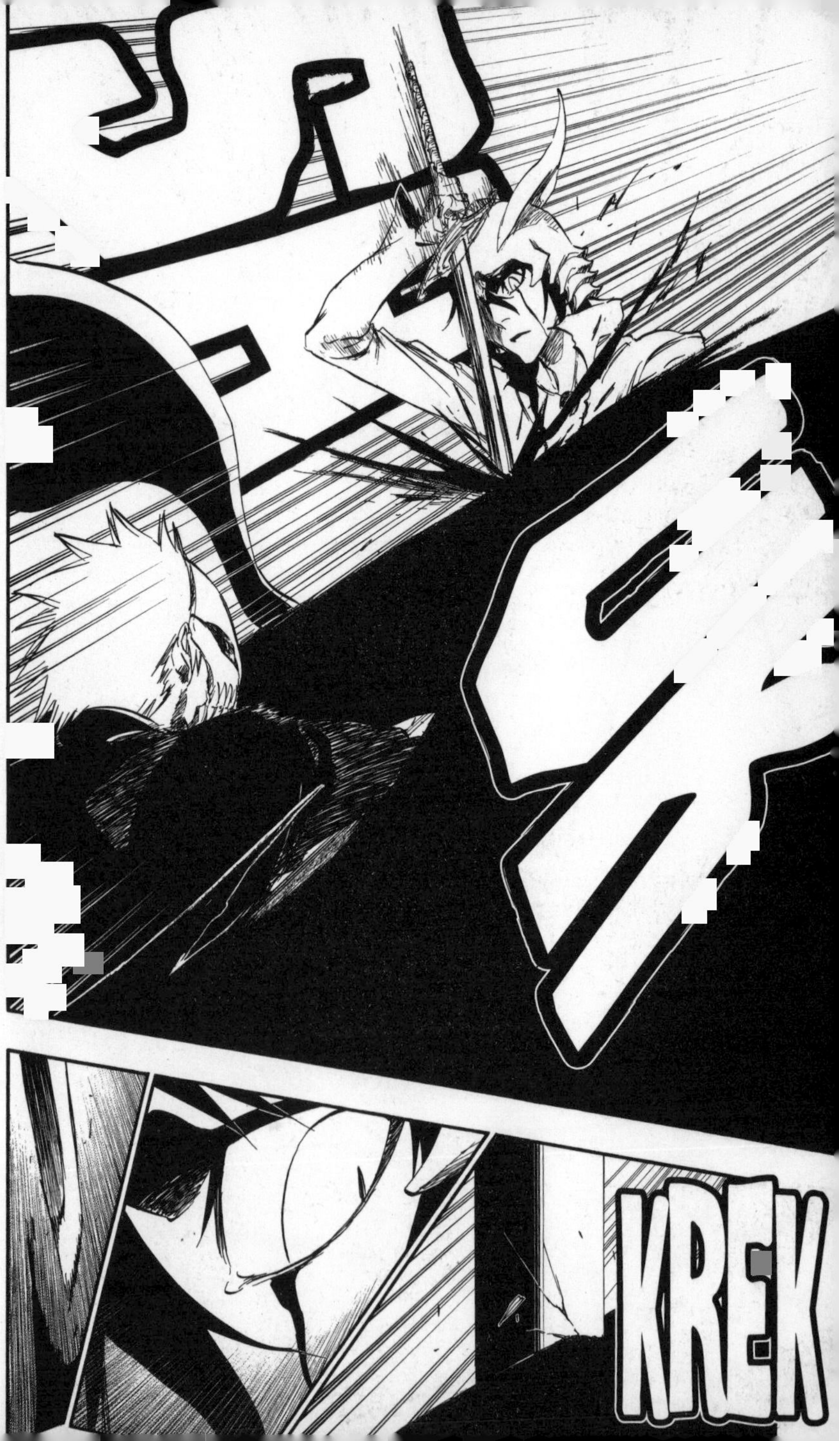
KREK

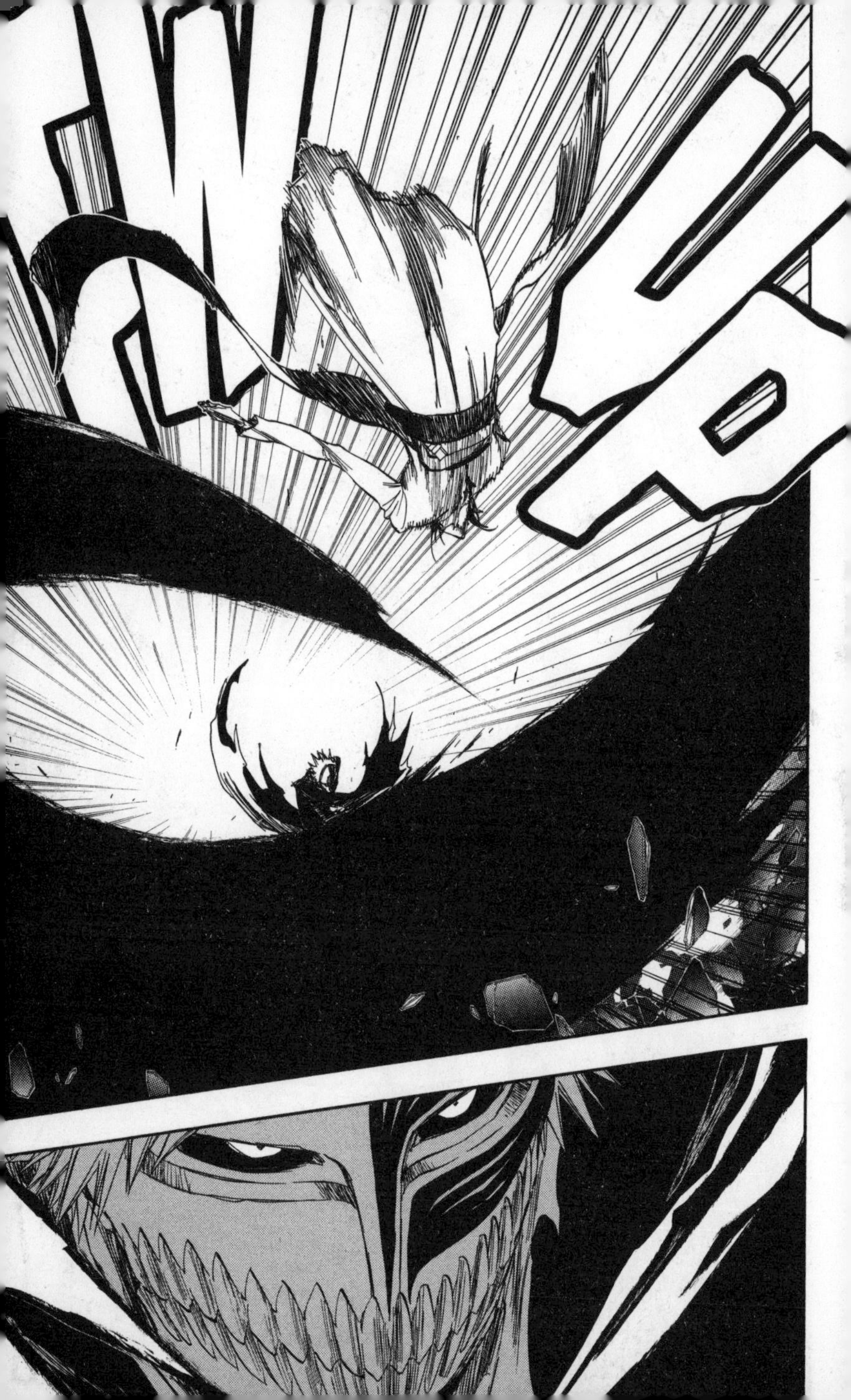

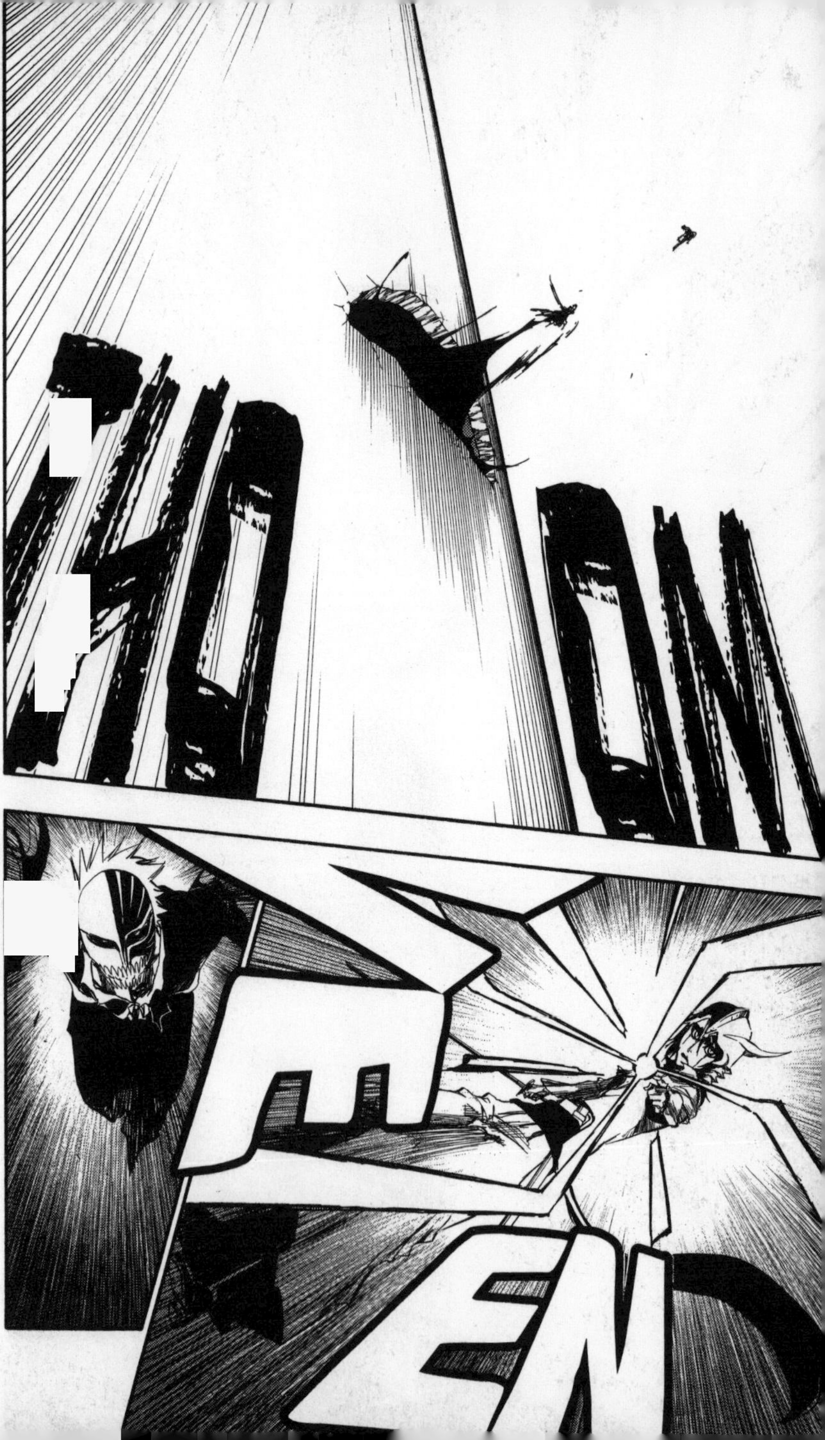

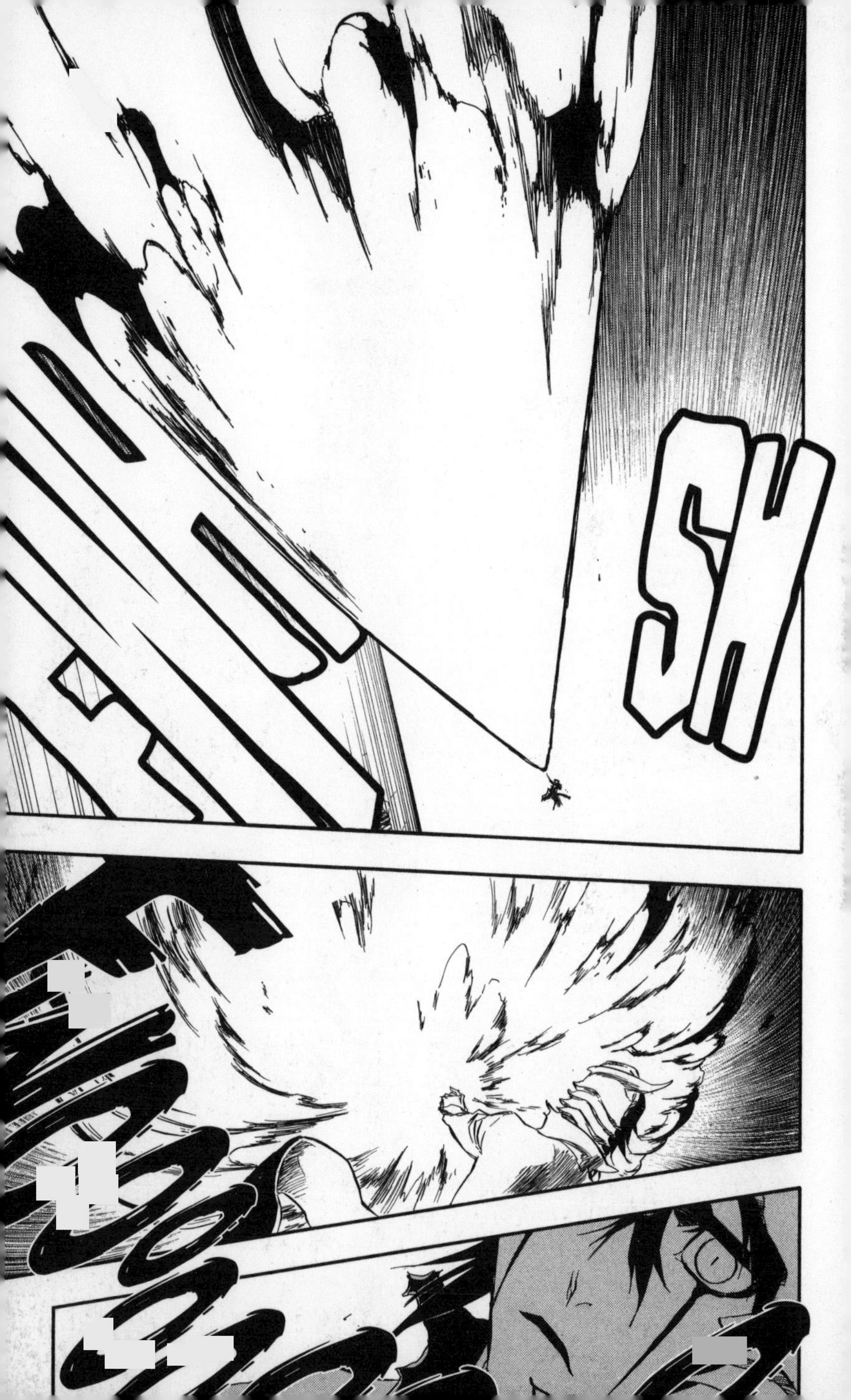
SH

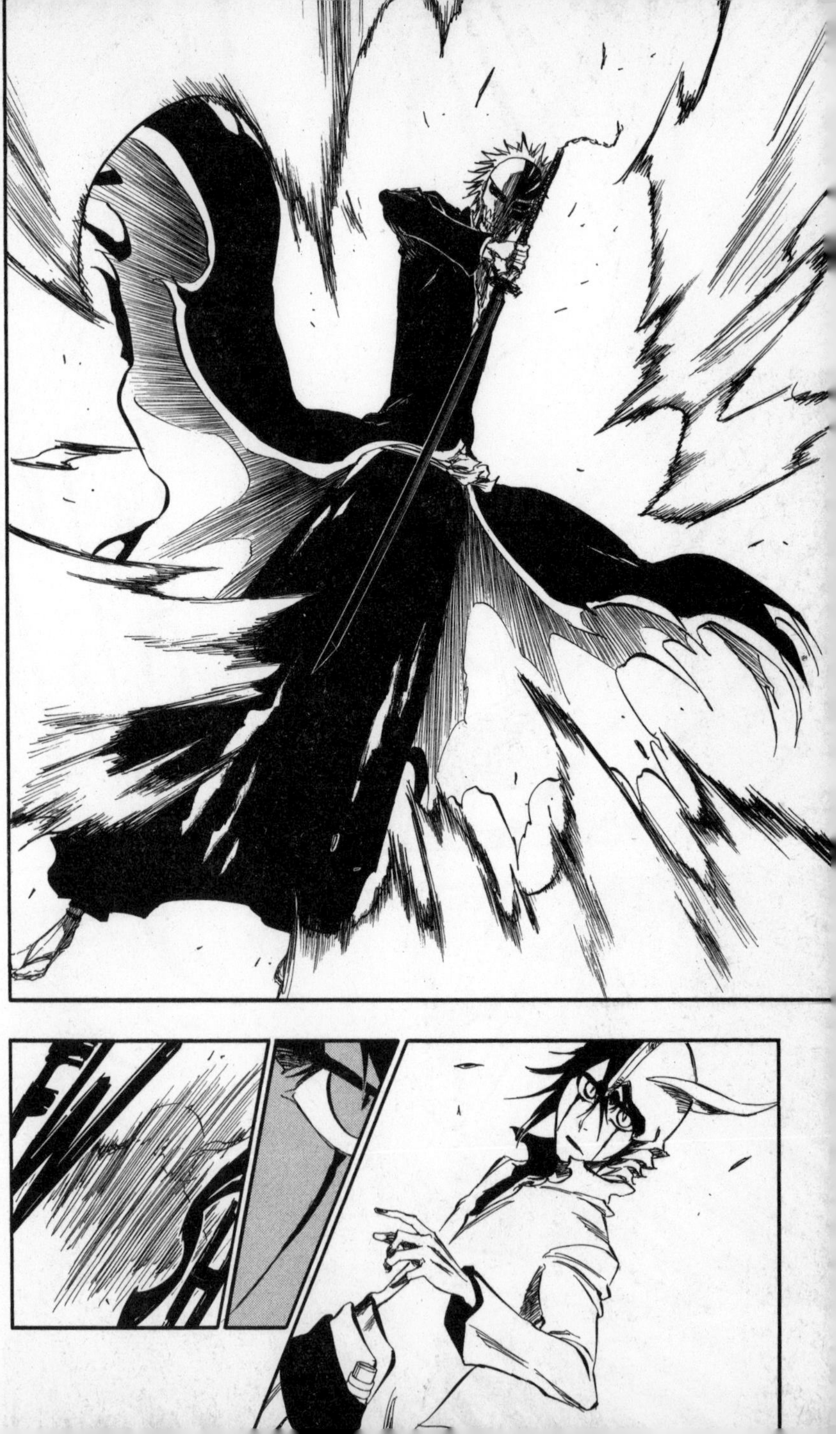

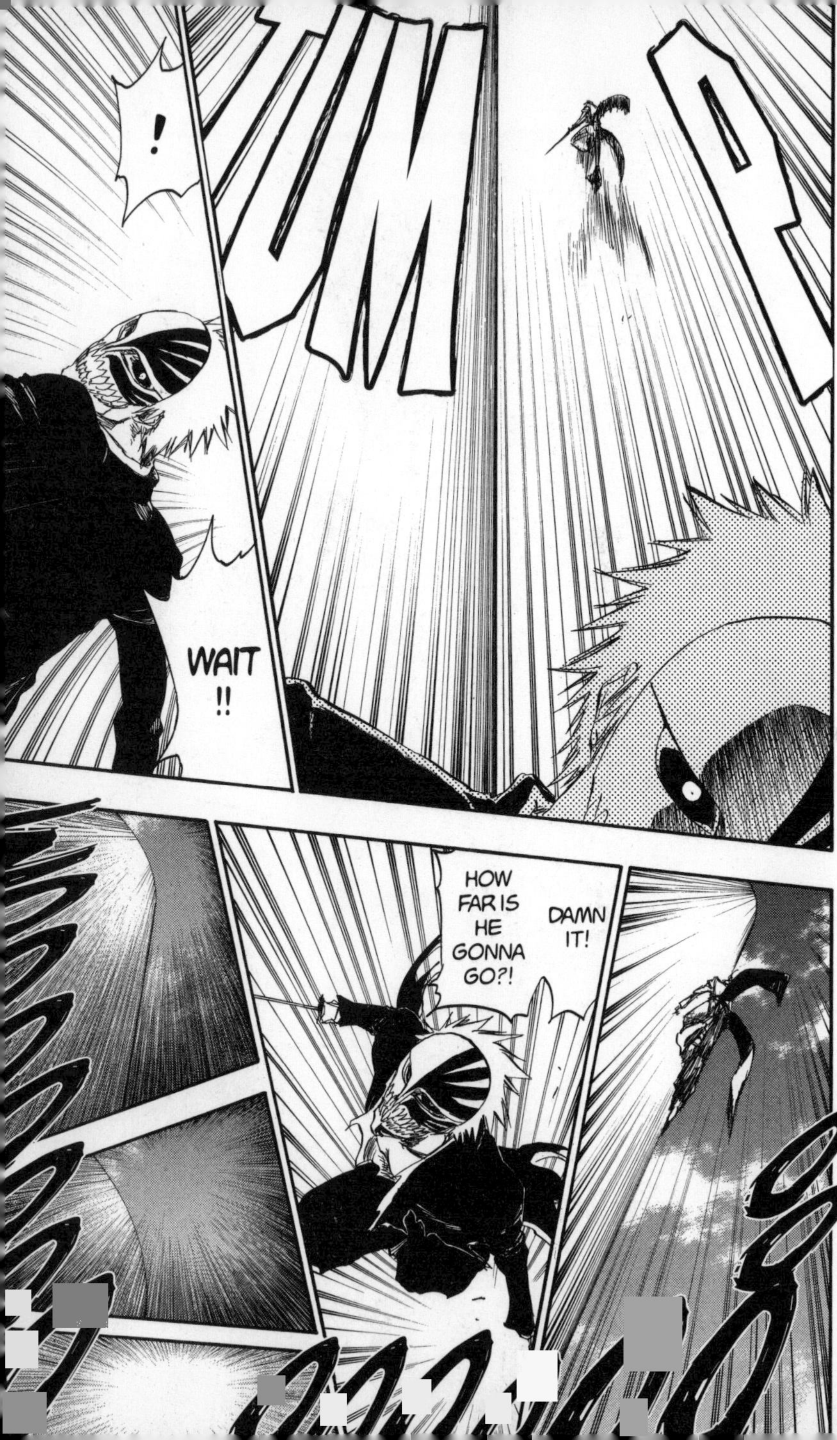
!
WAIT !!
DAMN IT!
HOW FAR IS HE GONNA GO?!

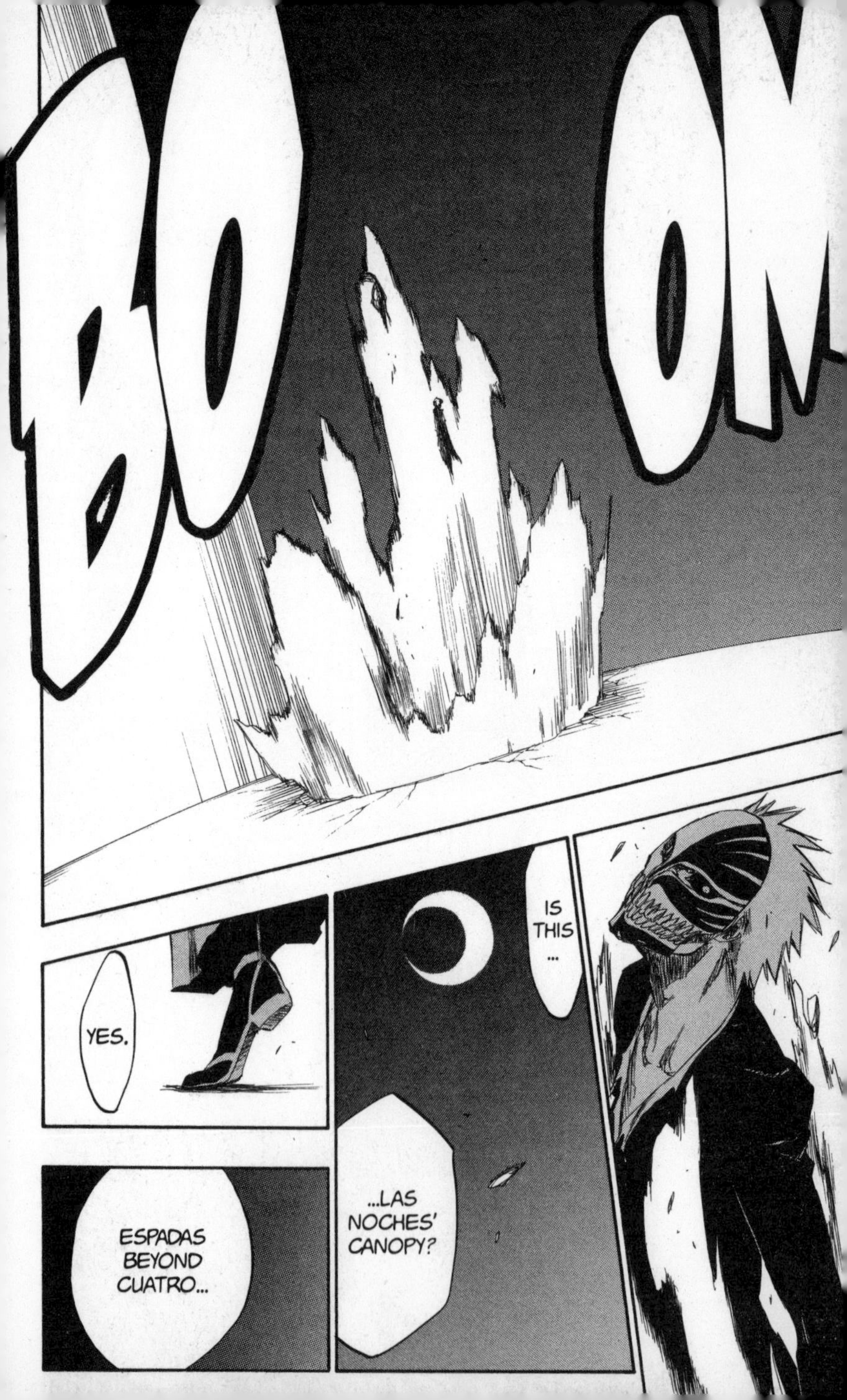
BOOM
IS THIS...
...LAS NOCHES' CANOPY?
YES.
ESPADAS BEYOND CUATRO...

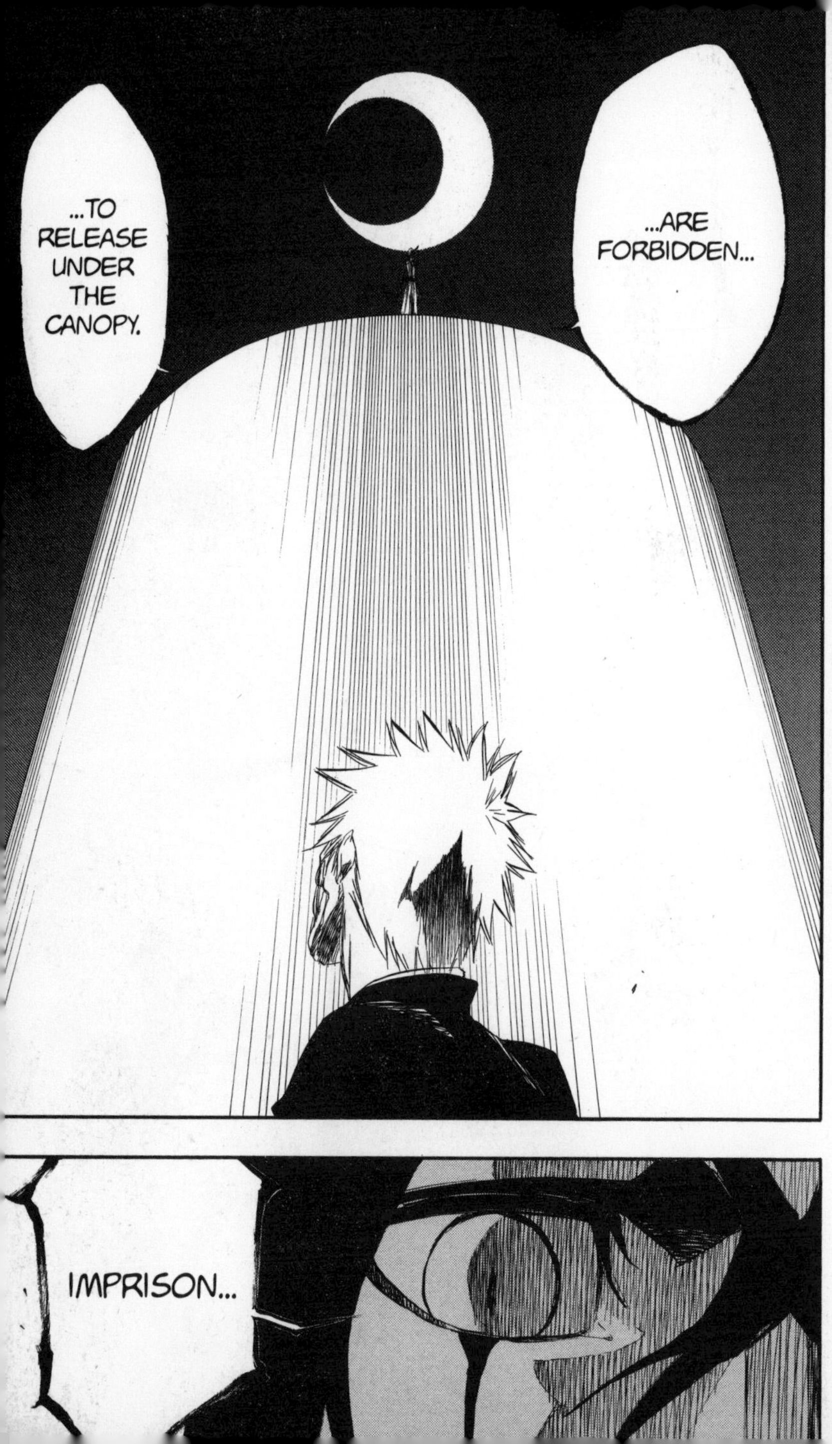
...ARE FORBIDDEN...
...TO RELEASE UNDER THE CANOPY.
IMPRISON...

the Pride

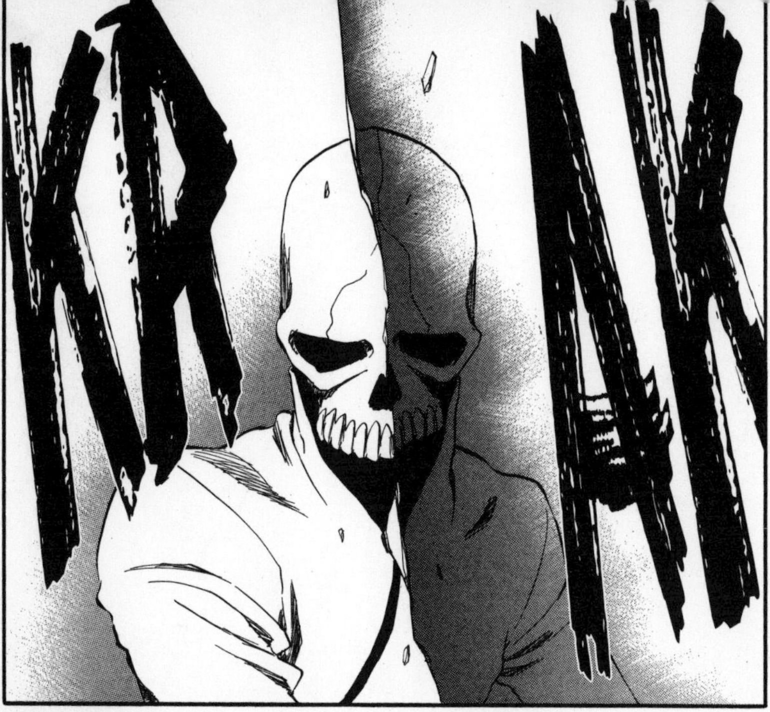
KRAK
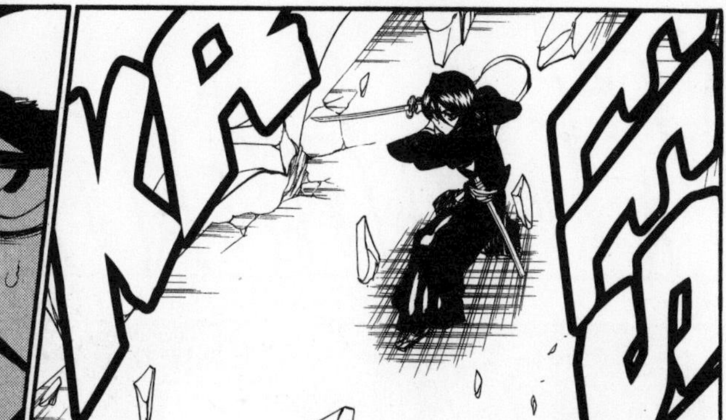
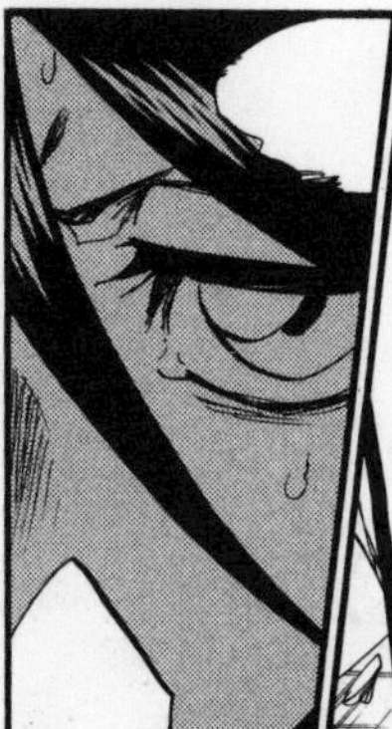
WHAT'S WRONG?

345. The Sloth

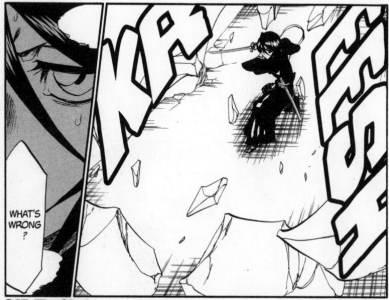

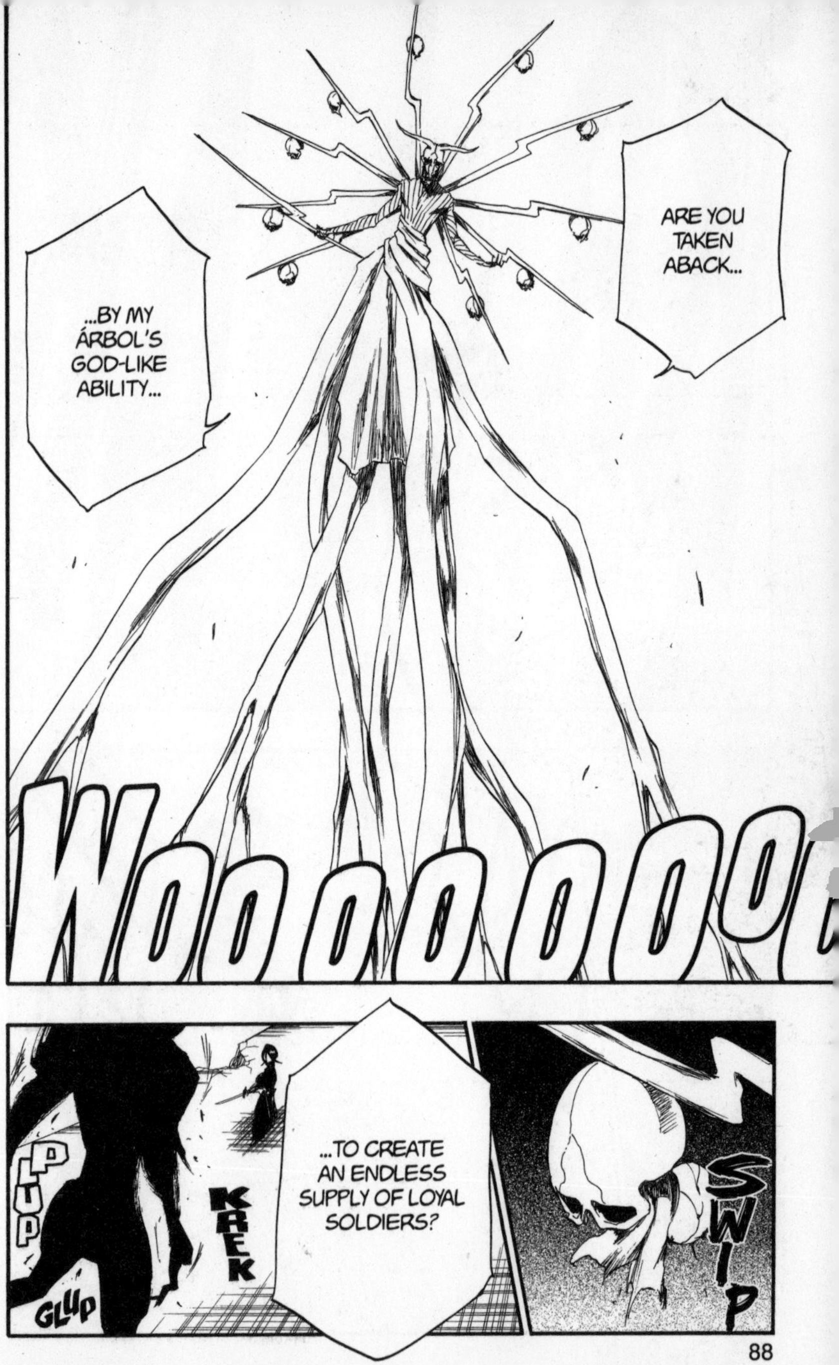
ARE YOU TAKEN ABACK...
...BY MY ÁRBOL'S GOD-LIKE ABILITY...
WOOOOOOO
SWIP
...TO CREATE AN ENDLESS SUPPLY OF LOYAL SOLDIERS?
KREK
PLUP
GLUP

READ THIS WAY

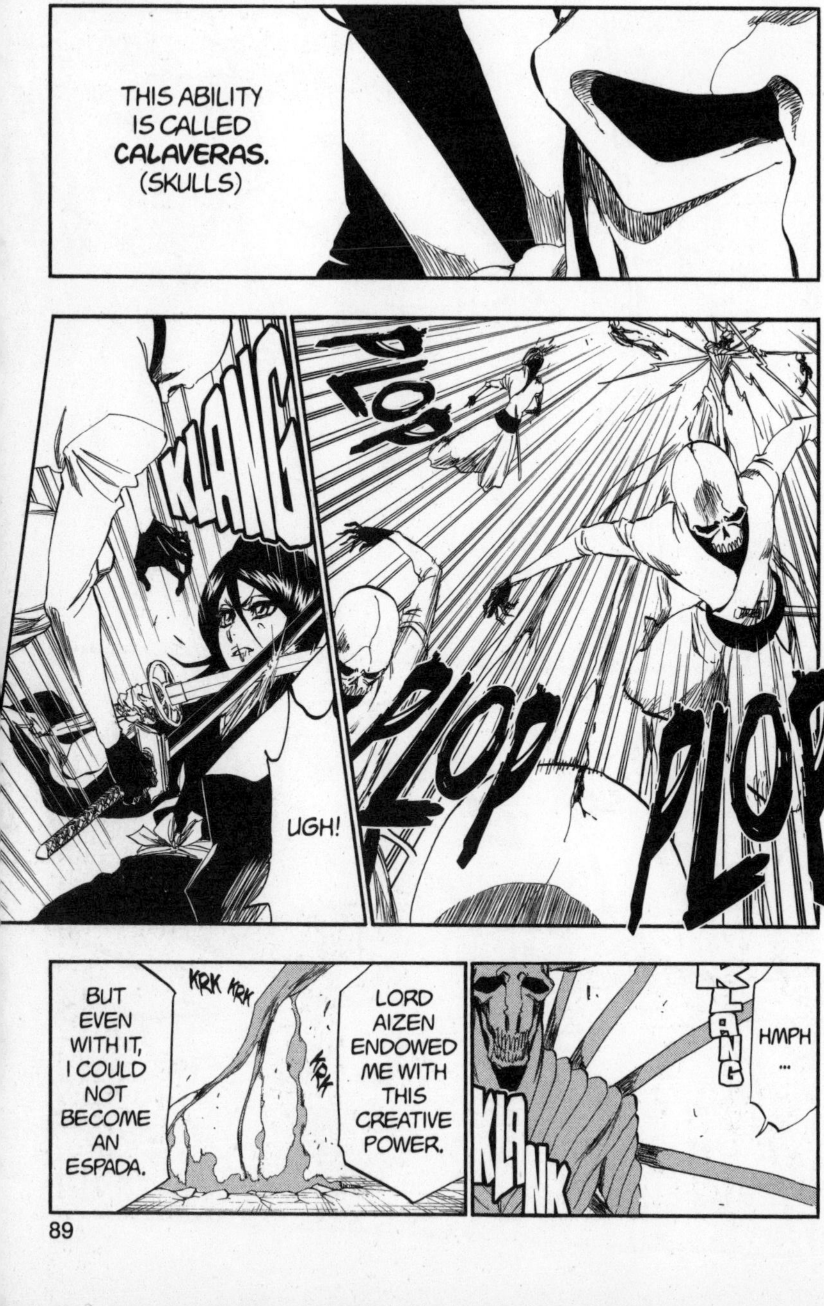
THIS ABILITY IS CALLED **CALAVERAS.** (SKULLS)
PLOP
PLOP
PLOP
KLANG
UGH!
KLANG
HMPH ...
KLANK
LORD AIZEN ENDOWED ME WITH THIS CREATIVE POWER.
KRK
KRK KRK
BUT EVEN WITH IT, I COULD NOT BECOME AN ESPADA.

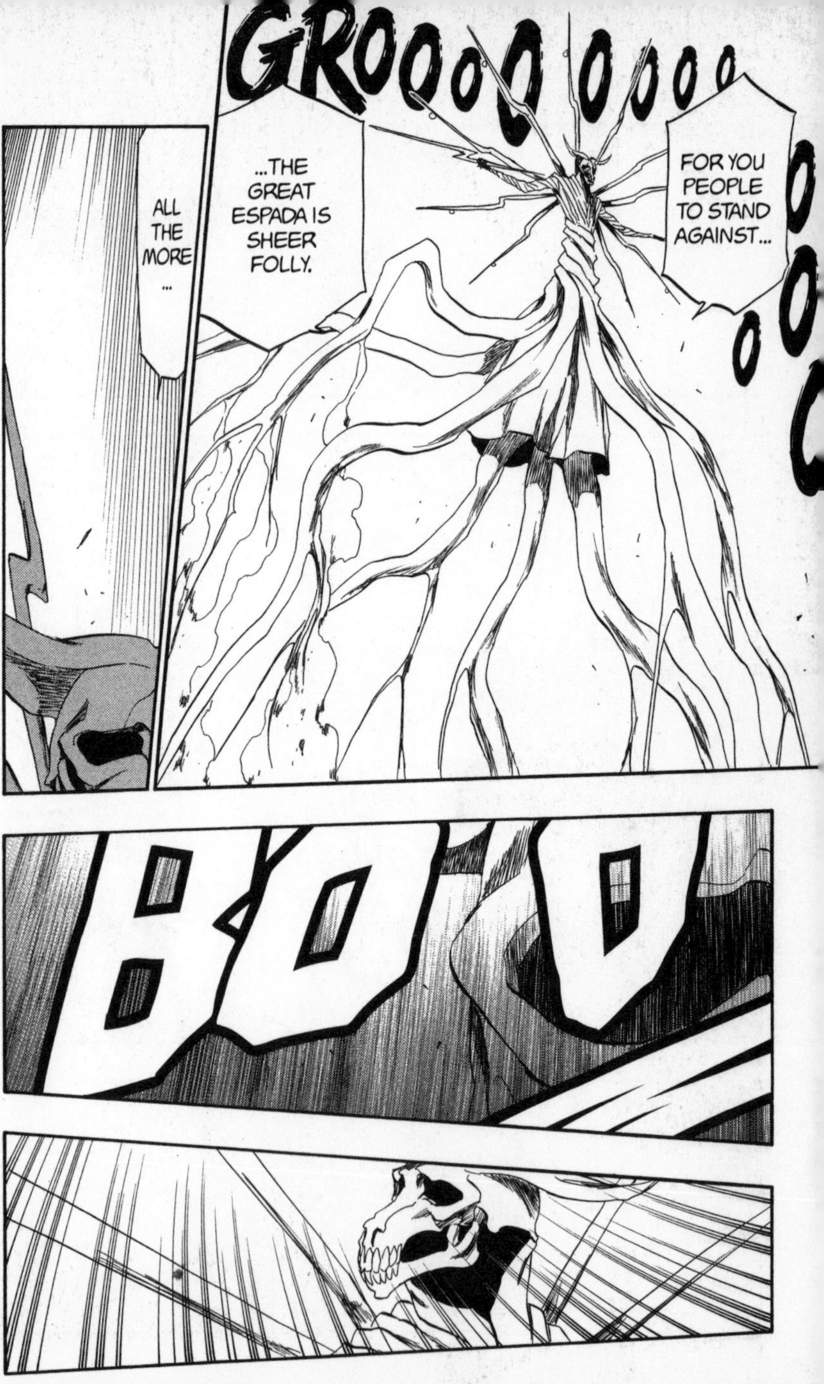
GROOOOOOOOOOOOO
FOR YOU PEOPLE TO STAND AGAINST...
...THE GREAT ESPADA IS SHEER FOLLY.
ALL THE MORE ...
BOOO

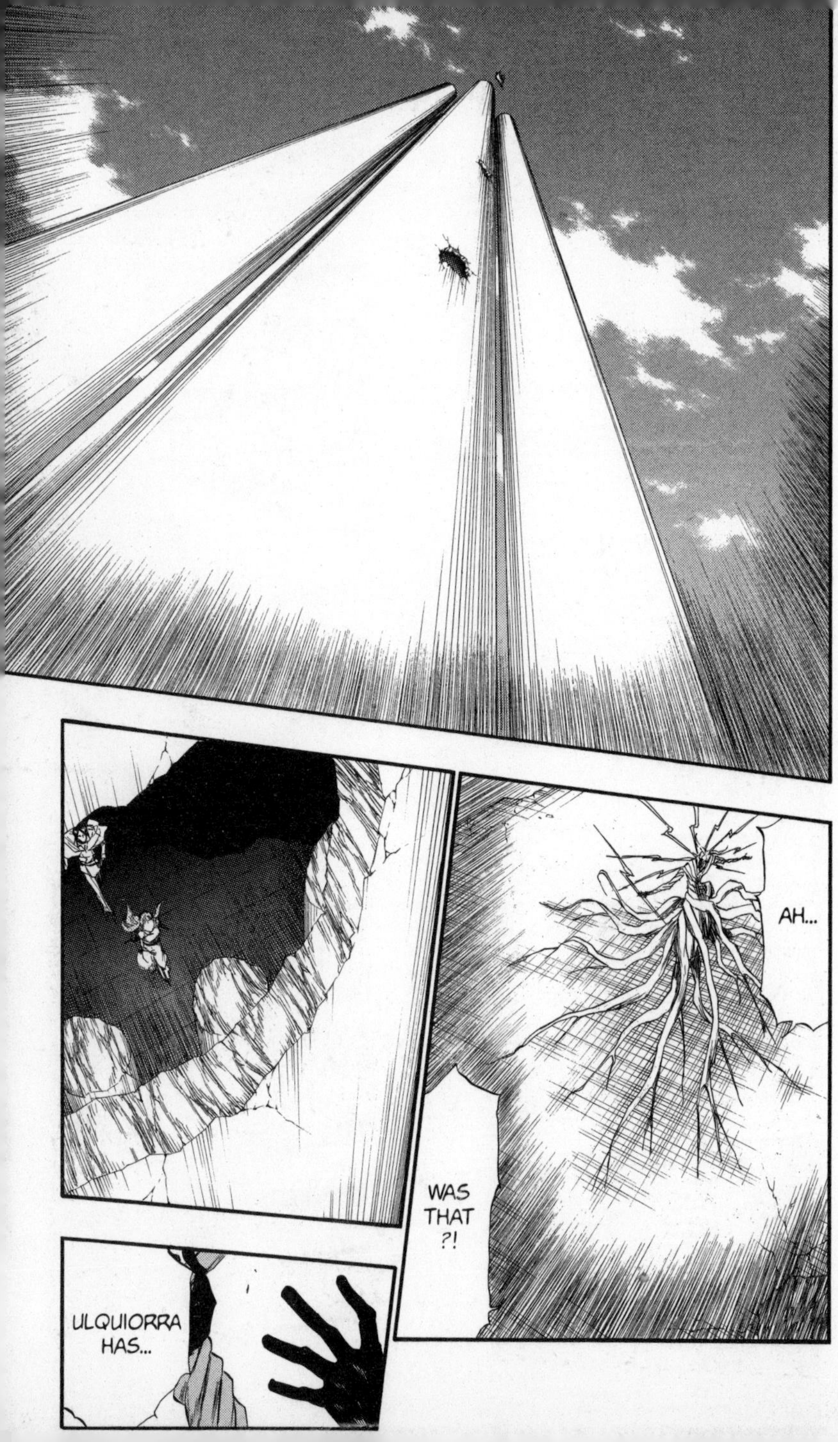
AH...
WAS THAT ?!
ULQUIORRA HAS...

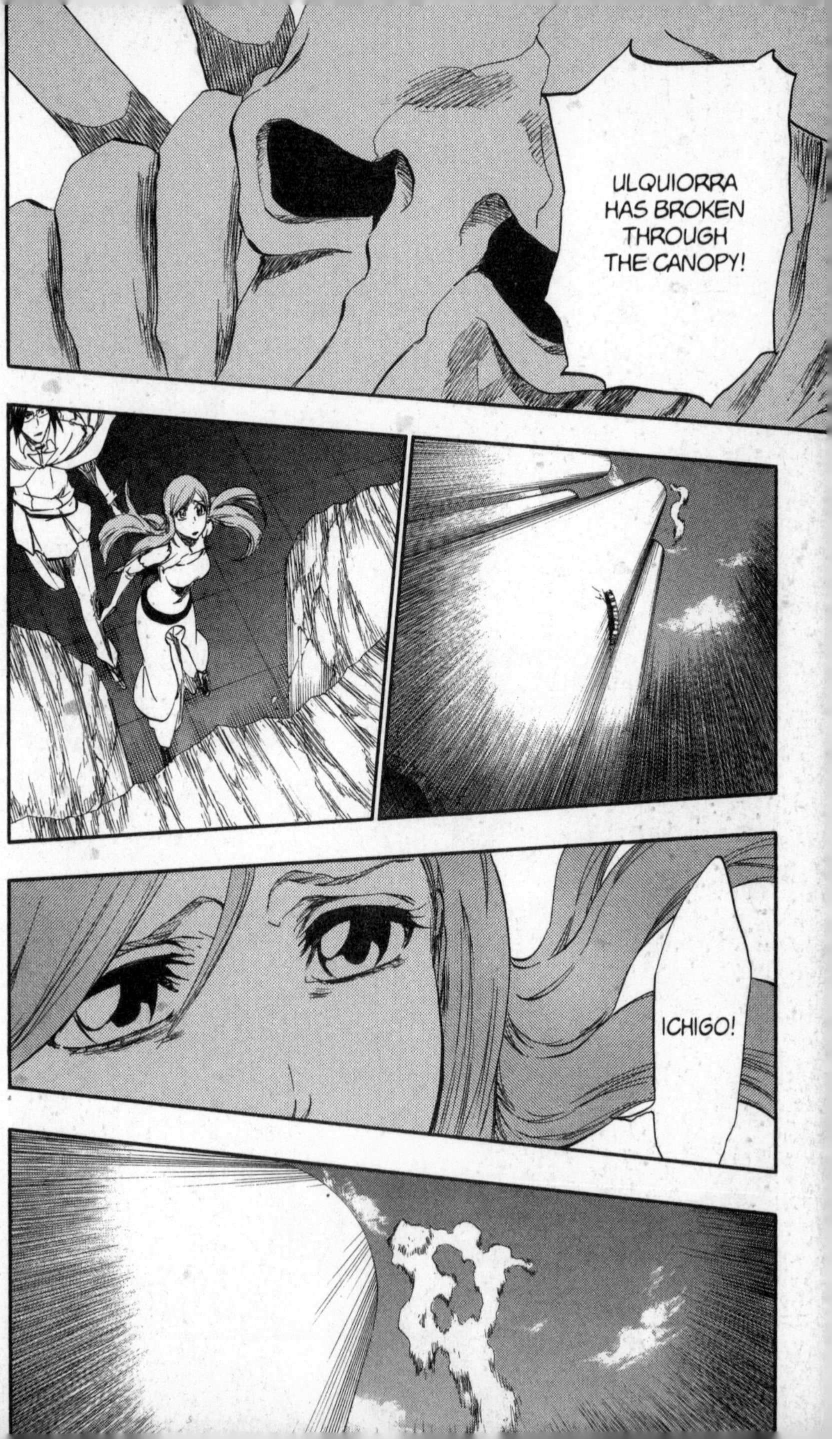
ULQUIORRA HAS BROKEN THROUGH THE CANOPY!
ICHIGO!

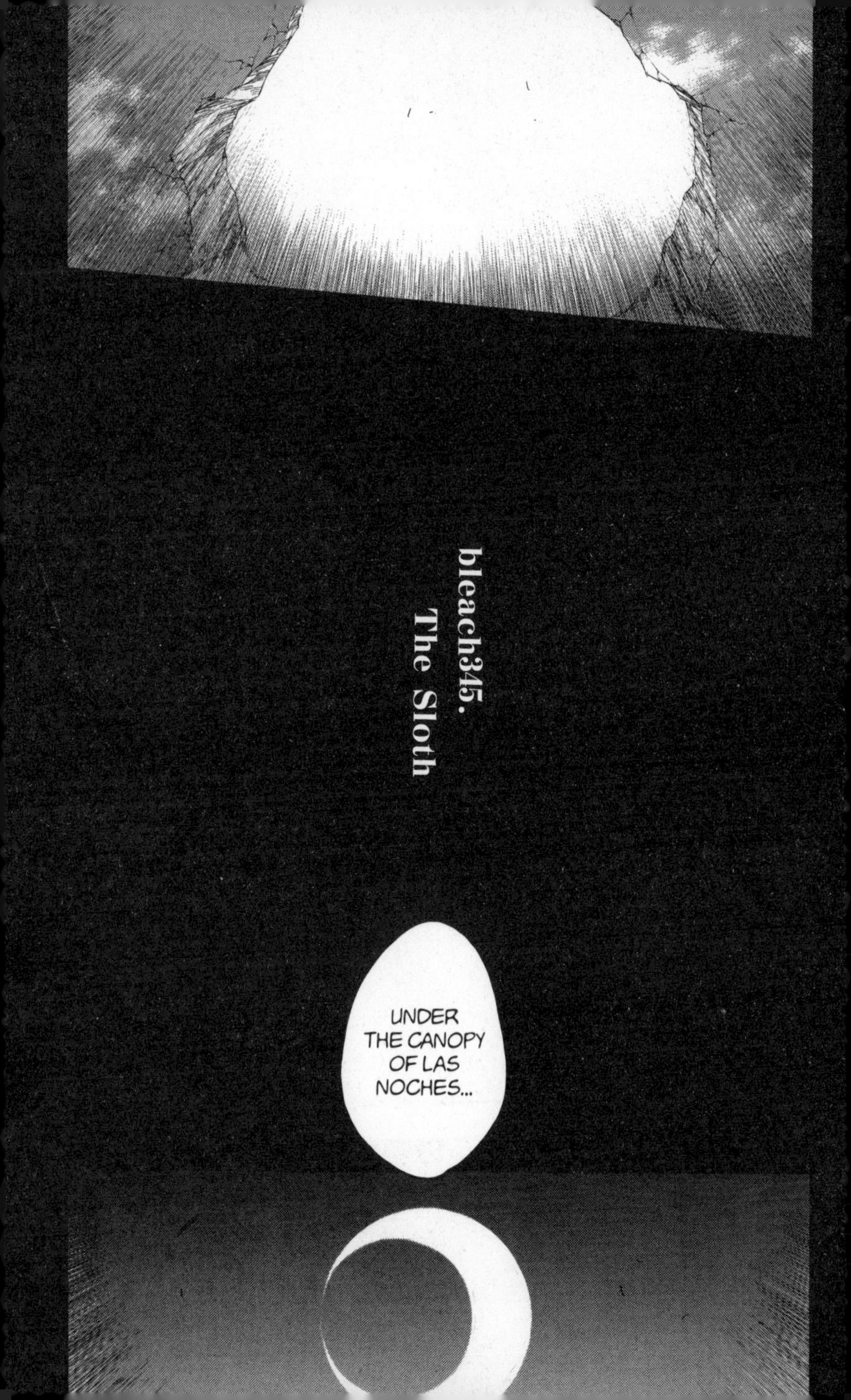
bleach345. The Sloth
UNDER THE CANOPY OF LAS NOCHES...

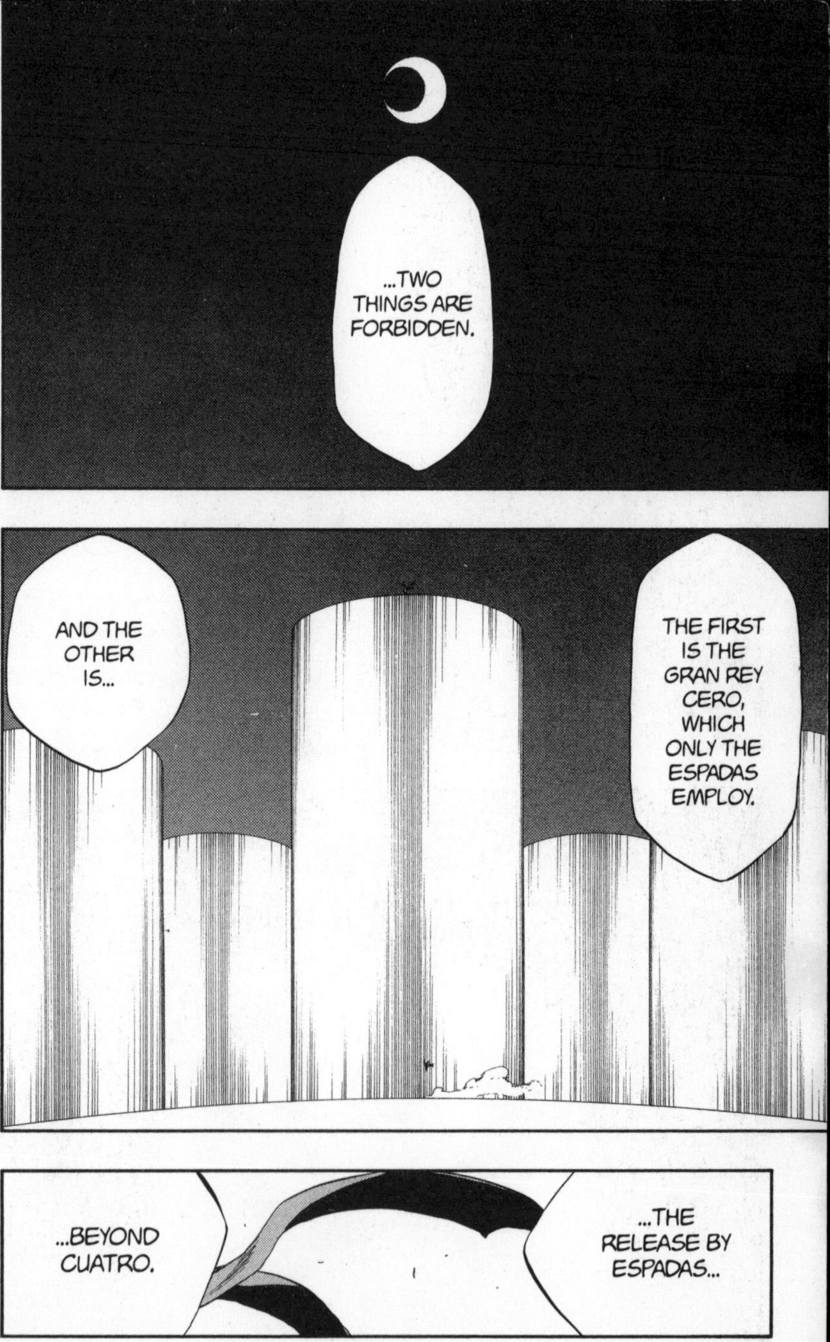
...TWO THINGS ARE FORBIDDEN.
THE FIRST IS THE GRAN REY CERO, WHICH ONLY THE ESPADAS EMPLOY.
AND THE OTHER IS...
...THE RELEASE BY ESPADAS...
...BEYOND CUATRO.

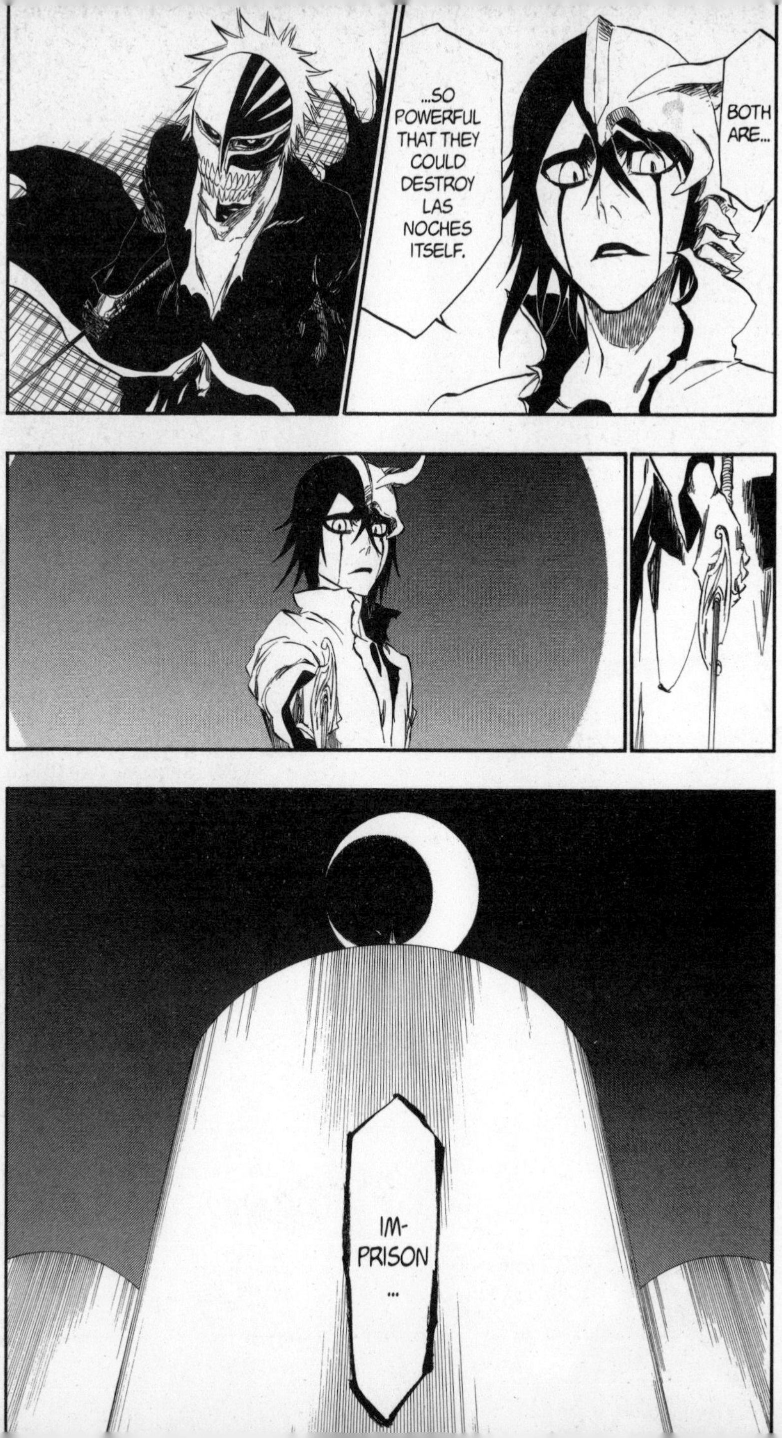
BOTH ARE...
...SO POWERFUL THAT THEY COULD DESTROY LAS NOCHES ITSELF.
IM-PRISON ...

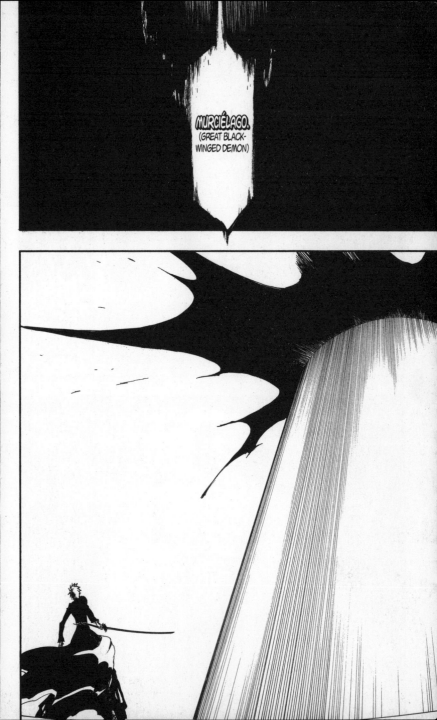

MURCIÉLAGO.
(GREAT BLACK-
WINGED DEMON)

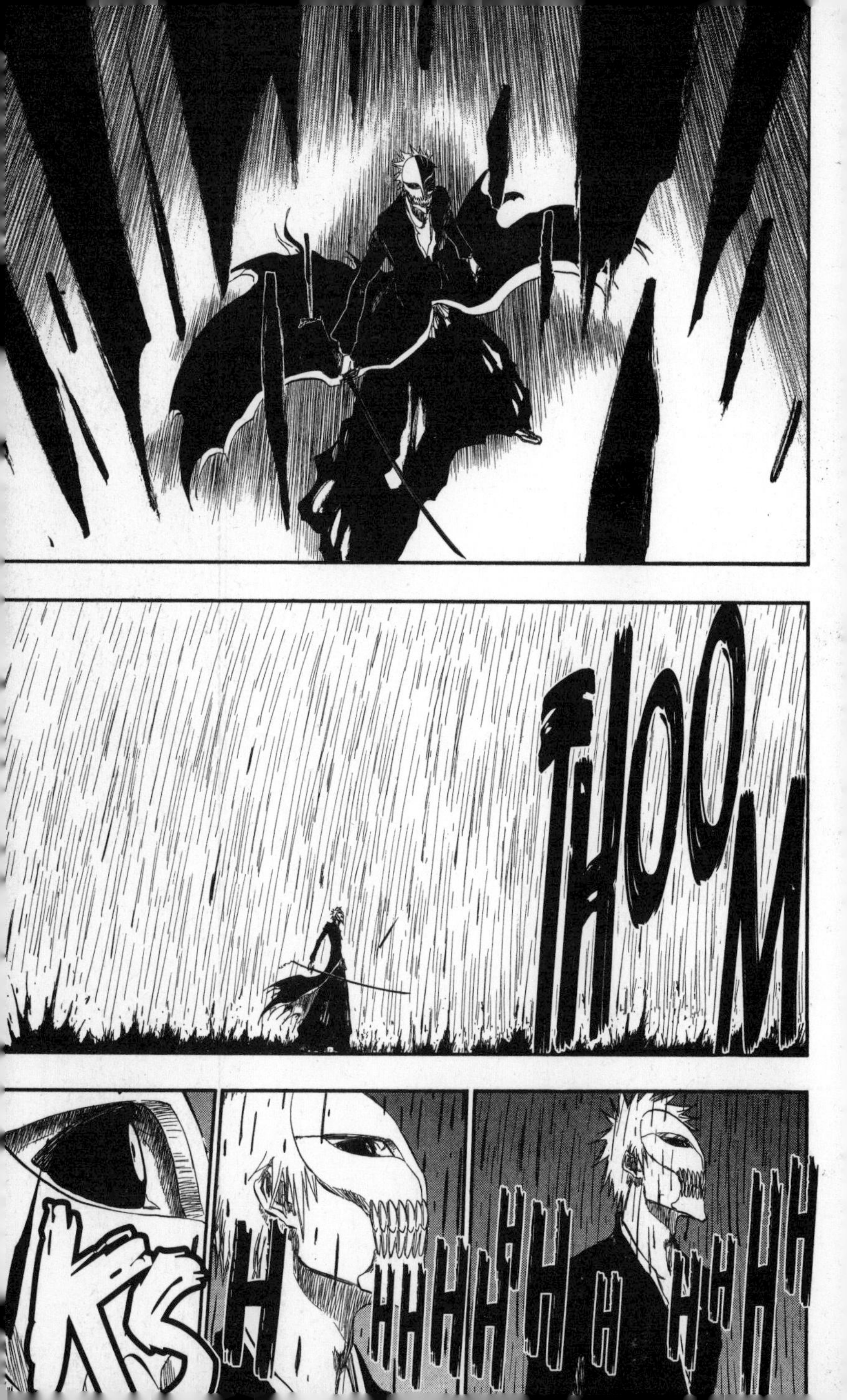
THOOM
KSHHHHHHHHHHHHH

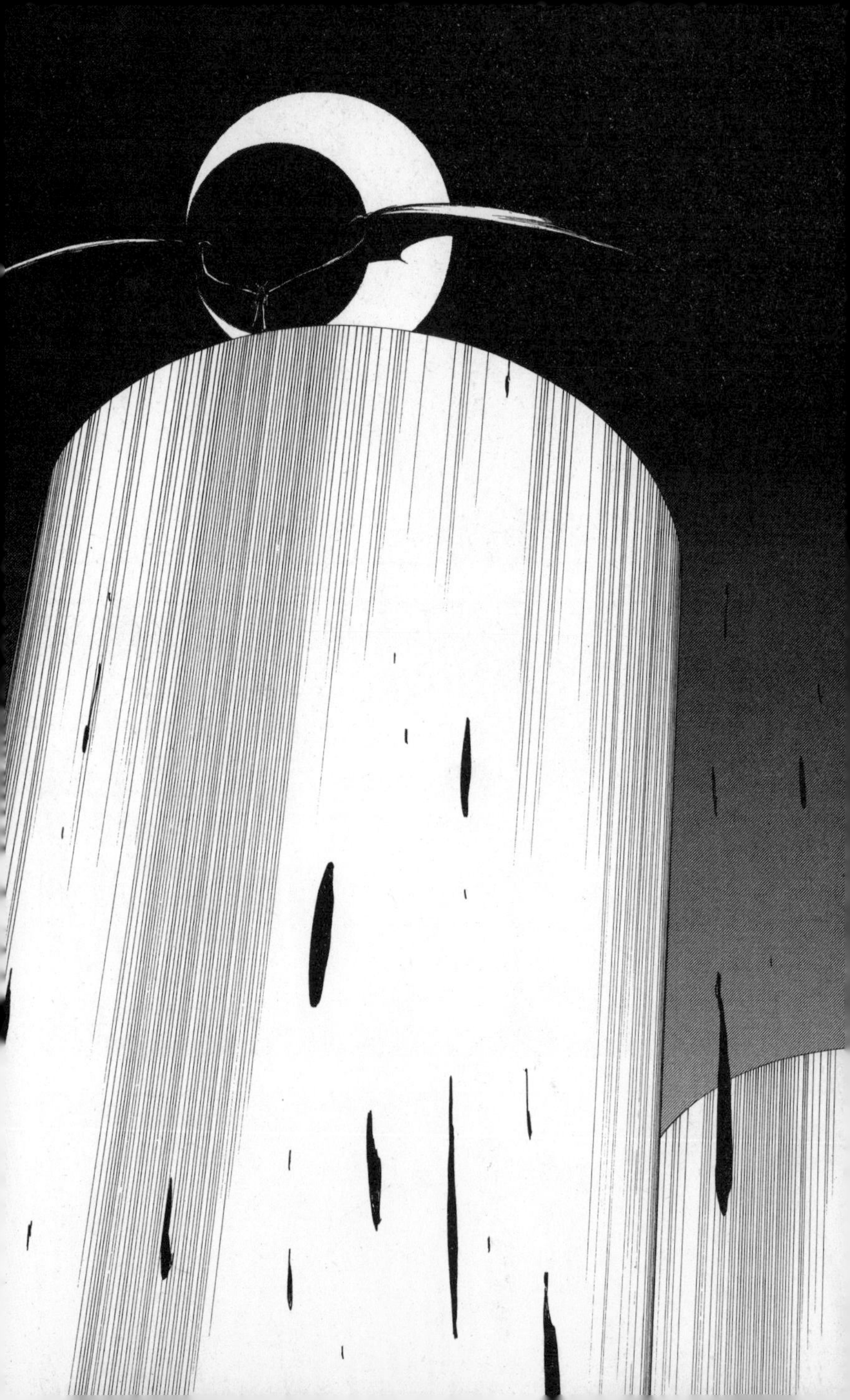

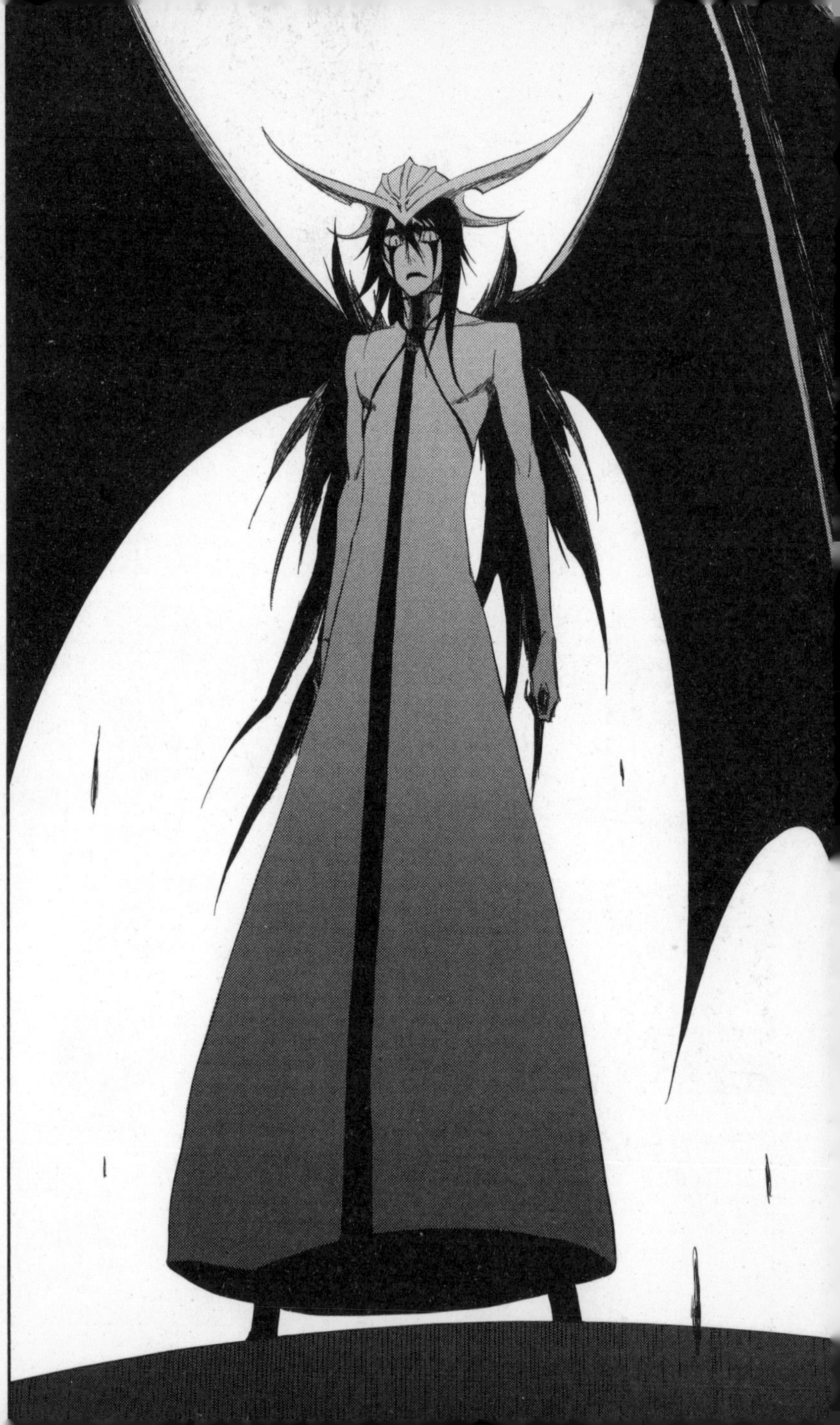

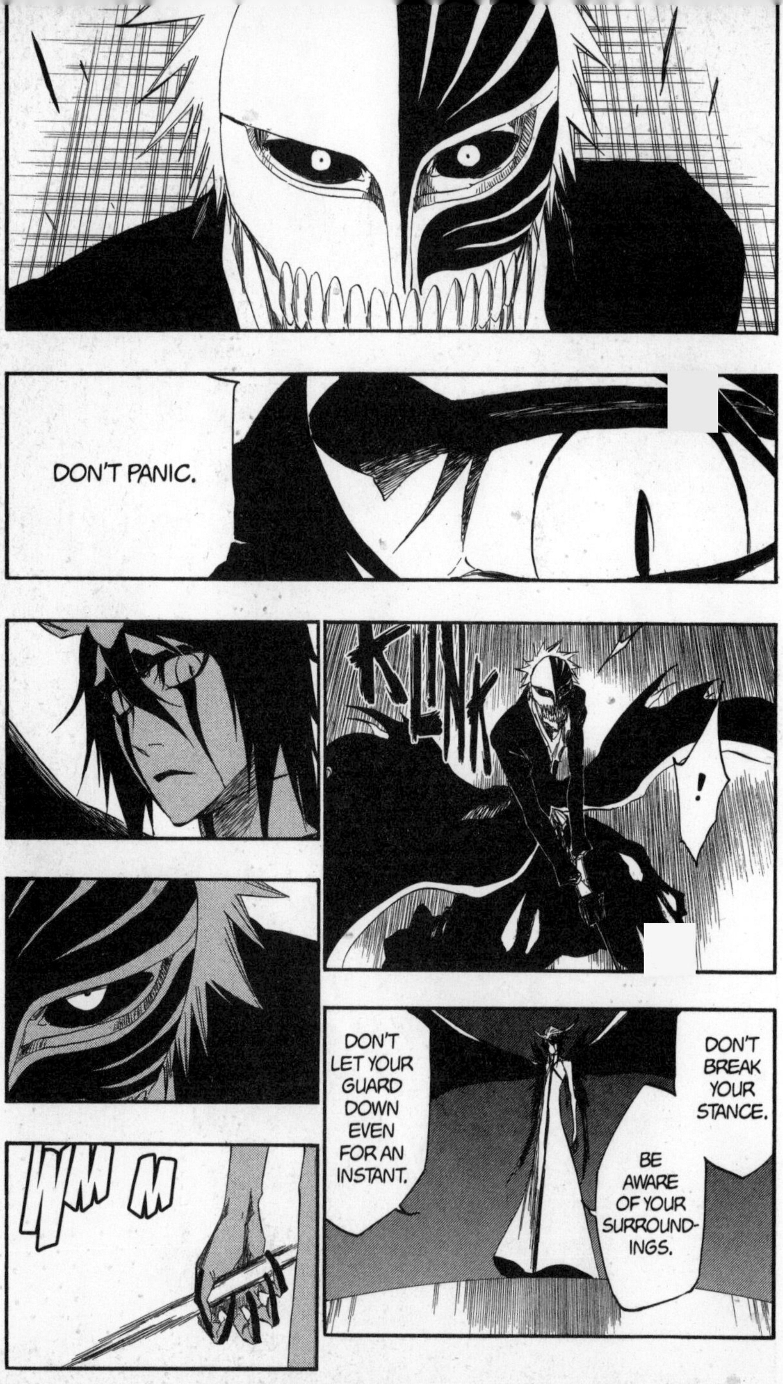
DON'T PANIC.
KLINK
!
DON'T BREAK YOUR STANCE.
BE AWARE OF YOUR SURROUND-INGS.
DON'T LET YOUR GUARD DOWN EVEN FOR AN INSTANT.
WMM

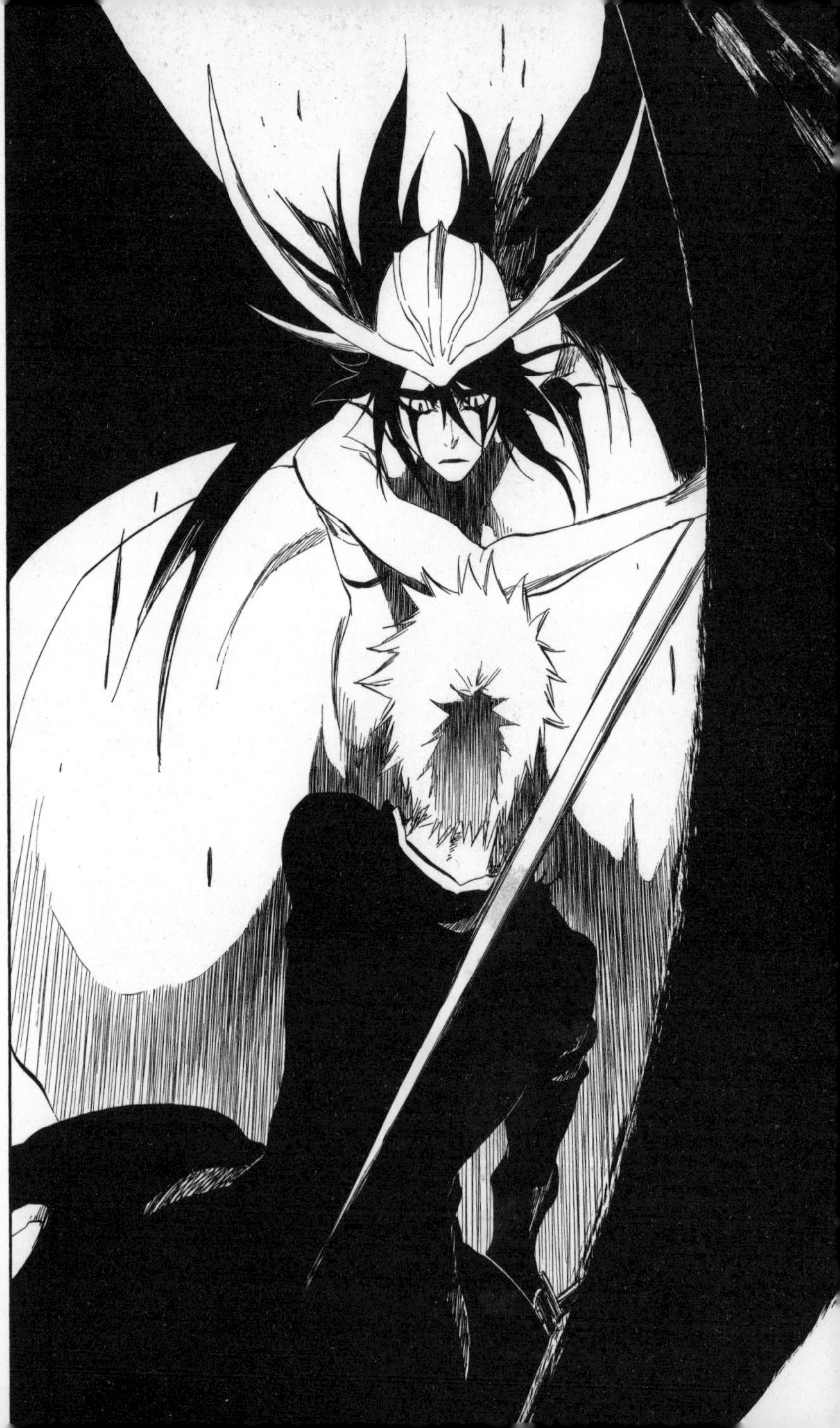

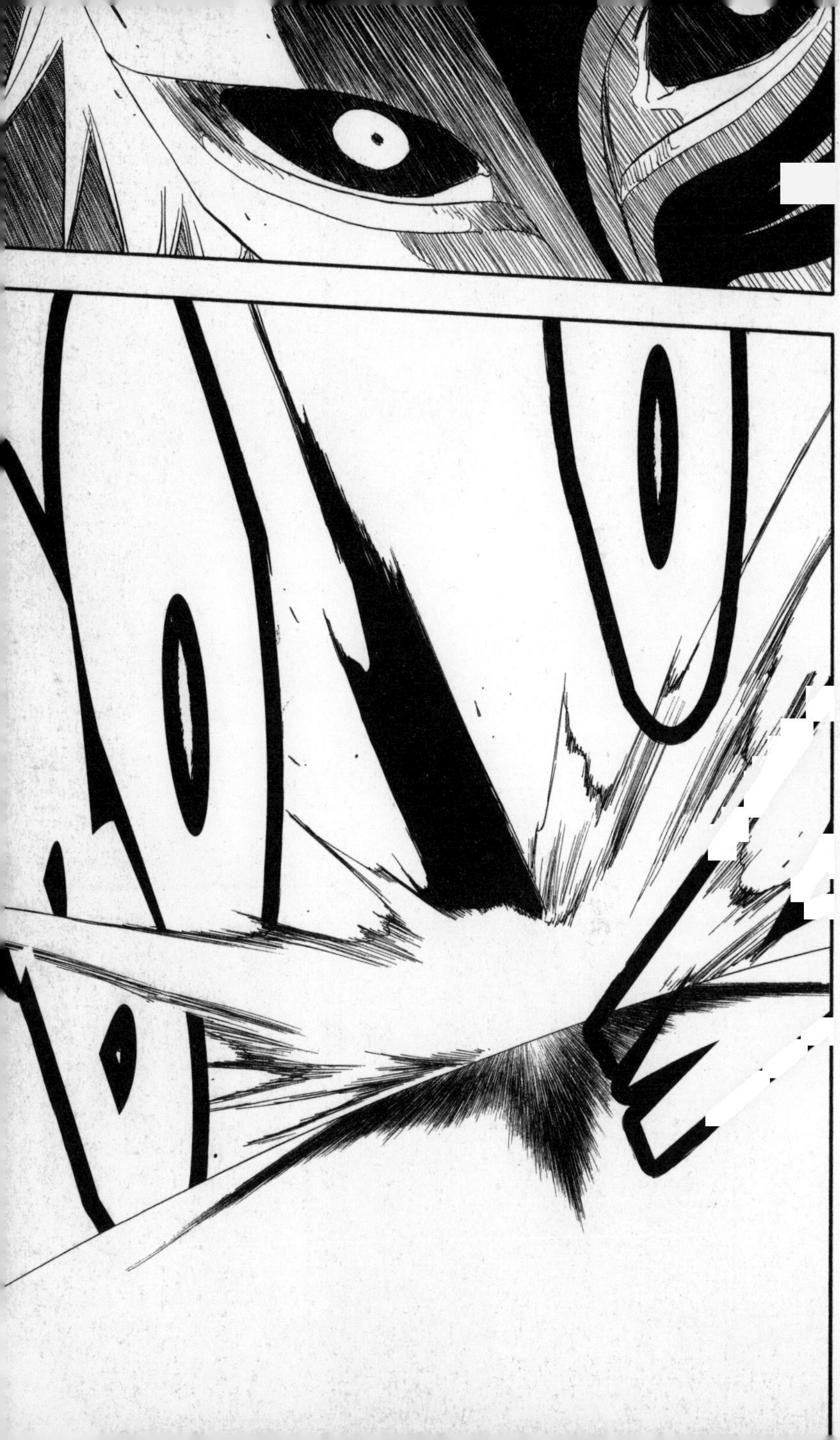

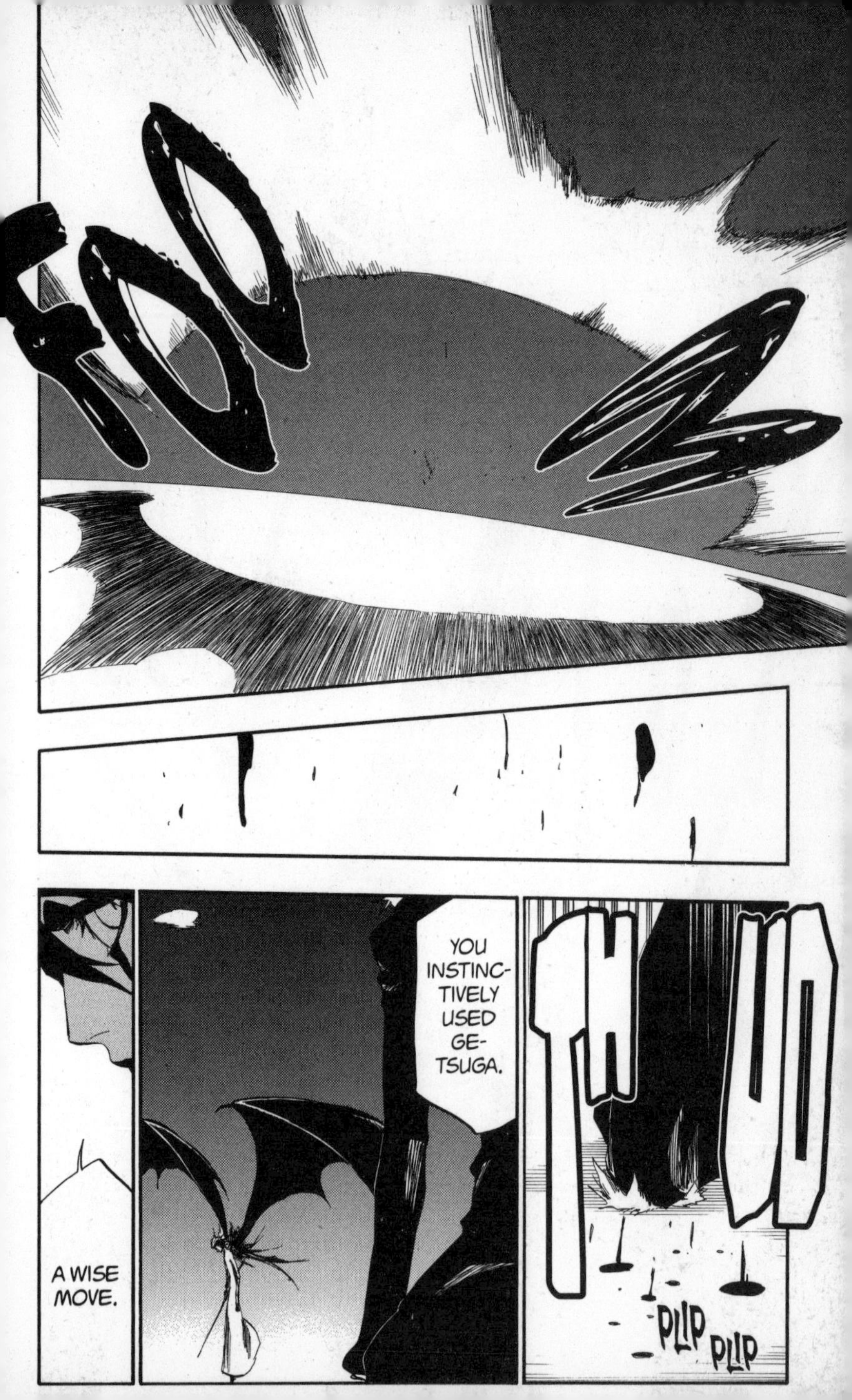
FOOM
THUD
PLIP PLIP
YOU INSTINCTIVELY USED GETSUGA.
A WISE MOVE.

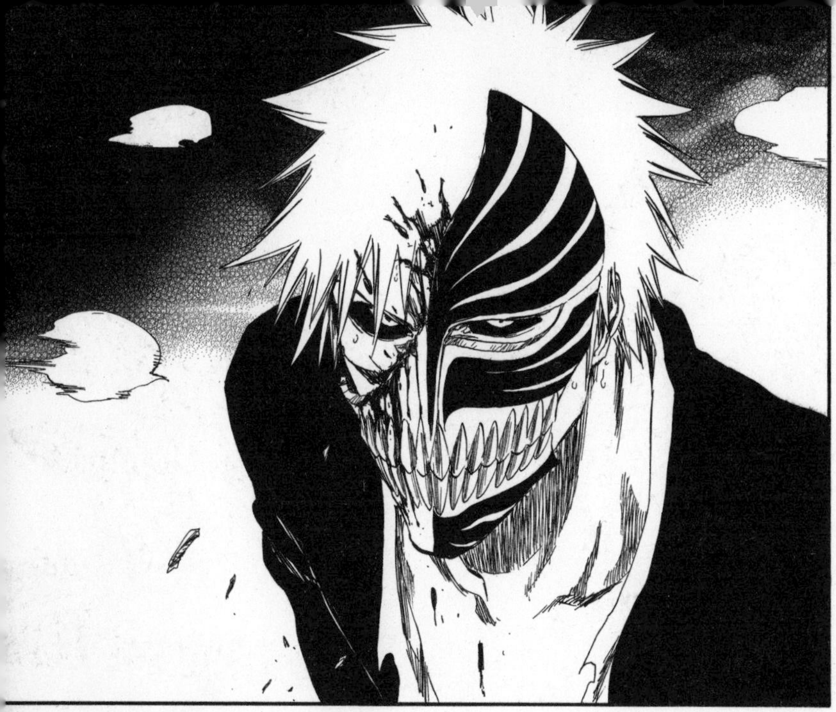

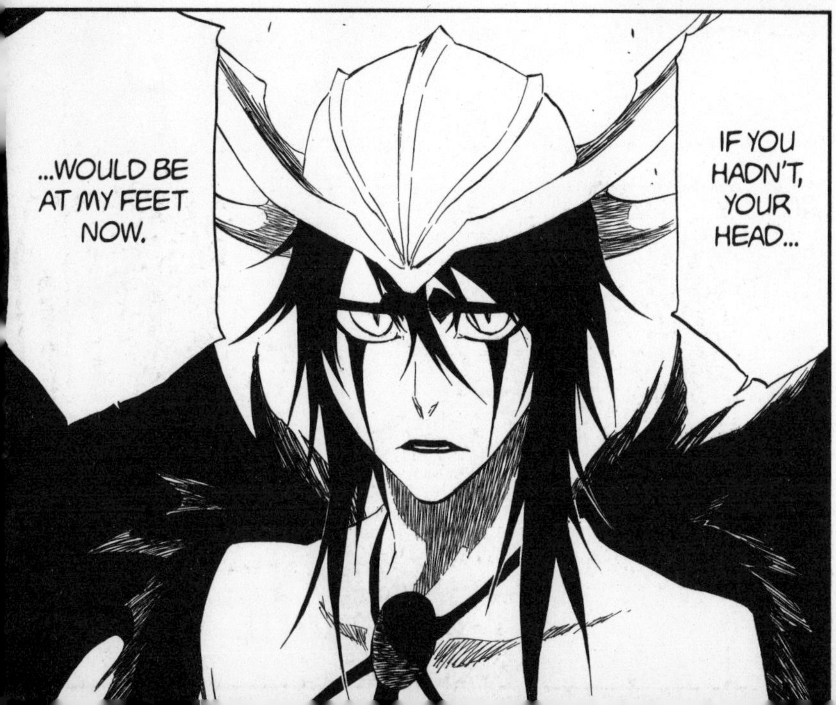
IF YOU HADN'T, YOUR HEAD...
...WOULD BE AT MY FEET NOW.

The Sloth

POP

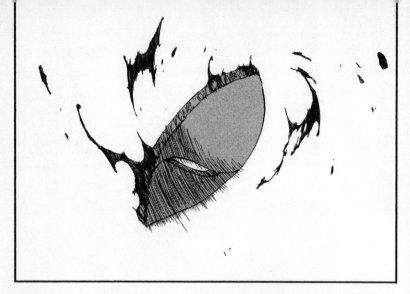

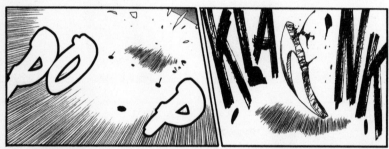

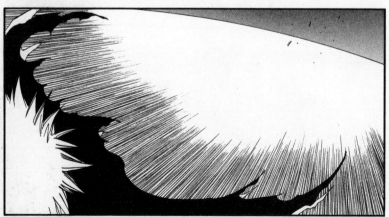

346. The Wrath

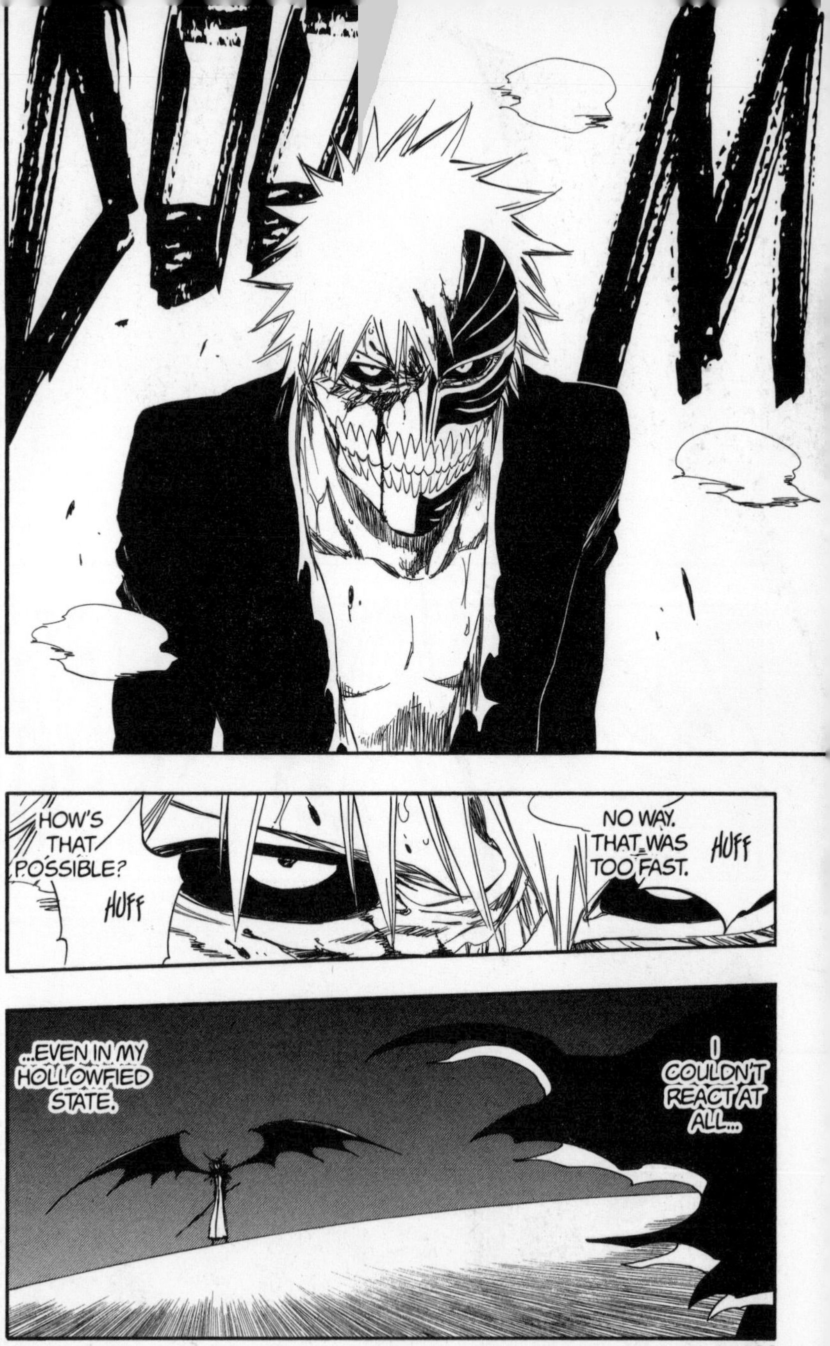

NO WAY. THAT WAS TOO FAST.
HUFF
HOW'S THAT POSSIBLE?
HUFF
I COULDN'T REACT AT ALL...
...EVEN IN MY HOLLOWFIED STATE.

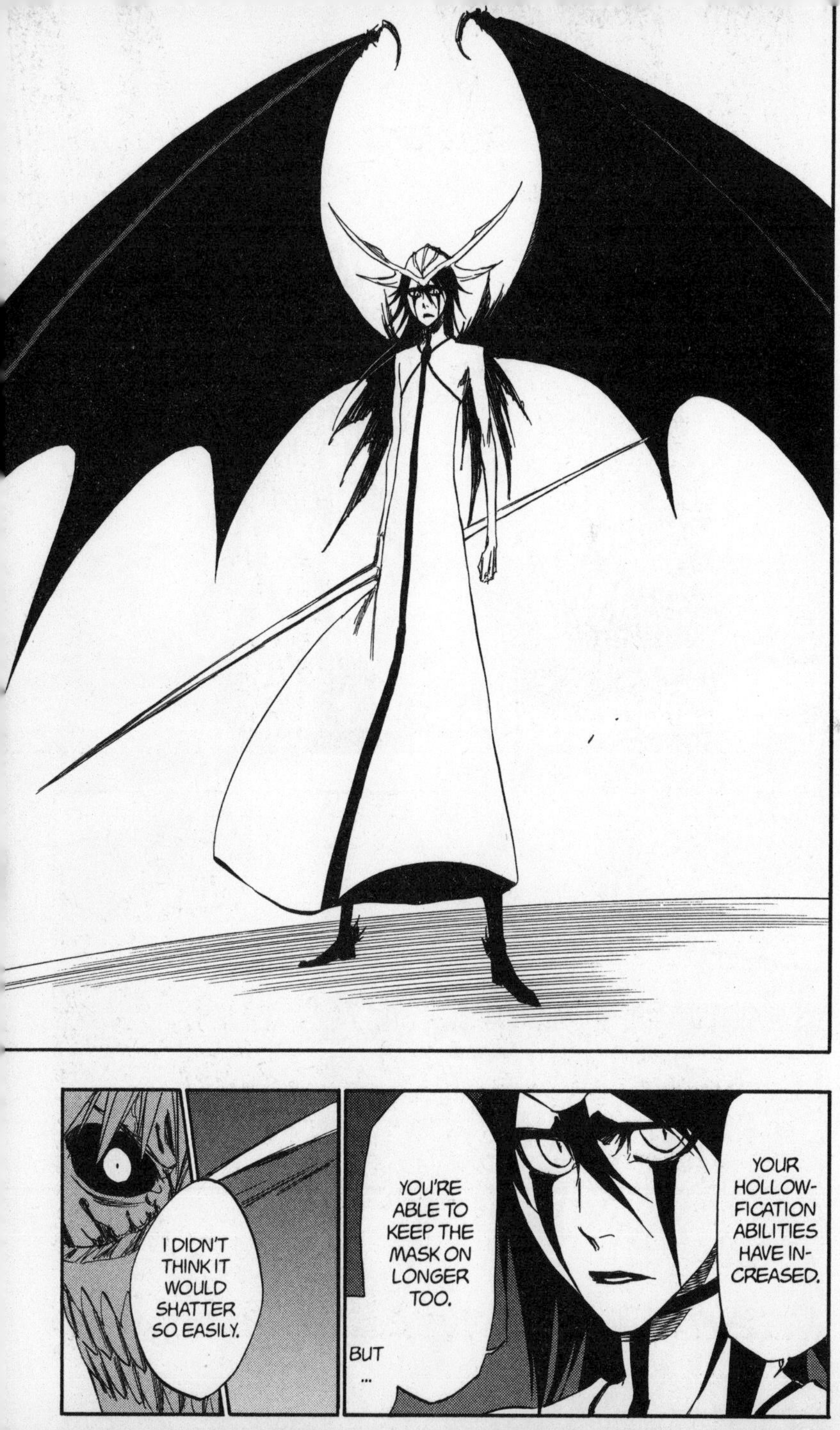
YOUR HOLLOW-FICATION ABILITIES HAVE IN-CREASED.
YOU'RE ABLE TO KEEP THE MASK ON LONGER TOO.
BUT ...
I DIDN'T THINK IT WOULD SHATTER SO EASILY.

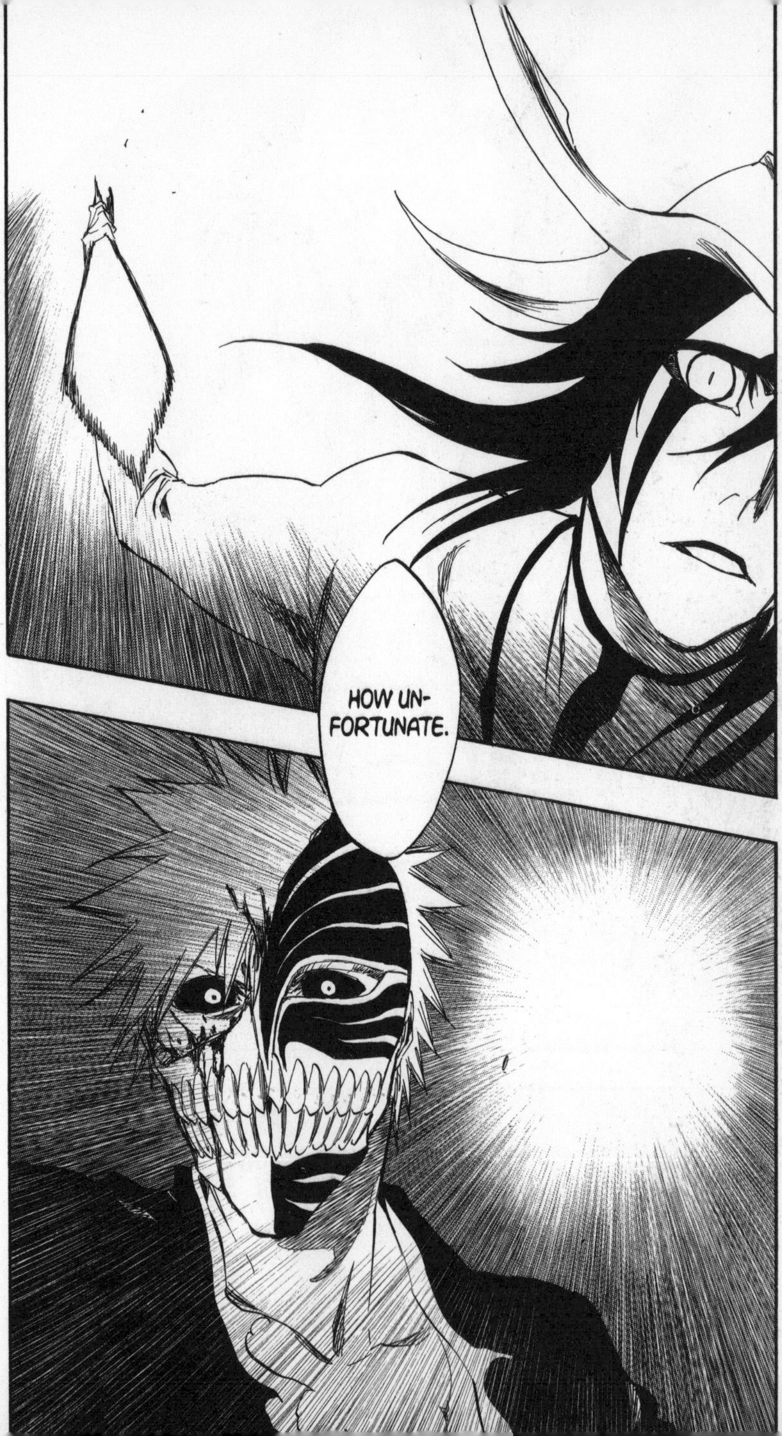
HOW UN-
FORTUNATE.

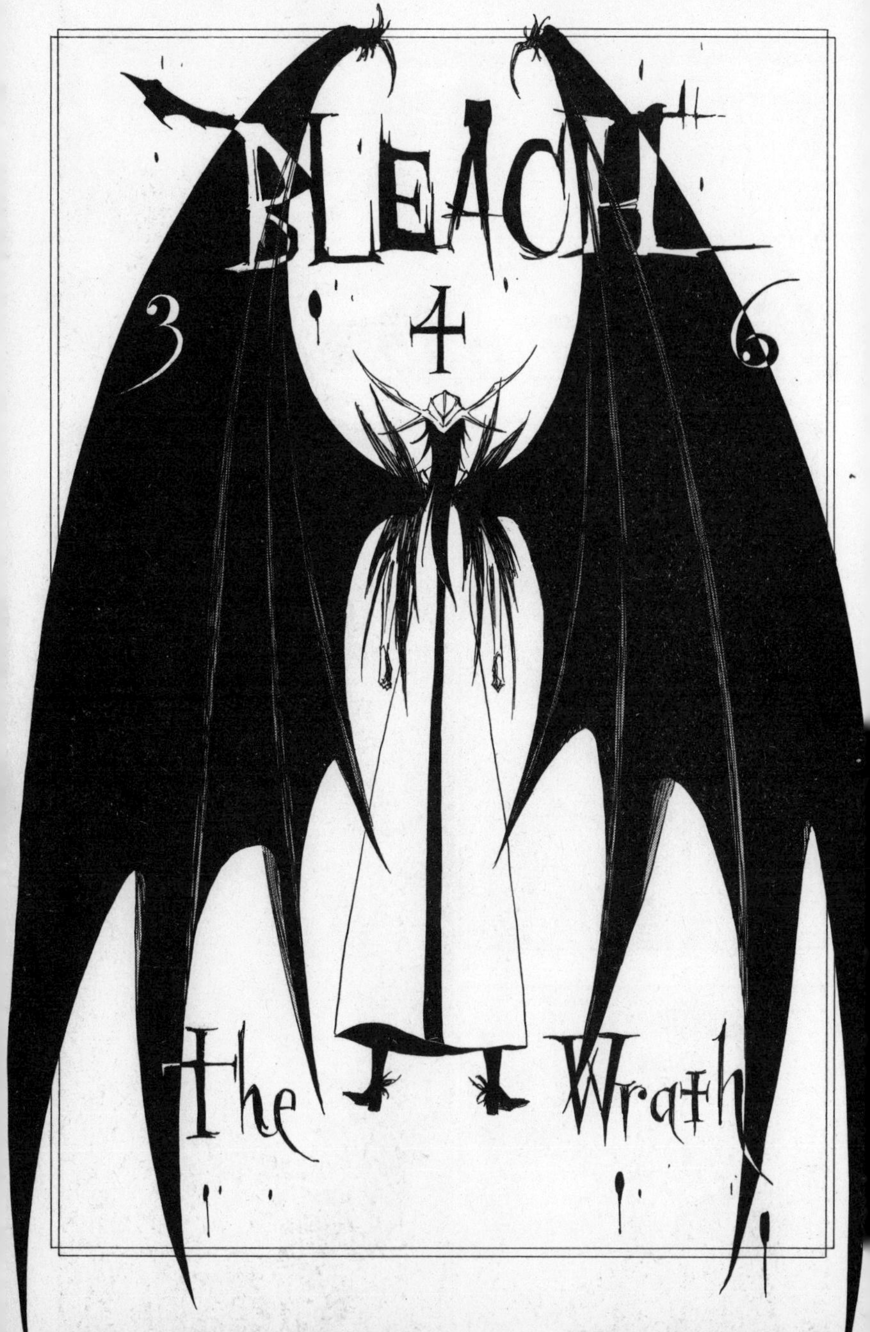
BLEACH
3
4
6
The Wrath

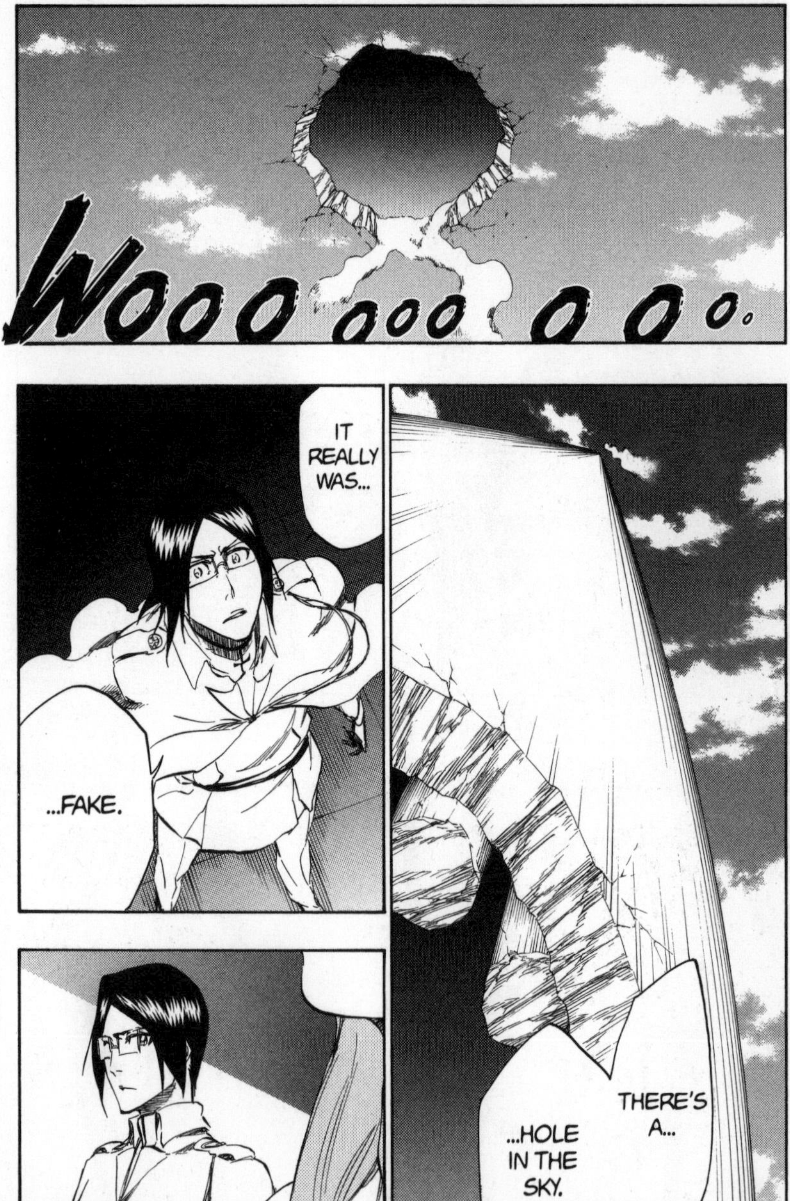
WOOO OOO O O O.
THERE'S A...
...HOLE IN THE SKY.
IT REALLY WAS...
...FAKE.

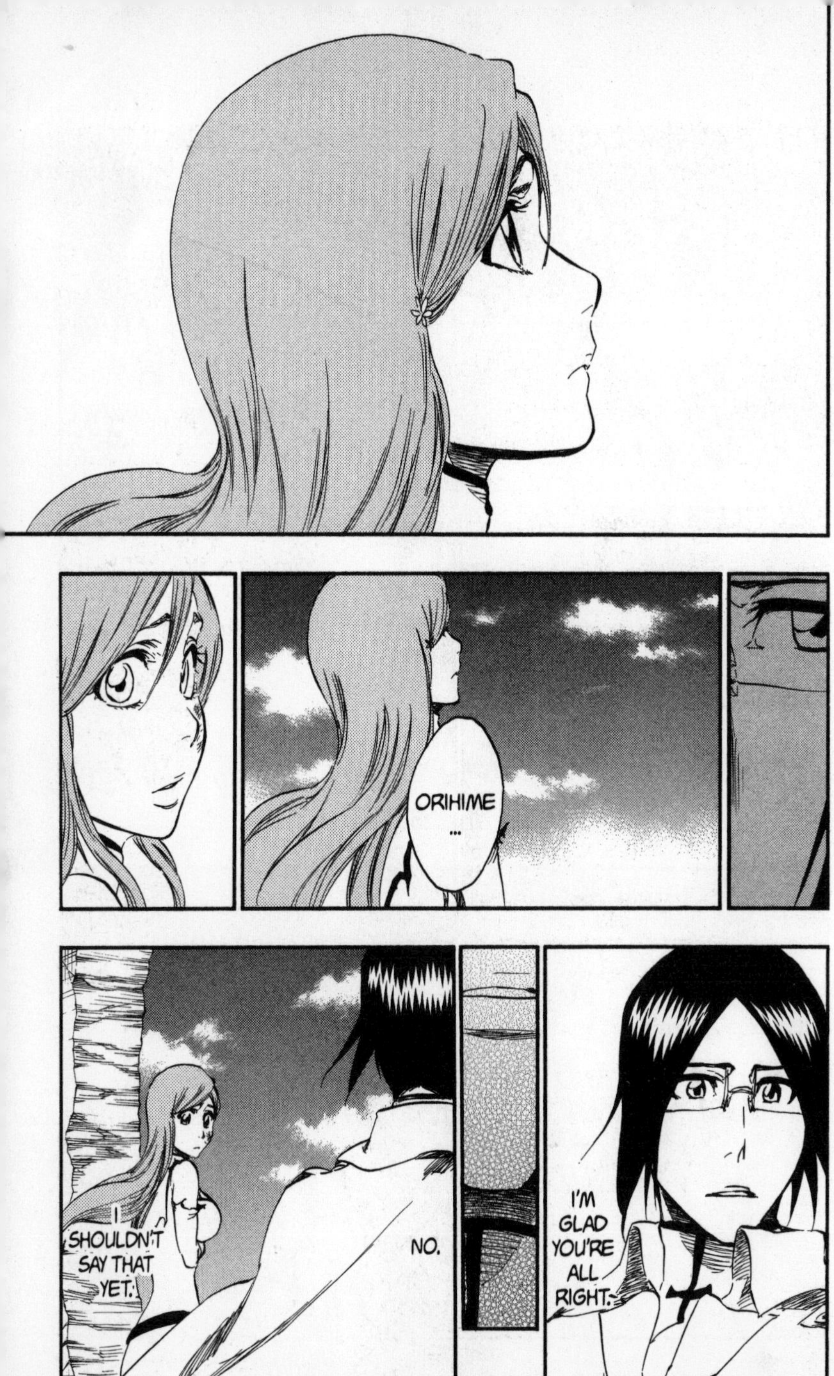
ORIHIME...
I'M GLAD YOU'RE ALL RIGHT.
NO.
I SHOULDN'T SAY THAT YET.

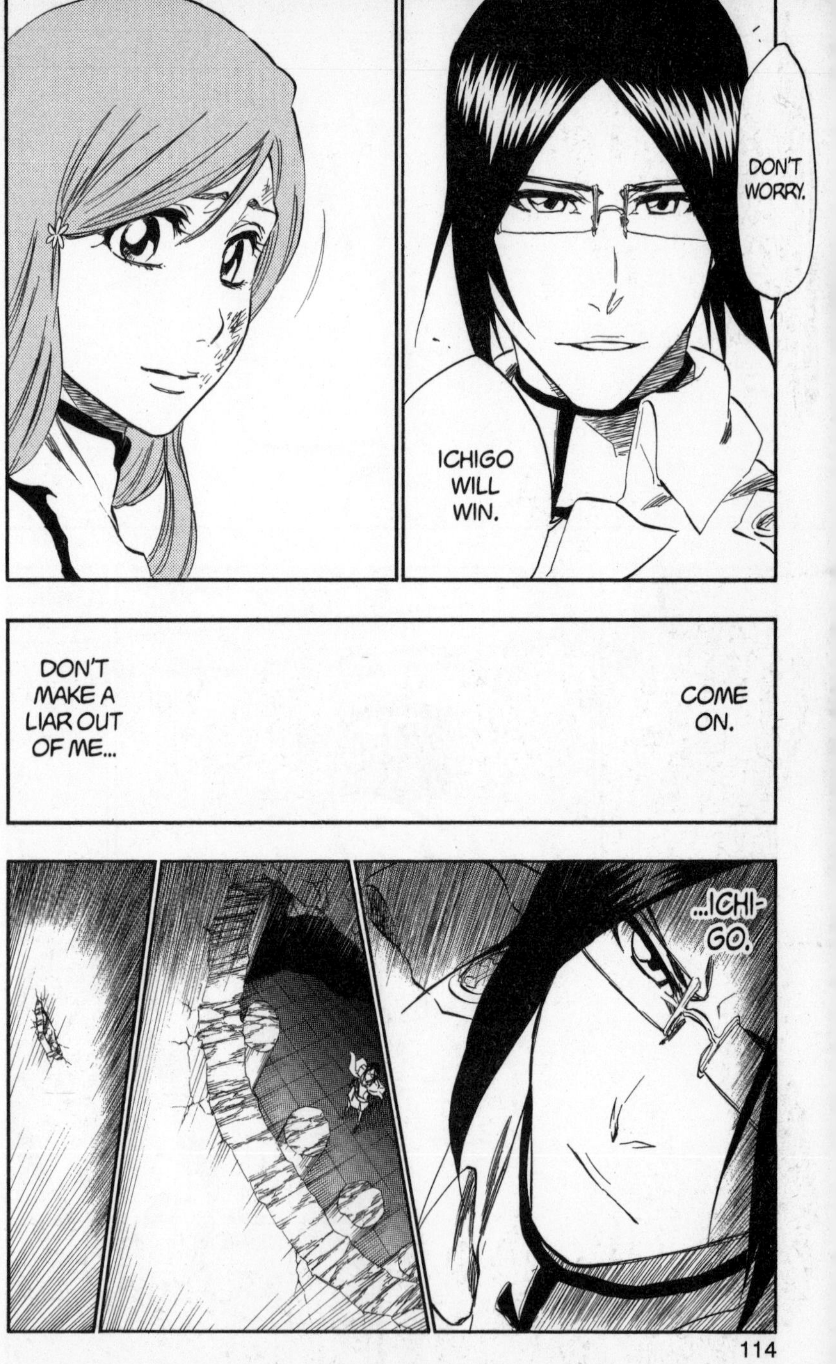
DON'T WORRY.
ICHIGO WILL WIN.
COME ON.
DON'T MAKE A LIAR OUT OF ME...
...ICHI-GO.

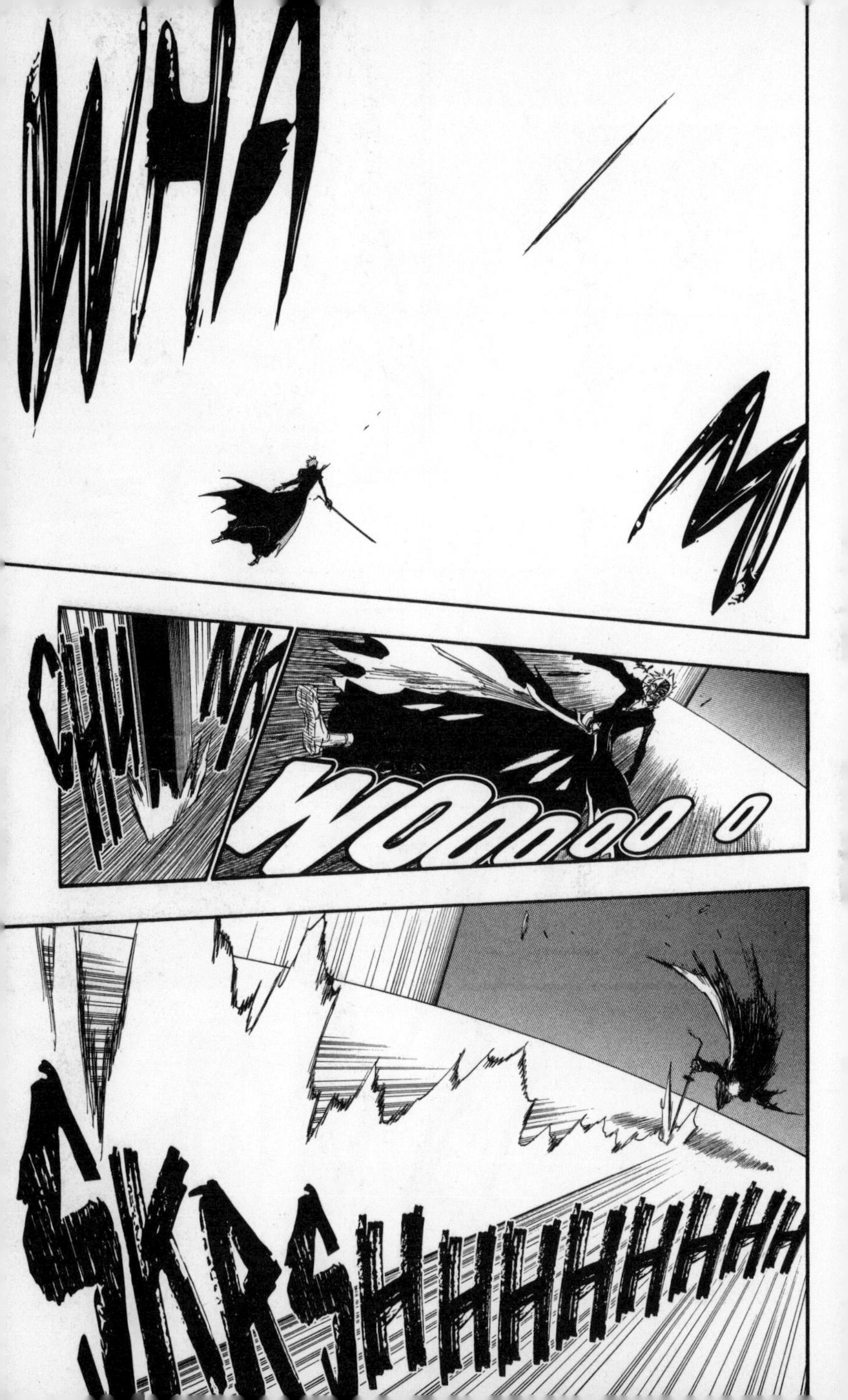
WHAM
WOOOOOOO
CHUNK
SKRSHHHHHHHHHHH

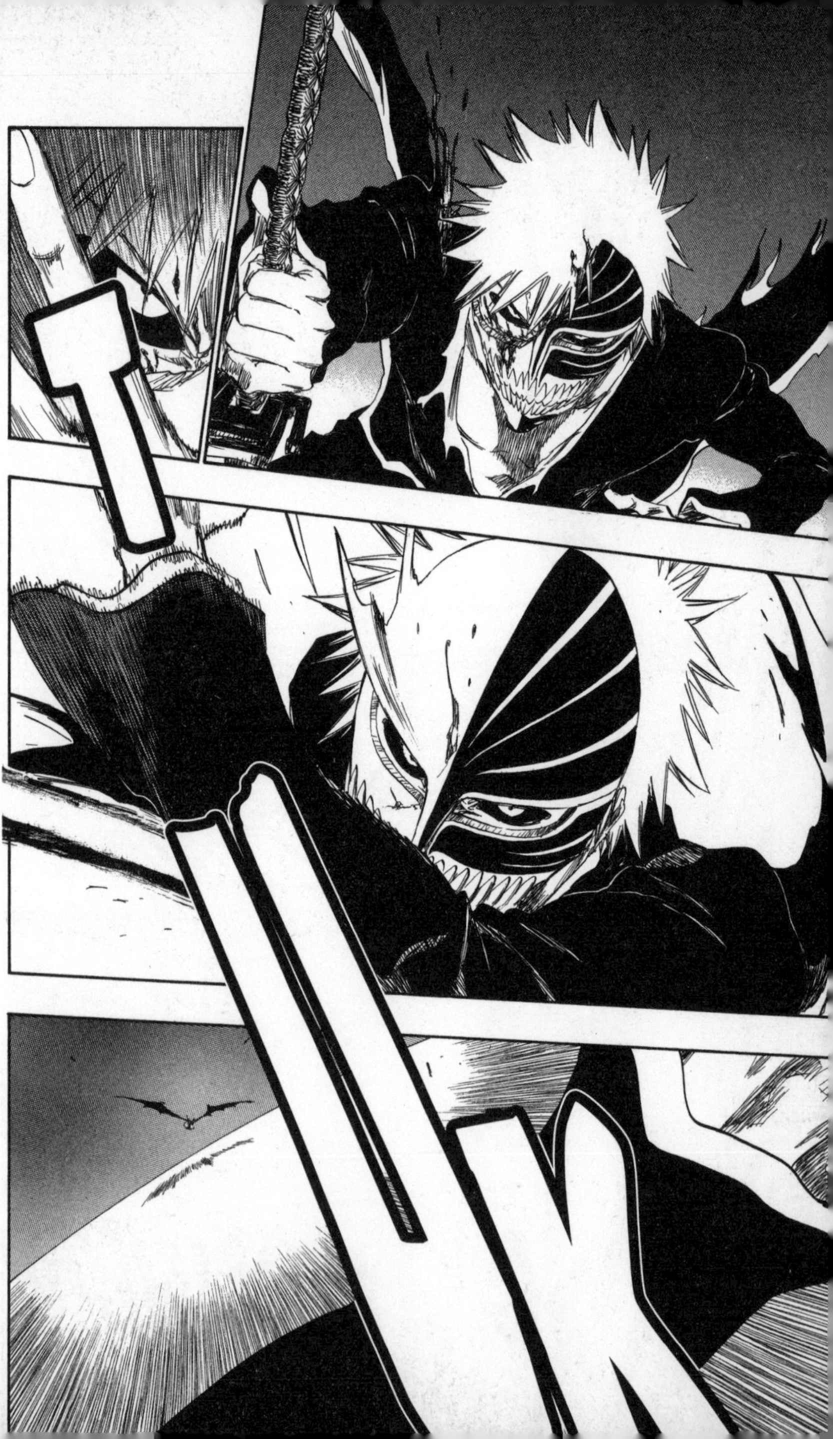

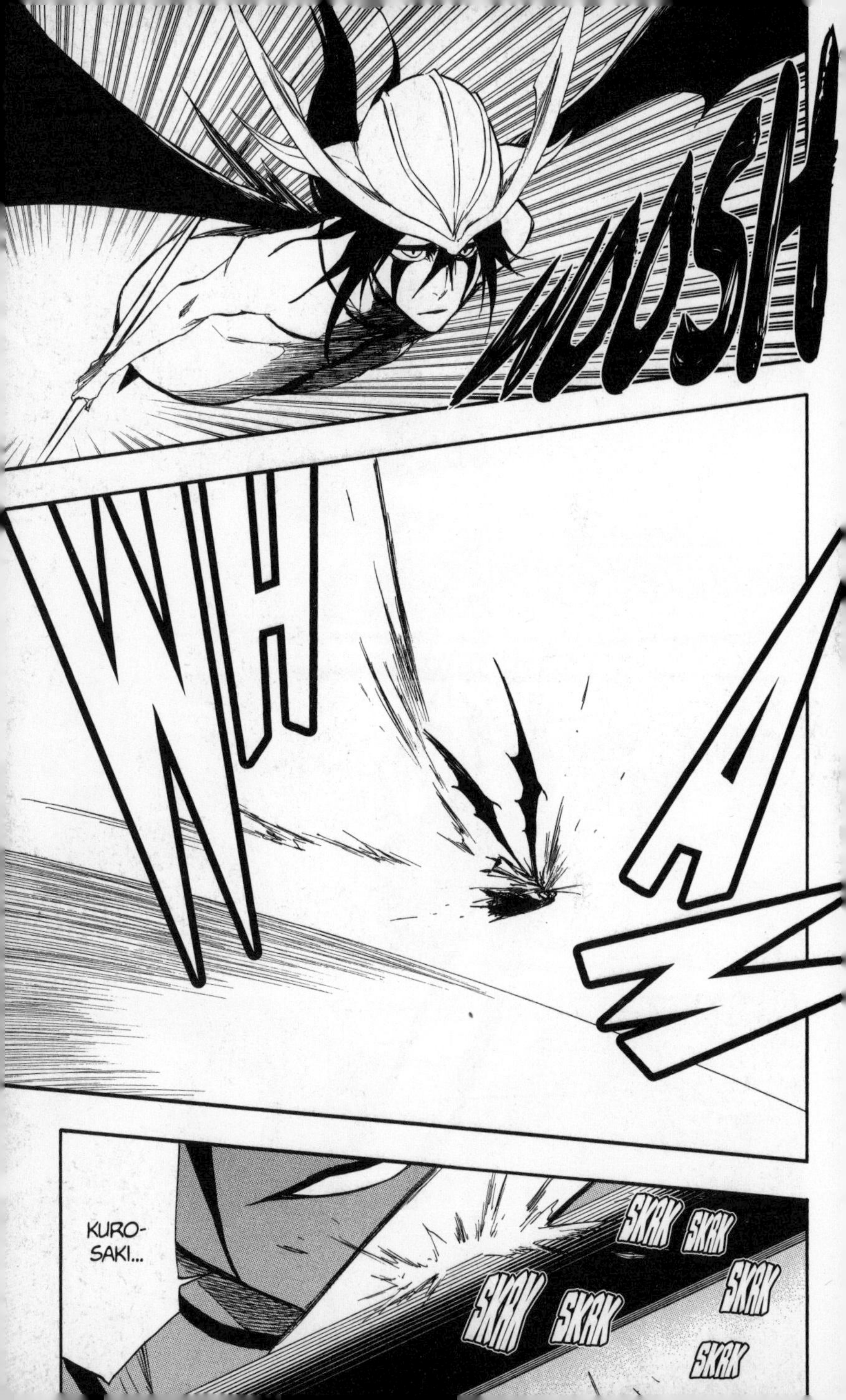
WHOOSH
WHAM
SKRK SKRK
SKRK
SKRK
SKRK SKRK
KURO-SAKI...

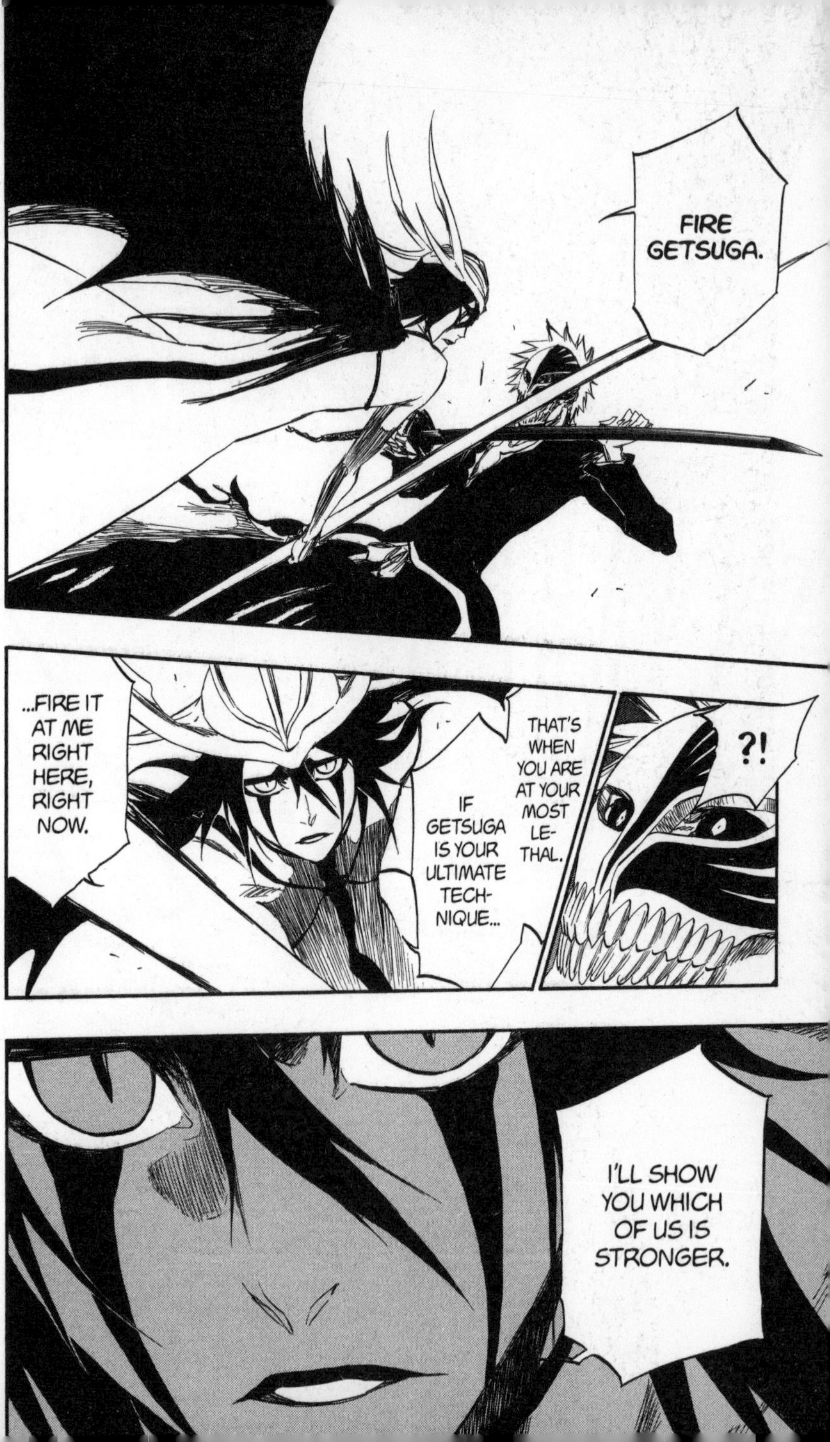
FIRE GETSUGA.
?!
IF GETSUGA IS YOUR ULTIMATE TECH-NIQUE...
THAT'S WHEN YOU ARE AT YOUR MOST LE-THAL.
...FIRE IT AT ME RIGHT HERE, RIGHT NOW.
I'LL SHOW YOU WHICH OF US IS STRONGER.

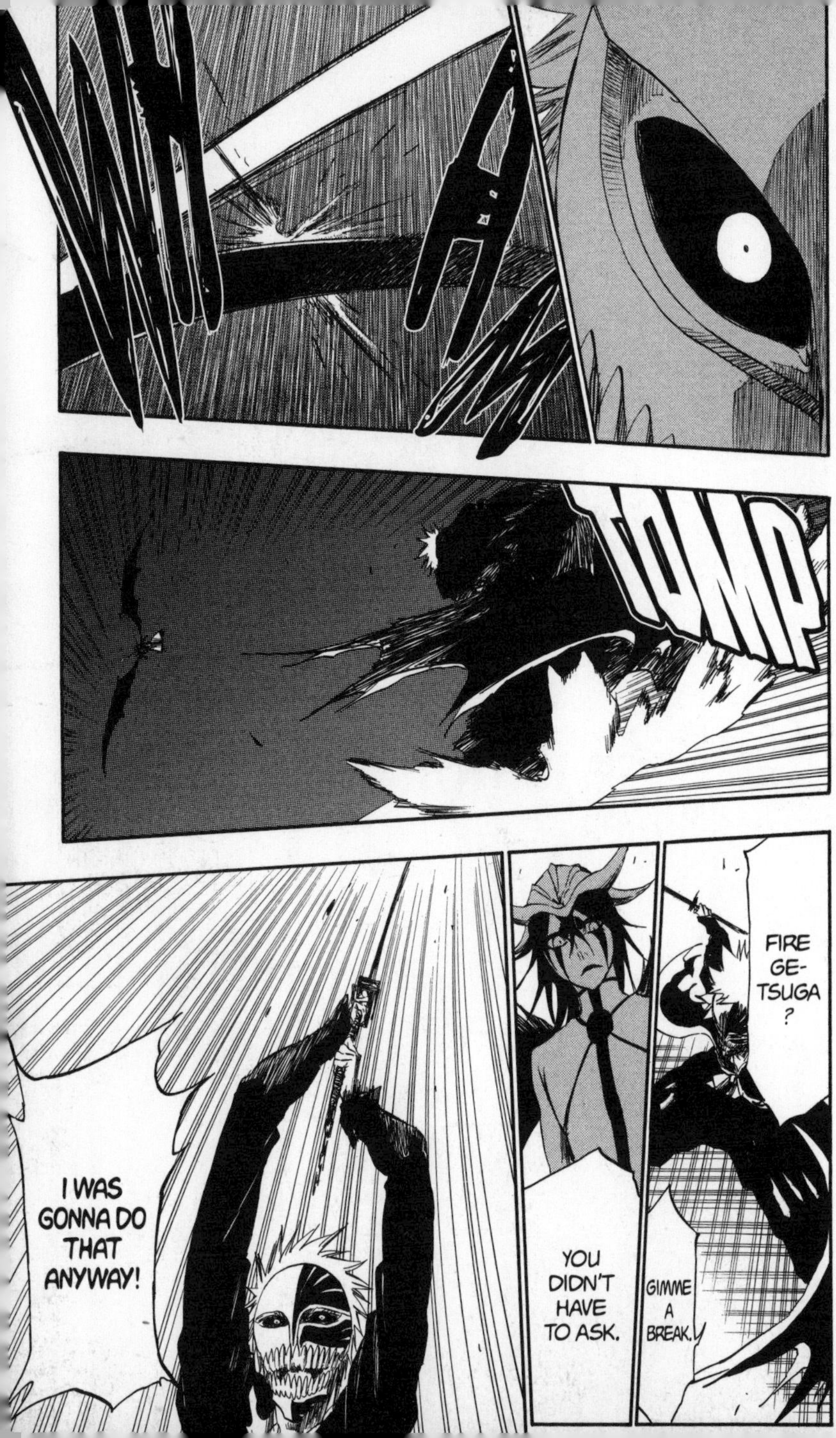
WHAM
TOMP
FIRE GE-TSUGA?
GIMME A BREAK.
YOU DIDN'T HAVE TO ASK.
I WAS GONNA DO THAT ANYWAY!

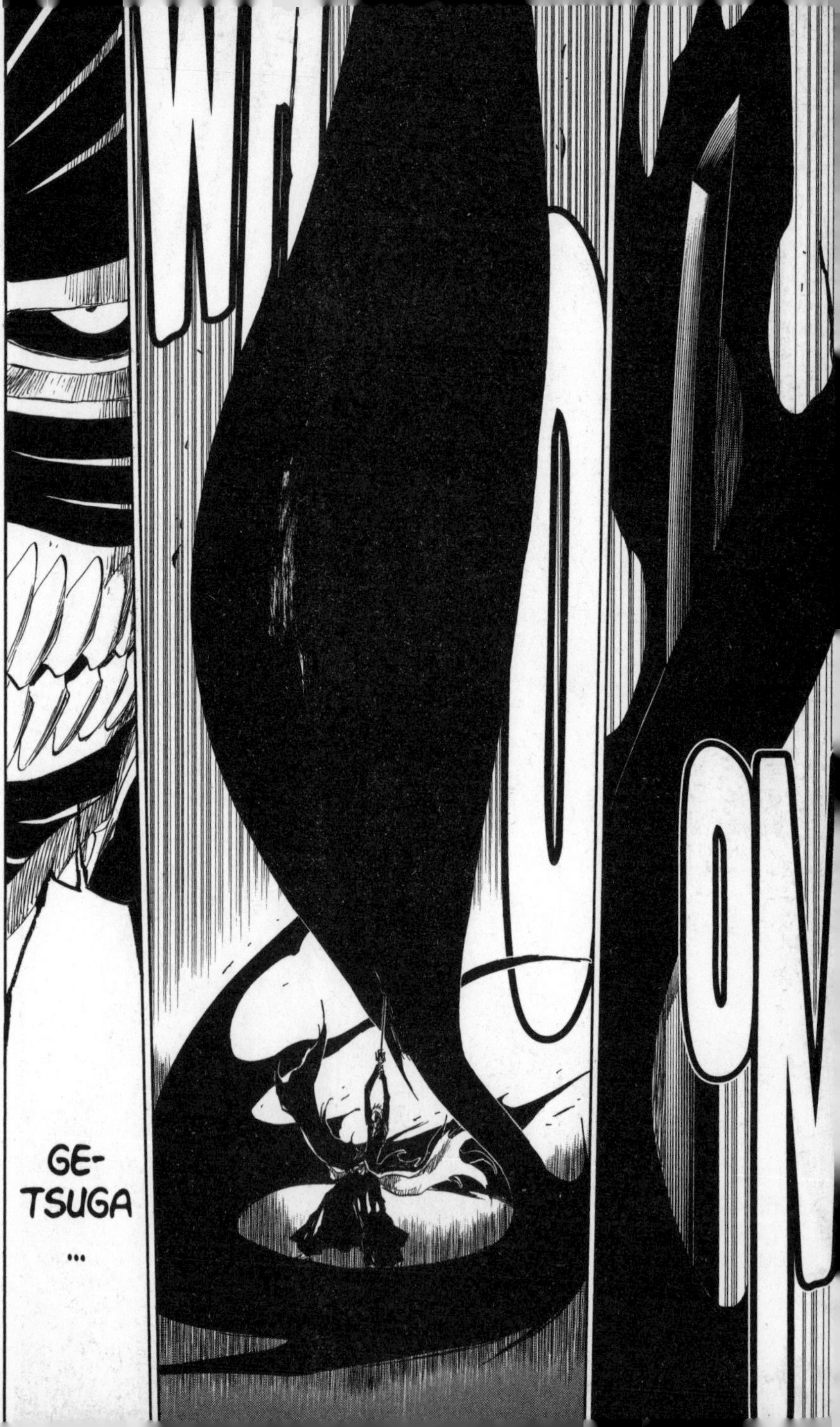
GE-
TSUGA
...

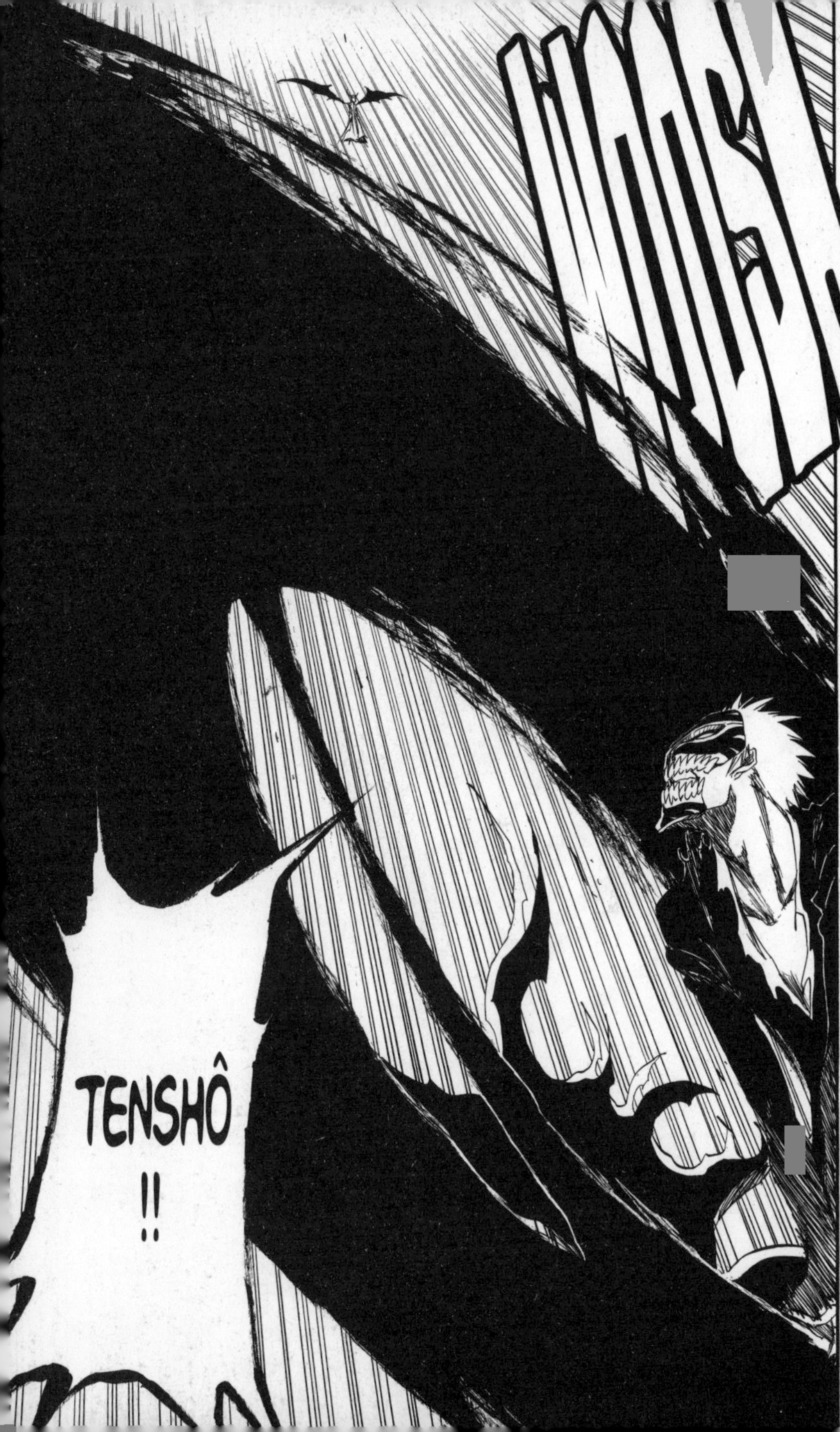
TENSHÔ !!

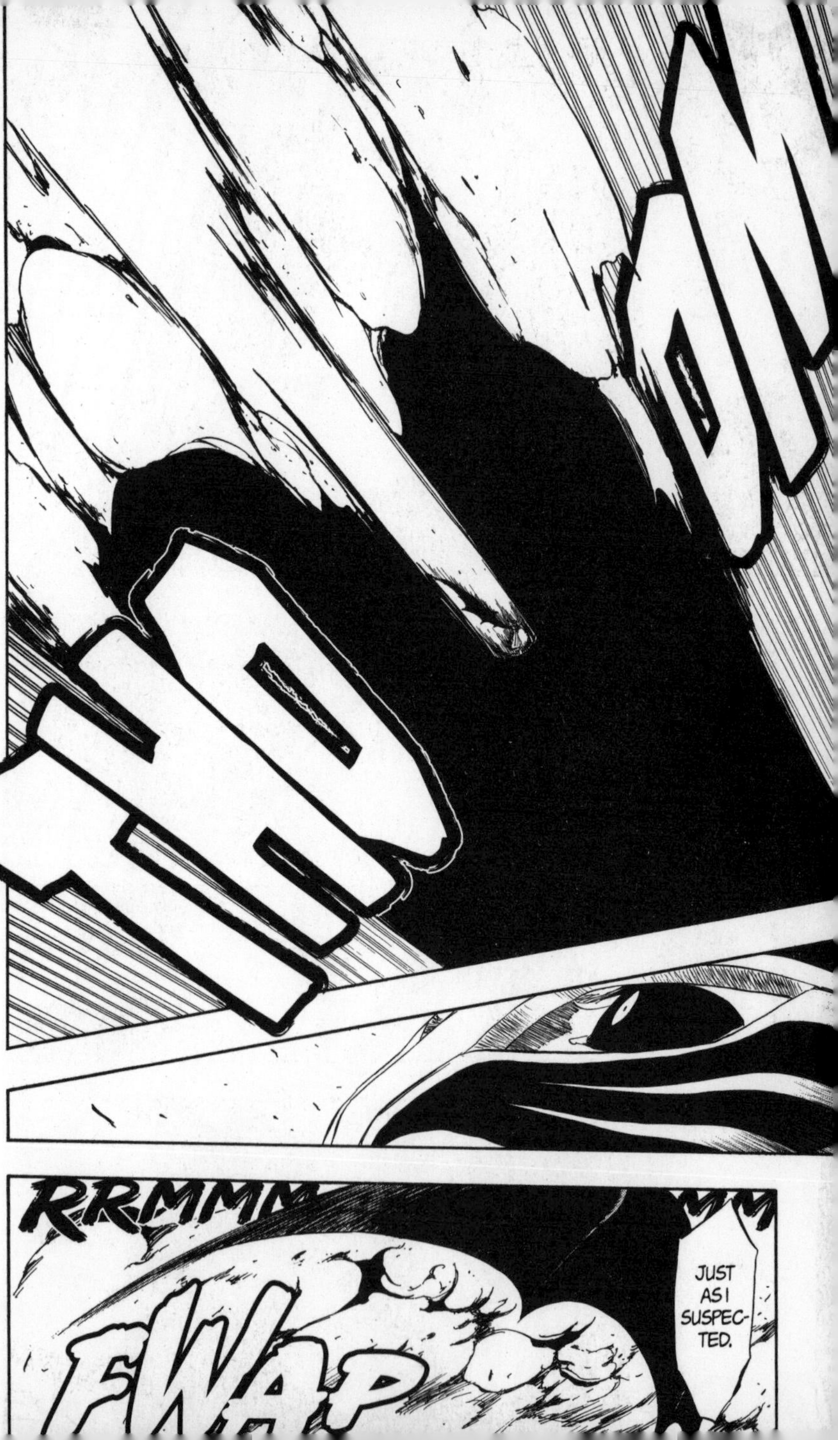
RRMMM
FWAP
JUST AS I SUSPECTED.

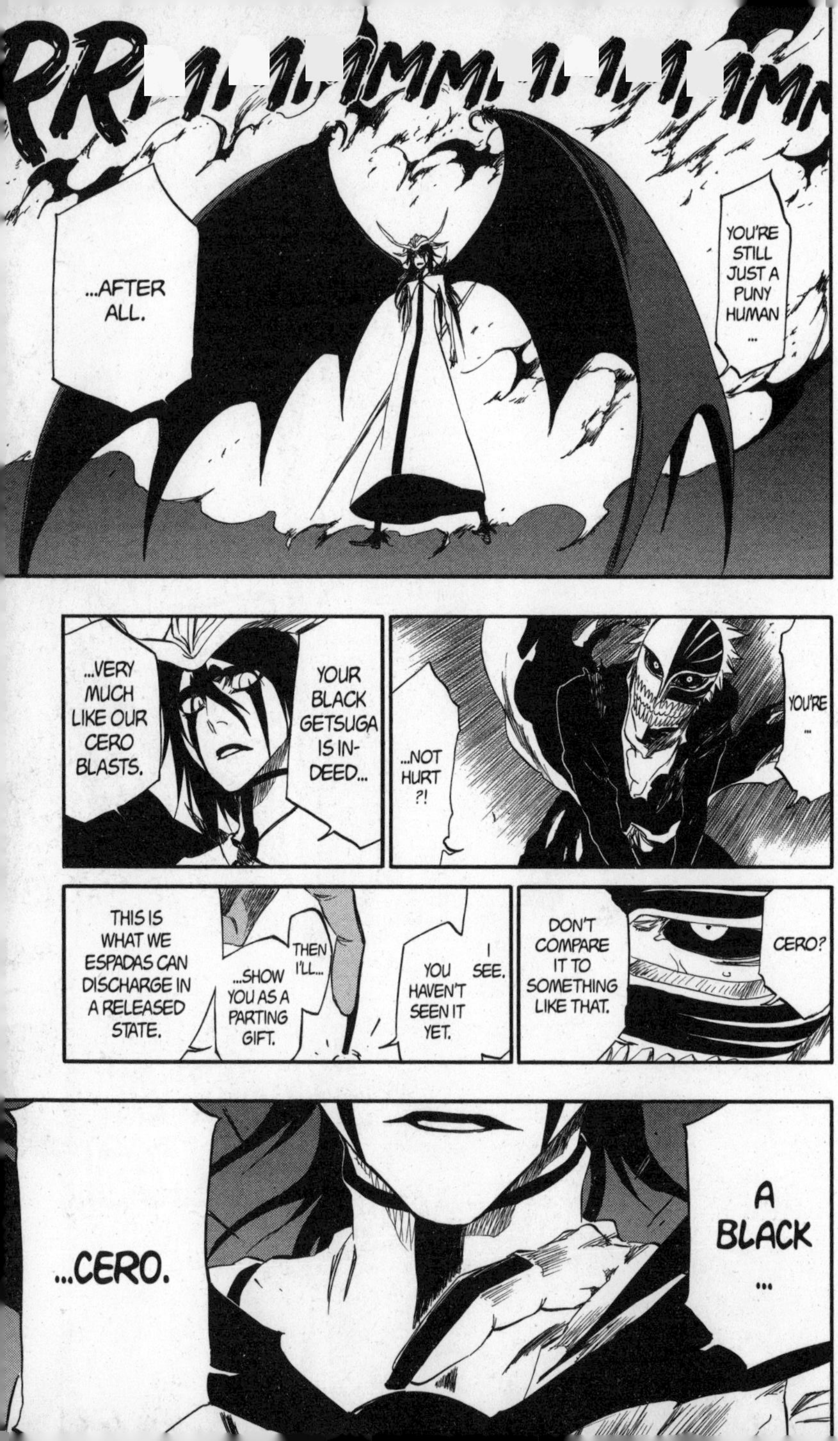
YOU'RE STILL JUST A PUNY HUMAN ...
...AFTER ALL.
YOU'RE ...
...NOT HURT ?!
YOUR BLACK GETSUGA IS IN-DEED...
...VERY MUCH LIKE OUR CERO BLASTS.
CERO?
DON'T COMPARE IT TO SOMETHING LIKE THAT.
I SEE.
YOU HAVEN'T SEEN IT YET.
THEN I'LL...
...SHOW YOU AS A PARTING GIFT.
THIS IS WHAT WE ESPADAS CAN DISCHARGE IN A RELEASED STATE.
A BLACK ...
...CERO.

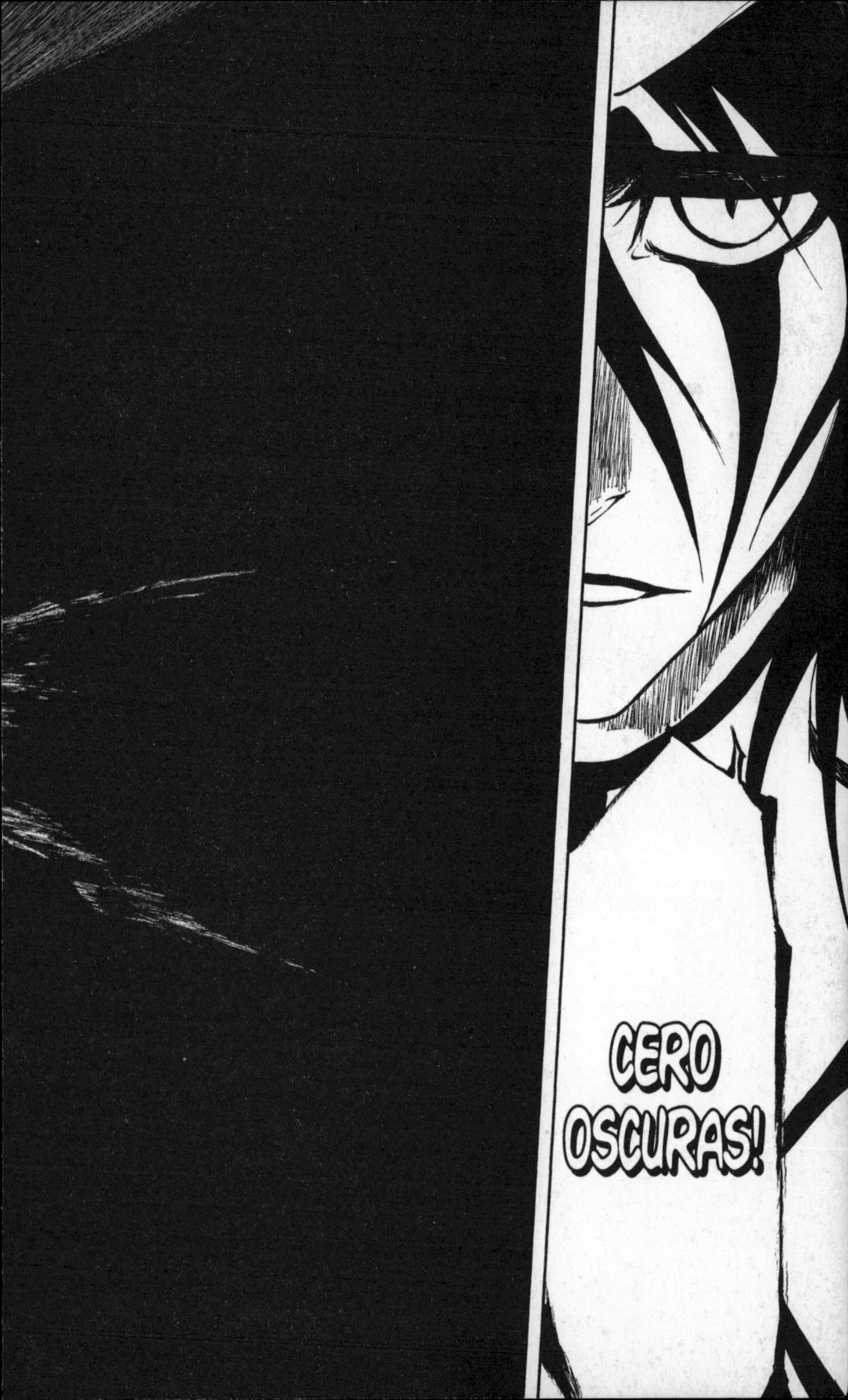
CERO OSCURAS!

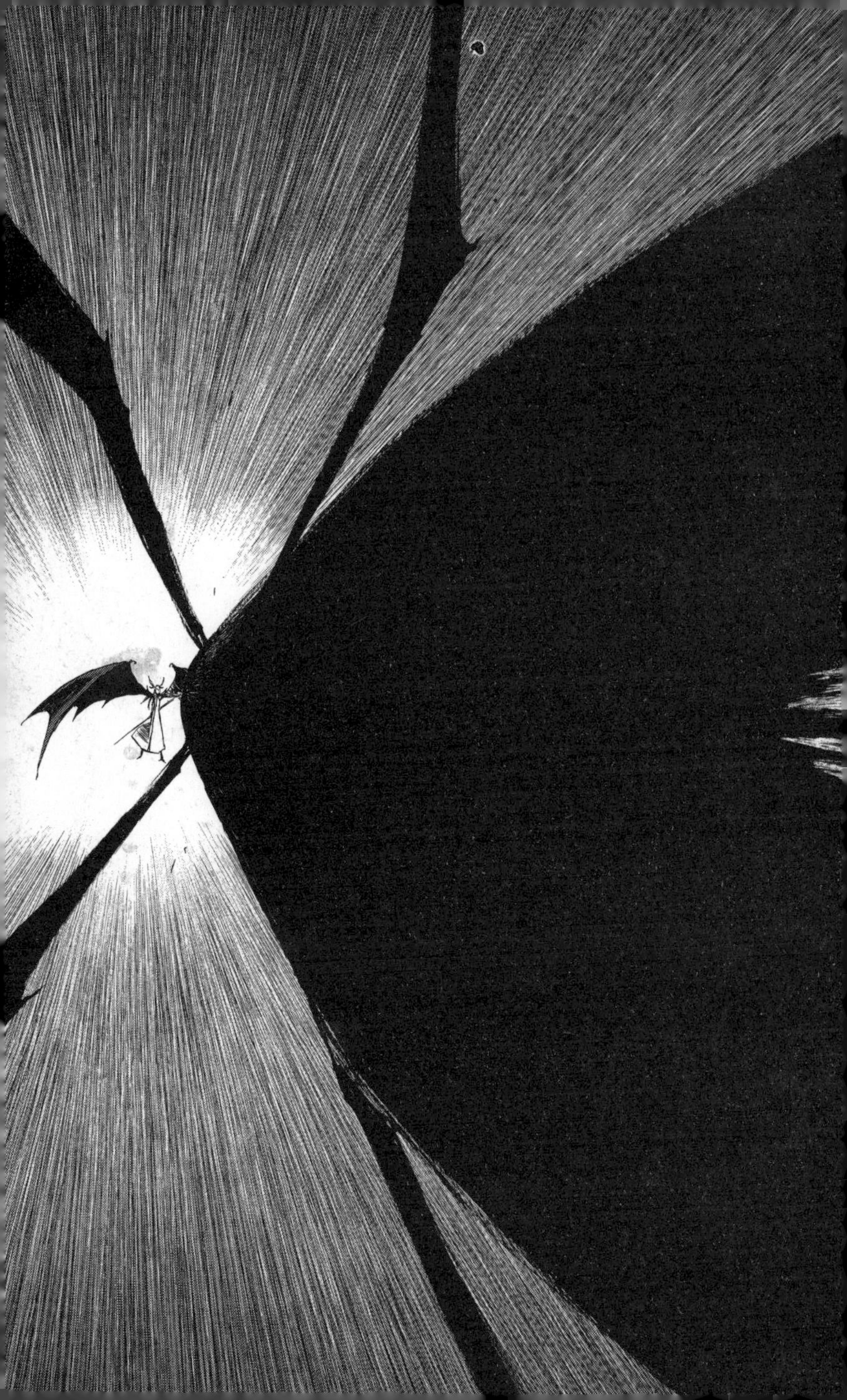

the
Wrath

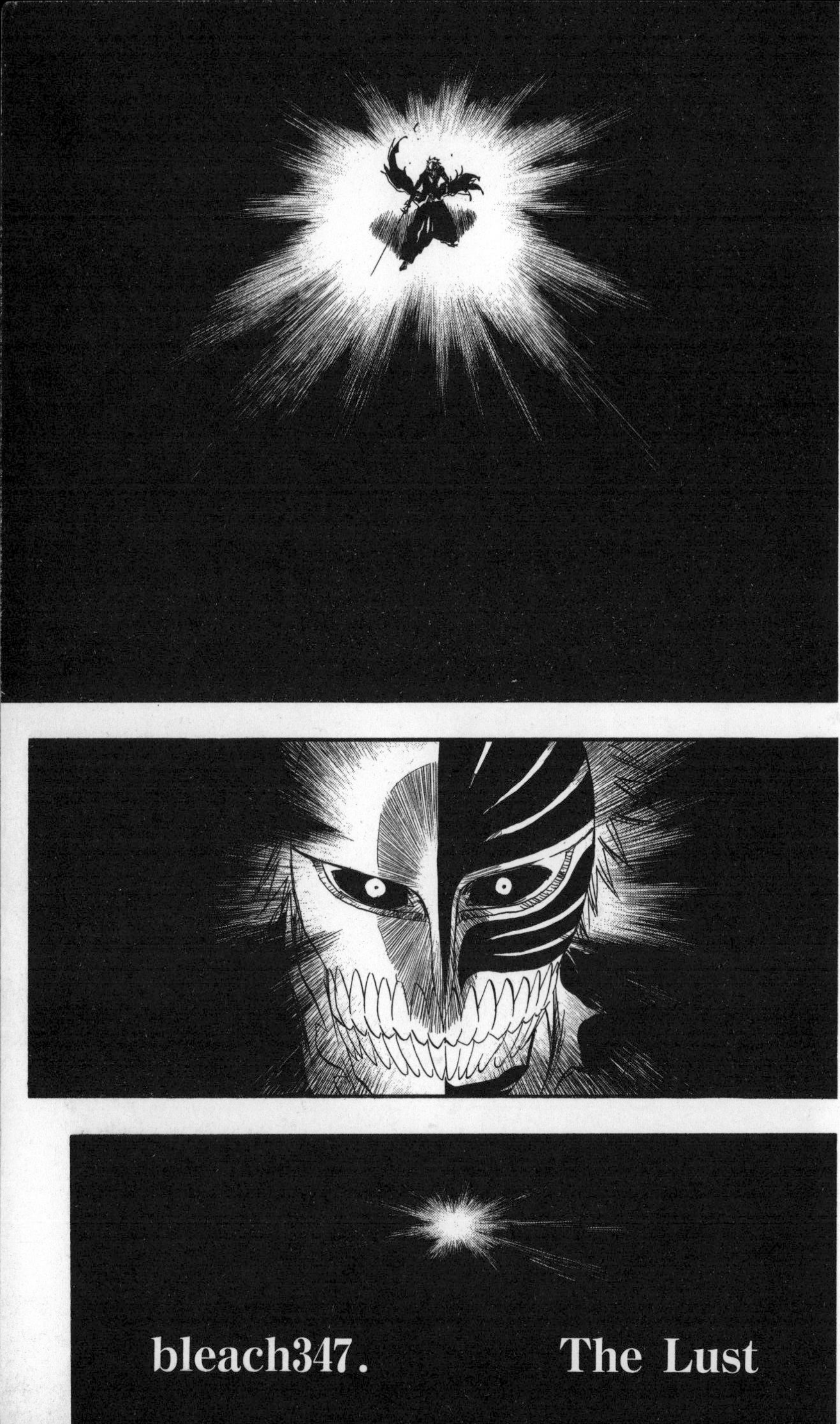
bleach347. The Lust

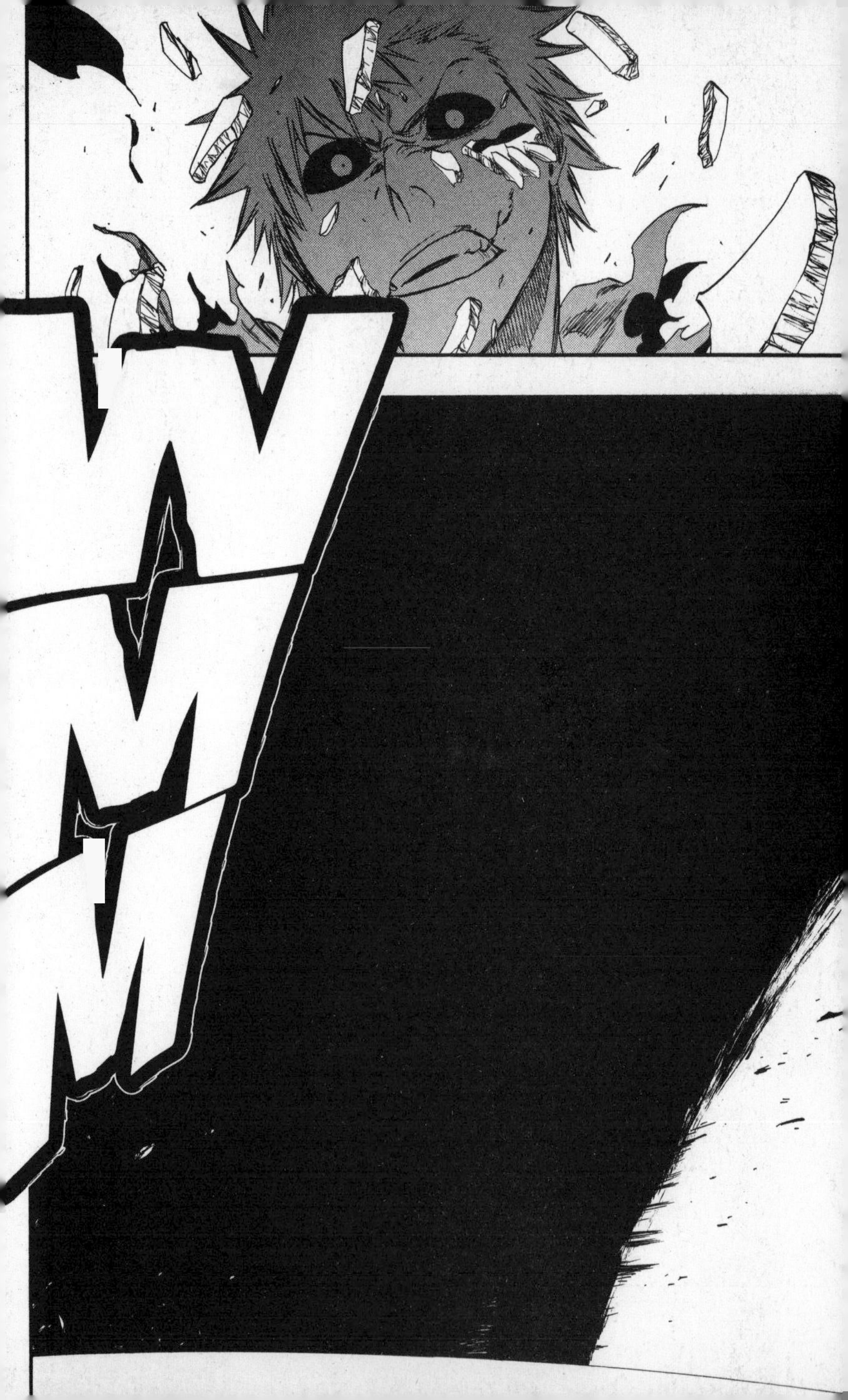

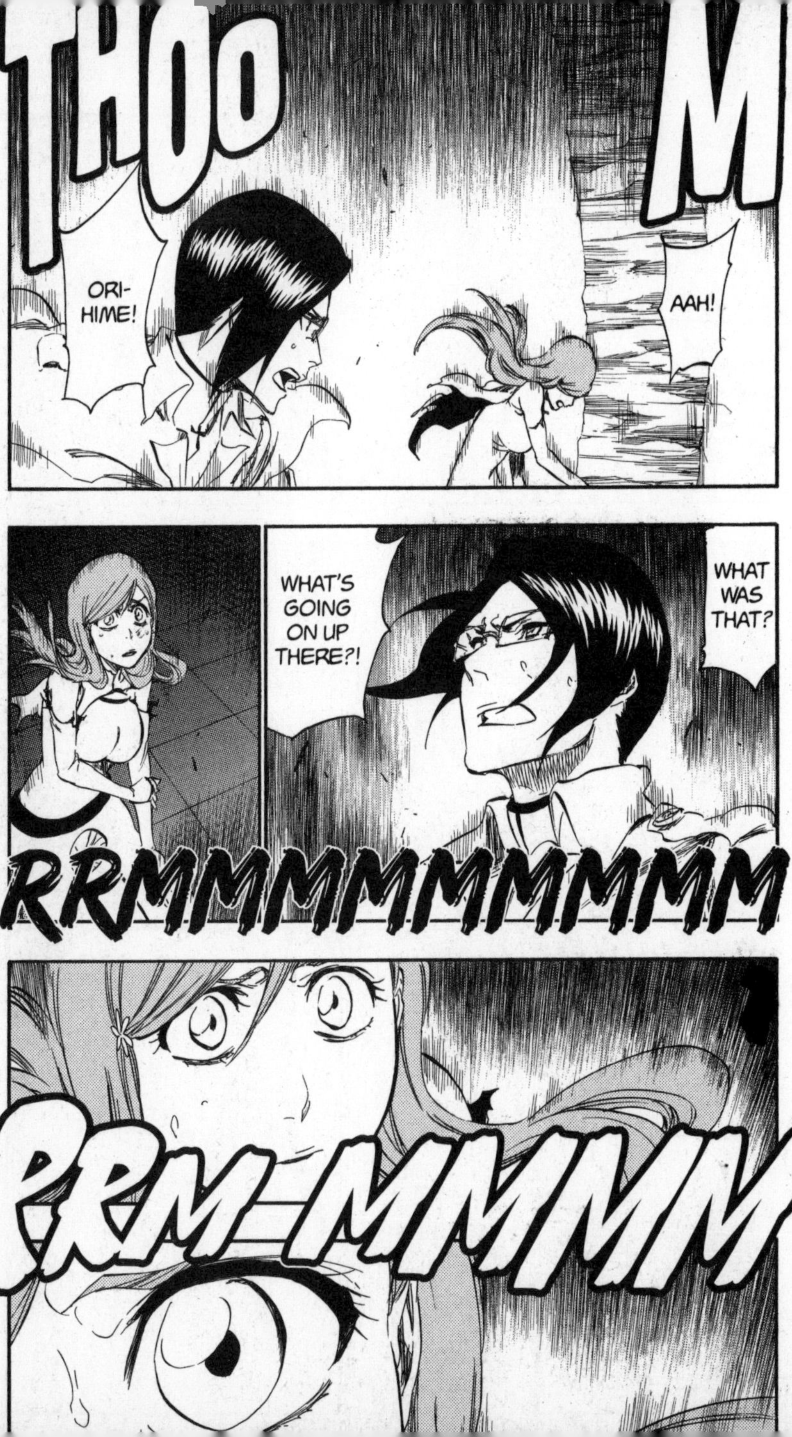
THOOM
AAH!
ORI-HIME!
WHAT WAS THAT?
WHAT'S GOING ON UP THERE?!
RRMMMMMMMMMMM
RRM MMMMM

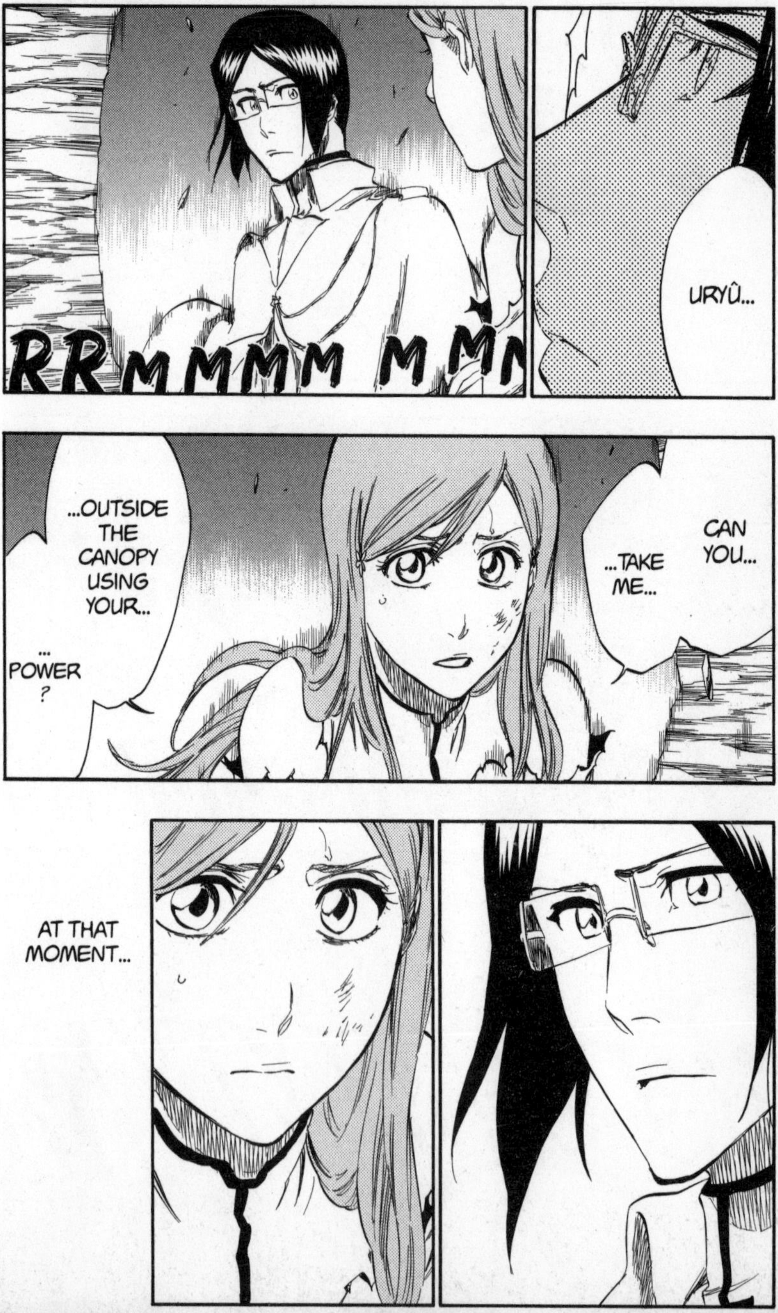
URYÛ...
RRMMMMM MMM
CAN YOU...
...TAKE ME...
...OUTSIDE THE CANOPY USING YOUR...
...POWER?
AT THAT MOMENT...

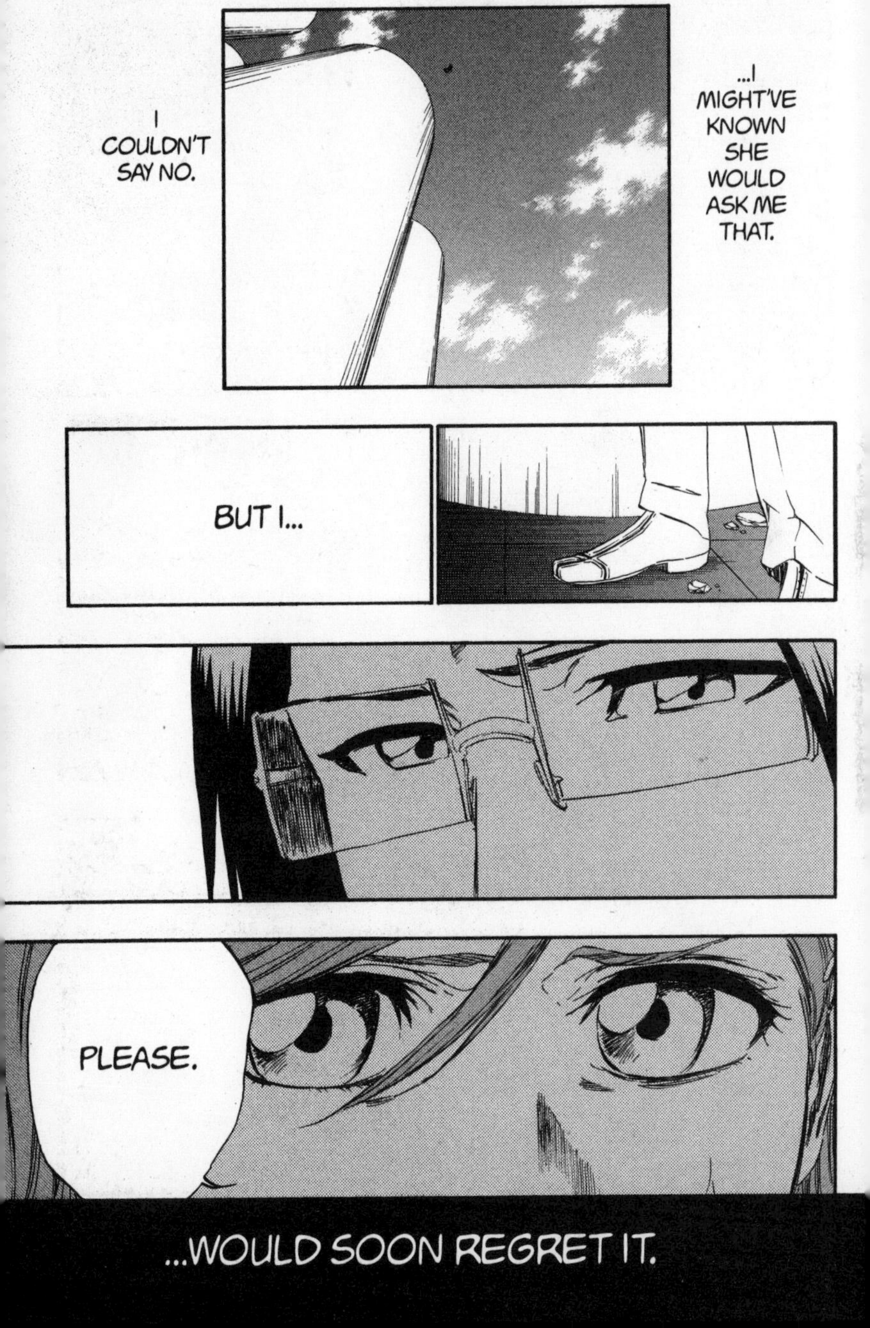
...I MIGHT'VE KNOWN SHE WOULD ASK ME THAT.
I COULDN'T SAY NO.
BUT I...
PLEASE.
...WOULD SOON REGRET IT.

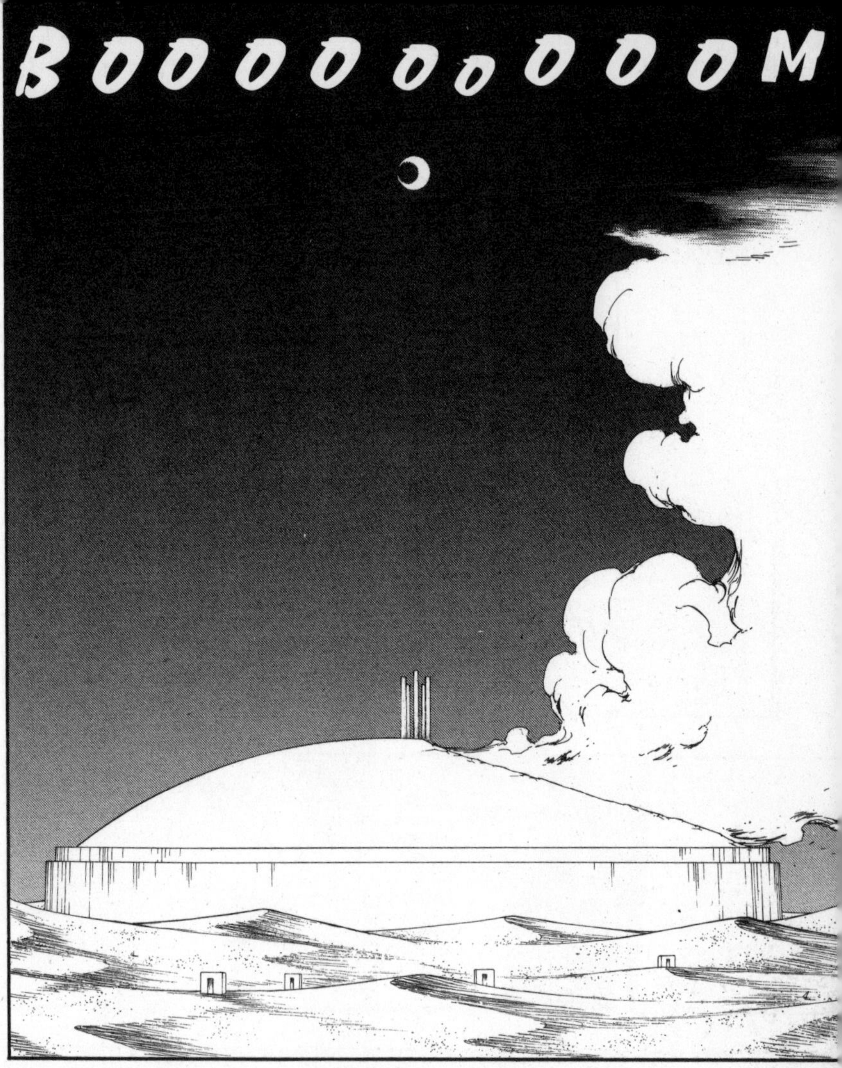
BOOOOOOOOOM
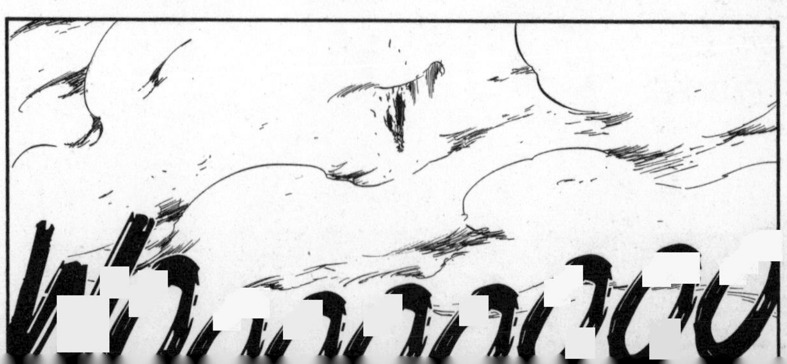

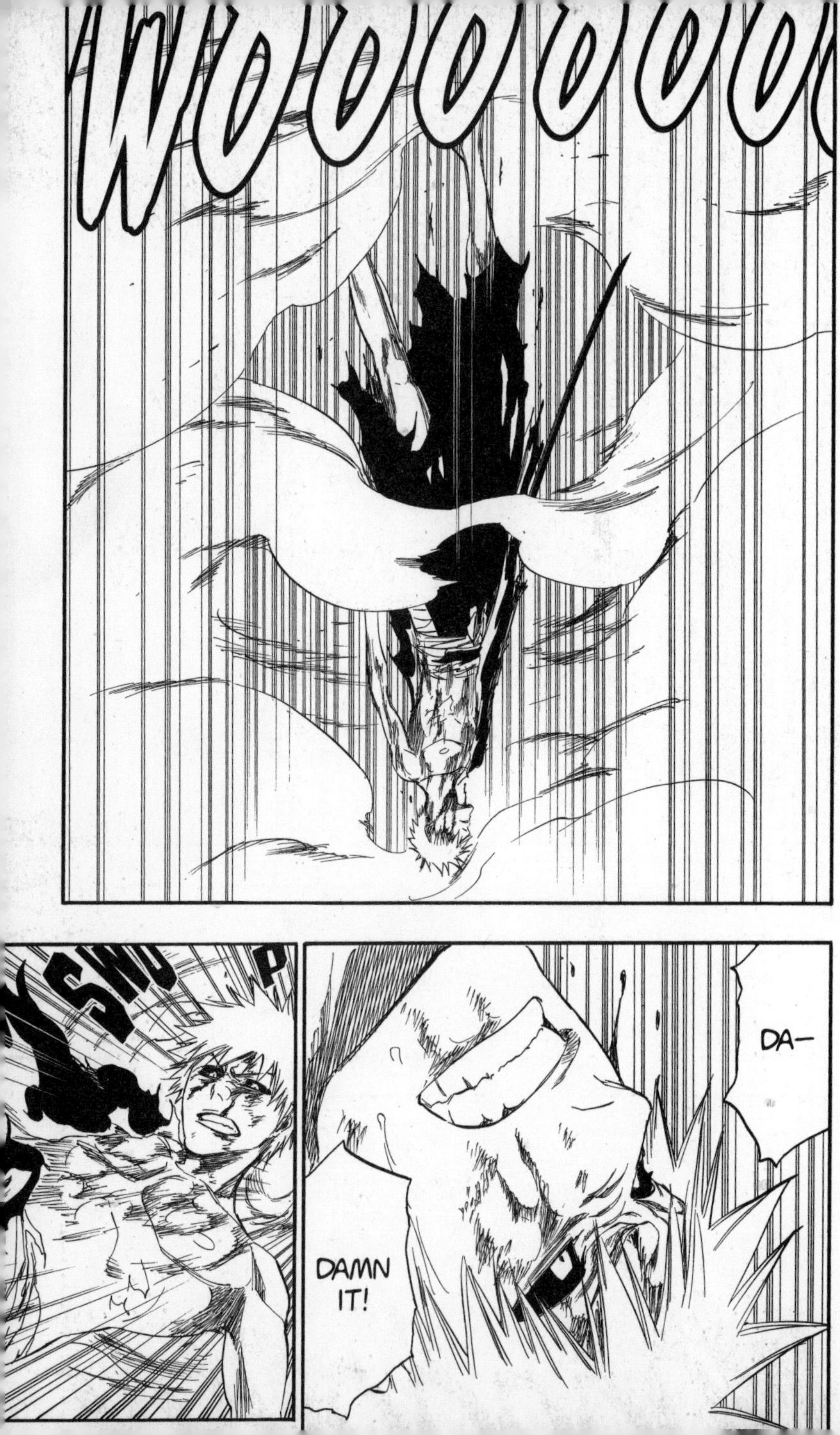
WOOOOOOO
DA-
DAMN IT!
SHUP

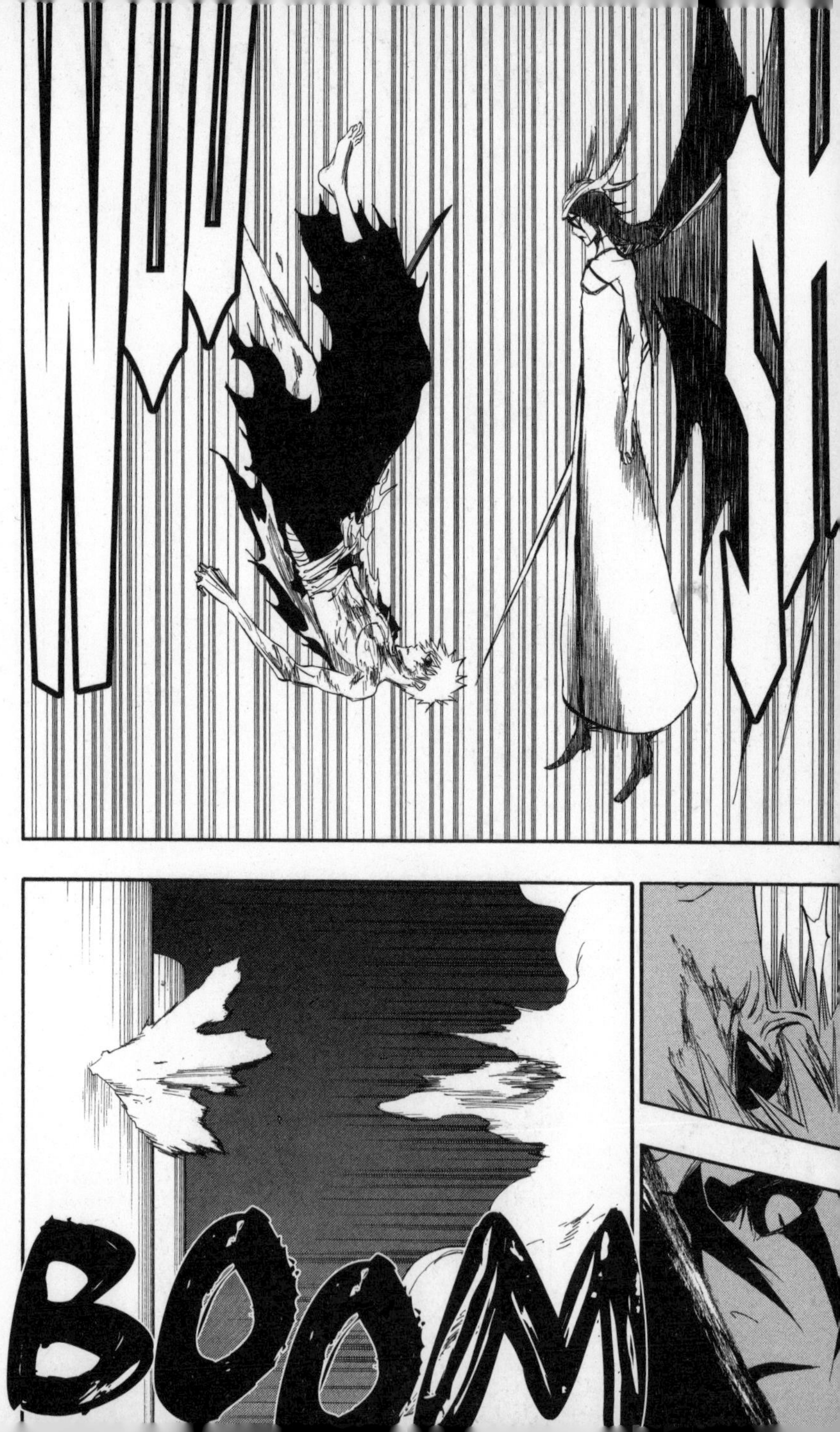
BOOM

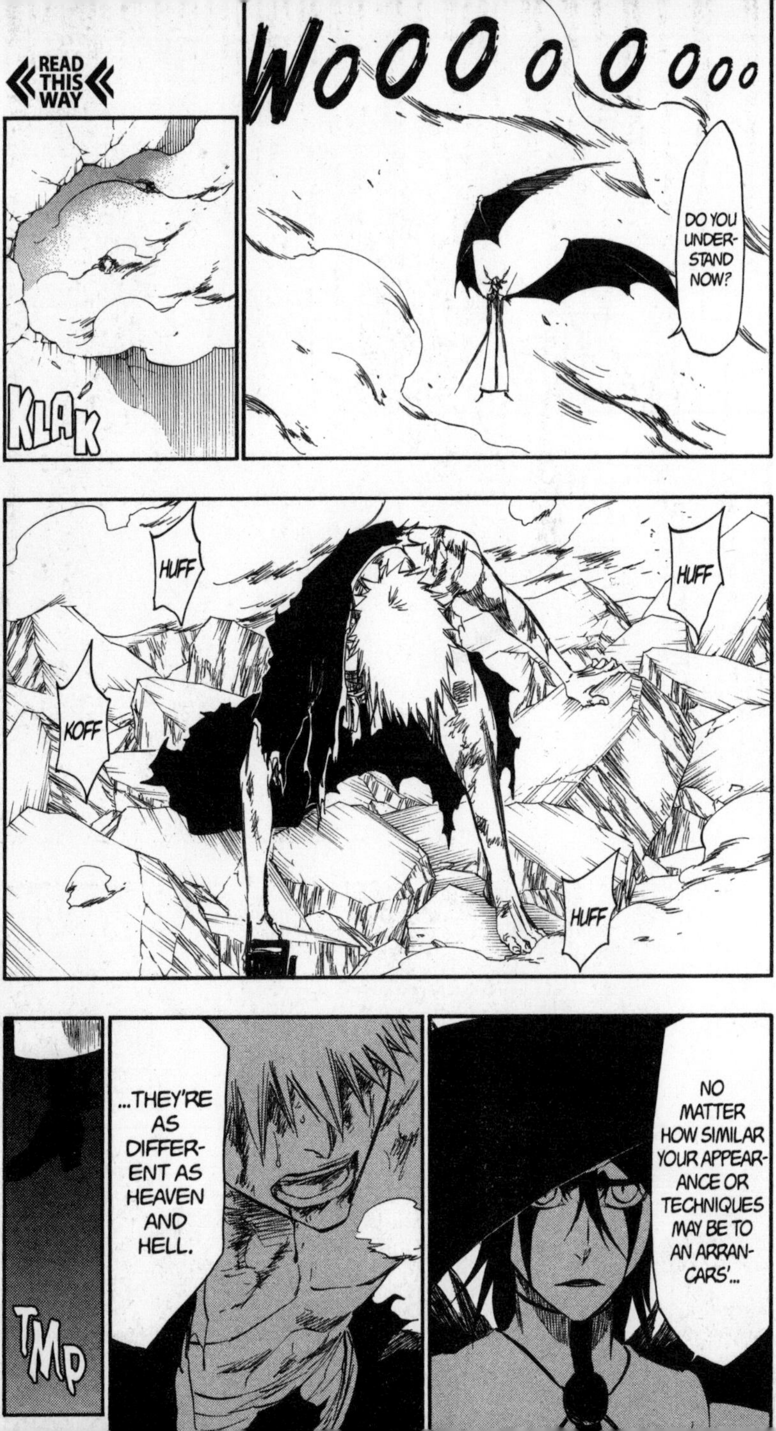
READ THIS WAY
WOOOOOOooo
DO YOU UNDERSTAND NOW?
KLAK
HUFF
HUFF
KOFF
HUFF
NO MATTER HOW SIMILAR YOUR APPEARANCE OR TECHNIQUES MAY BE TO AN ARRANCARS'...
...THEY'RE AS DIFFERENT AS HEAVEN AND HELL.
TMP

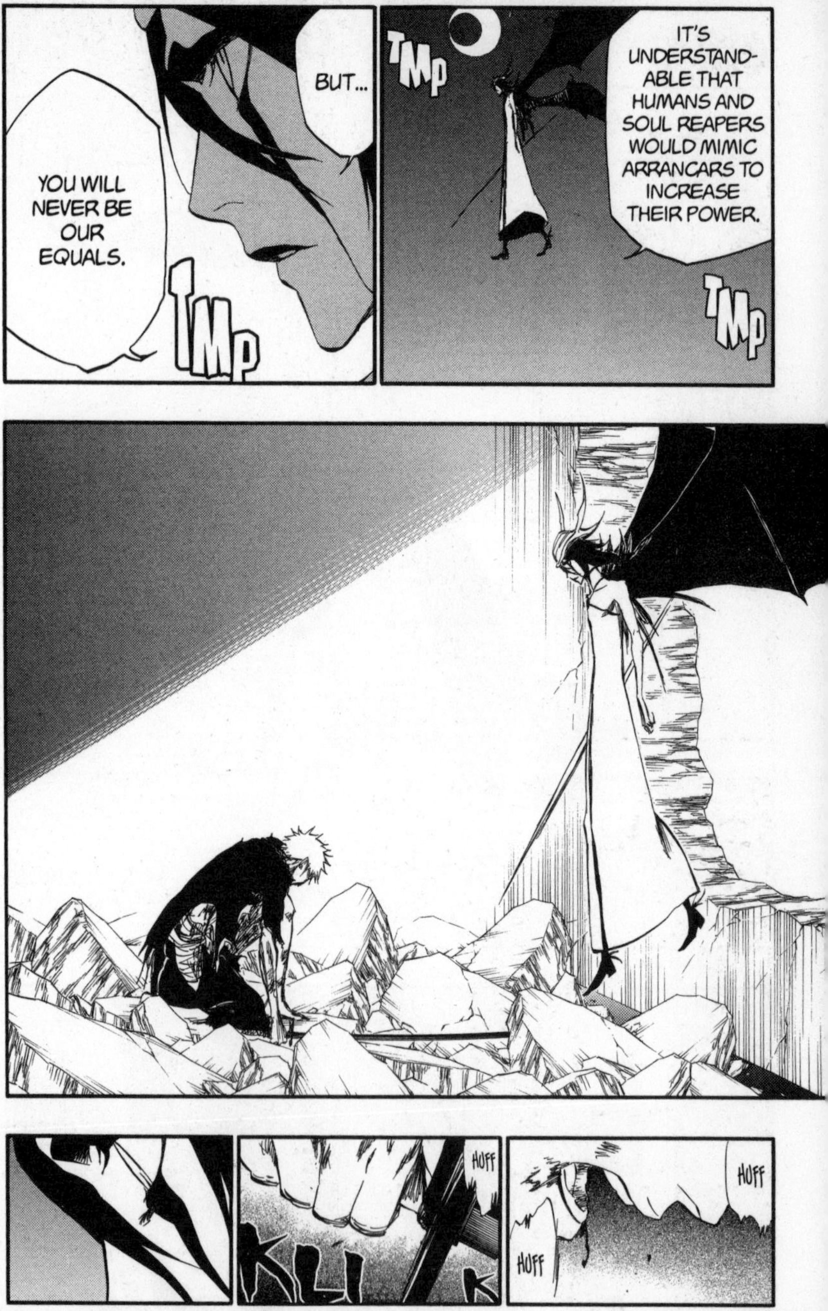

IT'S UNDERSTANDABLE THAT HUMANS AND SOUL REAPERS WOULD MIMIC ARRANCARS TO INCREASE THEIR POWER.
TMP
TMP
BUT...
YOU WILL NEVER BE OUR EQUALS.
TMP
HUFF
HUFF
HUFF
KLIK

TM

P

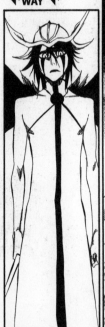

SNUFF

GE-
TSUGA

...

HUFF

HUFF

HUFF

HUFF

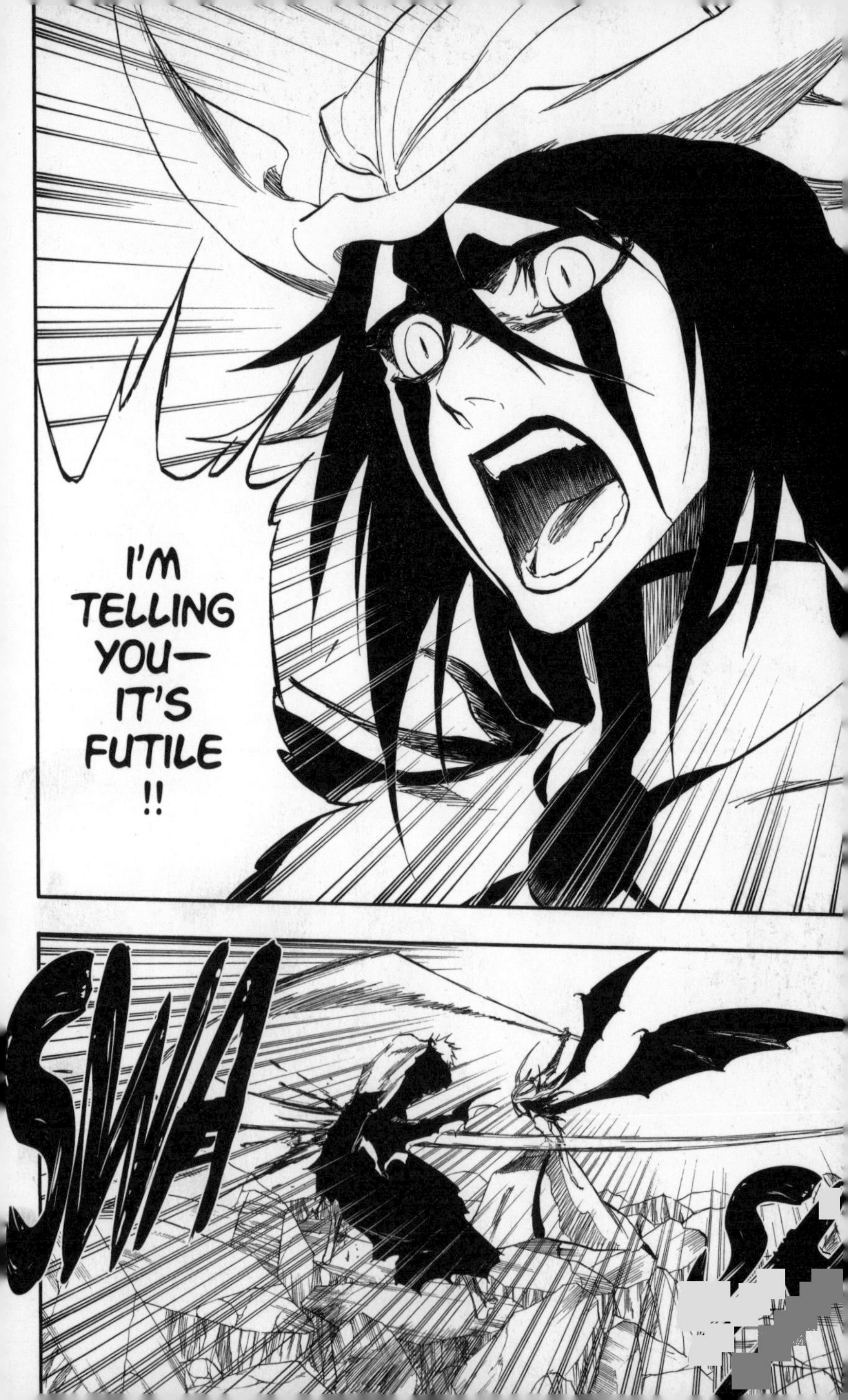
I'M TELLING YOU— IT'S FUTILE !!
SWA

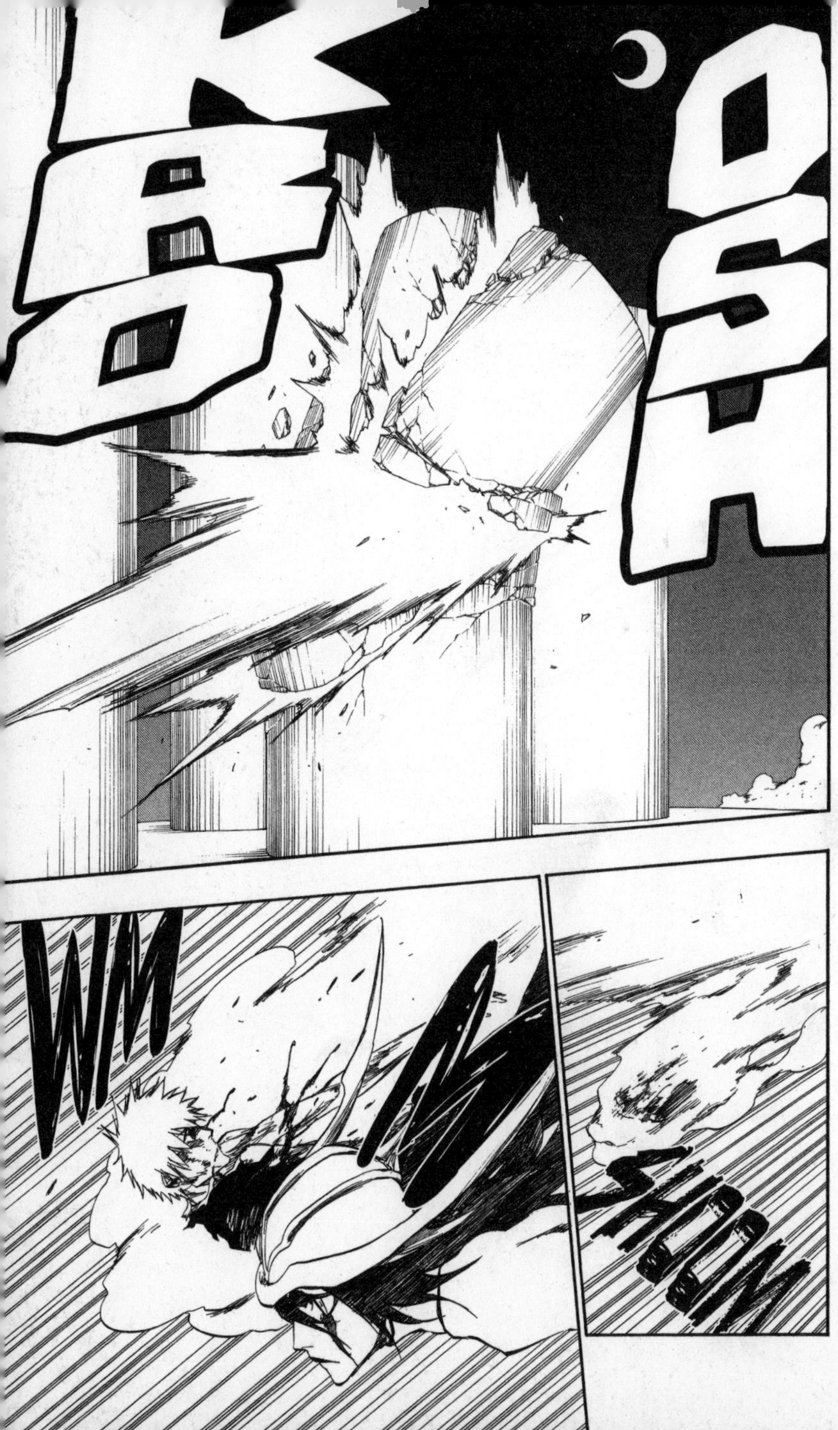

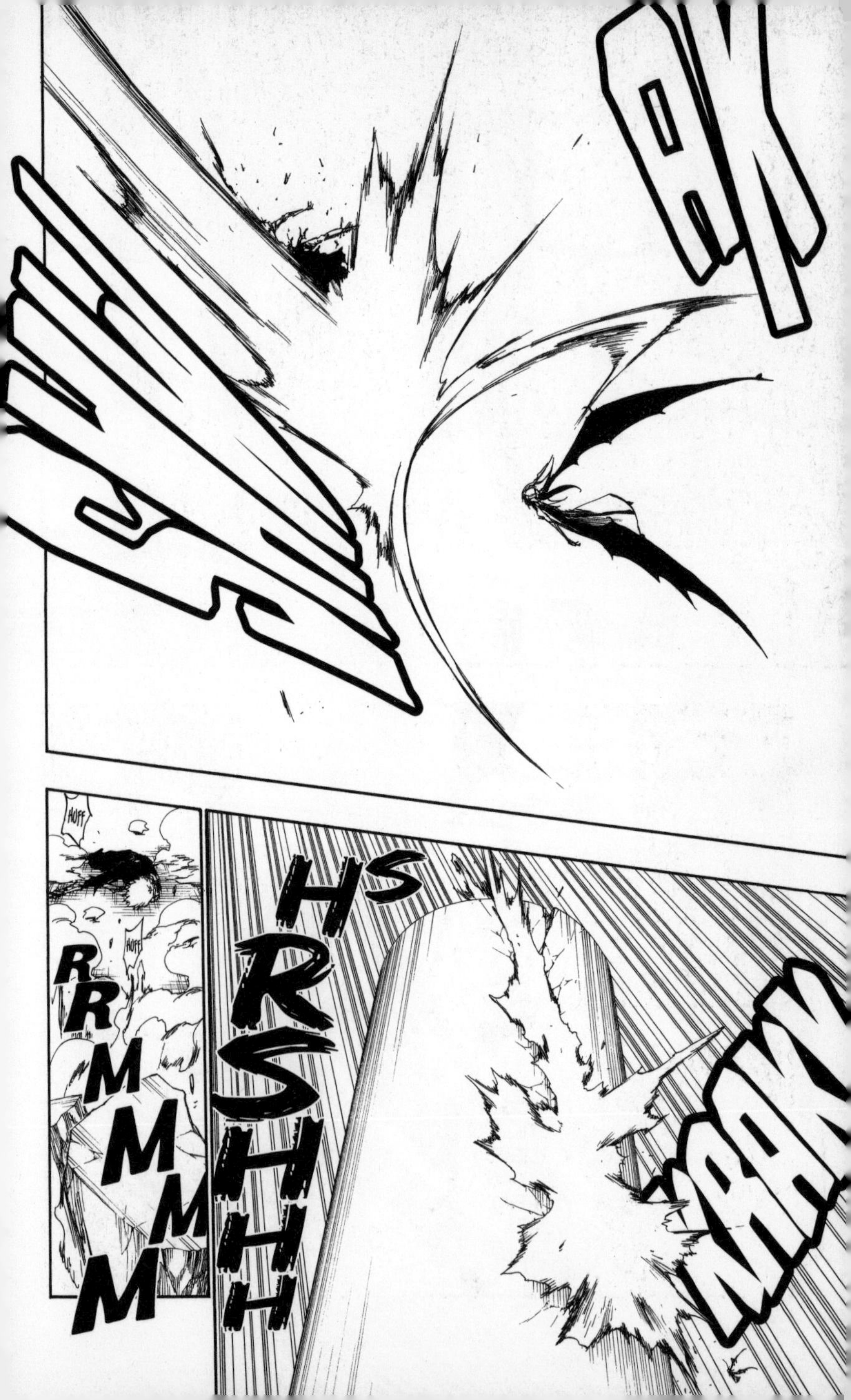
HSRSHHH
HUFF
HUFF
RRMMMMM

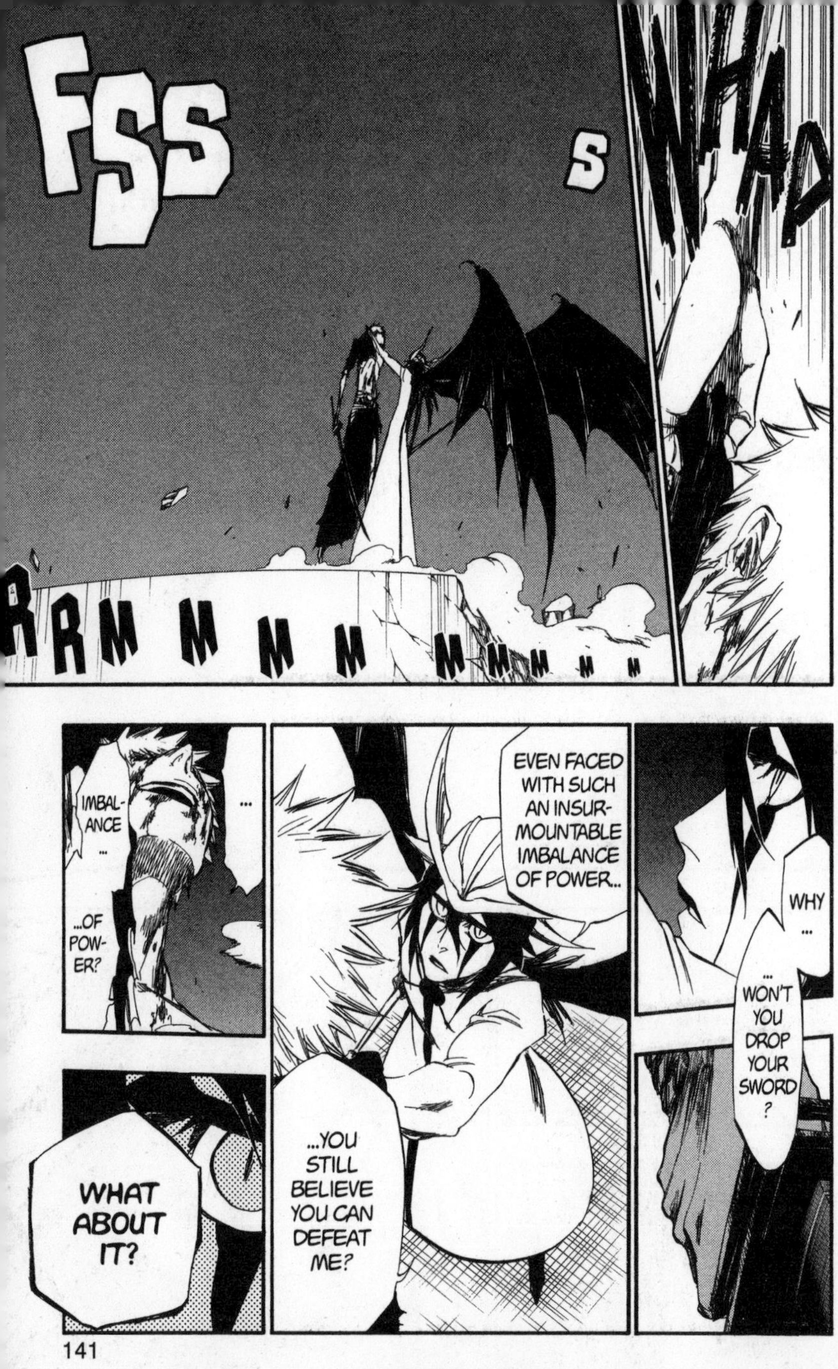
WHAD
FSS
S
RRMMMMMMMM
WHY ...
... WON'T YOU DROP YOUR SWORD?
EVEN FACED WITH SUCH AN INSUR-MOUNTABLE IMBALANCE OF POWER...
...YOU STILL BELIEVE YOU CAN DEFEAT ME?
...
IMBAL-ANCE ...
...OF POW-ER?
WHAT ABOUT IT?

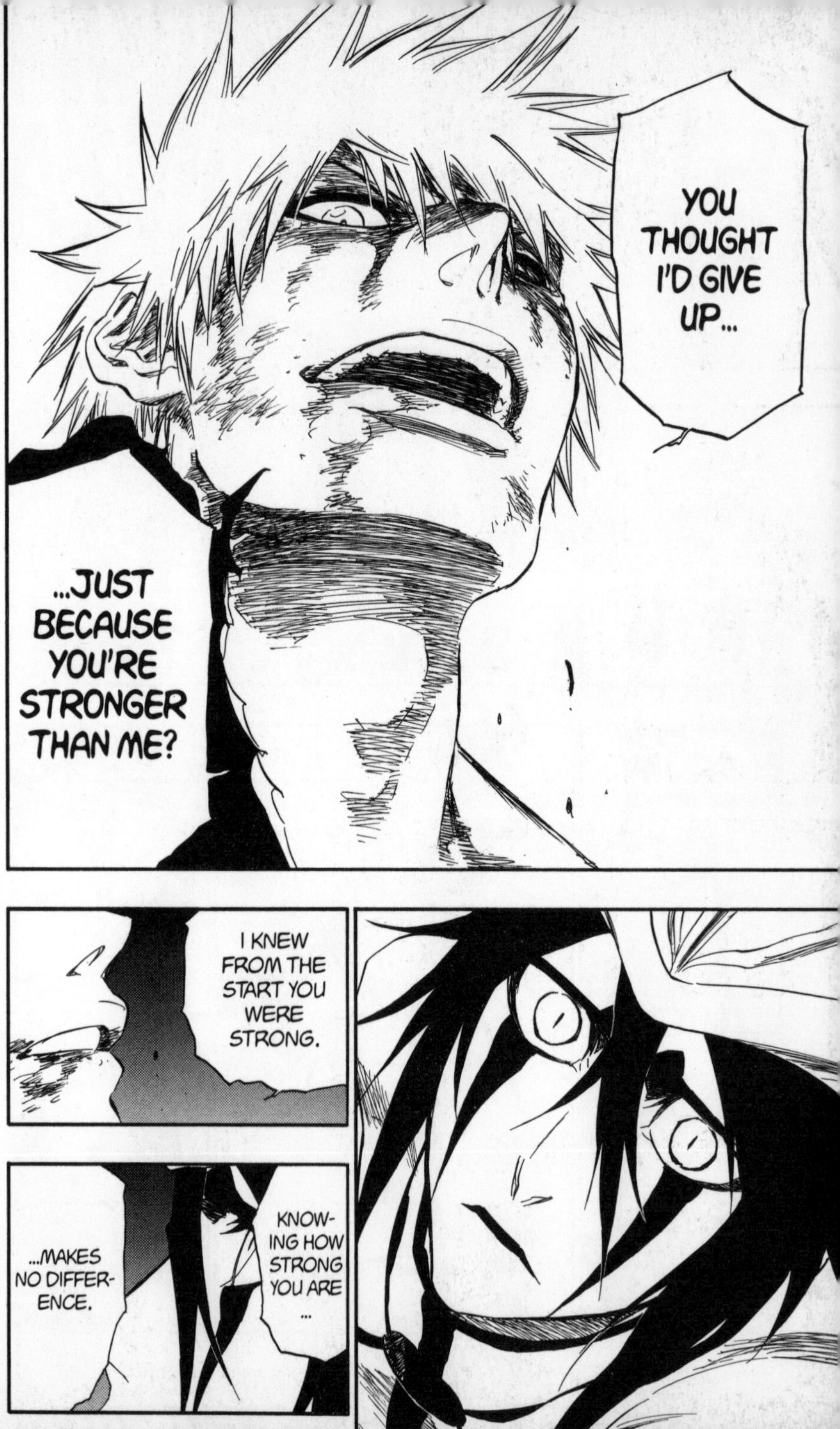
YOU THOUGHT I'D GIVE UP...
...JUST BECAUSE YOU'RE STRONGER THAN ME?
I KNEW FROM THE START YOU WERE STRONG.
KNOW-ING HOW STRONG YOU ARE ...
...MAKES NO DIFFER-ENCE.

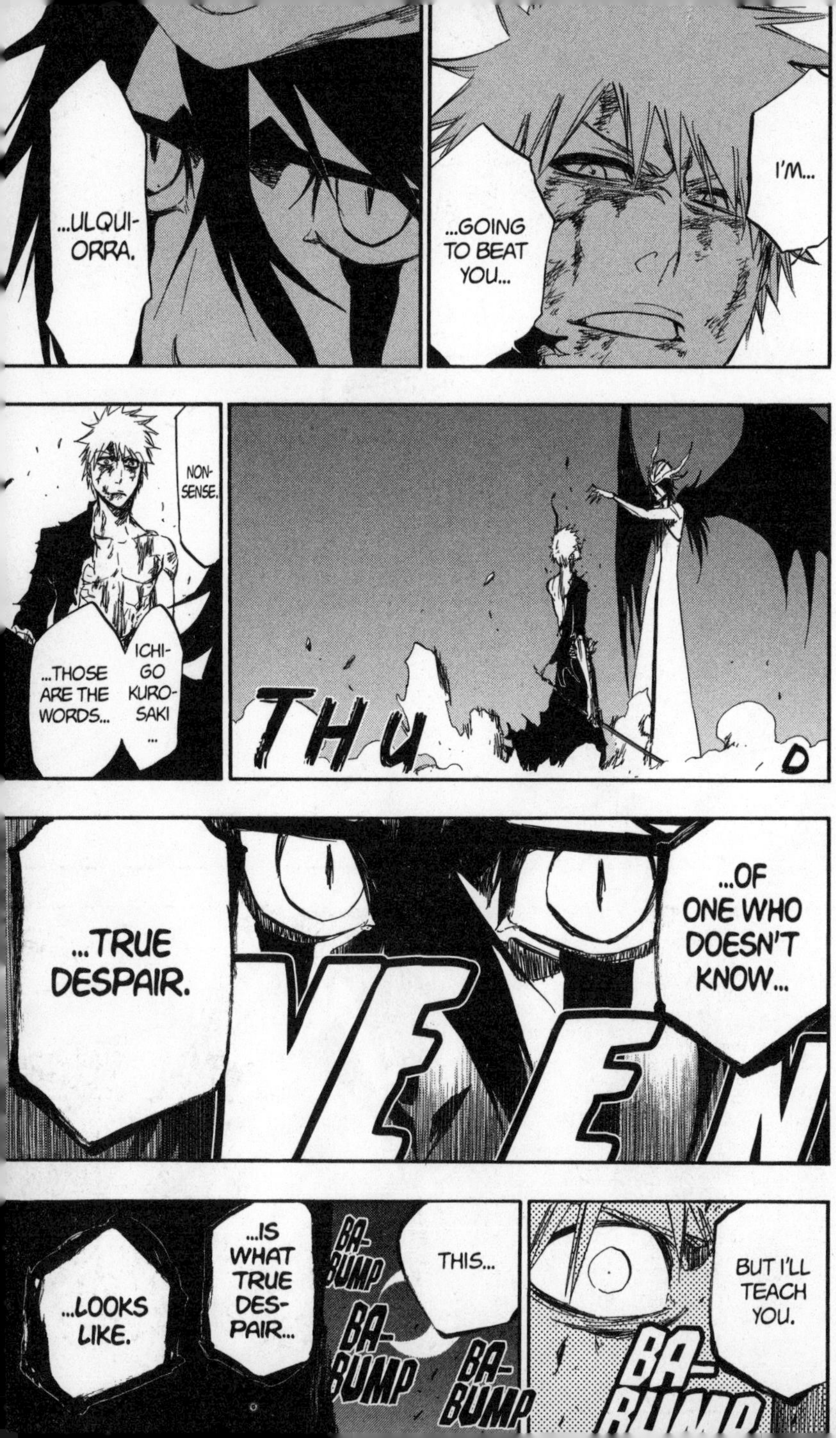
I'M...
...GOING TO BEAT YOU...
...ULQUIORRA.
THUD
NONSENSE.
ICHIGO KUROSAKI...
...THOSE ARE THE WORDS...
...OF ONE WHO DOESN'T KNOW...
...TRUE DESPAIR.
BUT I'LL TEACH YOU.
BA-BUMP
THIS...
BA-BUMP
BA-BUMP
BA-BUMP
...IS WHAT TRUE DESPAIR...
...LOOKS LIKE.

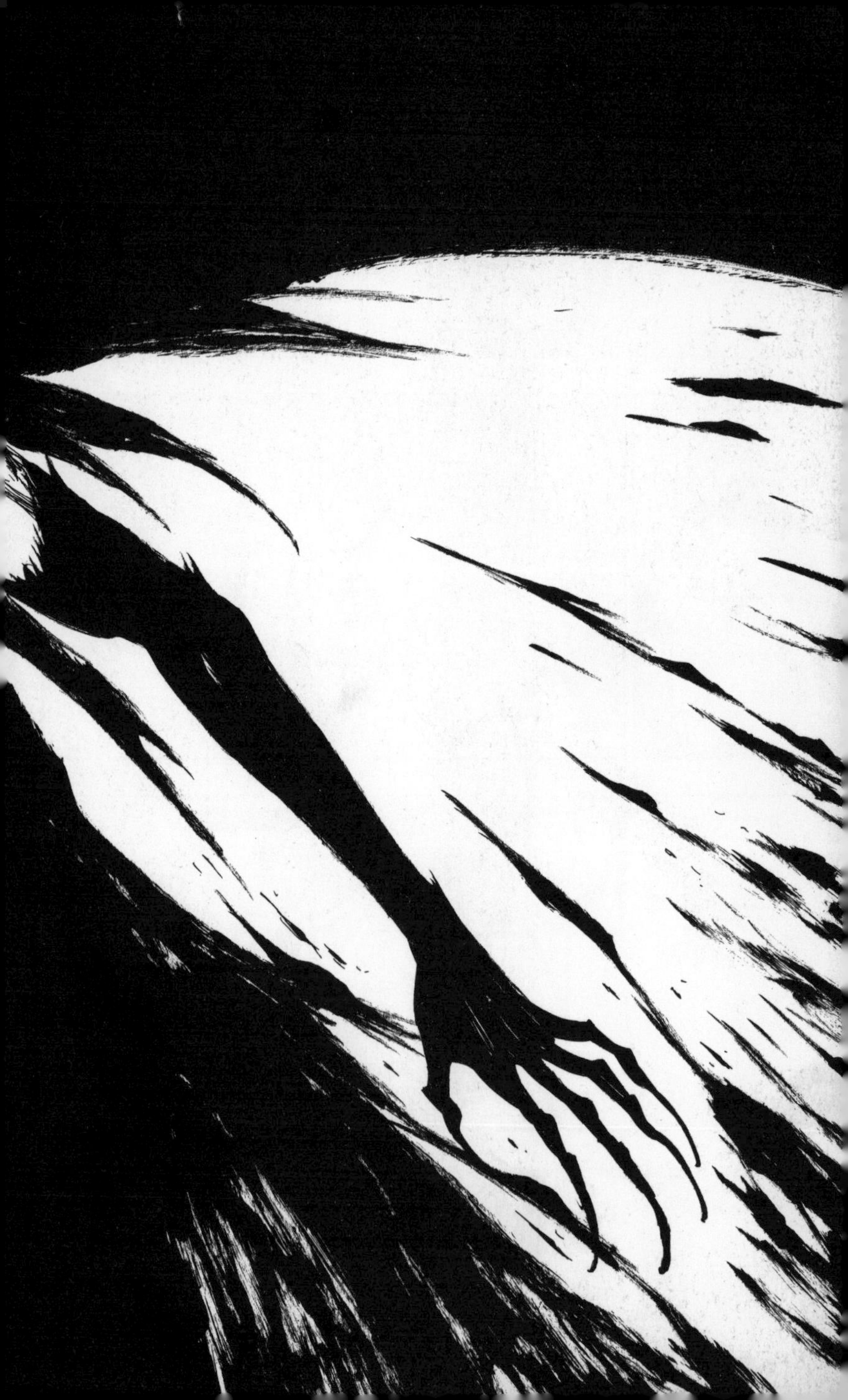

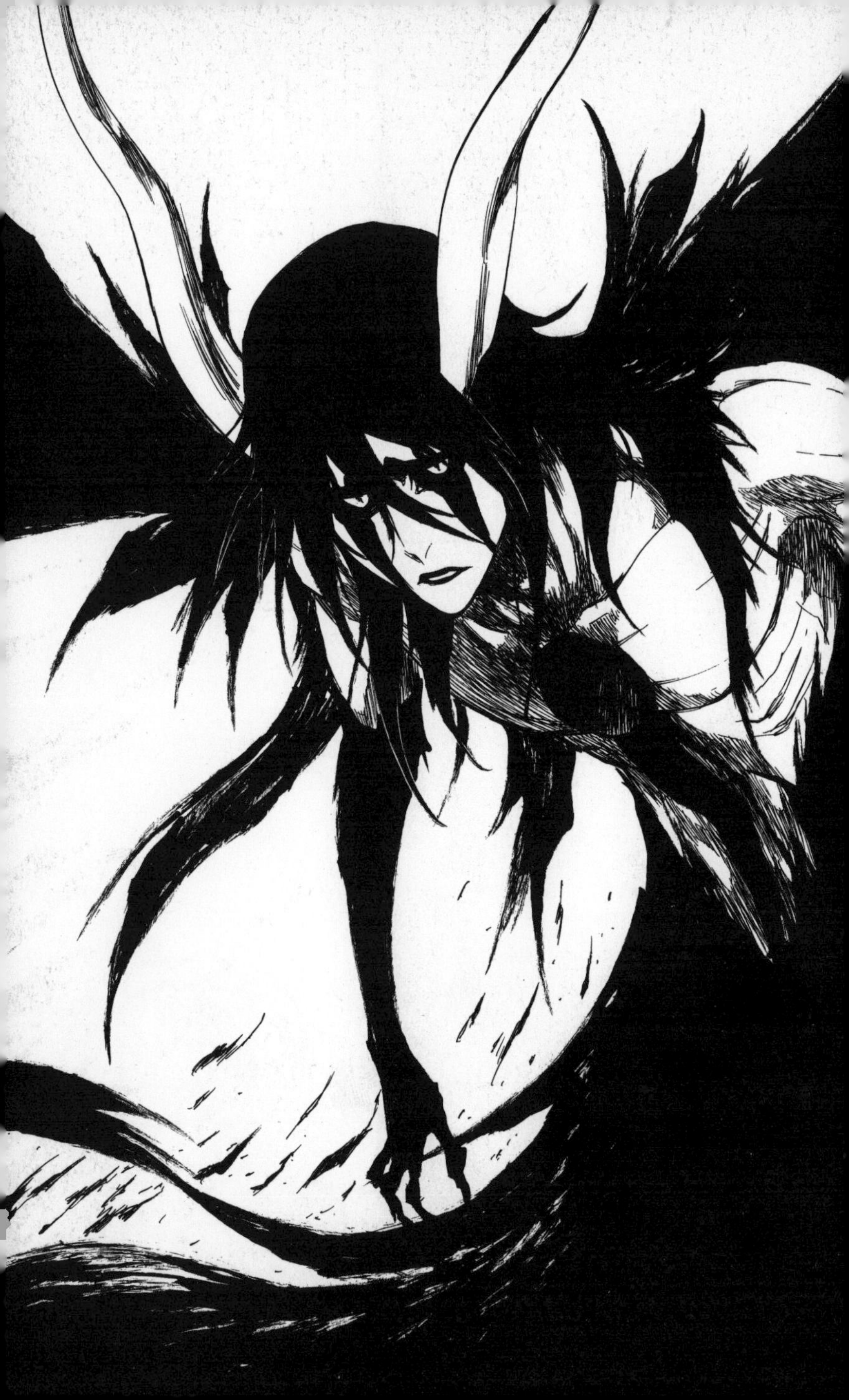

the Last

348. The Lust 2

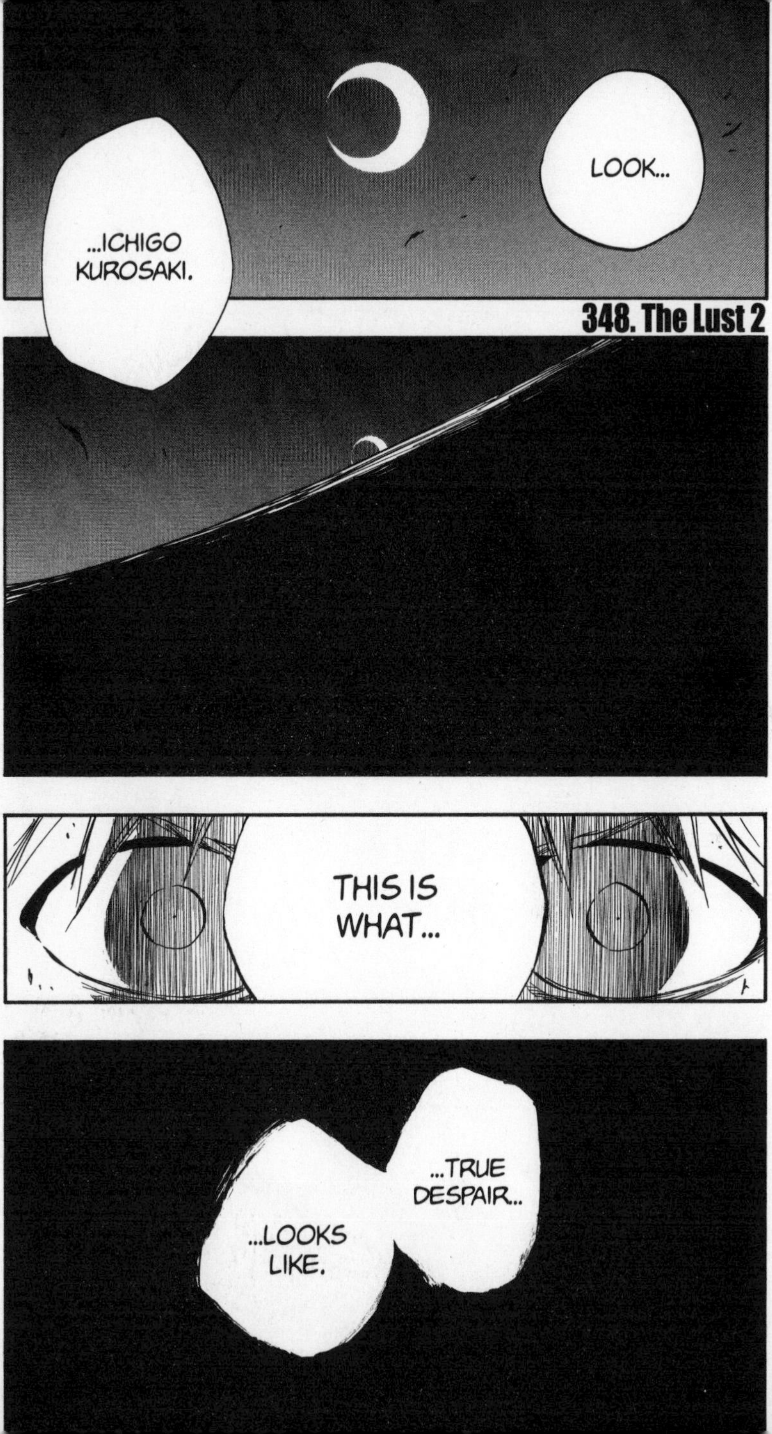
LOOK...
...ICHIGO KUROSAKI.
THIS IS WHAT...
...TRUE DESPAIR...
...LOOKS LIKE.

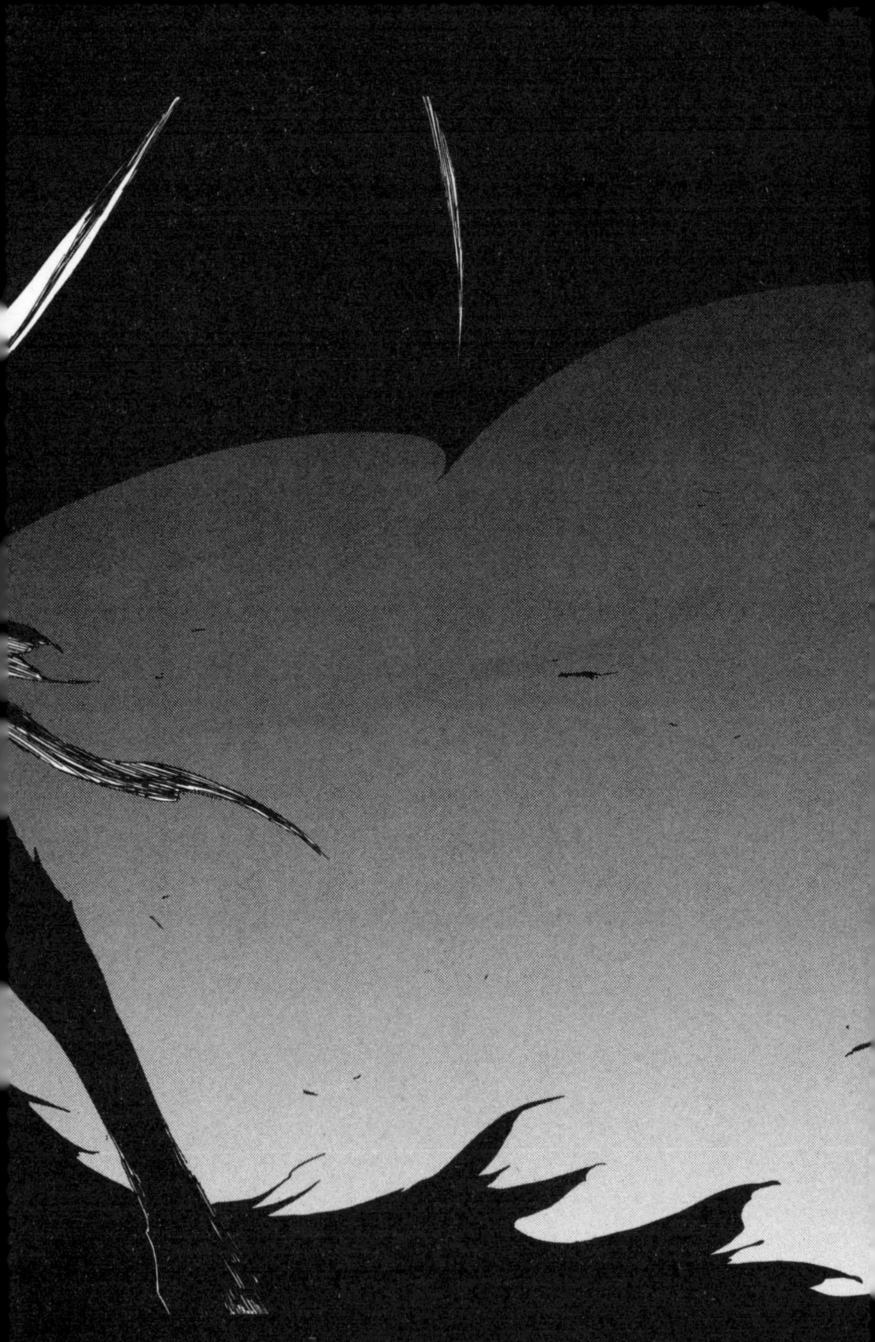

The Lust 2

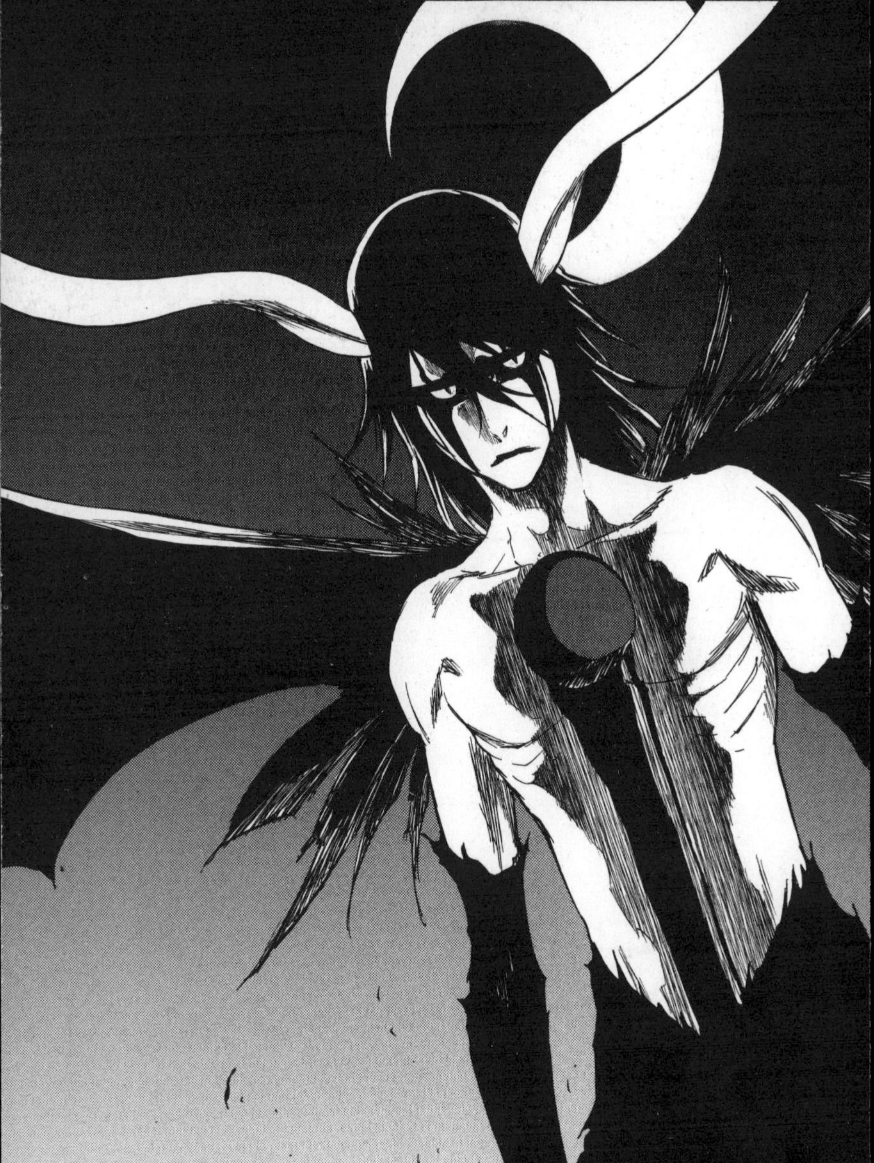

BLEACH 348.

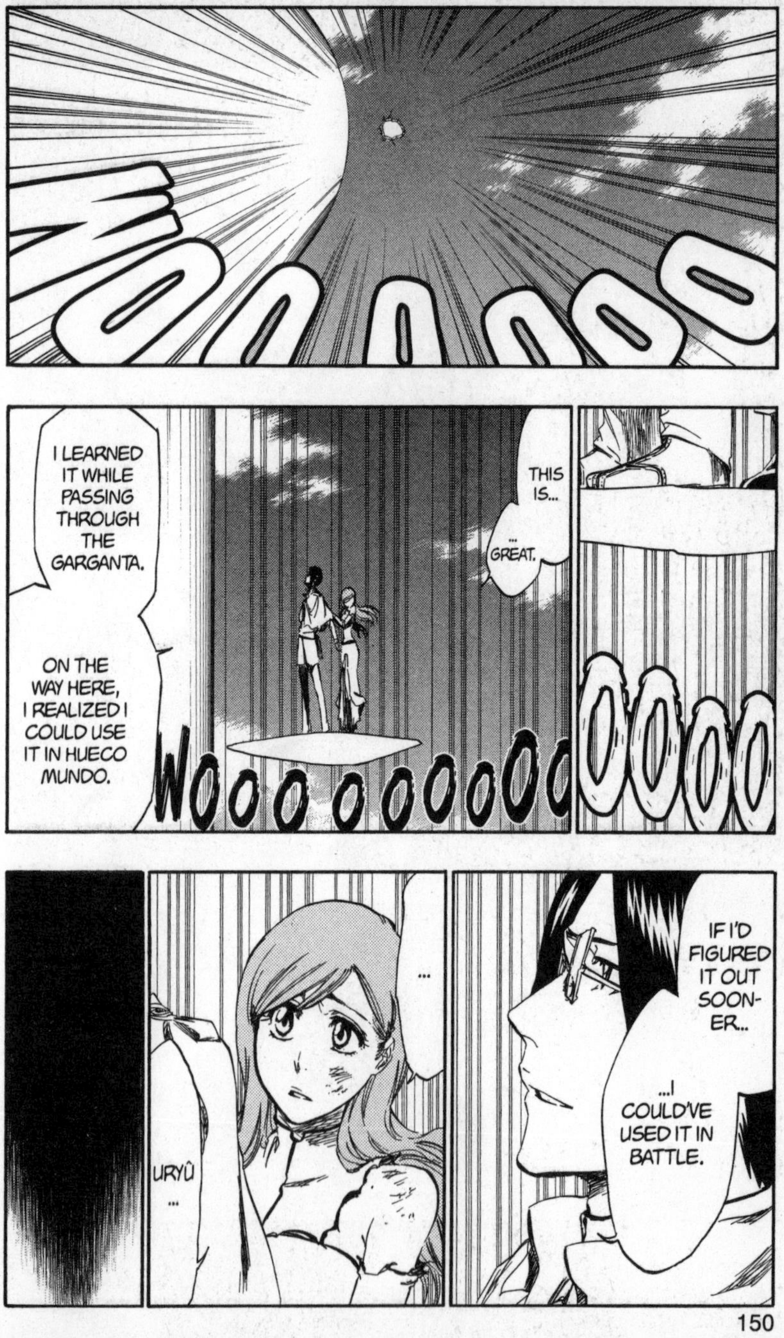
WOOOOOO
THIS IS...
...GREAT.
I LEARNED IT WHILE PASSING THROUGH THE GARGANTA.
ON THE WAY HERE, I REALIZED I COULD USE IT IN HUECO MUNDO.
WOOOOOOOOOOOOOOO
IF I'D FIGURED IT OUT SOON-ER...
...I COULD'VE USED IT IN BATTLE.
...
URYÛ ...

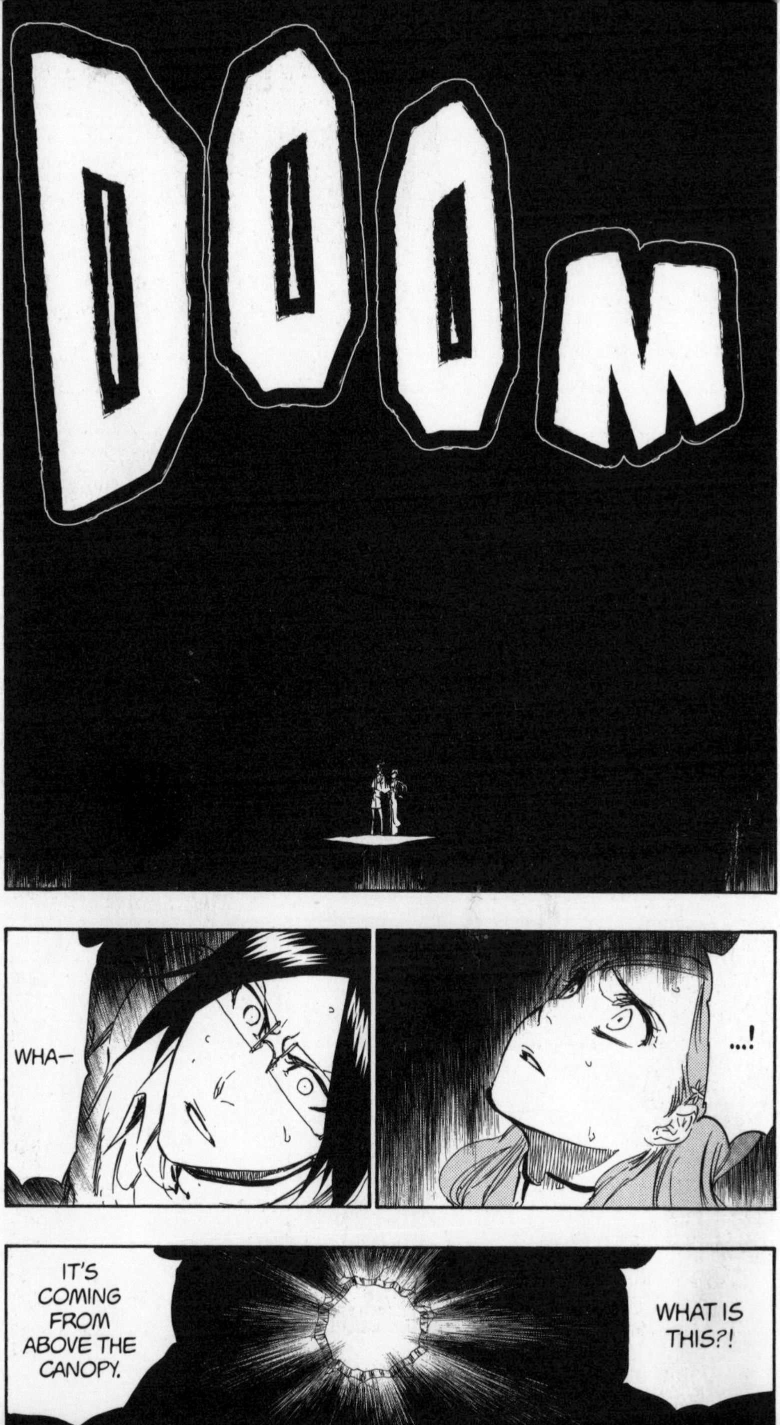
DOOM
...!
WHA—
WHAT IS THIS?!
IT'S COMING FROM ABOVE THE CANOPY.

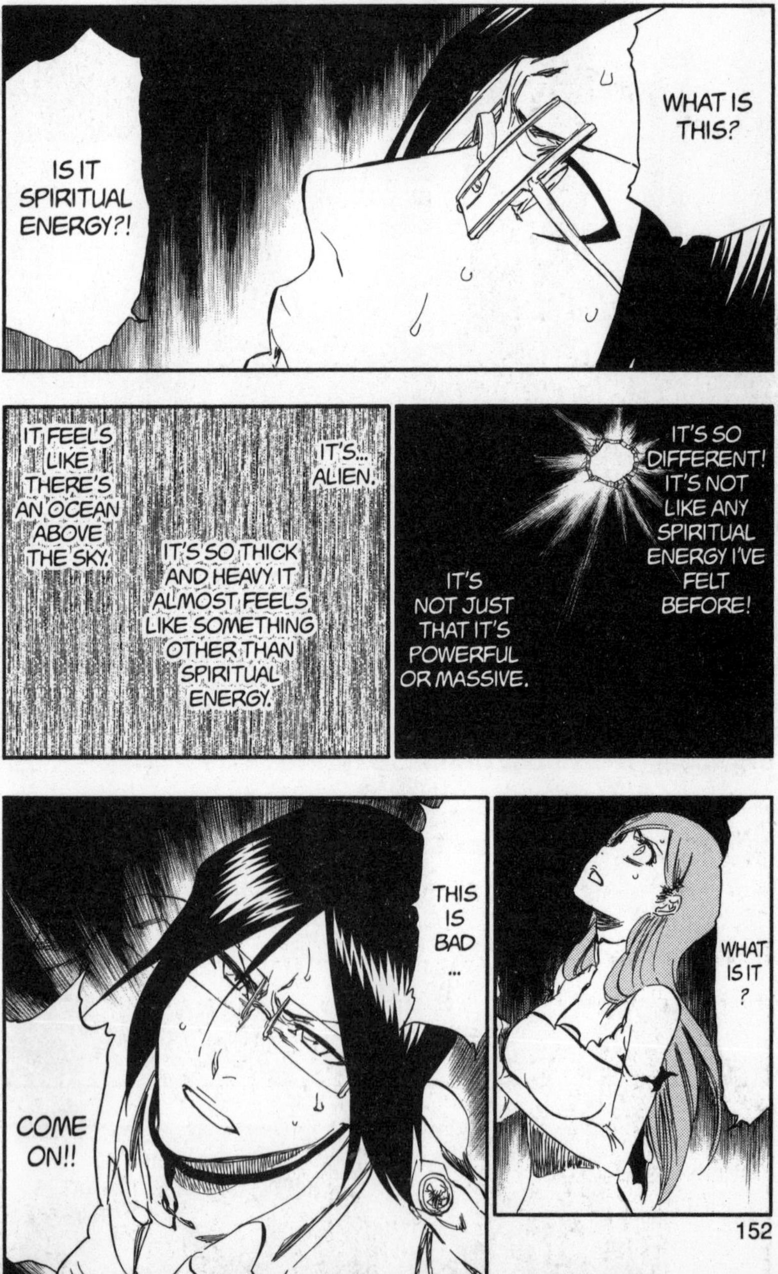
WHAT IS THIS?
IS IT SPIRITUAL ENERGY?!
IT'S SO DIFFERENT! IT'S NOT LIKE ANY SPIRITUAL ENERGY I'VE FELT BEFORE!
IT'S NOT JUST THAT IT'S POWERFUL OR MASSIVE.
IT'S... ALIEN.
IT'S SO THICK AND HEAVY IT ALMOST FEELS LIKE SOMETHING OTHER THAN SPIRITUAL ENERGY.
IT FEELS LIKE THERE'S AN OCEAN ABOVE THE SKY.
WHAT IS IT?
THIS IS BAD...
COME ON!!

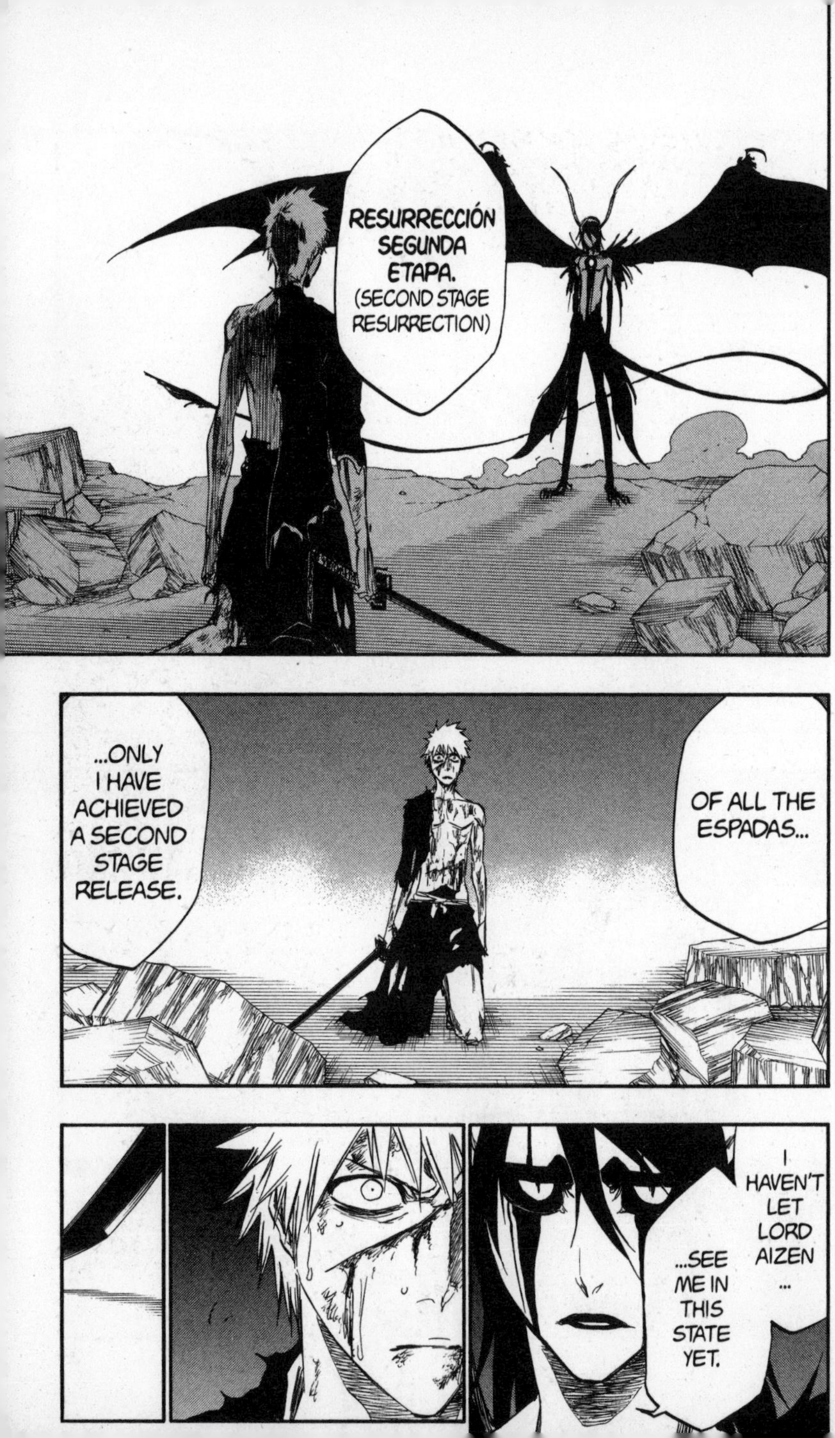
RESURRECCIÓN SEGUNDA ETAPA. (SECOND STAGE RESURRECTION)
OF ALL THE ESPADAS...
...ONLY I HAVE ACHIEVED A SECOND STAGE RELEASE.
I HAVEN'T LET LORD AIZEN ...
...SEE ME IN THIS STATE YET.

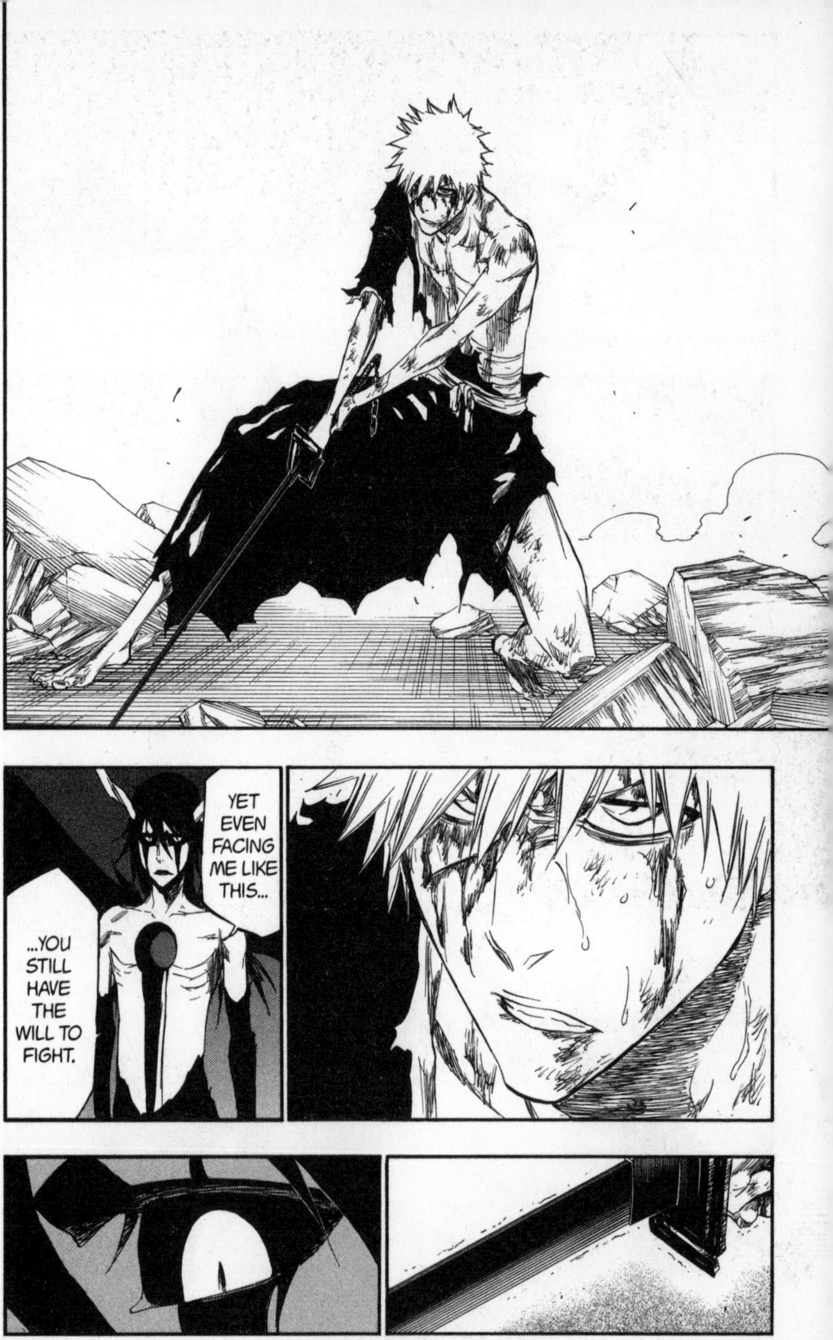
YET EVEN FACING ME LIKE THIS...
...YOU STILL HAVE THE WILL TO FIGHT.

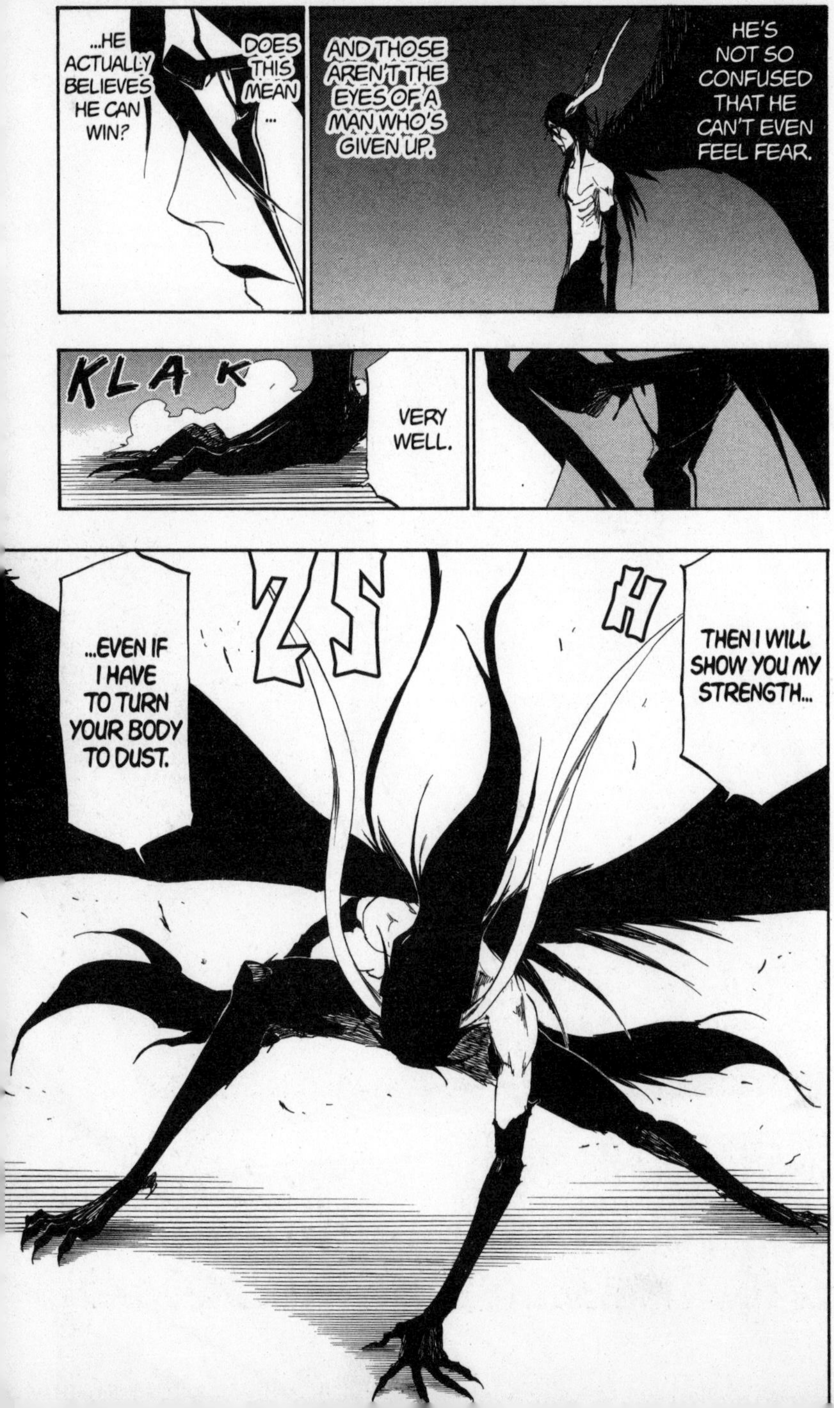
HE'S NOT SO CONFUSED THAT HE CAN'T EVEN FEEL FEAR.
AND THOSE AREN'T THE EYES OF A MAN WHO'S GIVEN UP.
DOES THIS MEAN ...
...HE ACTUALLY BELIEVES HE CAN WIN?
VERY WELL.
KLAK
THEN I WILL SHOW YOU MY STRENGTH...
ZSH
...EVEN IF I HAVE TO TURN YOUR BODY TO DUST.

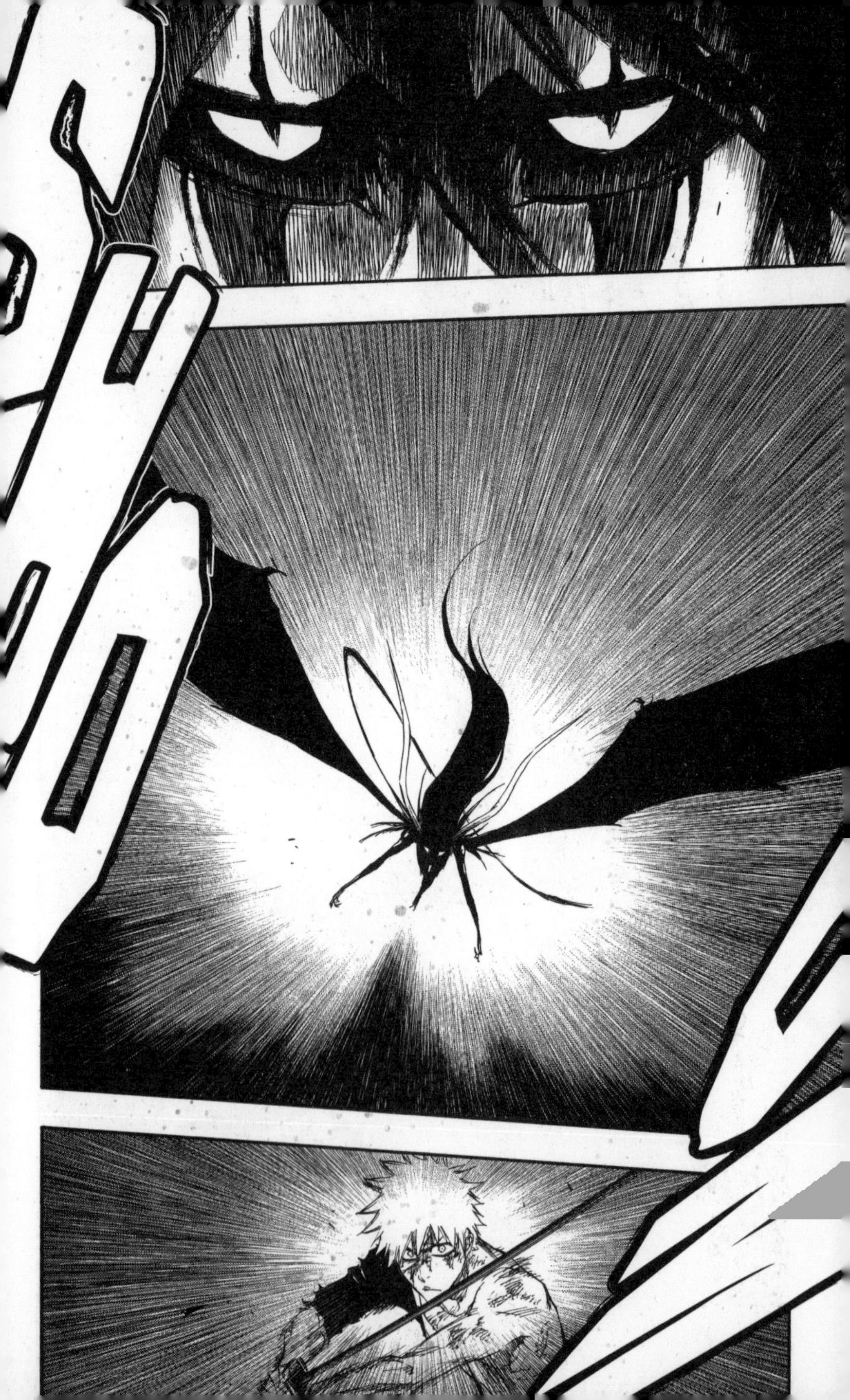

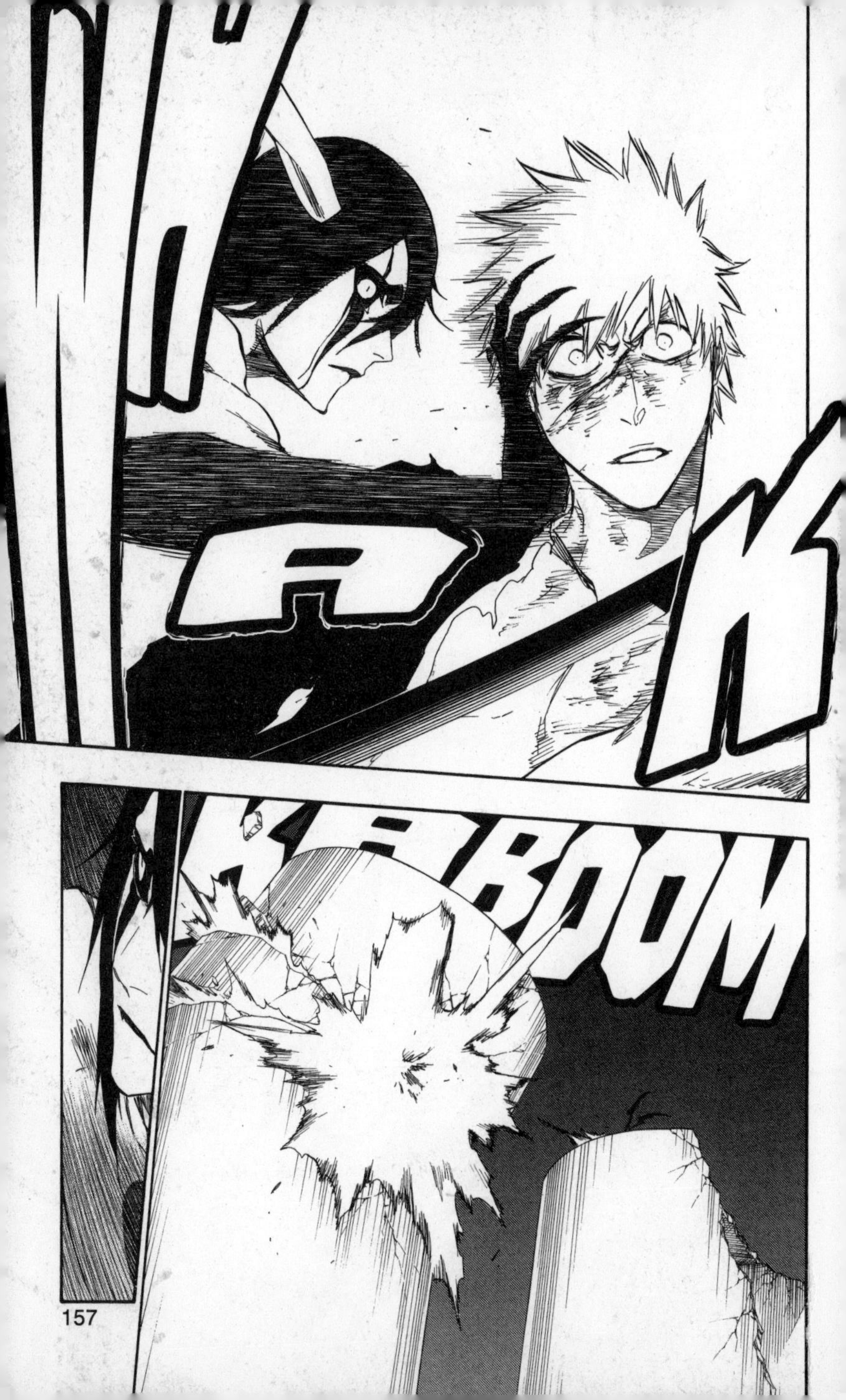
BOOM

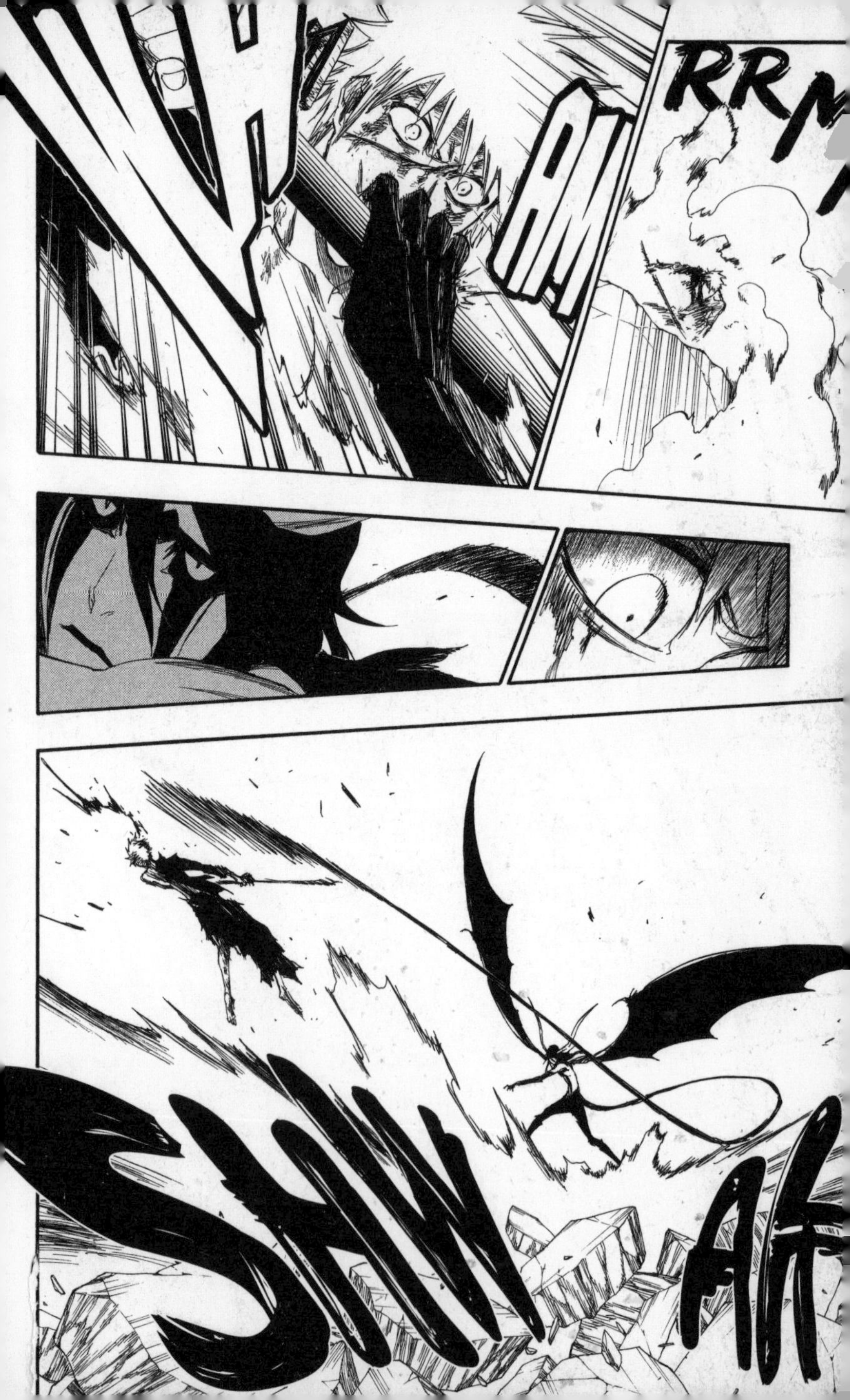
RRM
WHAM

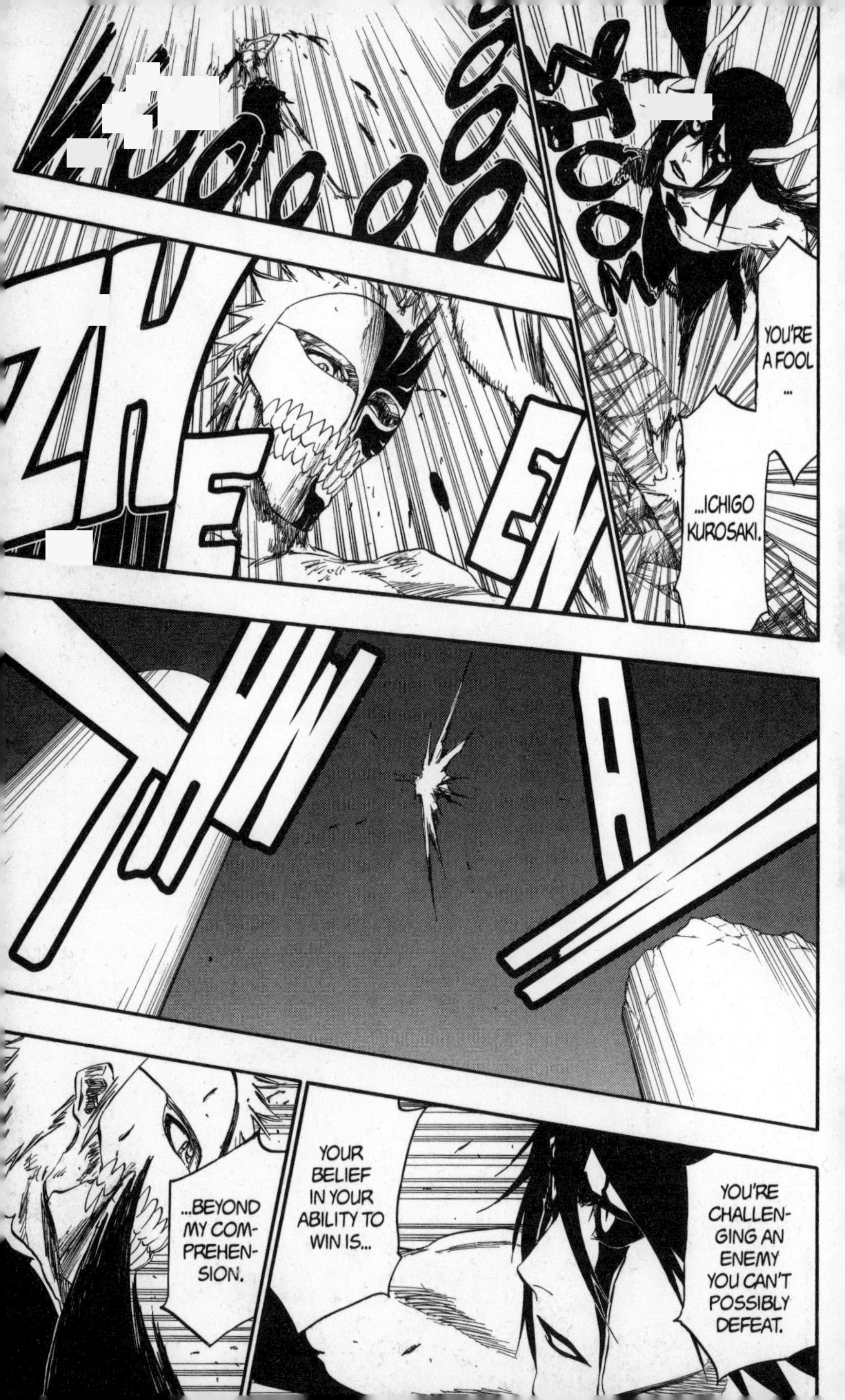
YOU'RE A FOOL ...
...ICHIGO KUROSAKI.
YOU'RE CHALLEN-GING AN ENEMY YOU CAN'T POSSIBLY DEFEAT.
YOUR BELIEF IN YOUR ABILITY TO WIN IS...
...BEYOND MY COM-PREHEN-SION.

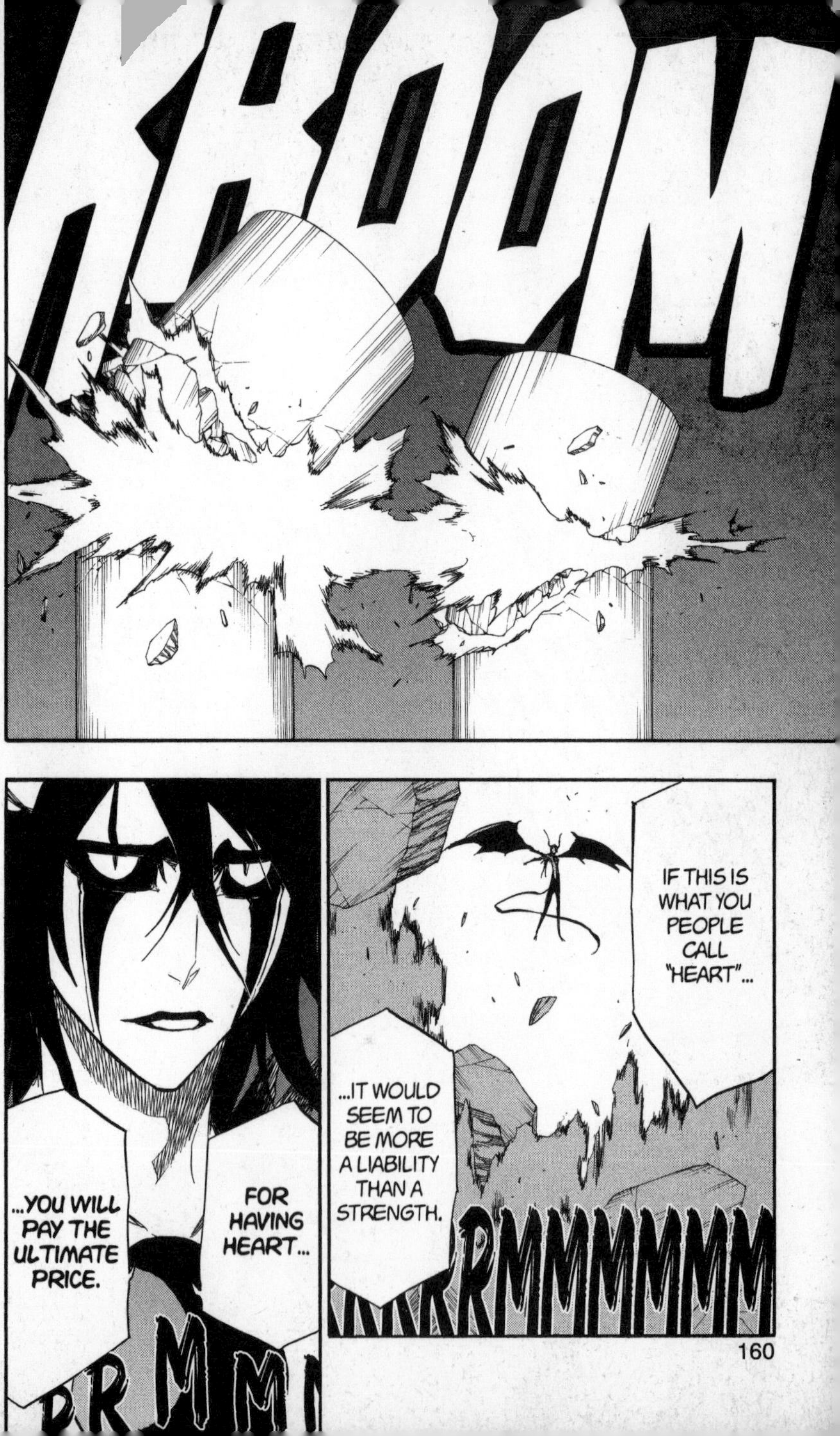
KBOOM
IF THIS IS WHAT YOU PEOPLE CALL "HEART"...
...IT WOULD SEEM TO BE MORE A LIABILITY THAN A STRENGTH.
RMMMMMMM
FOR HAVING HEART...
...YOU WILL PAY THE ULTIMATE PRICE.
DRMM

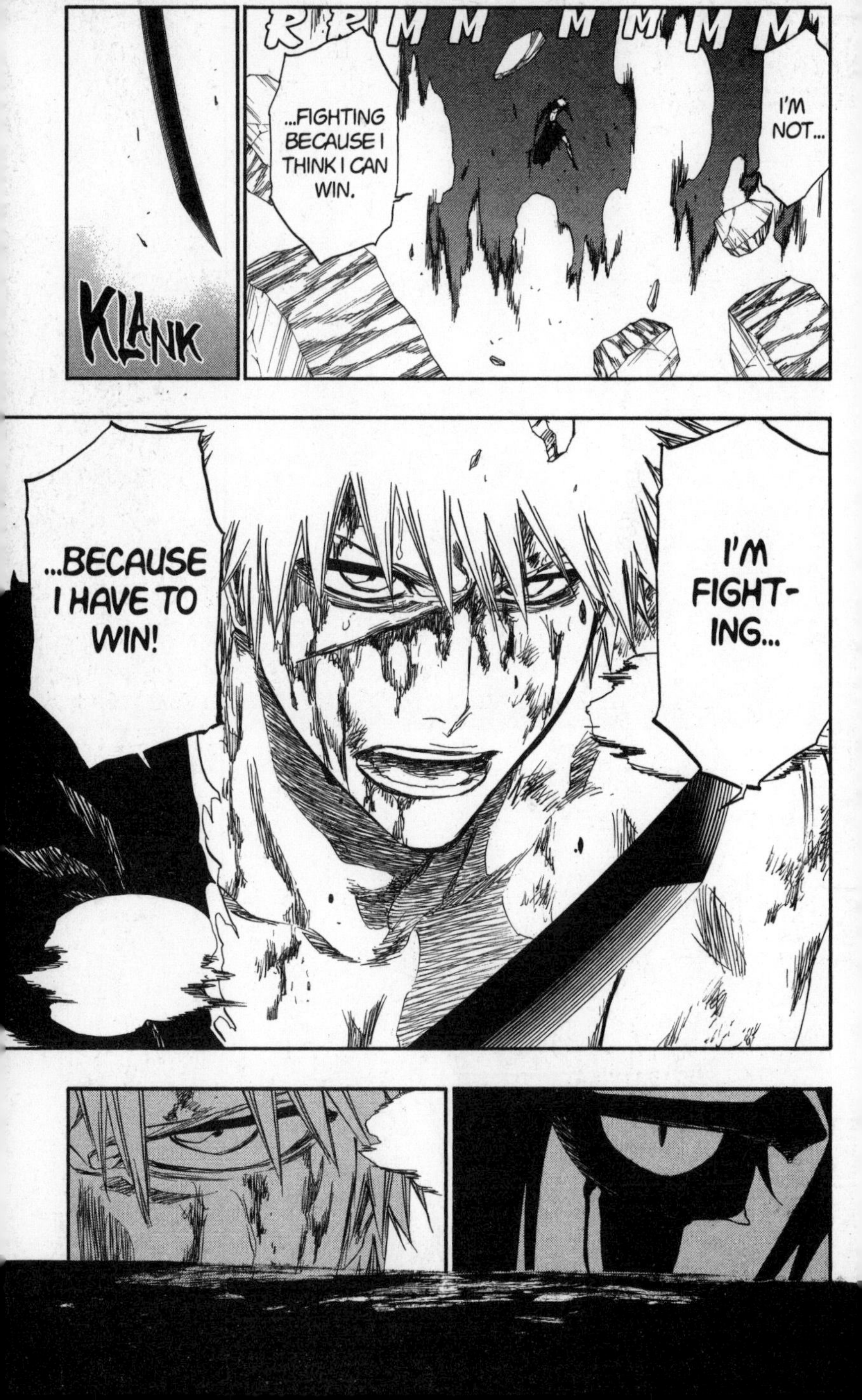
RRMM MMMM
I'M NOT...
...FIGHTING BECAUSE I THINK I CAN WIN.
KLANK
I'M FIGHT-ING...
...BECAUSE I HAVE TO WIN!

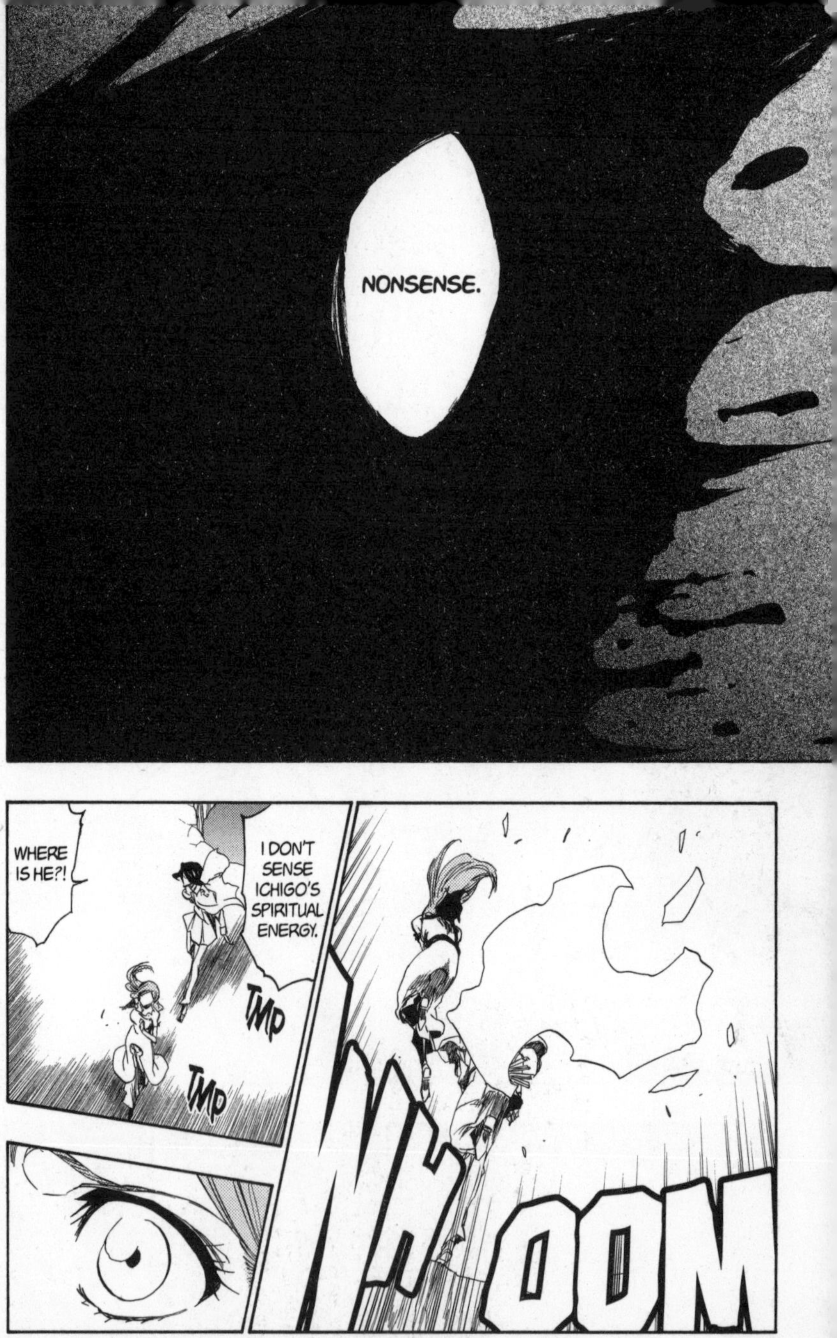
NONSENSE.
WHOOM
I DON'T SENSE ICHIGO'S SPIRITUAL ENERGY.
WHERE IS HE?!
TMP
TMP

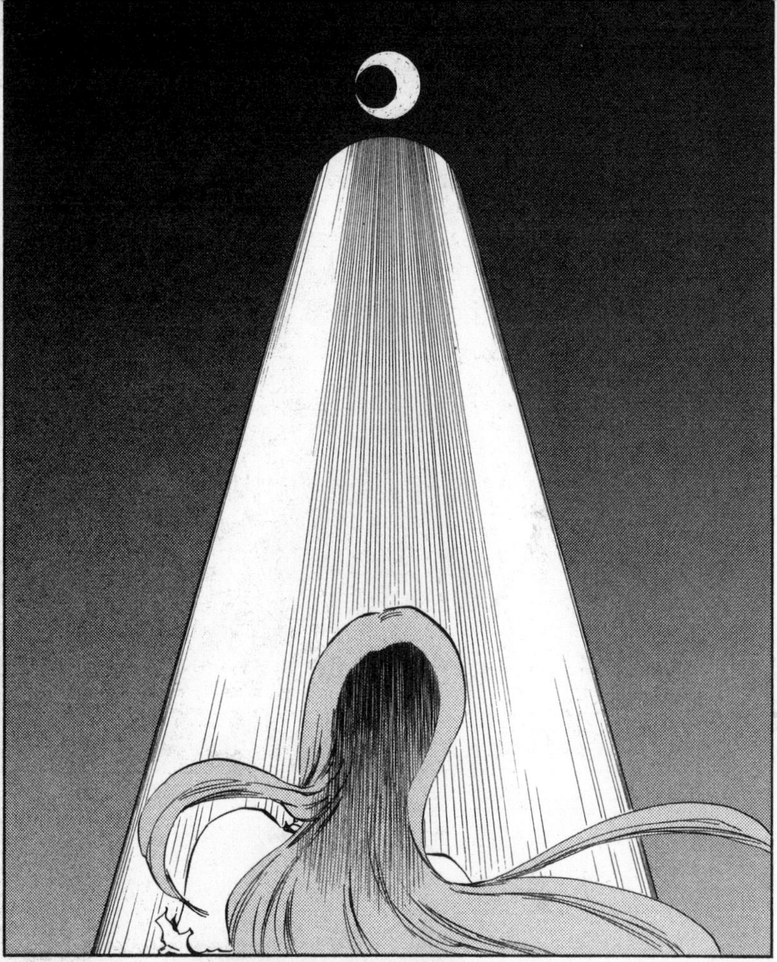

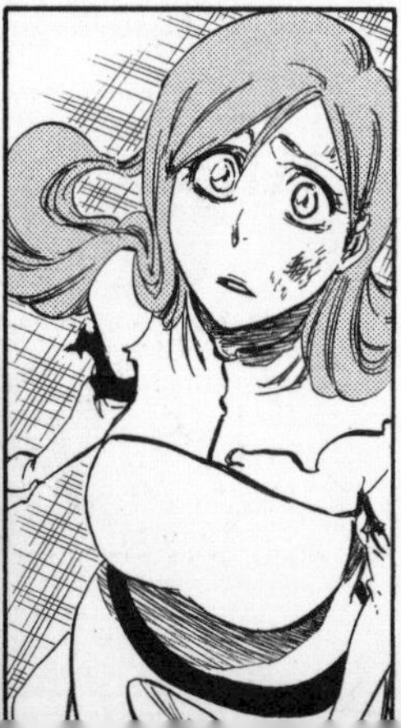

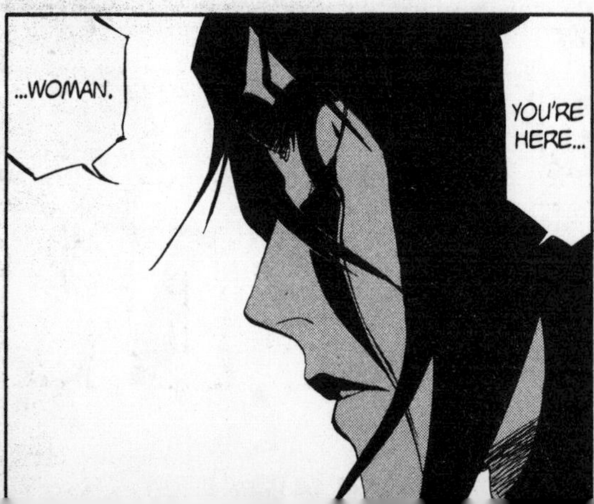
...WOMAN.
YOU'RE HERE...

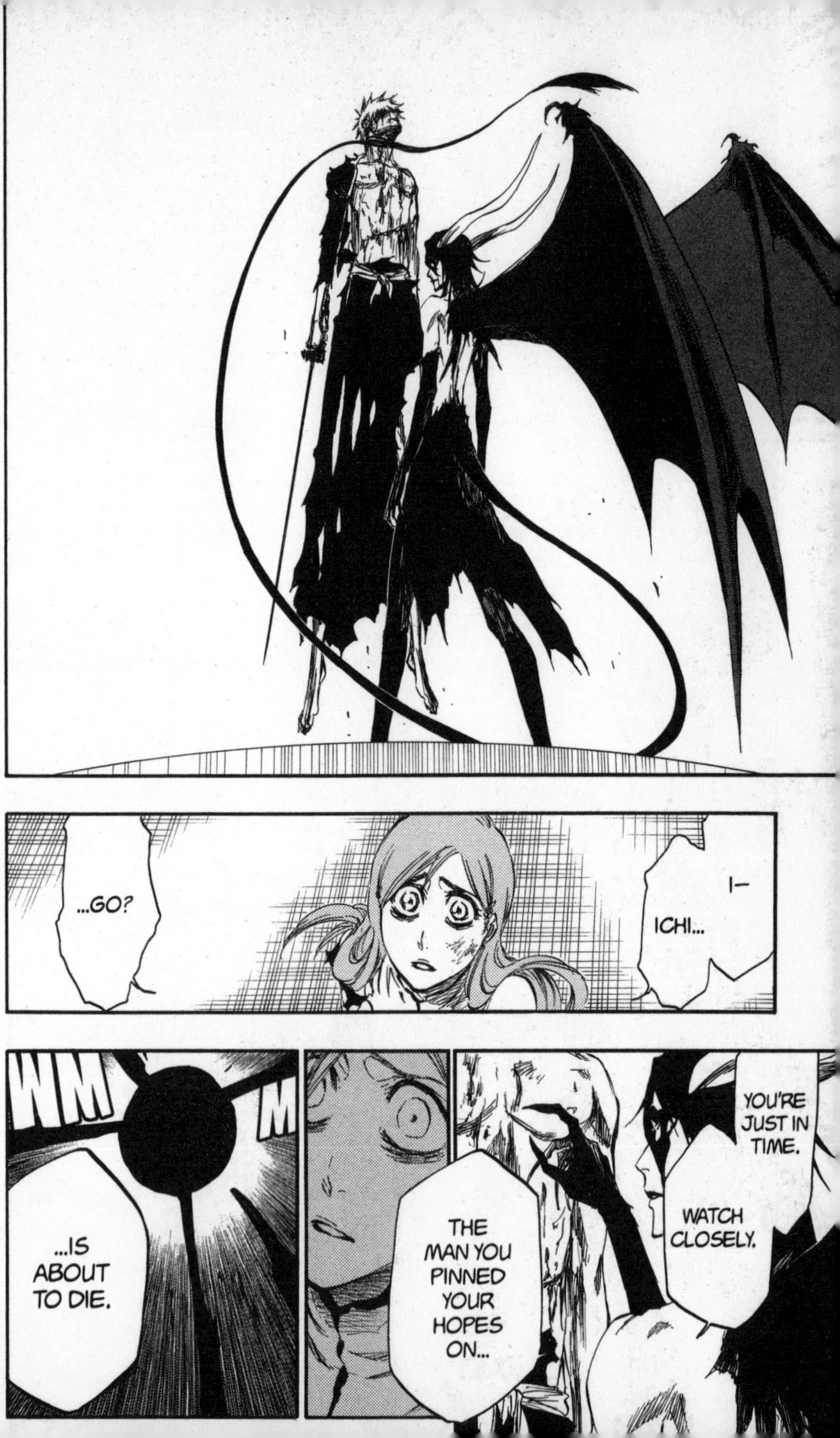
I— ICHI...
...GO?
YOU'RE JUST IN TIME.
WATCH CLOSELY.
THE MAN YOU PINNED YOUR HOPES ON...
WM
M
...IS ABOUT TO DIE.

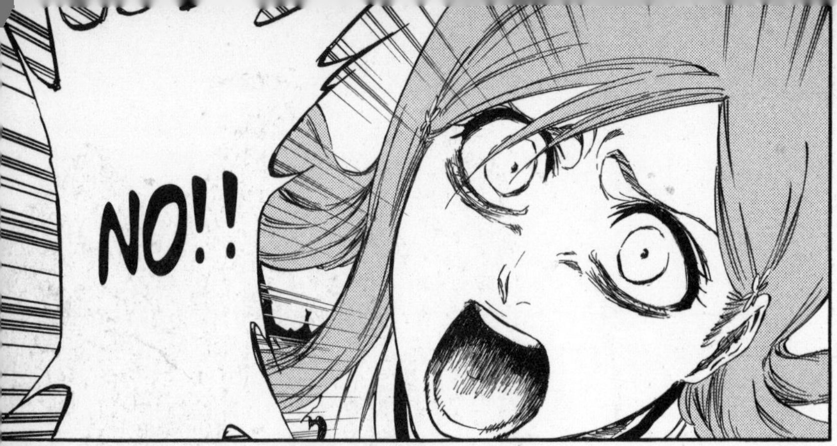
NO!!

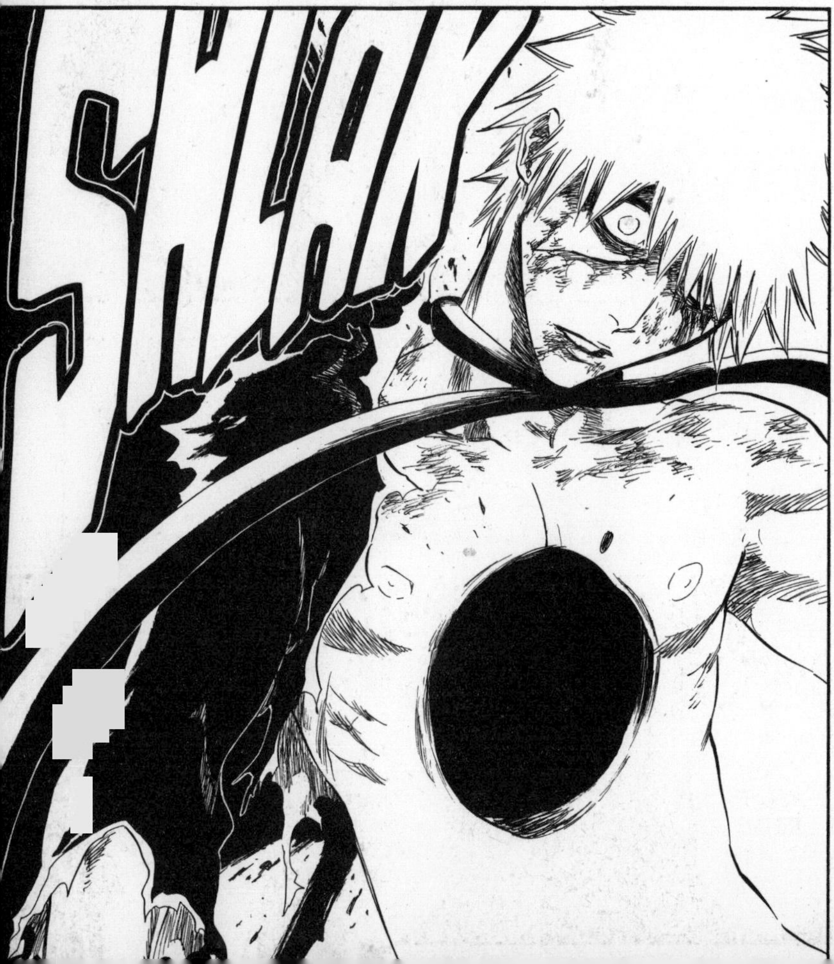

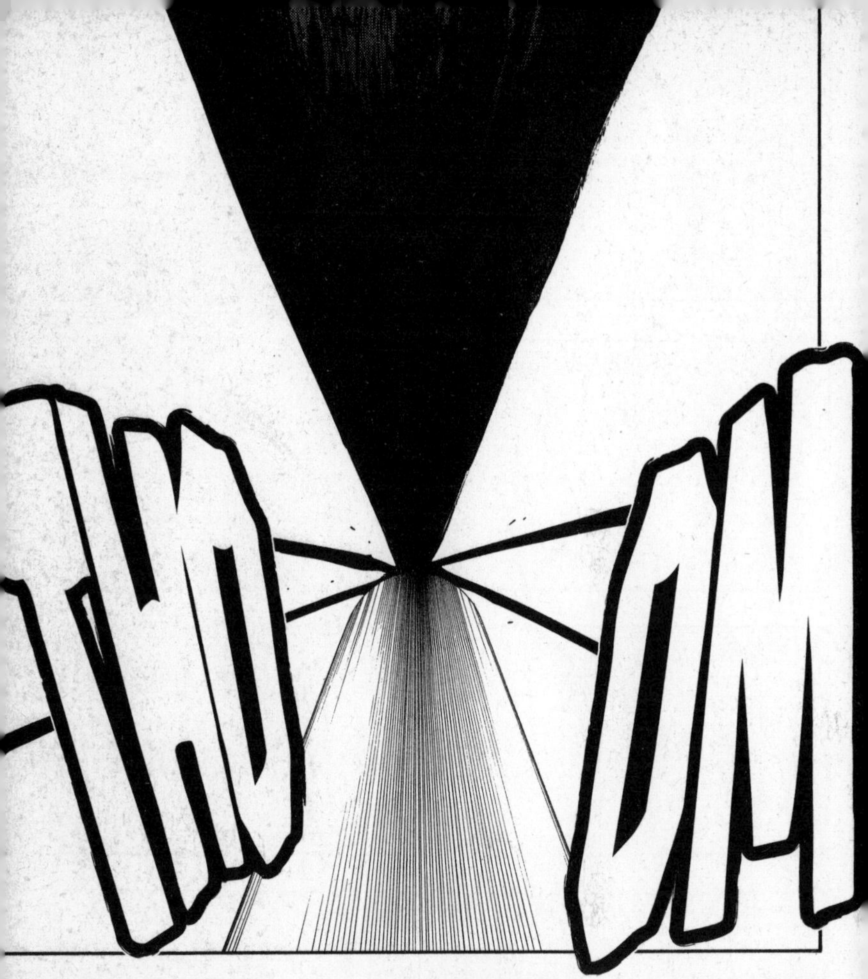
THOOM

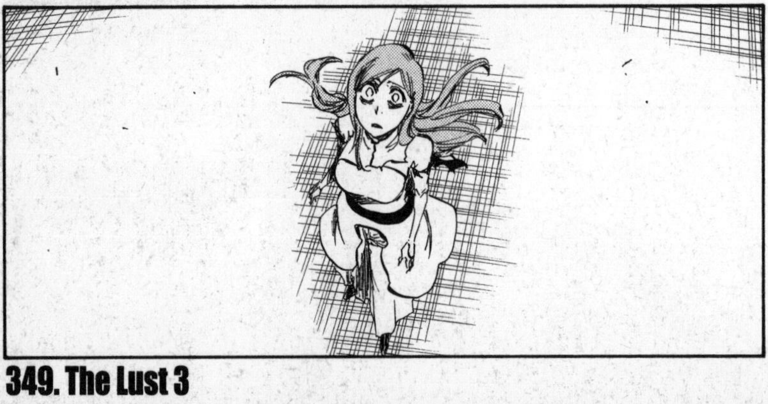

349. The Lust 3

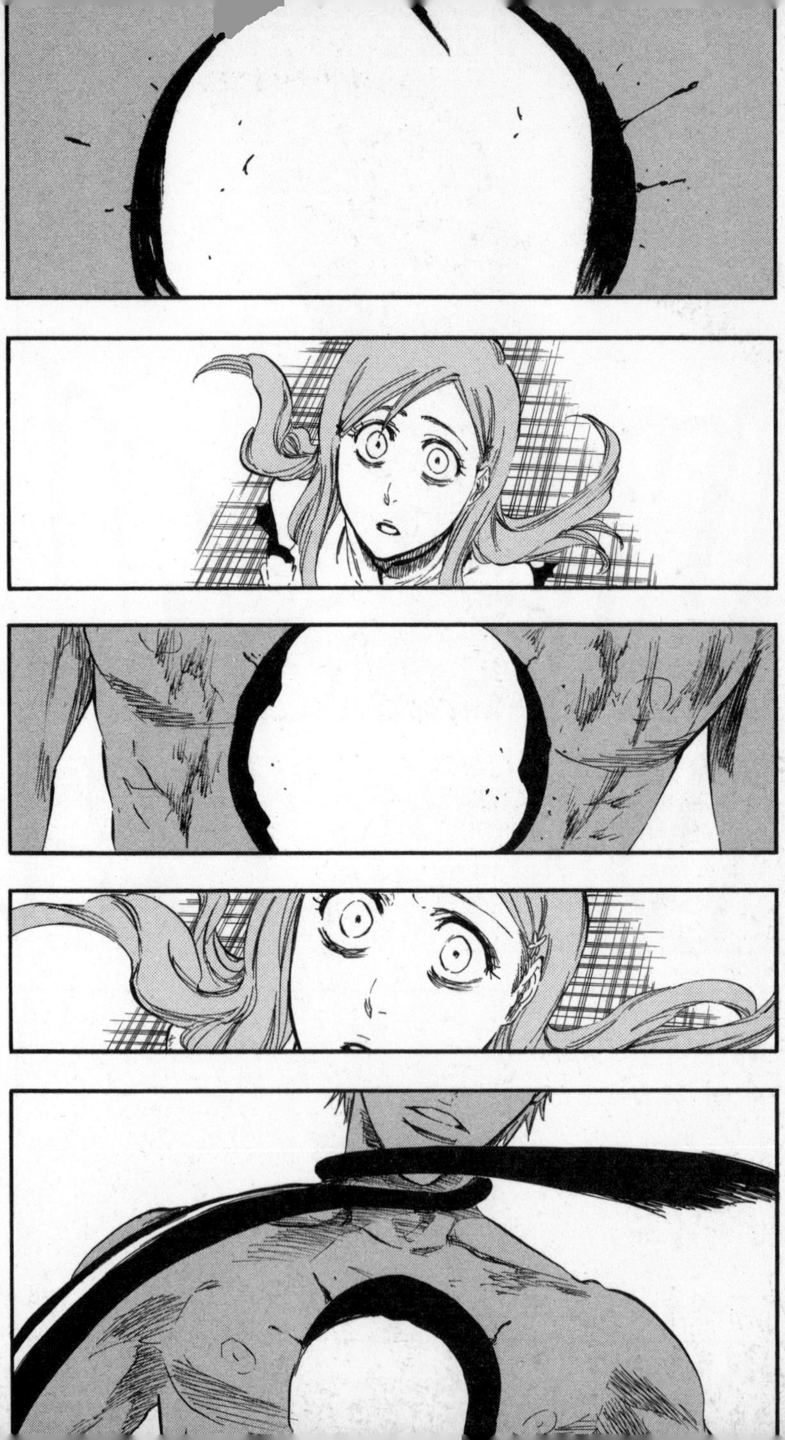

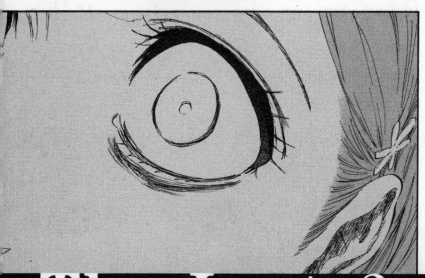

The Lust 3

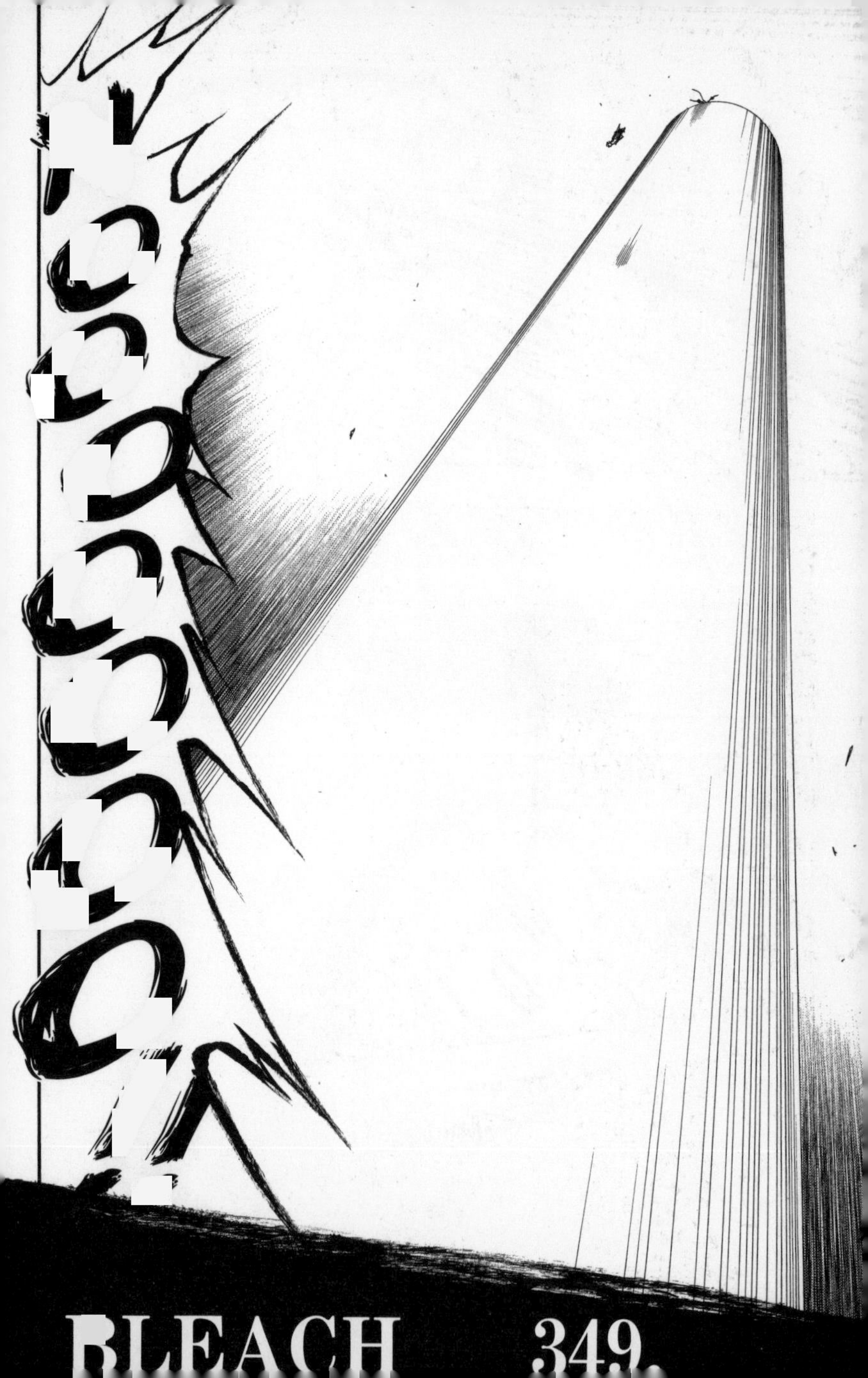
BLEACH 349.

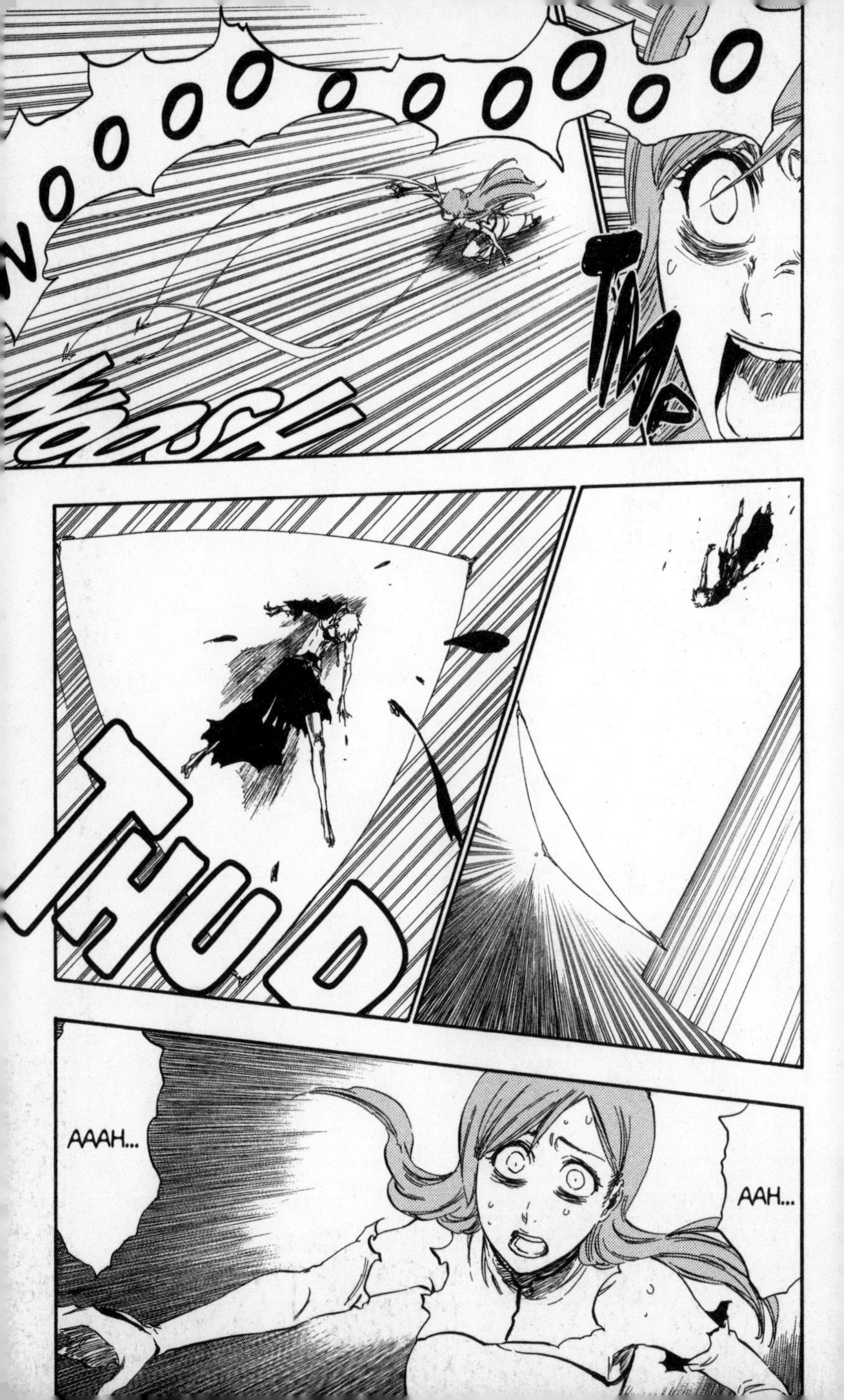
TMP
WOOOOOOOOOO
WOOSH!
THUD
AAH...
AAAH...

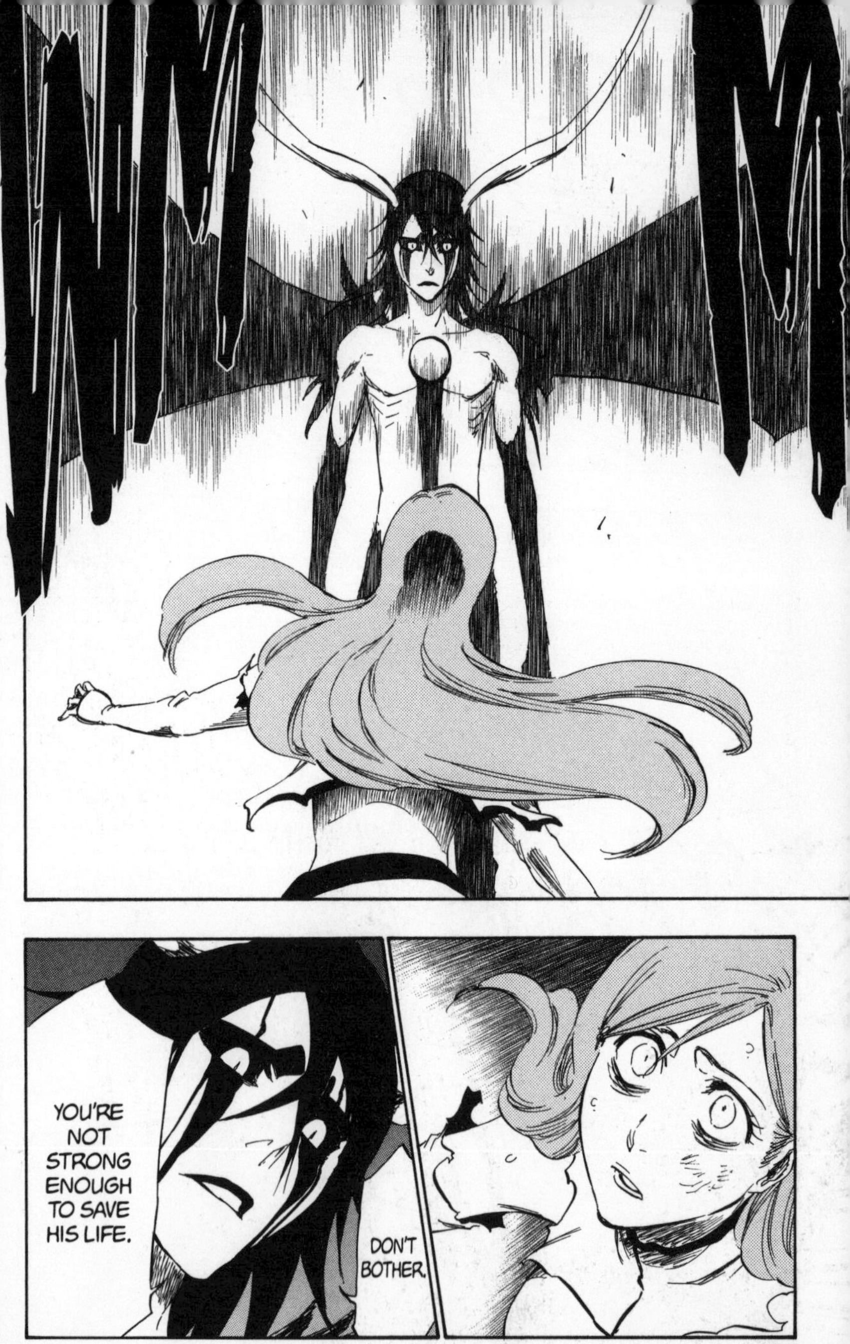
DON'T BOTHER.
YOU'RE NOT STRONG ENOUGH TO SAVE HIS LIFE.

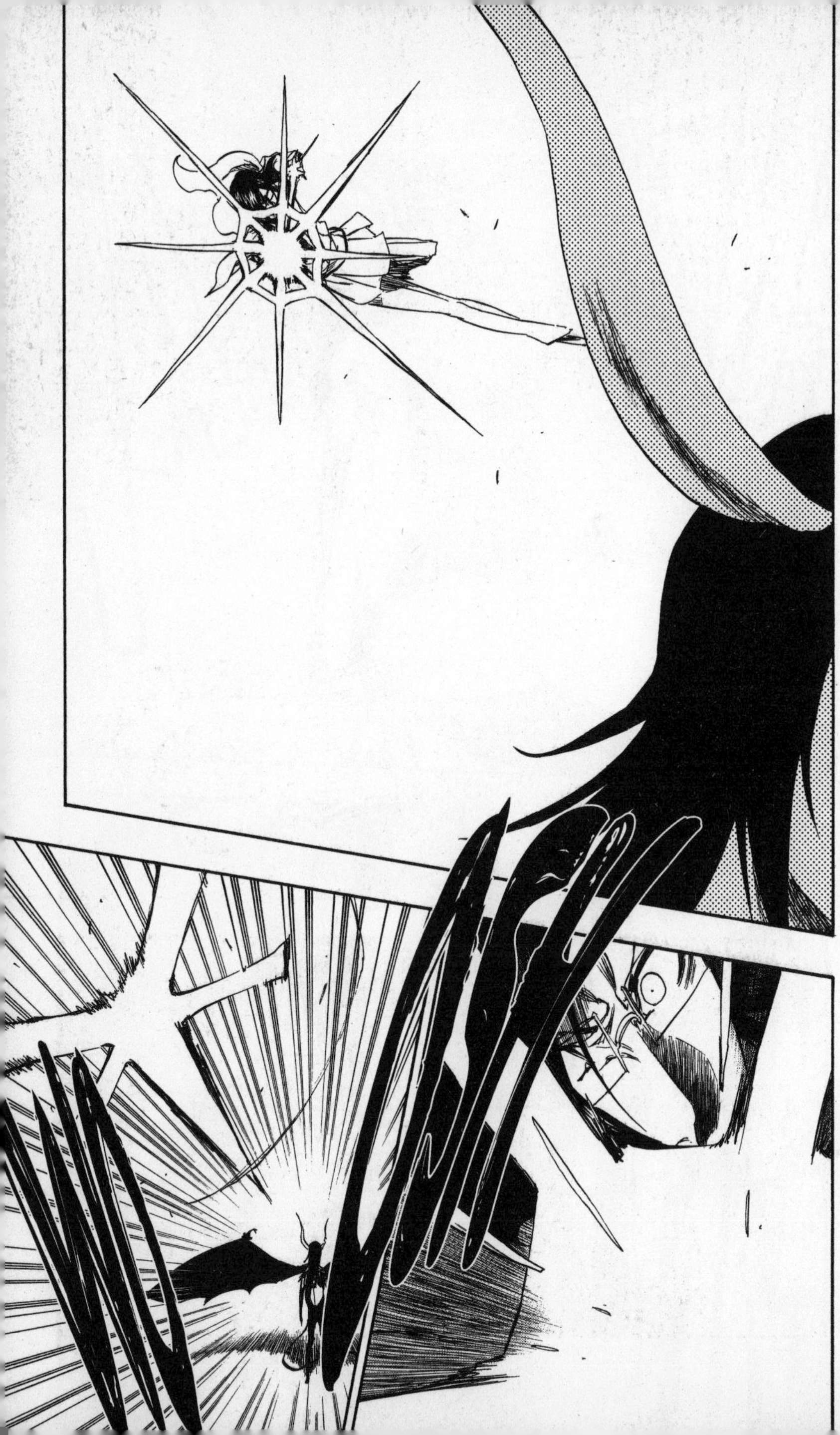

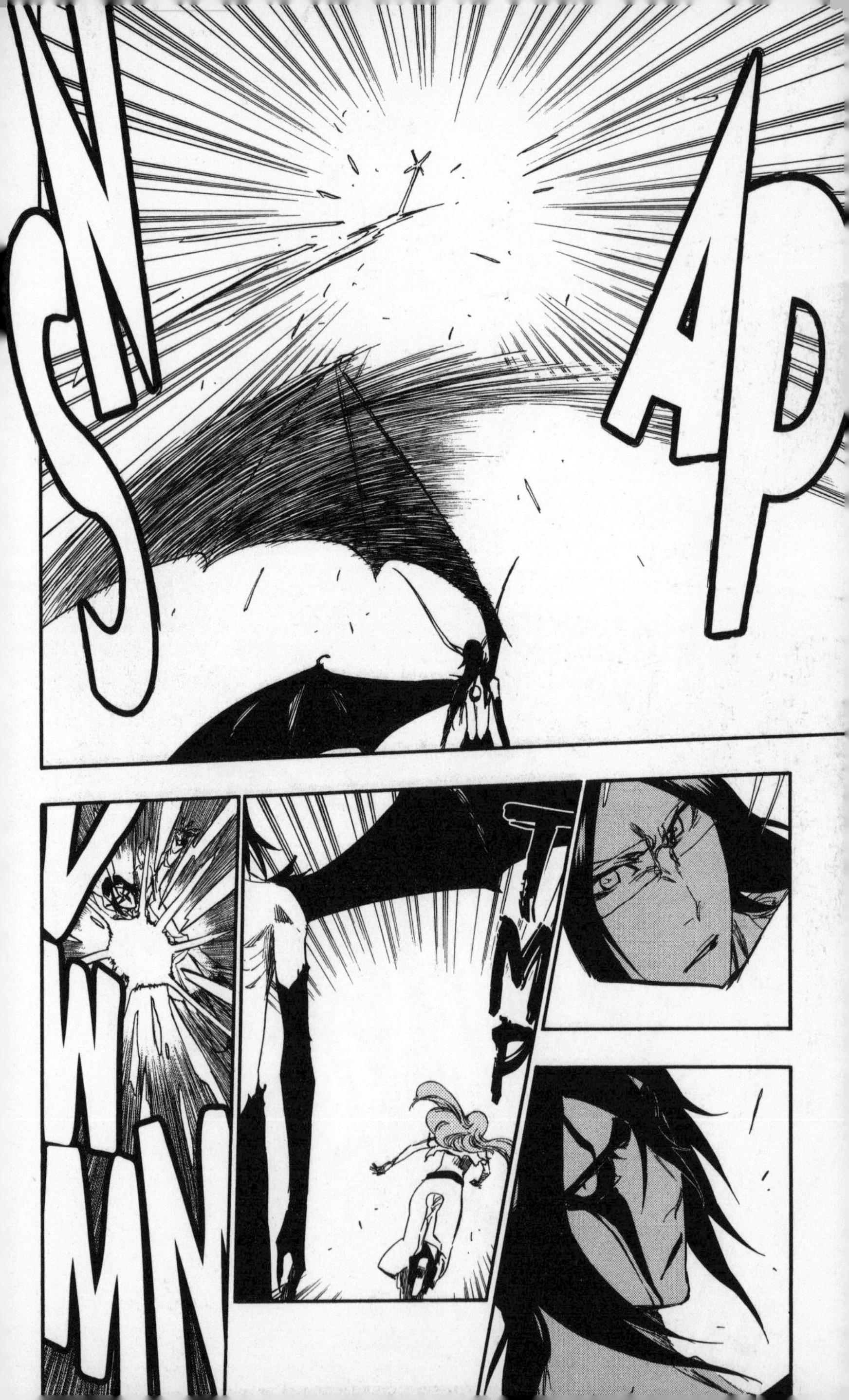
SNAP
TMP

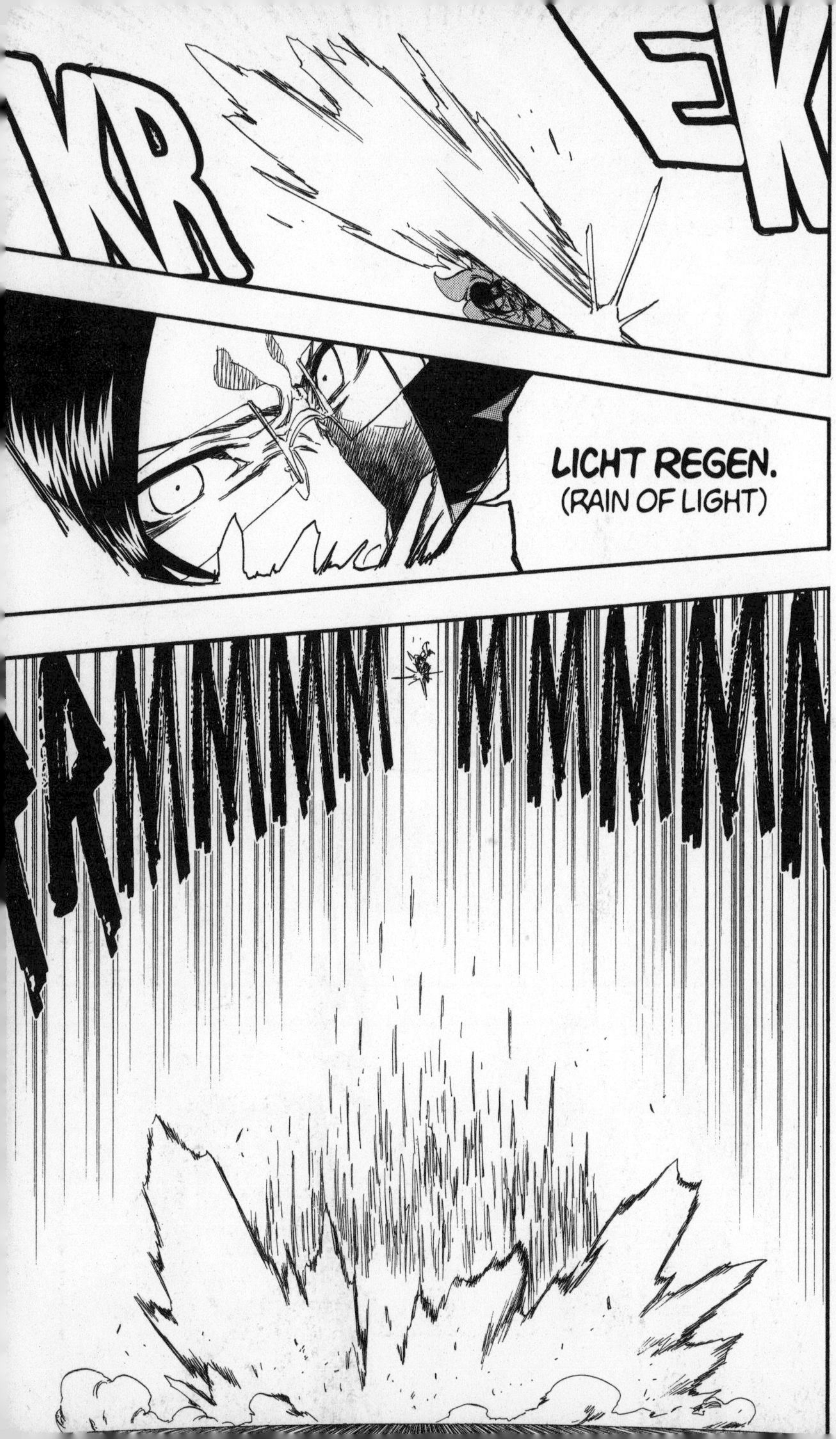
KR
EK
LICHT REGEN.
(RAIN OF LIGHT)
MMMMMM MMMMMM

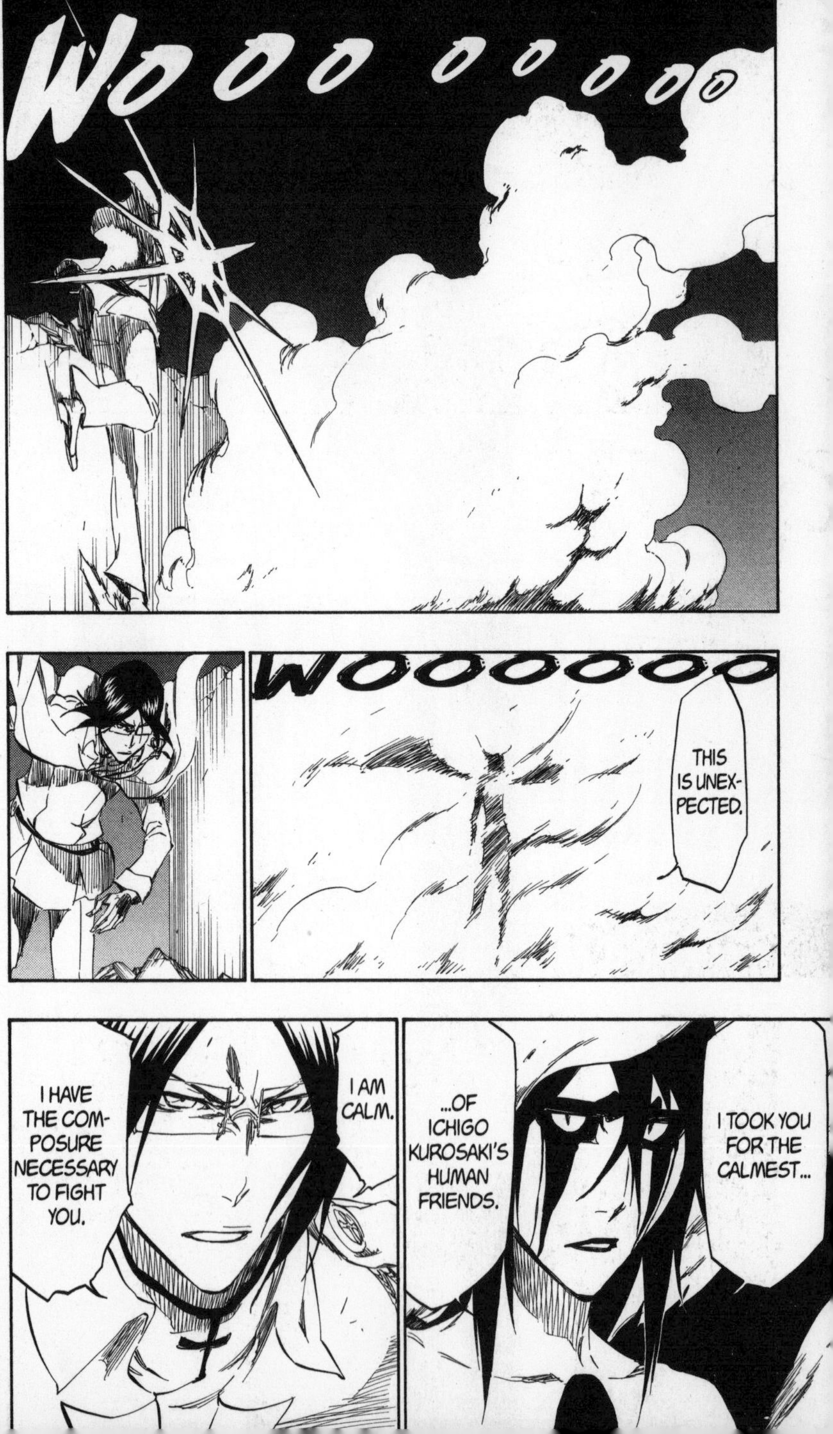
WOOOOOOOOO
WOOOOOOO
THIS IS UNEXPECTED.
I TOOK YOU FOR THE CALMEST...
...OF ICHIGO KUROSAKI'S HUMAN FRIENDS.
I AM CALM.
I HAVE THE COMPOSURE NECESSARY TO FIGHT YOU.

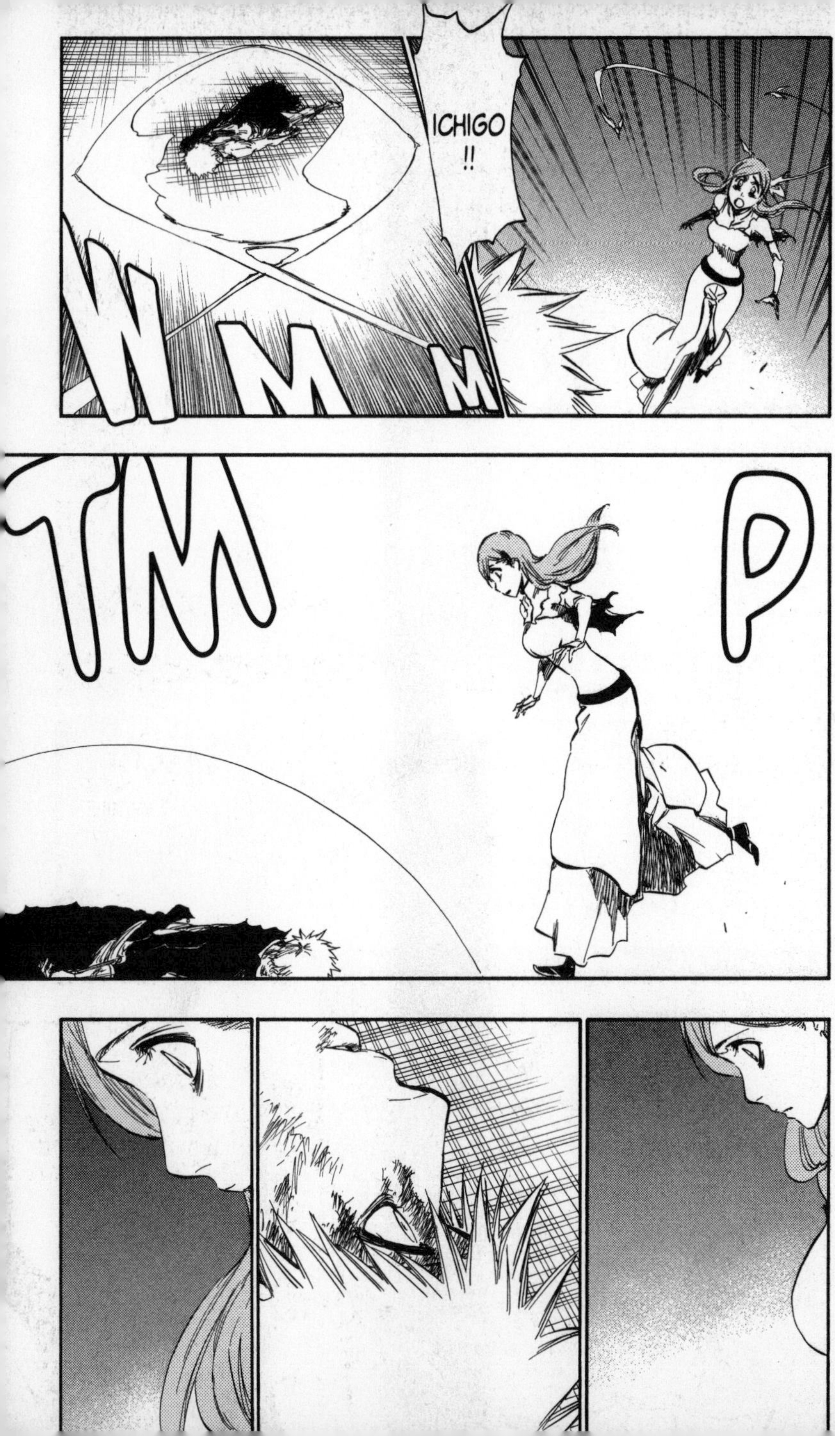
ICHIGO !!
WMMM
TMP

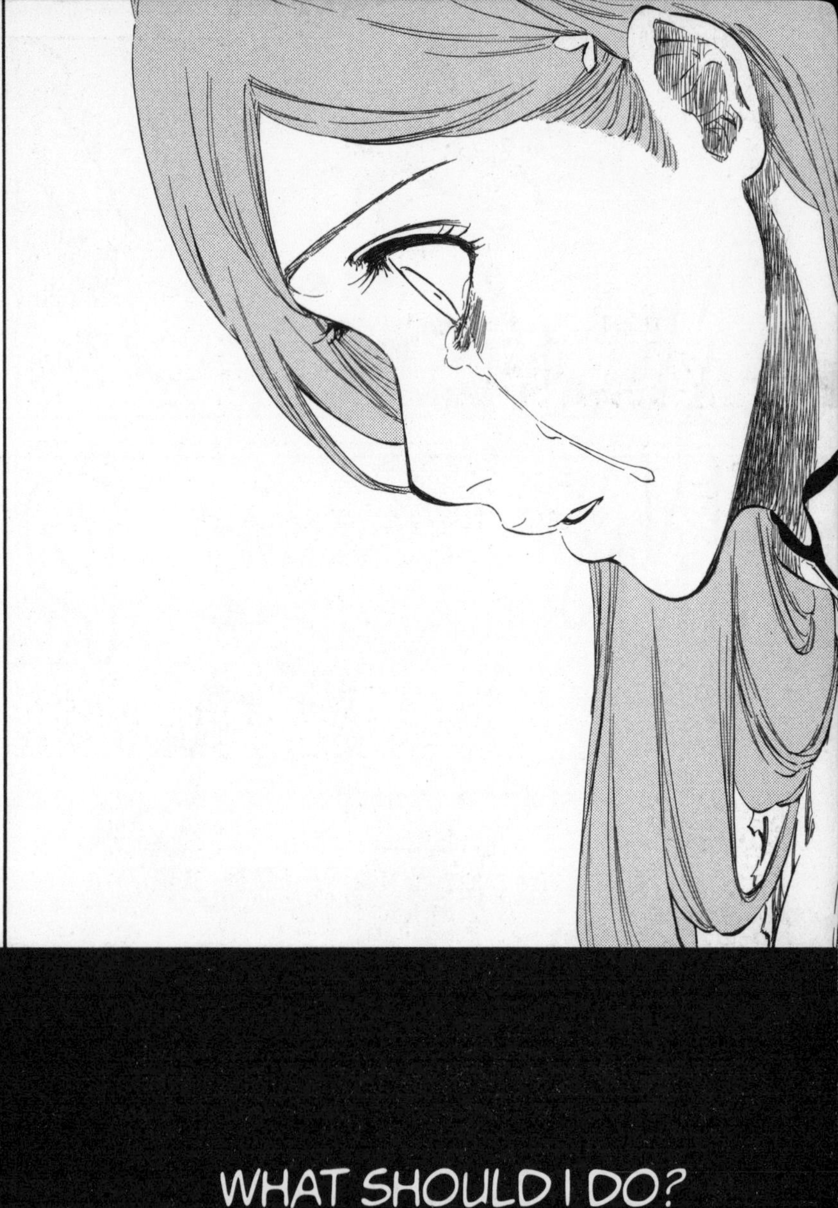
WHAT SHOULD I DO?

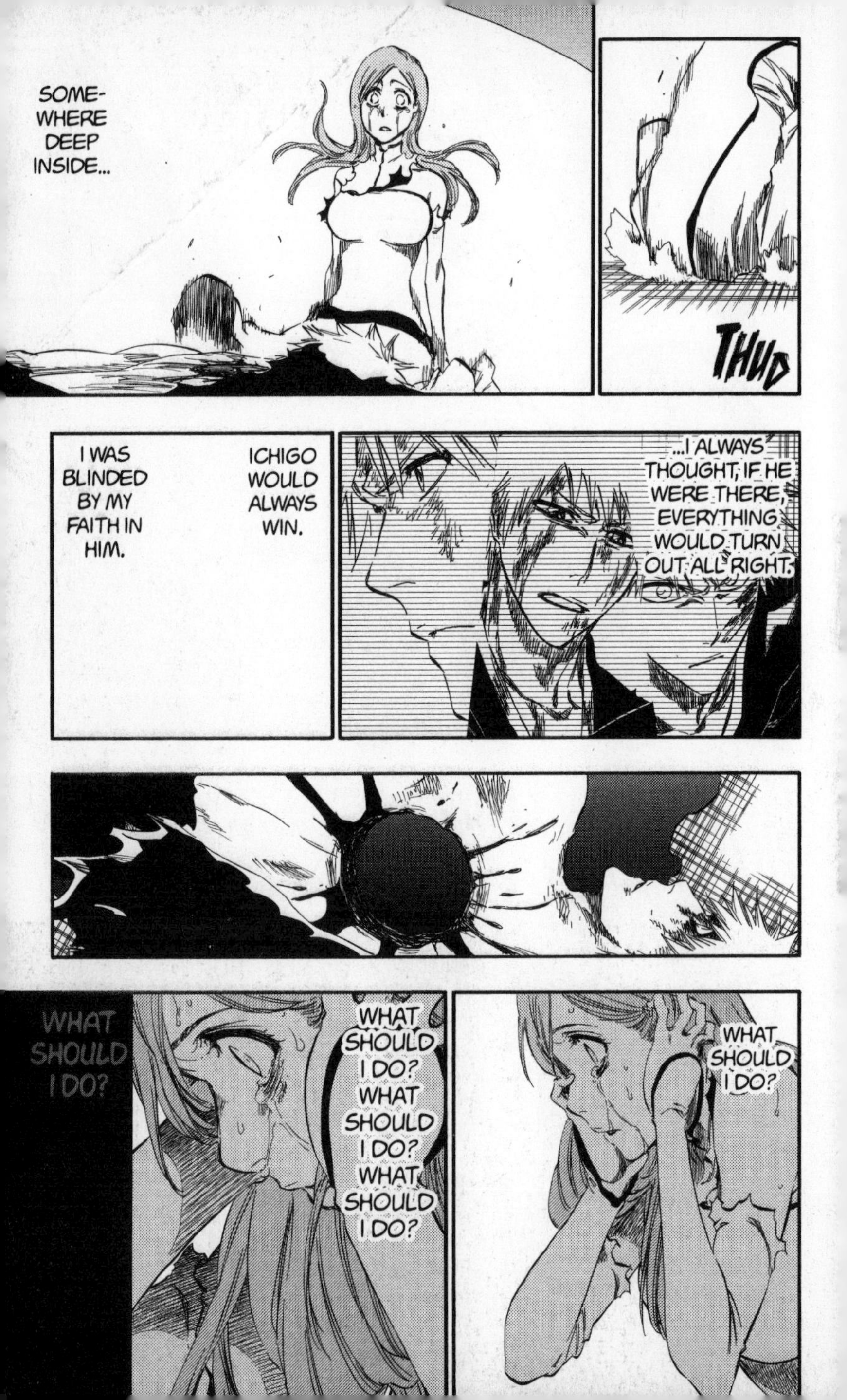
THUD
SOME-WHERE DEEP INSIDE...
...I ALWAYS THOUGHT, IF HE WERE THERE, EVERYTHING WOULD TURN OUT ALL RIGHT.
ICHIGO WOULD ALWAYS WIN.
I WAS BLINDED BY MY FAITH IN HIM.
WHAT SHOULD I DO?
WHAT SHOULD I DO? WHAT SHOULD I DO? WHAT SHOULD I DO?
WHAT SHOULD I DO?

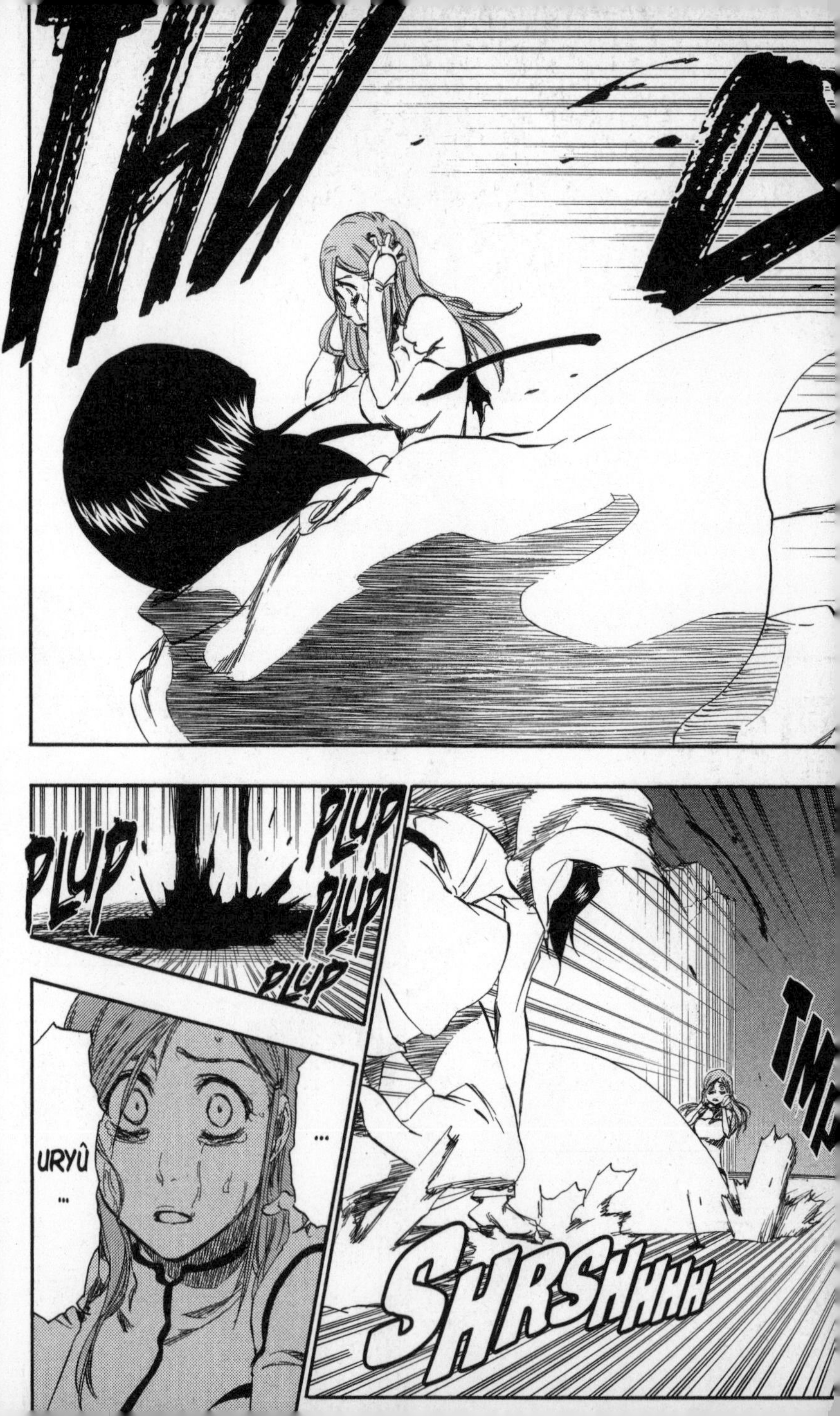
THUD
SHRSHHHH
PLUP
PLUP
PLUP
PLUP
...
URYÛ
...

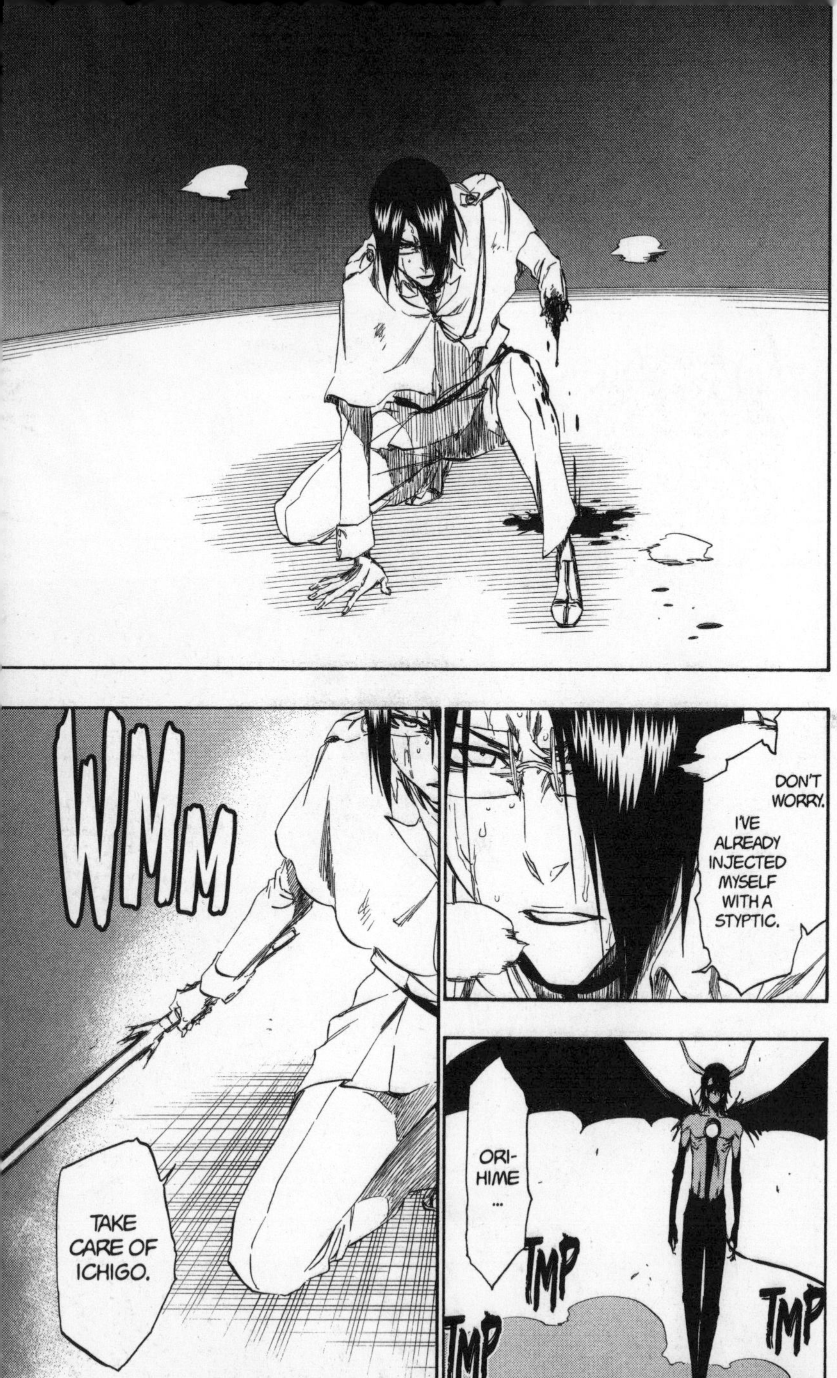
DON'T WORRY.
I'VE ALREADY INJECTED MYSELF WITH A STYPTIC.
ORI-HIME ...
TMP
TMP
TMP
WMM
TAKE CARE OF ICHIGO.

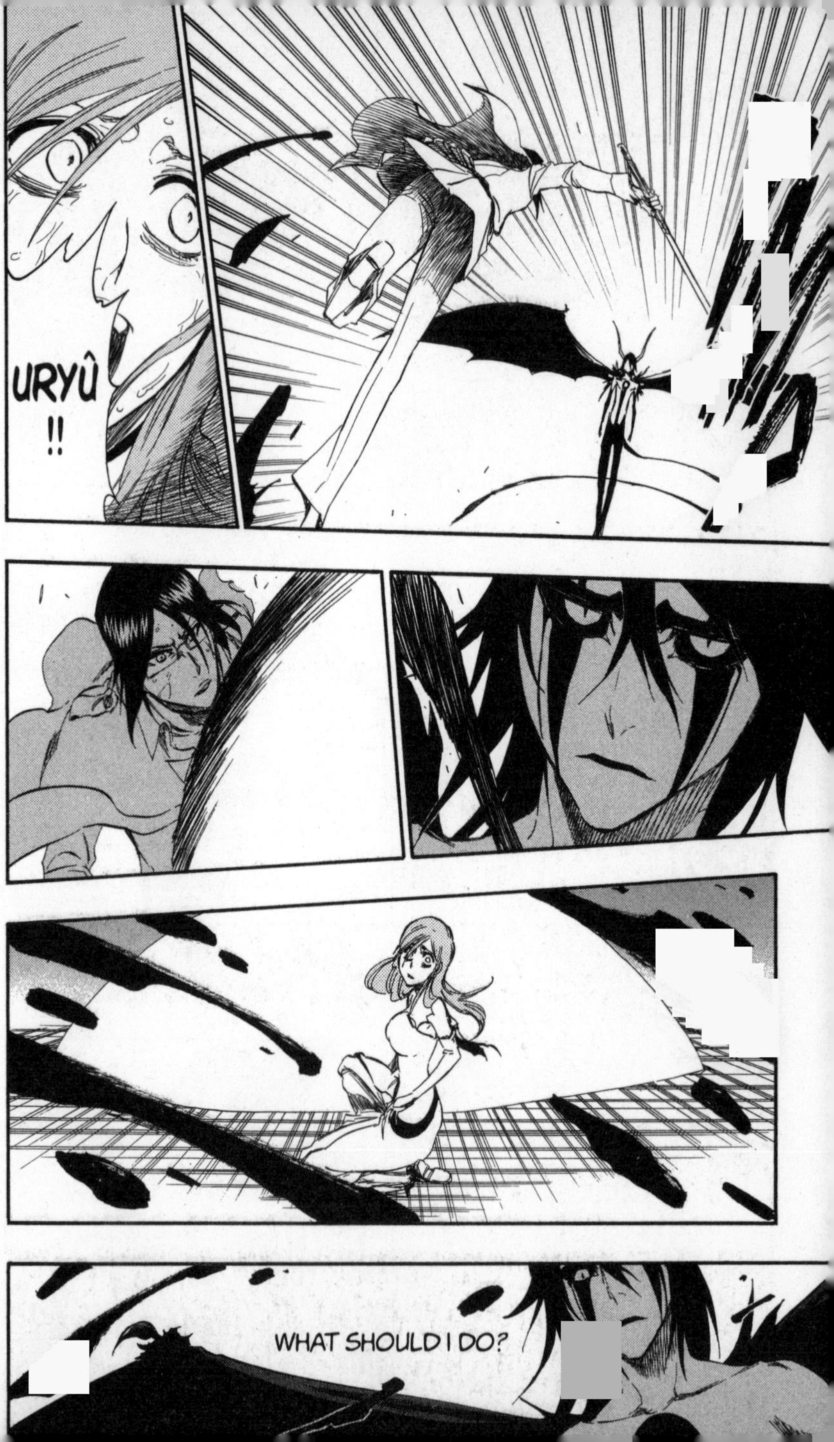
URYÛ !!
WHAT SHOULD I DO?

READ THIS WAY
WHAT SHOULD I DO, ICHIGO?
I DON'T KNOW WHAT TO DO!
I...
...DON'T KNOW ANYTHING.
ICHIGO...
ICHIGO...
ICHIGO...
ICHIGO, ICHIGO, ICHIGO...
ICHIGO...
HELP ME.

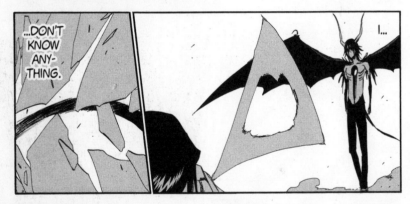

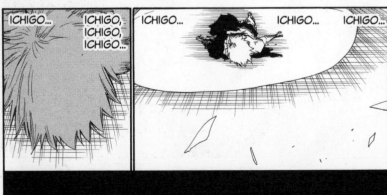

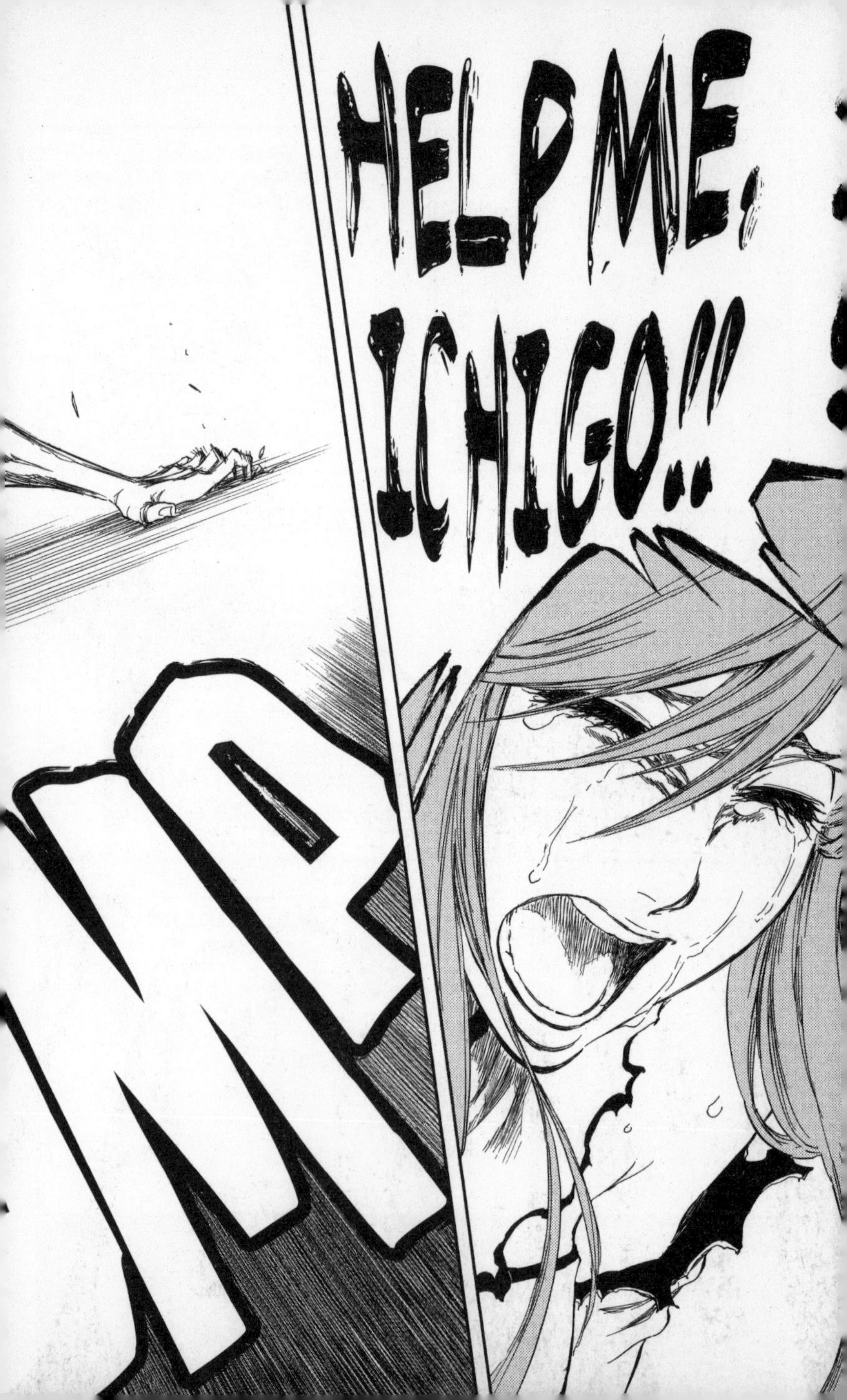
HELP ME, ICHIGO!!

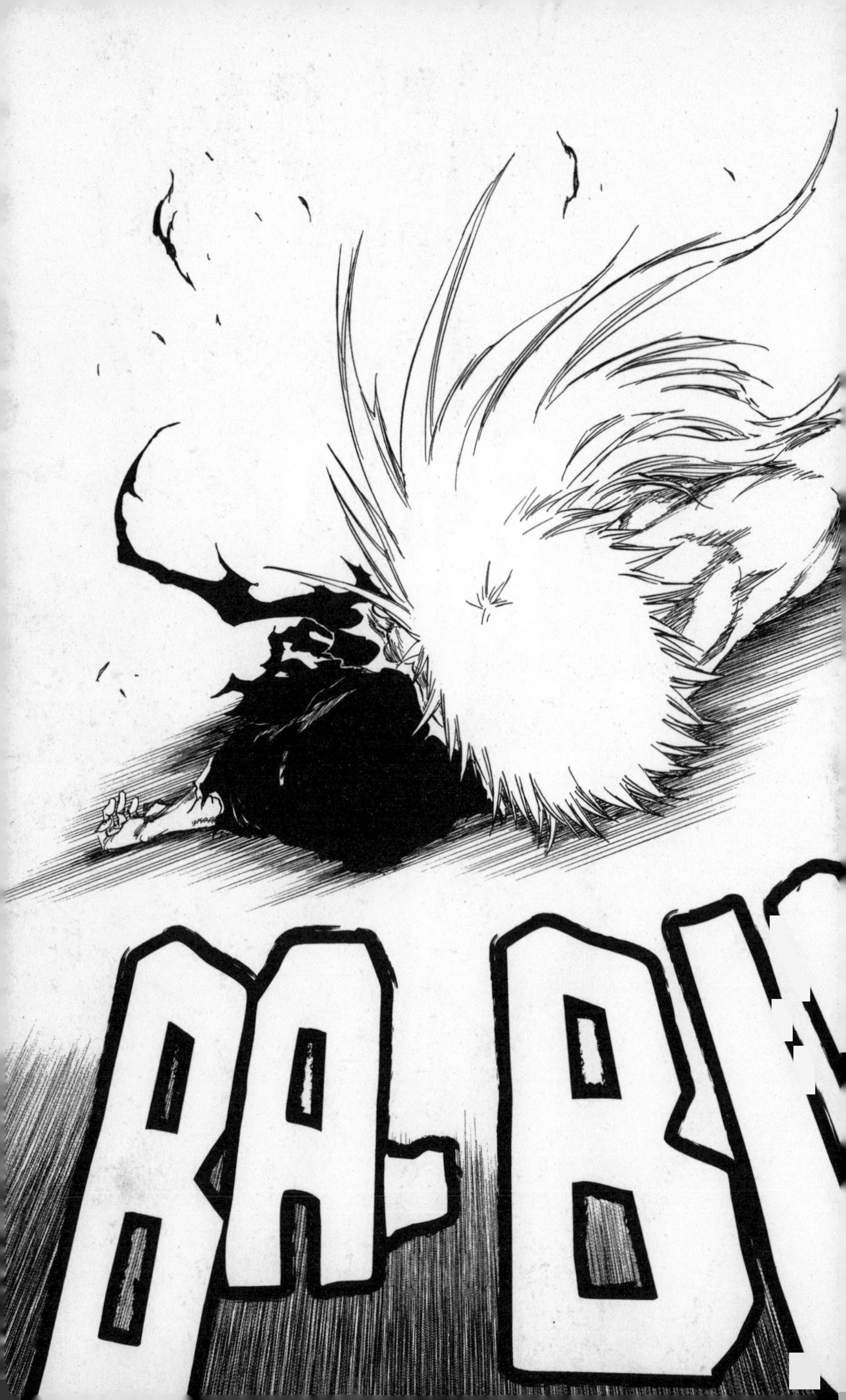
BA-B

CONTI
NUED
IN
BLEACH
41

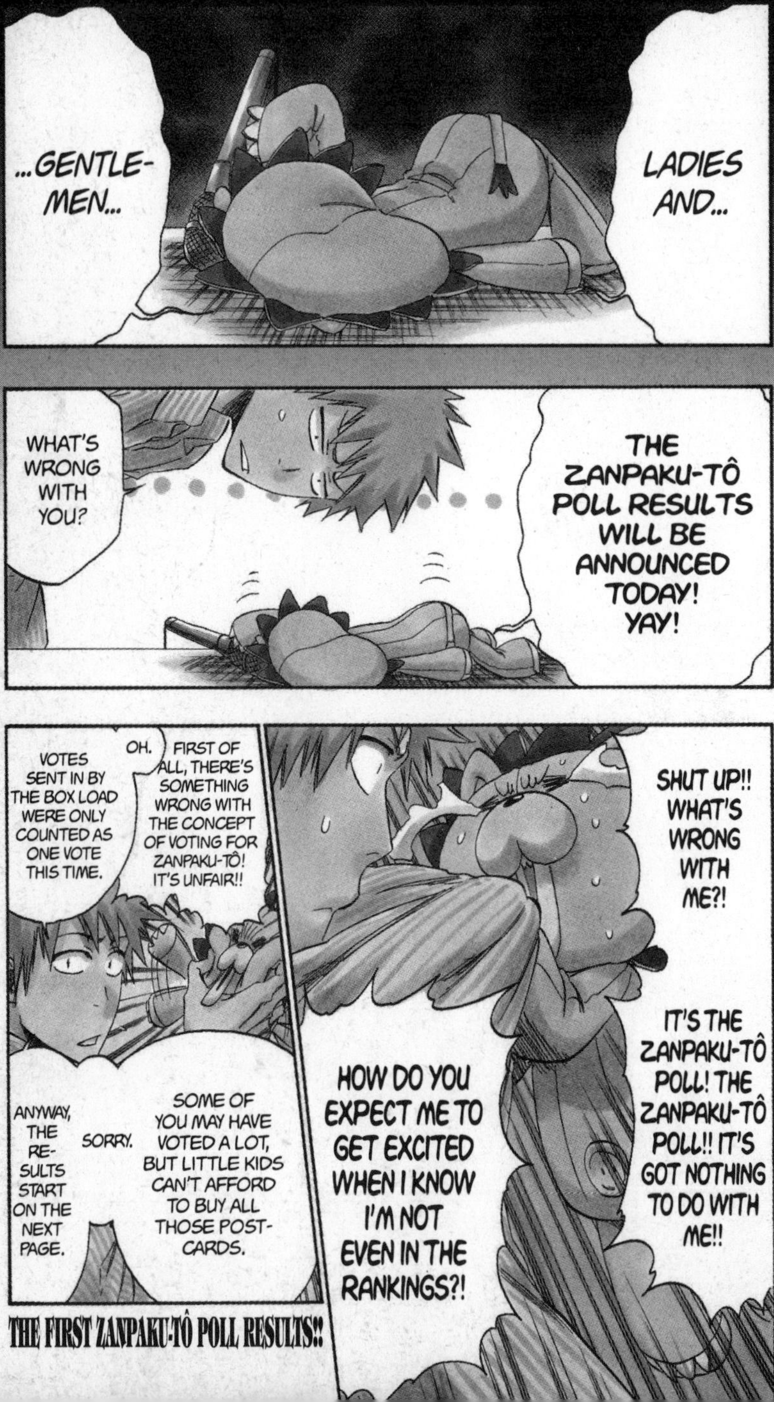
LADIES AND...
...GENTLEMEN...
THE ZANPAKU-TÔ POLL RESULTS WILL BE ANNOUNCED TODAY! YAY!
WHAT'S WRONG WITH YOU?
SHUT UP!! WHAT'S WRONG WITH ME?!
IT'S THE ZANPAKU-TÔ POLL! THE ZANPAKU-TÔ POLL!! IT'S GOT NOTHING TO DO WITH ME!!
HOW DO YOU EXPECT ME TO GET EXCITED WHEN I KNOW I'M NOT EVEN IN THE RANKINGS?!
FIRST OF ALL, THERE'S SOMETHING WRONG WITH THE CONCEPT OF VOTING FOR ZANPAKU-TÔ! IT'S UNFAIR!!
OH.
VOTES SENT IN BY THE BOX LOAD WERE ONLY COUNTED AS ONE VOTE THIS TIME.
SOME OF YOU MAY HAVE VOTED A LOT, BUT LITTLE KIDS CAN'T AFFORD TO BUY ALL THOSE POST-CARDS.
SORRY.
ANYWAY, THE RE-SULTS START ON THE NEXT PAGE.

THE FIRST ZANPAKU-TÔ POLL RESULTS!!

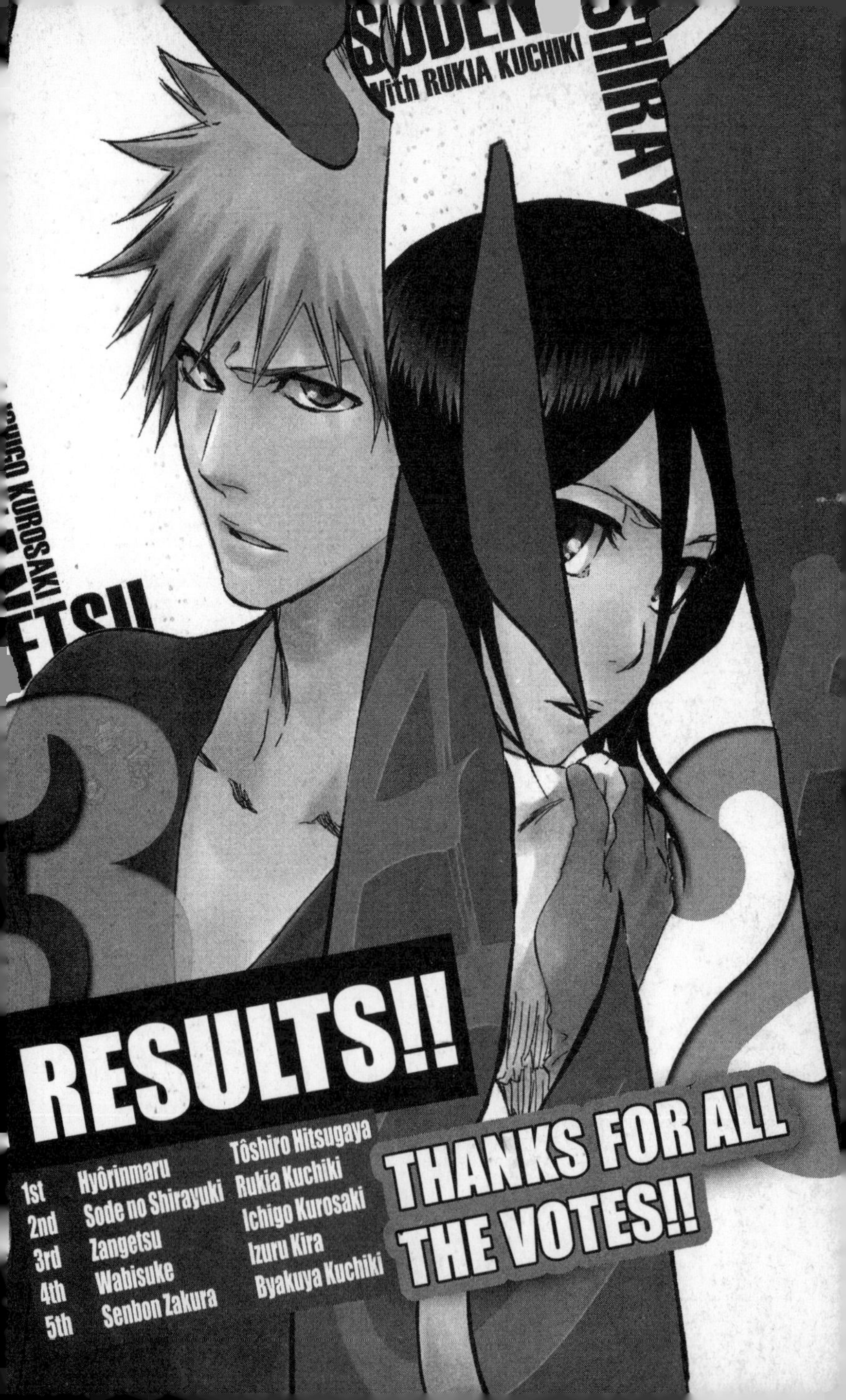
with RUKIA KUCHIKI
RESULTS!!
1st Hyôrinmaru Tôshiro Hitsugaya
2nd Sode no Shirayuki Rukia Kuchiki
3rd Zangetsu Ichigo Kurosaki
4th Wabisuke Izuru Kira
5th Senbon Zakura Byakuya Kuchiki
THANKS FOR ALL THE VOTES!!

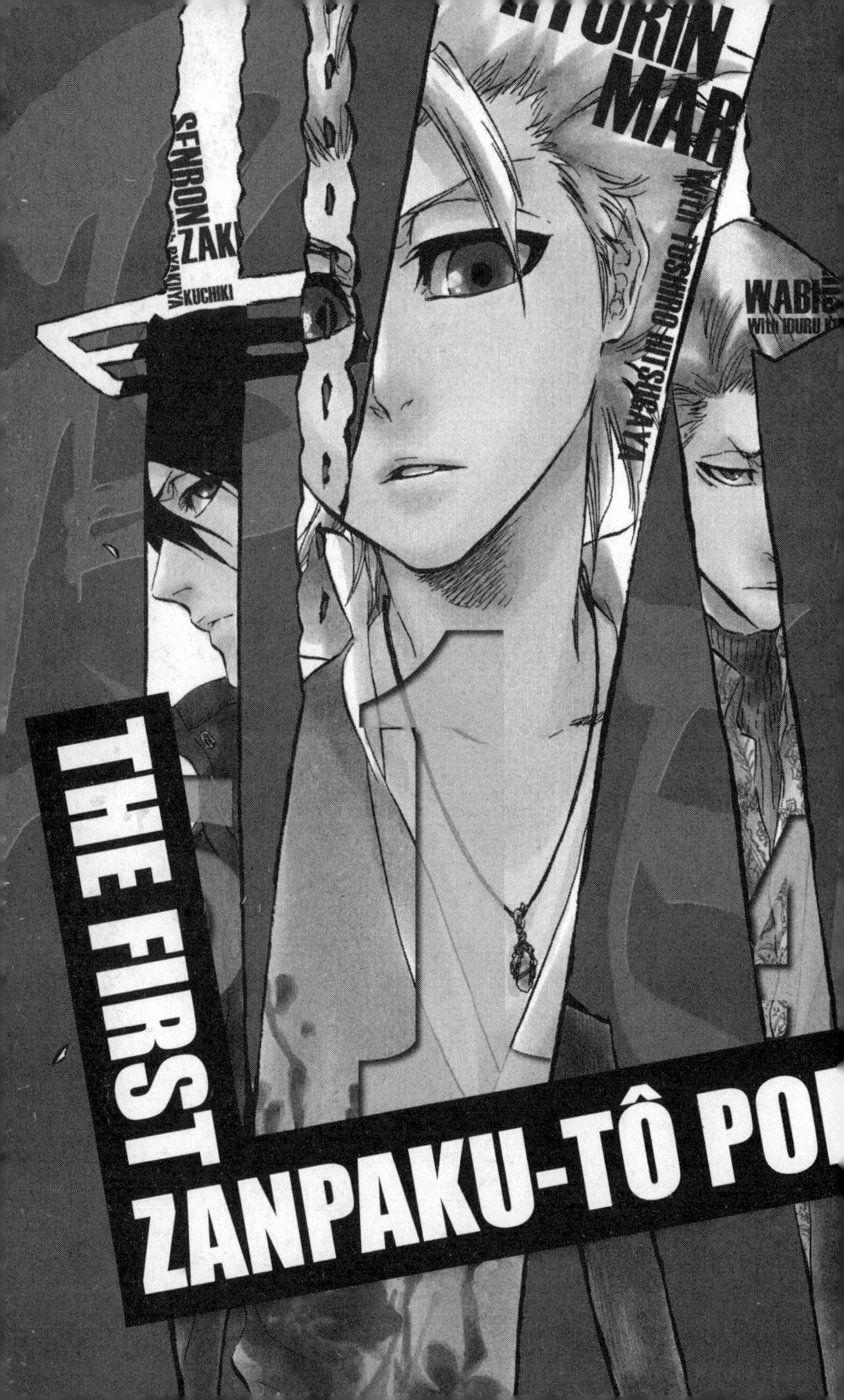

MAR
SENBON ZAKI
KUCHIKI
TOSHIRO HITSUGAYA
WABI
With IDURU
THE FIRST
ZANPAKU-TÔ PO

6th ▶ 64th!

6th
Kazeshini (Shuhei Hisagi)
7th
Zabimaru (Renji Abarai)
8th
Shinsô (Gin Ichimaru)
9th
Pantera (Grimmjow)
10th
Tensa Zangetsu (Ichigo Kurosaki)
11th
Ginrei Kojaku (Uryû Ishida)
12th
Benihime (Kisuke Urahara)
13th
Hôzuki-maru (Ikkaku Madarame)
14th
Ruri Iro Kujaku (Yumichika Ayasegawa)
15th
Suzumebachi (Soifon)
16th
Daiguren Hyôrinmaru (Tôshiro Hitsugaya)
17th
Sôgyo Kotowari (Jushiro Ukitake)
18th
Kyoka Suigetsu (Sousuke Aizen)
Neji Bana (Kaien Shiba)
Haineko (Rangiku Matsumoto)
21st
Seeleschneider (Uryû Ishida)
22nd
Kojaku (Uryû Ishida)
23rd
Tobiume (Momo Hinamori)
La Lujuriosa (Szayelaporro)
25th
Senbon Zakura Kageyoshi/Gôkei/Shûkei/Hakuteiken (Byakuya Kuchiki)
26th
Ashisogi Jizô (Mayuri Kurotsuchi)
27th
Fujikujaku (Yumichika Ayasegawa)
Ryûmon Hôzuki-Maru (Ikkaku Madarame)
29th
Kenpachi Zaraki's Zanpaku-tô
30th
Santa Teresa (Nnoitra)
31st
Hisago-maru (Hanataro Yamada)
32nd
Ryûjin Jakka (Shigekuni Genryûsai Yamamoto)
33rd
Katen Kyôkotsu (Shunsui Kyôraku)
Shunshun Rikka (Orihime Inoue)
Gamuza (Nelliel)
36th
Hihi-oh Zabimaru (Renji Abarai)
Mirokumaru (Senna)
38th
Tachikaze (Kensei Muguruma)
39th
Minazuki (Retsu Unohana)
40th
Suzumushi (Kaname Tôsen)
41st
Verruga (Tesla)
Tsuchi Namazu (Zennosuke Kurumadani)
43rd
Yachiru's Zanpaku-tô
Brazo Izquierda del Diablo (Yasutora Sado)
Konjiki Jizô (Mayuri Kurotsuchi)
46th
Ulquiorra's Sword
Del Toro (Ilfort)
Kokujôten Tengen Myo Oh (Sajin Komamura)
Tsunzaki Garasu (Jirôbô Ikkanzaka)
Trepadora (Luppi)
Reina De Rosas (Chuhlhourne)
52nd
Glotonería (Aaroniero)
Kotômaru (Matsuri Kudoh)
Beni-Shidare (Kenryû)
Tenra (Izuru Kira)
56th
Devorar Pluma (Abirama)
Golondrina (Cirruci)
White Zangetsu/Getsuga Tenshô (Ichigo Kurosaki)
Brujeria (Zommari)
Shinji Hirako's Zanpaku-tô
Tenken (Sajin Komamura)
Giralda (Dordoni)
64th
Asauchi
Rain Glove
Nanao Ise's eyeglasses' temple
Itegumo (Isane Kotetsu)
Tetsuzaemon Iba's Zanpaku-tô
Ulquiorra's Resurrección
Ulquiorra's eyeball
Ulquiorra's fingernails
Volcánica (Edorad)
Karin's soccer ball
Ultima (Pesche)
9th Company Shinobu Eishima's Zanpaku-tô
Brazo Derecha de Gigante (Yasutora Sado)
Águila (Abirama)
Sojiro Kusaki's Hyôrinmaru
Hôzan (Enjôji Tatsufusa)
Good Morning Ichigo!!
Gonryômaru (Chôjiro Sasakibe)
Chad's right arm that changed for the first time
Hiyori Sarugaki's Zanpaku-tô
Akei Hisagomaru (Hanataro Yamada)
Shunkô (Yoruichi Shihôin)
Hakuren (Rukia Kuchiki)
Tatsuki's fist
Pinza Aguda (Findorr)
Super Spirits Cane (Don Kannonji)
Kakushi Tsuijaku (Tsubaki/Orihime Inoue)
Uña Tirotear (Ice Ringer)
Kokyû Ryûjômaru (Fujimaru Kudoh)
Nijigasumi (Maki Ichinose)
Hinamori's "eye-glass cookie"
Desgarrón (Grimmjow)
Makimaki's Zanpaku-tô
Lanzador Verde (Nelliel)
Infinite Slick (Pesche)
Ms. Rangiku's breasts
Ryûjômaru (Matsuri Kudoh)

We decided to do a Zanpaku-tô Poll this time. A poll about Zanpaku-tô, techniques and Kidô was unprecedented, so there were some concerns, but it was interesting for those of us counting the votes to see the current stories (volumes 37 and 38) reflected in the results. As usual, non-*Bleach* things didn't count. So vote for Tôyako if you want, but we won't count it.

LOLY'S CURRENT SITUATION

Next Volume Preview

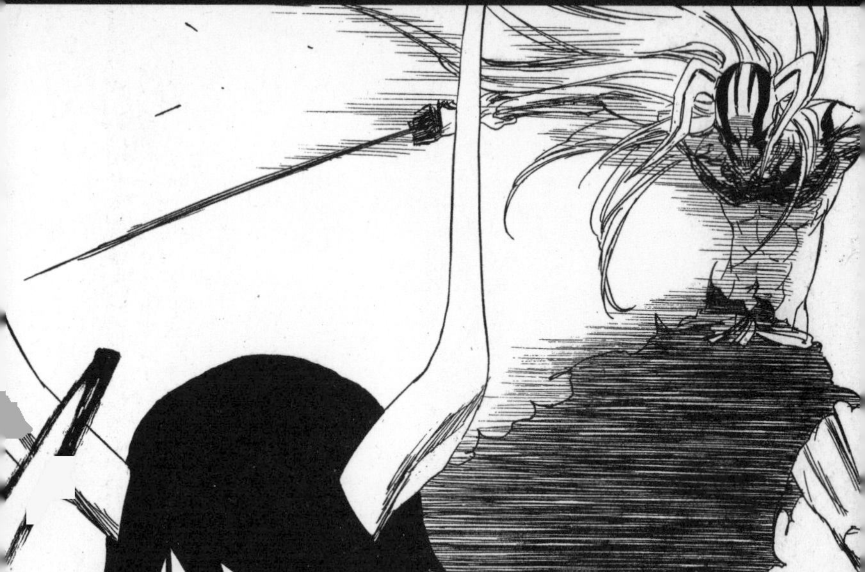

Taken to the brink of death, Ichigo's body undergoes a bizarre transformation. Can this new form finally defeat Ulquiorra? And is this new being even Ichigo any longer? The battle between rivals is settled once and for all!

On sale now!